The

BIBLE
and
LITERATURE
A READER

D0174001

The

BIBLE
and
LITERATURE
A READER

Edited by
DAVID JASPER *and* STEPHEN
PRICKETT

Assisted by
ANDREW HASS

Blackwell
Publishing

© 1999 by Blackwell Publishing Ltd
Introduction, selection, arrangement and apparatus © 1999 by David Jasper and
Stephen Prickett

BLACKWELL PUBLISHING
350 Main Street, Malden, MA 02148-5020, USA
9600 Garsington Road, Oxford OX4 2DQ, UK
550 Swanston Street, Carlton, Victoria 3053, Australia

All rights reserved. No part of this publication may be reproduced, stored in a retrieval
system, or transmitted, in any form or by any means, electronic, mechanical,
photocopying, recording or otherwise, except as permitted by the UK Copyright,
Designs, and Patents Act 1988, without the prior permission of the publisher.

First published 1999

8   2007

Library of Congress Cataloging-in-Publication Data

The Bible and literature : a reader / edited by David Jasper and Stephen
Prickett, assisted by Andrew Hass
    p. cm.
Includes bibliographical references and index.
1. Bible. English Authorized. 2. Bible as literature. 3. Bible-In literature.
4. Bible and literature. 5. English literature. 6. European literature.
I. Jasper, David. II. Prickett, Stephen. III. Hass, Andrew.
BS535.B487 1999
220.6'1—dc21   98–42662
                                                                    CIP

ISBN 978-0-631-20856-3 (alk. paper). — ISBN 978-0-631-20857-0 (pbk: alk.
paper)

A catalogue record for this title is available from the British Library.

Set in 10 on 12 pt StempelGaramond
by Pure Tech India Ltd, Pondicherry
Printed and bound in India
by TJ International Ltd, Padstow, Cornwall

The publisher's policy is to use permanent paper from mills that operate a sustainable
forestry policy, and which has been manufactured from pulp processed using acid-free
and elementary chlorine-free practices. Furthermore, the publisher ensures that the text
paper and cover board used have met acceptable environmental accreditation standards.

For further information on
Blackwell Publishing, visit our website:
www.blackwellpublishing.com

CONCORDIA UNIVERSITY LIBRARY
PORTLAND, OR 97211

Contents

CONTENTS

Contents

Contents

PREFACE

This reader is the result of many years of study, reflection and teaching. It makes no claims to be complete, but should serve rather as an introduction to the study of the Bible and literature, offering insights and ways of studying which, we hope, will bear fruit in further reading and research. We have, of necessity, taken only a small selection of familiar passages from the Bible, and we have based our work on the text of the King James Version, recently made more available to students and general readers through its inclusion in the Oxford World Classics series.

Our purpose is to help students who are studying both literature and theology. The notes to each passage, and the short introductions do not assume any prior familiarity with biblical criticism, though we hope that they are sufficiently challenging to appeal to readers more versed in both the Bible and literary studies. Most of the passages are drawn from English literature, though now and then we have included writings from authors as diverse as St Augustine and Jacques Derrida, where these are felt to be particularly illuminating. From time to time we have also included excerpts from critics such as Frank Kermode or Roland Barthes, though we have avoided the inclusion of technical biblical criticism. That may be found elsewhere, and the short bibliographies appended to each passage will offer some advice in this direction.

Obviously a work such as this rests on the shoulders of a great deal of earlier scholarship, even though its particular format and purpose is quite new. We would mention in particular David Lyle Jeffrey's splendid *A Dictionary of Biblical Tradition in English Literature* (Grand Rapids, 1992) as a gold-mine of information. Of the many people who have helped us on the way, we would thank especially Dr Andrew Hass of the University of Glasgow, who has worked tirelessly to bring together and bring to order a mass of material. Not only his scholarship, but also his skill with computers leave us deeply in his debt.

We hope that this book will not only serve academic and educational purposes, but may serve to bring the Bible alive to a wide range of readers both as a sacred text and as a source of endless inspiration to countless poets, novelists and writers within the traditions of English literature.

———— Acknowledgements ————

The editors and publishers gratefully acknowledge the following for permission to reproduce copyright material:

Anonymous, *The Brome: Abhraham and Isaac*, fourteenth-century passion play. Modernized by John Gassner from *Medieval and Tudor Drama*, Bantam Books, New York, 1963, copyright © the estate of John Gassner. The Wakefield Crucifixion, fifteenth century. Modernized by John Gassner from *Medieval and Tudor Drama*, Bantam Books, New York, 1963, copyright © the estate of John Gassner.
W. H. Auden, 'Victor', from *Collected Shorter Poems 1927–1957*, Faber & Faber Ltd, London, 1969.
Erich Auerbach, *Mimesis* (1946) tr. Willard R. Trask. Copyright © 1981 by Princeton University Press. Reprinted by permission of Princeton University Press.
Roland Barthes, 'The Struggle with the Angel', tr. Stephen Heath, from *Image-Music-Text*, Fontana Press, 1977.
Elizabeth Bishop, 'The Prodigal' from *The Complete Poems 1927–1979* by Elizabeth Bishop. Copyright © 1979, 1983 by Alice Helen Methfessel. Reprinted by permission of Farrer, Straus & Giroux, Inc.
Robert Bly, 'The Prodigal Son', from *The Man in the Black Coat Turns* by Robert Bly. Copyright © 1981 by Robert Bly. Used by permission of Doubleday, a division of Bantam Doubleday Dell Publishing Group Inc.
Samuel Taylor Coleridge, *Lectures on Revealed Religion* (1795), from Lecture 5, from *Collected Coleridge*, ed. Lewis Patton and Peter Mann. Copyright © 1971, Princeton University Press. Reprinted by permission of Princeton University Press.

Emily Dickinson, poems 59, 460 and 1651, from *The Poems of Emily Dickinson*. Reprinted by permission of the publishers and the Trustees of Amherst College from *The Poems of Emily Dickinson*, ed. Thomas H. Johnson Cambridge, Mass.: The Belknap Press of Harvard University Press. Copyright © 1951, 1955, 1979, 1983 by the President and Fellows of Harvard College.

T. S. Eliot, 'The Journey of the Magi' (1927) and Choruses from 'The Rock' (1934) from *The Collected Poems 1909–1962*, Faber & Faber, London 1969 and Harcourt Brace & Company.

William Golding, *Free Fall* (1959), Faber & Faber, London, 1961. Excerpt from *Free Fall*, copyright © 1959 by William Golding and renewed by W. Gerald Golding, reprinted by permission of Harcourt Brace & Company.

Joseph Heller, *God Knows* (1984), Transworld Publishers Ltd. Copyright © 1984 by Scapegoat Productions. Reprinted by permission of Alfred A. Knop Inc.

Geoffrey Hill, 'Canticle for Good Friday', from *For the Unfallen*, Andre Deutsch, London, 1959.

John Hollander, 'Psalms', from David Rosenberg, *Congregation: Contemporary Writers Read the Jewish Bible*. Copyright © 1987 by David Rosenberg. Reprinted by permission of Harcourt Brace & Company.

Howard Jacobson, *The Very Model of a Man*, Viking Penguin Books, 1993. Reprinted by permission of the Peters Fraser and Dunlop Group Ltd.

Søren Kierkegaard, 'Either/Or', from Thomas C. Oden, *Parables of Kierkegaard*. Copyright © 1978 by Princeton University Press. Reprinted by permission of Princeton University Press. *Fear and Trembling* (1843), tr. Walter Lowrie. Copyright © 1983 by Princeton University Press. Reprinted by permission of Princeton University Press.

D. H. Lawrence, *England, My England* (1922). Reprinted by permission of Laurence Pollinger Limited and the Estate of Frieda Lawrence Ravagli and Viking Penguin Inc., New York. 'Let There Be Light', from *The Complete Poems of D. H. Lawrence*, copyright © 1987, by Executors of the Estate of Frieda Lawrence Ravagli. Used by permission of Viking Penguin (USA). *St. Mawr* (1925). Reprinted with permission of Laurence Pollinger Limited and the Estate of Frieda Lawrence Ravagli: Alfred Knopf Inc.

Edwin Muir, 'The Annunciation', from *Collected Poems*, Faber & Faber, London. Copyright © 1960 by Willa Muir. Used by permission of Oxford University Press, Inc.

Wilfred Owen, 'At a Calvary near the Ancre' and 'The Parable of the Old Man and the Young', from *The Collected Poems*, ed. C. Day Lewis, Chatto & Windus, London, 1963.

ACKNOWLEDGEMENTS

David Schubert, 'A Successful Summer', from *Quarterly Review Poetry Series*, Vol. 24.

Wallace Stevens, 'An Ordinary Evening in New Haven', from *Collected Poems*, Faber & Faber Ltd, London, 1969.

Dylan Thomas, 'In the Beginning Was the Three-pointed Star', from *Collected Poems 1934–1952*, J. M. Dent, London, 1971. Reprinted by permission of David Higham Associates.

W. B. Yeats, 'The Lake Isle of Innisfree', from *The Collected Poems*, Macmillan, London, 1950. Reprinted by permission of A. P. Watt Ltd on behalf of Michael B. Yeats.

The publishers apologize for any errors or omissions in the above list and would be grateful to be notified of any corrections that should be incorporated in the next edition or reprint of this book.

— General Introduction —

It was not until the sixteenth century that the Bible began to find a central place in English literature with the great translations of men like William Tyndale and Miles Coverdale, culminating in the King James Bible of 1611 which was described by its translators as 'a treasury of most costly jewels against beggerly rudiments' and 'a fountain of most pure water springing up into everlasting life'. The aim of these devout scholars was to bring the Book of God to the common reader – a theological purpose which finally, in the theology of the Reformation, ensured that the sacred text was set apart from all other 'profane' literature. From then it was inevitable that biblical criticism should evolve largely apart from other forms of literary interpretation. This had not always been so. The gap between the Bible and other literature was far less clearly defined in the Middle Ages, and even so late a commentator as Erasmus could write in his *Enchiridion Militis Christiani* (1503) that 'a sensible reading of the pagan poets and philosophers is a good preparation for the Christian life'.[1] In 1534, however, Tyndale was quite clear why he was translating the New Testament into clear English from the best Greek sources:

Therefore (that I might be found faithful to my father and Lord in distributing to my brethren and fellows of one faith, their due and necessary food: so dressing and seasoning it, that the weak stomachs may receive it also, and be the better for it) I thought it my duty (most dear reader) to warn thee before, and to shew thee the right way in, and to give thee the true key to open it withal, and to arm thee against false prophets and malicious hypocrites, whose perpetual study is to leaven the scripture with glosses, and there to lock it up where it should save thy soul, and to make us shoot at a wrong mark, to put our trust in those things that profit their bellies only and slay our souls.[2]

Ironically, Tyndale's deeply religious project gave to English literature a treasury of phrases and language which ensured that it found a central place within the wider canon of poetry and prose. Even as the Bible was set apart as the sacred text, so it became embedded in the broad culture of 'secular' literature. Thus, that the Bible holds a unique status in the religious history of the western world is obvious enough; what is less obvious, but no less true, is that it holds an equally unique status in literary history and even in what might be called our collective cultural psyche. To begin with, we owe to it much of our notion of what constitutes a 'book'. As we shall see, any discussion of the relationship between the Bible and literature must start by recognizing the degree to which our notion of 'literature' is itself biblically based.

It would be tempting to see this in terms of the influence of the many literary genres contained in the Bible: narrative, history, poetry, proverbs etc., but even that is only half the story. Even the religious, or 'spiritual' content of the Bible is to a remarkable degree associated with its material conditions as a written text. We need to distinguish here between the 'sacred' and the 'spiritual'. The concept of the 'sacred' is common to almost every religious community the world over. It is attached most often to places, such as the sacred groves where, we are told, the ancient Druids used to worship in Britain, the sacred spots, such as Delphi, where the Greeks made pilgrimage to consult the Oracle, or the sacred sites of the Australian aboriginal peoples today. In contrast, the 'spiritual' is almost invariably associated with writing. At its simplest it usually involves a mode of awareness, a sense of transcendence, a linking of individuals to God and their fellow humans through time and space as mediated by the written word. 'Spiritual exercises' have traditionally involved prayer, meditation, and contemplation based around some holy text, or texts. Though no doubt one could find examples of such texts committed only to memory, or illiterate saints and mystics, in practice the vast majority of such spiritual practices, whether among Buddhists, Christians, Hindus, Muslims, Taoists or Zoroastrians, have been centred around written scriptures or holy books of some kind or another. Certainly the spiritual status of the Bible is, as it always has been, inescapably bound up with its material textuality.

Its material conditions have also shaped our idea of a book. Our English word 'Bible' is derived, via the French word *bible*, from the late

Latin *biblia*, a feminine singular noun that meant simply 'the book'. In its older Latin form, however, *biblia* was not understood as the feminine singular, but as the (identical) neuter plural form, which was, in turn, derived from the Greek *ta biblia*, which meant 'the books' – essentially no more than a collection of individual works. This shift in meaning reflects the changing physical conditions of the books themselves. Before the invention of the codex, or bound manuscript volume, the biblical texts were held as individual scrolls stored together in a wooden chest or cupboard. Under such conditions the question of the precise canon of which works did, or did not constitute the scriptures, or the exact order in which the constituent works should occur, though it might have been a matter of doctrinal debate, was not an immediately practical question. Since, just as today, one would rarely read from more than one section at once, the individual scrolls (representing what we would now call the biblical 'books') could (in theory at least) be assembled in more or less whatever order one chose.

With the invention of the codex, however, with its immediate practical advantages of compactness and ease of handling and storage, that flexibility of sequence was lost. From then on the books had to come in a specific order – and it is significant that the process of creating a canon for the Hebrew Bible and for the New Testament coincides historically with the widespread introduction of the codex form. What began as 'the books' had, literally and physically, become 'the book'.

As was to happen again later with the invention of printing, that change in physical conditions with the production of the codex was to have incalculable consequences for the meaning and reception of the Bible. To begin with, as we have just seen, this loose collection of very different kinds of material composed over a period of almost five hundred years – including in the Old Testament, history, prophecy, law, devotional verse, proverbs and even love poetry and fiction, as well as, in the New Testament, letters from named individuals – all had to be placed in a specific order. Juxtaposition always suggests meaning. The arrangement and sequence now necessary for the construction of the codex revealed that there were, in effect, several Bibles[3] – and the relationship between the various traditional sequences, or 'canons' is extremely complex.

Two other apparently accidental physical facts have made the relationship between the Bible and secular literature fundamentally different from that of the holy books of other religions. The first is that for Christian Europe the Bible has always been a translated book. Almost every line of its text serves to remind us that it is about the people of another time and place who belonged to other kinds of societies from our own and who spoke different languages from ourselves. We have grown so accustomed

3

to this curious fact that it is worth pausing for a moment to call attention to the obvious. Whatever its degree of borrowing from the Bible and other earlier writings, the Qur'an, for instance, is mediated to the Islamic world in the same Arabic in which it was written by the prophet Mohammed. A Muslim, whether in Glasgow, Mecca, Samarkand or Jakarta, is obliged to pray in the original and therefore sacred language dictated to the founder of his faith, it is said, by the Archangel Gabriel for that purpose – and for that reason there must be no tampering with the word of God. Three-quarters of the Christian Bible, by contrast, is acknowledged even by its most fundamentalist adherents to be originally the scriptures of another religion and written in a language never spoken by any Christian community.[4] Moreover, even that section, originally the Hebrew Bible, was never at any stage a linguistically homogeneous whole.

It is only when we contrast these basic assumptions about origins with the doctrine of the verbal stability of the Qur'an that we begin to realize just how great is the gulf separating Christianity and Islam in their unconscious preconceptions about the nature of a text. In spite of a strong fundamentalist tradition in certain parts of evangelical Protestantism, Christianity, by the very appropriative eclecticism of its origins, has always been at least dimly conscious of its own distance from its sacred writings. In other words, the problem of its own origins has always warranted a theory of reading, a hermeneutic system of interpretation – even if, as in some cases, that appears to be largely in the form of an insistence on the inspired nature of the King James Version. In contrast, though English language versions of the Qur'an are, of course, now available,[5] it is nevertheless clearly understood by Muslims that these are *not* translations; they do not, and cannot carry the force of the original inspired Arabic wording. Moreover, whatever earlier sources or degrees of appropriation modern scholars may detect behind the various Surahs of the Qur'an, there is, officially at least, no countenancing of the idea that the way in which we understand the past might be conditioned by the cultural circumstances of the present. This has, of course, been made easier by the fact that for contingent historical reasons, until large-scale migration of Islamic communities to Europe and North America began in this century, it was possible for most of the Islamic world not to feel any problematic or disturbing cultural gap between itself and its sacred texts. Though it had spread outward from the countries of its origin in the Arabian peninsula, unlike Christianity, Islam had never been forced to decamp entirely from its own geographical heartland. This is the second physical and historical condition under which the Bible comes to us: not merely is it not in its original languages; it is also uprooted from its original territory. It is a book in exile.

This physical, cultural, and linguistic gap between Christianity and its sacred texts has always meant that the Bible has related to its social context in a quite different way from either the Qur'an or any of the scriptures of the other world religions. Since the Reformation, moreover, it has been available, almost everywhere, if not in the local vernacular (the language of the King James Bible was never the ordinary language of the people) then at least in a form intelligible to most people. This sense that it was both very distant, and, at the same time an integral part of the local culture has led to a constant demand for biblical stories to be re-told in plays, in verse, and later even in prose narrative. Significantly, there was never a prohibition on paraphrase, or on re-telling biblical stories, as there was for a long time on direct translation – indeed, the initial pre-Reformation feeling that translation was blasphemy does not seem to have carried over into this process of re-telling in other words. Moreover, as we shall see, however much sixteenth-century Protestantism might resemble Catholicism in its capacity for dogmatism and persecution, the printing presses that had brought it into existence also ensured that it had effectively lost control of its own texts. The production of Bibles was a commercial matter, and with the power to read and interpret went the capacity to innovate. Furthermore, for the first time the invention of the printing press ensured that the text of the Bible was stable – Martin Luther's class on the Epistle to the Galatians in 1503 was revolutionary inasmuch as all his students were individually reading the *same* text, freed from the vagaries of the hitherto hand copied manuscripts. From the 'poor man's Bible' in the stained glass of the great medieval cathedrals, to the metrical psalms of the Scottish Covenanters, the stories and poems of the Bible were told and re-told, adapted, appropriated, and re-used until any original boundary between 'sacred' and 'profane' texts (despite the claims of theology) was blurred in a way that made the Bible a part of English literature, as Shakespeare was also to become – and the element of religion as less a dogmatic system than a running argument, already present in the ancient Hebrew, entered into and enriched a new fictional tradition. Biblical quotations, biblical plots, biblical references became a part of ordinary speech and writing to the point where many people were simply unaware of the origins of the sayings and metaphors they were using.

In the case of English this process was greatly enhanced by particular qualities of the King James Bible itself. Though it was not at first popular, by the eighteenth century it had come to have an enormous influence on the development and vocabulary of the English language. David Norton, for instance, gives a whole series of examples of words which appear in the 1611 Bible that were current or familiar archaisms in the sixteenth century but which had dropped out of use by the eighteenth century, and were later revived into common speech in the nineteenth century.[6] These include such words as 'ate', 'discomfiture', 'eschewed', 'laden', 'nurture', 'ponder' and 'unwittingly'. Many, though not all, of these can be shown to have made their comeback with the increasing popularity of the Authorized Version. The word 'ponder', for instance, seems to have survived on the strength of one famous verse, taken by the Authorized Version straight from Tyndale: Luke 2: 19: 'but Mary kept all these things and pondered them in her heart'. By the mid-eighteenth century it is listed as being obsolete, and its revived sense reflects all the solemnity of Luke's Annunciation. The point here is not just that, as Norton very convincingly argues, the Authorized Version has acted 'as a kind of uncrowded Noah's ark for vocabulary for perhaps two hundred years'[7] but also that such words, even where not specifically coined for the needs of translation, are restored to us from the ark subtly transformed, and often with added value.

But this was not simply a matter of vocabulary. When the Revised Version of the New Testament was published in 1855 the *Edinburgh Review* was one of a number of sources that criticized it for bending the native English idiom to conform with the Greek[8] – the reviewer being apparently unaware that precisely this criticism had been thrown by an earlier generation of critics against the Authorized Version itself. In the intervening two and a half centuries, however, those archaic and sometimes tortured phrases produced by literal renderings of Greek and Hebrew into English had themselves been assimilated and hallowed by time and custom so that we no longer recognize such phrases as 'the skin of my teeth', 'lick the dust' or 'fell flat on his face' as the alien semitic intruders that they once were.[9]

It should come, then, as little surprise to find that by the end of the eighteenth century the Bible is being read almost as if it were itself a contemporary work of fiction – not so much in the sense that people questioned its truth (though many were prepared to do just that) but that even devotional readers were looking at biblical stories in terms of plot, character, or motivation, rather than in the typological ways that had once been normal. In one of his numerous ironic asides to the reader in *Tom Jones*, Fielding warns that we must not be too hasty in our judgements of what is going on, because, unlike him, we are not the creator, and can have no sense of the whole picture that will be eventually revealed.[10] This oblique reference to himself as a Calvinistic God is less blasphemous than prophetic. Here, for instance, is precisely the same argument, in reverse, only a few years later in Mrs Trimmer's (1741–1810) introduction to her popular *Help to the Unlearned in the Study of the Holy Scriptures*:

The Books that follow, as far as the BOOK OF ESTHER, are called the HISTORICAL BOOKS. The Histories they contain differ from all the other histories that ever were written, for they give an account of the ways of GOD; and explain *why* GOD *protected and rewarded* some persons and nations, and *why* he *punished* others; also, *what led* particular persons mentioned in Scripture to *do* certain things for which they were approved or condemned; whereas writers who compose histories in a common way, without being *inspired of God*, can only form guesses and conjectures concerning God's dealings with mankind, neither can they know what passed in the hearts of those they write about; such knowledge as this, belongs to *God* alone, whose ways are *unsearchable and past finding out*, and *to whom all hearts are open, all desires known!*[11]

It is only a comparatively short step from regarding God as the supreme novelist, to reading the Bible as 'literature' in an aesthetic rather than a devotional sense, but we need here to distinguish between two very different meanings of the phrase 'the Bible as literature' that are often confused, and which have frequently bedevilled recent literary discussions of the biblical texts.

The first is a product of post-Enlightenment secularization, and involves a *replacement* of the Bible's 'religious' content by aesthetic values – a process taken to its logical conclusion in the 1930s with the publication of a version of the Bible 'Designed to be Read as Literature', and a number of subsequent works purporting to deal with the Bible as a purely secular collection, freed from all theological presuppositions.[12]

As far back as the early nineteenth century, Shelley, the radical atheist poet, could treasure the poetry of the Hebrews primarily as monuments to the freedom of the human spirit and superb examples of his craft; two generations later, Matthew Arnold, discounting the accretion of super-natural 'folk-stories' around the basic human narratives of the Old and New Testaments could urge us to value them not for their historical content but for their 'poetic' value. Though, as we shall see, Arnold's position was not a simple aesthetic one, it was read by many of his contemporaries simply as a way of enjoying the great prose style of the King James Bible once one had ceased to believe in any of its contents. This was a position sharply attacked in the twentieth century by T. S. Eliot, who argued in 1935, paradoxically, that when the Bible is discussed as 'litera-ture', its literary influence is, in reality, already at an end, since, according to him, the aesthetic values we find in literature are ultimately dependent on other values imported from outside. This view of aesthetics as an essentially second-order system, whose values are always acquired, as it were second-hand from somewhere else, was made more plausible for the

English-speaking world by the fact that such debates almost invariably centred on the supposed literary qualities of the King James Authorized Version of 1611.[13] As C. S. Lewis after Eliot drily commented, 'it is very generally implied that those who have rejected its theological pretensions nevertheless continue to enjoy it as a treasure-house of English prose. It may be so ... But I never happen to meet them ... I cannot help suspecting ... that those who read the Bible as literature do not read the Bible'.[14]

That aesthetics might mean more than the appreciation of artistic and formal qualities in a work whose content had ceased to carry conviction of itself was rarely understood or discussed in the English-speaking world, but in Germany from the end of the eighteenth century a quite different meaning to the word had evolved. Kant's suggestion that art might provide the necessary link between 'Reason' (the realm of pure and immediate apprehension) and 'Understanding' (which concerns our world of everyday appearances) had given a new potential status and importance to art and literature.[15] For the group of young self-consciously styled 'Romantics' in Jena in the 1790s this was to offer a quite new way of defining truth. Though the group centred on the literary critics August and Friedrich Schlegel, together with Caroline Michaelis, August's mistress (later to marry Schelling) and Dorothea Mendelssohn, who was later to marry Friedrich, it also included poets, such as Novalis (Friedrich von Hardenberg), Tieck, and Hölderlin, philosophers, including Fichte, Schelling, and, somewhat more distantly and intermittently, Hegel, as well as the most important theologian of the period, Friedrich Schleiermacher. From this literary, philosophical and theological matrix was to emerge the idea that there were two very different conceptions of truth: one relating to verifiable statements about the world (what one might call 'scientific truth'); the other derived from the hermeneutic tradition, linking truth to art via the claim that art reveals the world in ways which would not be possible without the existence of art itself. Truth is thus seen in terms of the capacity of forms of articulation to 'disclose' the world.[16] Novalis, for instance, claimed that by engaging in the play of the resources within the dynamic web of relationships that surround us all, we can reveal 'truths' that cannot emerge if we wish to define the relationships or find a grounding proposition. As Andrew Bowie puts it, 'the world thus constituted is not a realm of fixed objects, but rather a world in which "truths" arise by combining different *articulations* of what there is'.[17] Aesthetic truth reveals the world through creation rather than mere description.

It was from this tradition that we find developing a second approach which saw a literary understanding of the Bible not as a replacement of its religious content, but as an *adjunct* to it, leading, so it was argued, to a greater understanding of it as a whole. Thus Johann Gottfried Herder's *The Spirit of Hebrew Poetry* (1782–3) was written both from the point of view of a pious Christian believer, and as a romantic nationalist who believed that the poetry of a people displayed the unique qualities and values of their language and culture. The 'genius of the [Hebrew] language', he writes in his Preface, 'we can nowhere study better...than in its poetry, and indeed, so far as possible, in its most ancient poetry...Let the scholar then study the Old Testament, even if it be only as a human book full of ancient poetry, with kindred feeling and affection'.[18] Herder uses the broader meaning of the German concept of 'poetry' to embrace, for instance, the whole of Genesis and the book of Job, without questioning (as others were already doing) their historical content. 'Among the Hebrews,' he writes, 'history itself is properly poetry'.[19] Hebrew poetry expresses 'the earliest perceptions, the simplest forms, by which the human soul expressed its thoughts, the most uncorrupted affections that bound and guided it'.[20]

These two broad understandings of 'the Bible as literature' have haunted recent developments in literary 'approaches' to the interpretation of the Bible in which scholars of literature have begun to stake claims to read the Bible outside the academic and ecclesiastical guild of specialist biblical critics. As long ago as the 1940s, the theologian and biblical scholar Austin Farrer published studies of the gospels and Revelation with a poetic and literary flair which resulted in his ostracism from the community of his fellow critics, and the suspicion of more conservative literary critics. When Helen Gardner read these excursions in 'literary readings' of the Bible, and their development in the work of literary scholars like Frank Kermode, she admitted that she 'was dismayed at the combination of great intellectual activity, and great enjoyment in the exercise of interpretative ingenuities, with the melancholy negativism of the confusion: the sense that the whole enterprise was a kind of game played for its own sake, which was ultimately pointless'.[21]

The dam, however, was broken, and the dilemma inherited from the Reformation – that the Bible was *the* sacred text, and at the same time at the heart of a literary culture – has become central to an increasingly diverse debate which is the subject of the second of our Introductory Essays. It has become, more than ever, an 'open text',[22] subject to varieties of reading and its religious claims opened up anew by the reading strategies of feminist readings, deconstructive readings, new approaches in rhetorical studies and so on almost *ad infinitum*. Such readings have broken down barriers between Christian and Jewish interpreters, whose ancient midrashic hermeneutics have found a new voice by way of developments in literary theory, such that even some of the more conservative of the 'literary critics' of the Bible have become nervous of the consequences. In their General Introduction to the now standard *Literary Guide to the Bible* (1987), Frank Kermode and Robert Alter admit:

Given our aim to provide illumination, we have not included critics who use the text as a springboard for cultural or metaphysical ruminations, nor those like the Deconstructionists and some feminist critics who seek to demonstrate that the text is necessarily divided against itself.[23]

But the flood cannot be stemmed, and it is the purpose of this reader to indicate that the Bible has always been at the heart of the life of poetry and literature, in dialogue with creative writers through the ages in spite (or perhaps because) of its special status as a text. This interplay could be expanded into the visual arts and music, but these are out of the scope of our task here. Even the biblical critics themselves have begun to acknowledge the essentially creative nature of their academic endeavour, one recently remarking that he is 'eager to reply to the Gospels in kind, to write in a related idiom'.[24] The great English translations of the sixteenth century rediscovered the Bible as literature, and the tensions which resulted from this have, devoutly, uncomfortably, scurrilously, beautifully sustained these texts, in the words of the King James Version translators, 'a whole paradise of trees of life, which brings forth fruits every month, and the fruit thereof is for meat, and the leaves for medicine'.

Notes

1 *The Essential Erasmus*, selected and translated by John P. Dolan (New York and Scarsborough, Ontario: Mentor Books, 1964), p. 36.
2 W. T. Unto the Reader, *Tyndale's New Testament*, ed. David Daniell (New Haven, CT: Yale University Press, 1995), pp. 3–4.
3 See, for instance, Robert P. Carroll, *Wolf in the Sheepfold: The Bible as a Problem for Christianity* (London: SPCK 1991), p. 7; and John Romer, *Testament: The Bible and History* (London: Michael O'Mara Books, 1988), p. 227.
4 The problem of the Old Testament's relationship to Christianity is, of course, too complex to be so swiftly dismissed. See, for instance, John Bright, *The Authority of the Old Testament* (Grand Rapids, Michigan: Baker Book House, 1980) ch. 2, for a lucid exposition of the 'classical' solutions to this fundamental problem of Christian origins.
5 See, for instance, that of Mohammed Marmaduke Pickthall (1930) (London: Star Books, 1989).

6 Norton, *A History of the Bible as Literature* (Cambridge: Cambridge University Press, 1993) Vol. 2, pp. 80–5.

7 Ibid., p. 85.

8 Ibid., p. 237.

9 Job 19: 20; Psalms 72: 9; Numbers 22: 31; Norton, *A History*, Vol. 2, p. 342.

10 Henry Fielding, *Tom Jones*, ed. R. P. C. Mutter (Harmondsworth: Penguin, 1966), p. 467.

11 Mrs. (Sarah) Trimmer, *Help to the Unlearned in the Study of the Holy Scriptures* (2nd edn, 1806).

12 See, for instance, T. R. Henn, *The Bible as Literature* (London: Lutterworth, 1970); John B. Gabel and Charles B. Wheeler, *The Bible as Literature: An Introduction* (New York: Oxford University Press, 1986); and Robert Alter and Frank Kermode (eds), *The Literary Guide to the Bible* (London: Collins, 1987).

13 A view of the Authorized Version that did not become prevalent until some two hundred years after its publication. See Norton, *A History*.

14 C. S. Lewis, 'The Literary Influence of the Authorised Version', in *They Asked for a Paper* (London: Geoffrey Bles, 1962) p. 46.

15 See Stephen Prickett, *Origins of Narrative: The Romantic Appropriation of the Bible* (Cambridge: Cambridge University Press, 1996), pp. 184–90.

16 See Andrew Bowie, *From Romanticism to Critical Theory: The Philosophy of German Literary Theory* (London: Routledge, 1997), p. 17.

17 Ibid., p. 69.

18 J. G. Herder, *The Spirit of Hebrew Poetry*, tr. James Marsh (Burlington: Vermont, 1833), pp. 22–3.

19 Ibid., p. 37.

20 Ibid., pp. 45–6.

21 Helen Gardner, *In Defence of the Imagination* (Oxford: Oxford University Press, 1982), p. 114.

22 See, Francis Watson (ed.), *The Open Text: New Directions for Biblical Studies* (London: SCM, 1993).

23 Frank Kermode and Robert Alter, *The Literary Guide to the Bible* (London: Collins, 1987), p. 6.

24 Stephen D. Moore, *Mark and Luke in Poststructuralist Perspectives* (New Haven, CT: Yale University Press, 1992), p. xviii.

BIBLICAL AND LITERARY
— CRITICISM: A HISTORY OF —
INTERACTION
STEPHEN PRICKETT

—— 1 The Bible as Criticism ——

The distinction between scripture and criticism, text and commentary, is a relatively recent one in the history of the Bible – remembering that 'recent' here means post-canonical, that is, since the third century CE when the books of the Christian Bible were assembled into more or less their final form. Though it is not difficult to see that large sections of the New Testament are, in fact, commentaries on parts of the Hebrew Bible, later re-arranged and edited by Christians as the 'Old Testament', it may be less obvious that much of the Hebrew Bible itself also consists of a running commentary – both on earlier books, and, as we are now beginning to learn, on other, older, near-eastern religious texts. Indeed, even the selection of books, or 'canon', of the Bible and the order of their arrangement is a critical and polemical act. Just as the Christian Old Testament is a deliberate ideological re-structuring of the Hebrew Bible, so the Protestant Bible – most familiar to English-speakers in the Authorized or King James Version – is a no less ideologically motivated re-arrangement of the Catholic Vulgate, in which the so-called 'deutero-canonical' texts have been withdrawn and placed into a new, third, grouping, the Apocrypha. There are many Bibles, and the textual differences between them witness to centuries of critical controversy and, often, persecution.[1]

In the only specifically Christian part of the Bible, the New Testament, only the four Gospels and Acts purport to offer straight historical narrative, telling the story of the life and death of Jesus and the subsequent spread of the Church from Palestine across the eastern Mediterranean as far as the imperial centre, Rome. Of the rest, the Epistles are mostly direct commentaries on passages of the Hebrew Scriptures, drawing out, in the light of Jesus' fulfilment of them, what the various writers see as their philosophical, practical, and ethical consequences. The remaining book, Revelation, is the most astonishing intertextual commentary on the Hebrew scriptures, creating, from their open-ended longings, closure and apocalypse on a cosmic scale. Even the Gospels, however, are careful literary constructs, constantly relating the life and actions of Jesus to specific Hebrew texts. The phrase 'This he did according to the scriptures', and its many variants, regularly punctuate the synoptic Gospels (Matthew, Mark and Luke) and it is clear that where John's Gospel differs from these, it is in response to the needs of an even more complex critical structure, part literary, part philosophical, that attempts to provide a commentary and interpretation on the events of Jesus' life.

Nor are these origins of the New Testament in a critical gloss on the Old in any sense an aberration. The Bible is a monument to intertextuality. As we have seen, according to the Gospels, Jesus himself presented much of his teaching in the form of a commentary on the Hebrew scriptures. The belief of Paul and the other early Church leaders that Jesus was the predicted Messiah of the Hebrew prophets, only reinforced the importance of the Hebrew Bible as the major section of the Christian scriptures, but, at the same time, emphasized the need for those scriptures to be radically reinterpreted. In this sense, Christianity was born of a critical debate about the nature and meaning of texts. Every canon is an act of interpretation.

The first attempt to put together a collection of Christian books to form a putative New Testament was made in the second century by Marcion – who wanted to drop the Hebrew scriptures altogether from the Christian canon. He was denounced as a 'heretic', and all his works were later destroyed. Ironically, we only know the contents of the Marcion canon from the attacks that were made upon it by his enemies: it apparently consisted of one gospel (Luke's) and some of Paul's letters. In response to Marcion, however, the early Church, led by Irenaeus of Lyon, then had to define orthodoxy by putting together its own canon and declaring it to be a single, sacred and unalterable corpus. That process of canon-formation was accompanied by intense and often acrimonious debate, with fierce conflict between different Christian communities and traditions, and (in the case of the Catholic Vulgate) was only more or less completed by Eusebius after the Council of Nicaea. As has been mentioned, the Anglican Protestant canon of the King James Bible only dates from the sixteenth-century Reformation.

But by its very formation, a canon tends to loosen a text from its particular historical setting and to make it transcend its original purpose.[2] Thus the existing cultic language of Judaism was given new life by being redeployed by Christian writers with reference to Jesus as its paradigm example.[3] In the Epistle to the Hebrews, for instance, the Old Testament idea of sacrifice is re-read to encompass the crucifixion of Jesus – which is then read back as the supreme example of the earlier ritual. What we see happening very early in the Christian era is, in effect, a two- or even arguably three-fold process of appropriation. At the same time as the Hebrew, Aramaic, and Greek of the Christian Bible were being translated into Latin, the very terms of the translation were also being transformed with radically new metaphorical meanings. For instance, by identifying Jesus with the sacrificial Passover lamb of Jewish ritual, not merely was the idea of sacrifice being given a new focal point and meaning, but in addition a rich vein of figurative pastoral typology was simultaneously being opened up and appropriated from the Hebrew scriptures to link with similar imagery in the New Testament – as numerous popular translations of the twenty-third Psalm bear witness.

This process of appropriating the Hebrew scriptures for Christian purposes also involved a massive metaphorical re-interpretation of their contents – creating what Austin Farrer has called a 're-birth of images'.[4] Many of the books of the Hebrew canon involved prescriptions for Jewish rituals which had little or no relevance to the practices or beliefs of the new Hellenistic Christian communities scattered around the eastern Mediterranean. In some cases their narratives, laws, and even ethical teachings actually seemed to contradict those of the New Testament. If Marcion's open dismissal of the Hebrew scriptures was seen as over-reacting, it was nevertheless a response to an obvious common difficulty. For those more 'orthodox' authorities like Irenaeus and Eusebius, who believed the Hebrew writings to be divinely inspired, and therefore indispensable, some method had to be found to harmonize them with what was now believed to be their fulfilment. Jewish interpreters had already shown with their allegorizing of the Song of Songs how texts could be given other meanings apart from their obvious literal one, and this existing tradition was now reinforced and made more easily acceptable by the adoption of similar Greek methods of exegesis. In the first century, Philo, a Hellenized Jew, foreshadowed the later Christian synthesis of Hebrew and Greek traditions by claiming that not only were the Hebrew scriptures compatible with Greek philosophy, but that in many cases the Greek writers had been influenced by the Hebrew ones.[5] In so doing he showed how Greek allegorical methods could be used on other Hebrew scriptural books. Soon the general claim that Christianity was the key to understanding the Hebrew scriptures – the message of Philip to the Ethiopian in Acts 8 – was supported by an increasingly elaborate system of figurative and allegorical interpretation. Some writers were even prepared to appropriate pagan classical texts for Christianity by the same process: Virgil's *Aeneid*, for instance, was read as an allegory of the Christian soul's journey through life. Later commentators, such as Origen and Augustine were to lay the foundations of a complex and polysemous system of exegesis covering the entire Bible.

2 The Bible and the Classics

No amount of allegorization, however, could wholly evade the cultural clash between the literature of the Bible and that of the Greek and Latin classics. One of the earliest references to the Bible from the pagan classical world comes from a critical treatise in the early Christian era by Longinus, dealing, among other things, with the concept of 'the sublime'.[6] After some lengthy examples of sublimity from the Greek classics, he suddenly cites 'the lawgiver of the Hebrews', who said 'Let there be light.' This sublime 'lawgiver' is not, of course, God, but Moses – the presumed human author of the first five books of the Old Testament, the Pentateuch. Though the actual reference is fleeting enough, given that Longinus was writing for an educated pagan Roman audience, it suggests that such people might have been much more familiar with the Hebrew Bible than has commonly been assumed. If this is so, and the Hebrew scriptures were at least to some degree already known to the wider Roman society, it would certainly help to account for the dramatic spread of Christianity in the first few centuries of the common era. After the rediscovery of Longinus in the fifteenth century, for many classically educated Europeans, however, the reference meant much more. It was nothing less than the formal acknowledgement by the Roman world that not merely were the Judeo-Christian scriptures morally and spiritually superior to pagan religions, but that they were also aesthetically superior to classical literature. Isaac Watts, for instance, writing in the eighteenth century, observes the manifest inferiority of the (classical) 'Gentiles...when brought into Comparison with MOSES, whom LONGINUS himself, a Gentile Critic, cites as a Master of the sublime stile, when he chose to use it'.[7]

Such an aesthetic endorsement would have astonished the Church Fathers. So far from matching the measured periods of the English King James Bible, the *koiné* Greek of the New Testament is not a literary language at all – and certainly not the language of the great classical writers – but a low-status common patois spoken amongst non-native

15

Greek speakers in the trading communities of the eastern Mediterranean. For the classically trained scholars who were to lead the Church in the second, third, and fourth centuries, the bastard Greek of the New Testament was a continual aesthetic barrier. Augustine, Jerome, Gregory, and Tertullian were all troubled by what they saw as the sheer barbarity of the gospels' style. Unless the whole wealth of the classical literary tradition was to be rejected out of hand, some way had to be found of explaining why the Holy Spirit, which was believed to have inspired the New Testament writers, had such a poor prose style.

For Tertullian (writing *c.*200 CE) the answer was to avoid comparison. 'What has Athens to do with Jerusalem?...We must seek the Lord in purity of heart...Since Christ Jesus, there is no room for further curiosity, since the gospel no need for further research.'[8] Similarly, for Gregory, 'the same lips cannot sound the praises of both Jupiter and Christ'. At first sight Ambrose too seemed to agree, arguing like Tertullian that the scriptures contained all necessary instruction,[9] yet he clearly saw nothing wrong in openly structuring his *De officiis ministrorum*, written for the clergy of Milan, on Cicero's *De officiis*. Ambrose's pupil, Augustine, likewise admits in his *Confessions* that it was Cicero's philosophy that had set him on the road to conversion by giving him a passion for true wisdom. Perhaps the most agonizing conflict of aesthetic loyalties is recorded by Jerome, another avid Ciceronian. Compared with the classics, the 'uncultivated language' of the Old Latin Bible was so offensive that, he wrote, it made his 'skin crawl'.[10] Soon after he fell ill and dreamed that he had died. Asked before the judgement seat what manner of man he was, he replied that he was a Christian. 'Thou liest,' came the reply, 'thou art a Ciceronian, not a Christian.'[11] In 382 he was commissioned by Pope Damasus to begin his great new Latin translation of the Bible, now known as the Vulgate.

Though Jerome would have preferred to give his new version the style and polish of the classical rhetoric in which he had been trained, his new task faced him with a unique problem: how far could any translator be expected to know the full meaning of the words God had originally dictated? He had, he felt, no choice but to follow the original, whatever the result, and, if necessary, allow its oddity and uncouthness to show through. Though his translation is nevertheless written in characteristically good Latin, this decision was to change the future development of the Latin language and, with hindsight, the Vulgate marks the beginning of the historic division between the antique rhetoric of classical Latin (in effect from then on a dead language) and the form in which it was to survive into the Middle Ages – Church Latin. For later generations, reared not on the Latin of the classics but on that of Jerome's Bible itself, the original critical problem had disappeared – but, as we shall see, it was in time replaced by a similar veneration for the Latin of Jerome's Vulgate. In the meantime the new *lingua franca* of Europe was a direct product of the uneasy encounter between the classical and Jewish traditions.

——— 3 Medieval Critical Theory ———

In one respect, however, the classical tradition was to triumph. Though there is at least one allegory in the Old Testament,[12] it is not a characteristic form of Jewish narration. But, as we have seen, given the allegorizing cast of the later classical world and Jesus' own use of allegorical and figurative forms in many of his parables, it was natural that the Christian re-interpretation of the Hebrew scriptures should have relied heavily on this technique. In the following centuries this was elaborated into a multi-layered system of reading that, in a context where there was still no distinction between sacred and secular texts, embraced the whole of literature. Thus Virgil's fourth *Eclogue*, with its prophecy of a coming ruler, was understood as a parallel to Isaiah and a foretelling of Christ.

Different schools of thought differed as to the precise number of figural interpretations possible to a given passage of scripture. Some Alexandrian authorities detected as many as twelve, but four was by far the most widely accepted number.[13] Even this number could itself be arrived at by typological reasoning. Irenaeus, for example, argued for the canonical primacy of the four gospels from the fact that God's world was supplied in fours: as there were 'four zones', and 'four winds', so there were four gospels. From this four levels of interpretation followed easily. According to St John Cassian in the fourth century these were a literal, or historical sense, an allegorical, a tropological (or moral) and an anagogical. Tropological related to the Word, or doctrine conveyed by it, and therefore carried a moral sense; the anagogical concerns eternal things. Cassian takes as his example the figure of Jerusalem. Historically it may be seen as the earthly city; allegorically, it stands for the Church; tropologically it represents the souls of all faithful Christians; anagogically, it is the heavenly city of God.[14] As a later Latin rhyme has it:

> *Littera gesta docet, quid credes allegoria,*
> *Moralis quid agas, quo tendas anagogia.*

[The letter teaches what happened, the allegorical what to believe, The moral what to do, the anagogical toward what to aspire.][15]

This new Christian sense of 'allegory' (from the Greek *allegoria*) came to carry a quite different sense from the original classical one of a fiction, fable or personification with another meaning – of the sort used by Aesop. For the Church the historical actuality of the person or event actually served to guarantee its inner spiritual meaning.[16] Even more important, allegorization of the canon further helped to prise stories loose from their original setting and to give them the possibility of universal significance. Erich Auerbach argues convincingly that this new Christian interpretative theory was an essential ingredient in its becoming a world religion.

Figural interpretation changed the Old Testament from a book of laws and a history of the people of Israel into a series of figures of Christ and the Redemption – so Celtic and Germanic peoples, for example, could accept the Old Testament as part of the universal religion of salvation and a necessary component of the equally magnificent and universal vision of history conveyed to them along with this religion...Its integral, firmly teleological, view of history and the providential order of the world gave it the power to capture the imagination...of the convert nations. Figural interpretation was a fresh beginning and a rebirth of man's creative powers.[17]

It was, in effect, the prime tool not merely of the Christian appropriation of the Hebrew scriptures, but of the evangelization of Europe. As Auerbach also significantly observes, this appropriation was accompanied by a new outburst of creative energies – even if some figural interpretations strike the modern reader as little short of grotesque. A sermon among the *spuria* of Chrysostom interprets the Massacre of the Innocents by noting that the fact that children of two years old and under were murdered, while those of three presumably were spared, is meant to teach us that those who hold the Trinitarian faith will be saved whereas Binitarians and Unitarians will undoubtedly perish.[18] By the Middle Ages the literal meaning of even such writings as Paul's letters had taken second place to figurative meanings.

The effect of this, now almost-invisible, tradition upon the subsequent development of European literature can scarcely be over-estimated. Until almost the end of the eighteenth century, for instance, the literal meaning of the Bible was seen as only one among many ways of understanding it. Not merely did allegorical, figural, and typological modes of reading co-exist with the literal one, but, because they were more generalized, they were often in practice given higher status. Moreover, since the Bible, together still with the classics, was the model for all secular literature, such multi-levelled modes of reading naturally also influenced the way in which other books were read. Allegorical levels in Dante's *Divine Comedy*, or the popular medieval love story, *The Romance of the Rose*, were not optional extras, but a normal and integral part of what was expected from literature. The idea of a primary literal meaning to a given text is an essentially modern one – dating, in effect, from the rise in status and popularity of the novel. Though it is easy to see Bunyan's seventeenth-century *Pilgrim's Progress* as standing at the end of a 1,500-year-old allegorical tradition, in many ways it is better understood as a transitional work, anticipating the modern novel. In spite of the clearly allegorical names of the characters, its surface narrative is unusual in being the more complex and interesting of its two levels. Even then the tradition of allegorical names for characters, familiar to us from the medieval play, *Everyman*, and continued in such characters as Sir Politick Would-Be, in Ben Jonson's *Volpone*, runs straight through into the English novel. One thinks of Fielding's Squire Alworthy in *Tom Jones*, Pip in Dickens' *Great Expectations*, or Dotheboys Hall in *Nicholas Nickleby* – and, in the drama, even Mr Chasuble in Oscar Wilde's *The Importance of Being Earnest*. Similarly, the ghost of polysemous reference haunts modern secular critical theory, as it did that of the Romantics. Theories of symbolism, the psychological readings of Freud and his many successors, and the deconstructive readings of Derrida alike depend on medieval and ultimately biblical interpretative practices.

—— **4 The Reformation** ——

It is significant that the first European printed book, by Gutenberg, had been the Vulgate (1456). What is significant about it, however, is that it does not seem to have been either an act of piety or of political correctness, but a straight business venture.[19] The Bible had ceased to be the 'property' of the institutional Church, copied by monks in *scriptoria* and read aloud to the people, and became a commercial artefact in the public domain. If you could afford it, and read it (still two big ifs in the fifteenth century) you could study it for yourself. In that sense the Protestant Reformation of the sixteenth century was the product of new technology. Without the printing-press knowledge of the Bible could never have become widespread enough for there to be dissent about its meaning, and it is notable that, whatever other social and political factors may have been at work, Protestantism spread and took hold in those countries with (relatively) high literacy rates. But the printing-press affected even the illiterate, for the polemical conflicts of the Reformation were as much visual as verbal. One modern historian has described them as a 'woodcut war': for every reader who could understand Luther's objections to the sale of indulgences, there were ten who could understand a printed woodcut of the whore of Rome copulating with Antichrist or the Pope shitting lies.[20] Not merely did printing make the Bible available as never before, but it had also changed the Bible itself in ways that were quite unforeseen. Above all, the market for the Latin Bible was never going to equal the potential commercial demand for local vernacular versions.

Wyclif's first English translation of the Bible (c.1380) had been suppressed by the Convocation of Oxford, which, in 1408, forbade anyone, on pain of excommunication, to translate any part of the scriptures into the vernacular unless authorized by a bishop. No such authorization was subsequently given, and, in case the Church's views on the subject were not clear enough, after his death Wyclif's body was dug up from his grave at Lutterworth and thrown into the local river. When, in the early sixteenth century, the Protestant William Tyndale, approached the Bishop of London for assistance for a new translation it was refused in terms that made it clear 'not only that there was no room in my Lord of London's palace to translate the New Testament, but also that there was no place to do it in all England'. Tyndale moved to Wittenberg, the city of Luther, and finished his translation of the New Testament in 1525. He began printing it in Cologne, but by the time he had reached the end of Matthew's Gospel the town council intervened, and Tyndale was forced to flee, with his printed sheets, to Worms, where it was completed. In pre-Reformation England it was immediately attacked by the bishops, the Lord Chancellor, Sir Thomas More, and by the King, Henry VIII, who was still rejoicing in the title of 'Defender of the Faith' bestowed on him by a grateful Pope. Copies were burned and readers persecuted. In 1531 Henry attempted to have Tyndale extradited, and, when that failed, to have him kidnapped from Antwerp, where he was then living. Tyndale was finally seized by the orders of another enemy, the (Holy Roman) Emperor in 1535, strangled, and burned at the stake at Vilvorde in the Netherlands.

In 1546 the attack on vernacular versions was renewed by the counter-Reformation Council of Trent, which (to the astonishment of many Catholic biblical scholars) re-affirmed the supremacy of the Vulgate. So great indeed was the Church's horror at the idea of translation from the now sacred text of Jerome's Vulgate that one modern critic, David Lawton, has suggested that this vehemence of response to the idea of translation may well betray not merely an unwillingness to allow the Bible to be removed from the institutional controls imposed by Latin, but also, at a much deeper level, a feeling that, when applied to holy things, the English language, or indeed any vernacular form, was a kind of blasphemy.[21]

The Church's sense that translation somehow involved much more than simply reproducing the Bible in another language was indeed correct – if not necessarily for the reasons contemporaries supposed. Among other unforeseen changes were the demands made by printing on the new translations. Spelling had to be standardized – in many cases for the first time – and that, in turn, meant that in languages like both German and English, where there were a wide variety of dialects, many with works already written in them, one literary dialect, or 'grapholect',[22] now had to be created as the standard form of the language. Though this might involve privileging one particular dialect – in Germany, *Hochdeutsch*; in England, that of the south east – in both cases the demands of such new translations went far beyond the existing resources of any dialectal form. New words, phrases, and concepts had to be introduced, immeasurably enriching the existing language and transforming its capacities to absorb and appropriate. In the case of German, Luther's great translation was to produce virtually a new language, and scholars date modern 'High German' from the publication of his Bible. In the case of English, the language was already in a process of rapid change and vocabulary growth throughout the sixteenth century, but successive biblical translations, by Tyndale, Coverdale, Rogers and others, culminating in the King James Bible of 1611, together with the work of Shakespeare, Jonson, and other Elizabethan writers and dramatists all contributed to the vast vocabulary and technical resource of the English of the seventeenth century.

Nevertheless, the Reformation was not, as it is sometimes presented today, a conflict between authority and individual freedom, but between two equally dogmatic kinds of authority. For Luther and Calvin, as for Wyclif and Tyndale, the question was not over the need for authority, but whether in the last resort that authority resided in the interpretative tradition of the Catholic Church, or with the text of holy scripture itself. For those Protestants who believed the latter was the case, it was axiomatic that, properly understood, the scriptures would provide their own secure interpretation. Calvin's original training had not been as a theologian, but as a lawyer, and if, in practice, Calvinist Geneva proved to be even less tolerant of dissent than Catholicism, it was not least because the written text of the Bible, interpreted within a primarily legal framework of thought, seemed to offer a quite new degree of divinely inspired certainty.

But it was certainty of a new kind. Though the Catholic Church had always sought, through sacraments such as confession and penance, to internalize its moral teachings, and insisted that the pious believer should, similarly, see Christ's life and teachings as applying to them personally, the sheer rarity of Bibles in a world before printing meant that for the mass of ordinary people a parallel stress on internalizing the meaning of scripture was hardly an option. For Calvin, however, leading a literate and Bible-reading community in Geneva, the act of understanding scripture was evidence of divine inspiration. For him, 'the secrete testimony of the holy ghoste' was superior to human reason; those 'whom the holy ghost hath inwardly taught, doe wholly reste uppon the Scripture, and that... Scripture is to be credited for it self sake'.[23] In England William Whitaker agreed that

we determine that the supreme right, authority, and judgement of interpreting the scriptures, is lodged with the Holy Ghost and the scripture itself...We say that the Holy Spirit is the supreme interpreter of scripture, because we must be illuminated by the Holy Spirit to be certainly persuaded of the true sense of scripture.[24]

Though there was general agreement that the literal sense was central, this did not mean uniformity of interpretation, or even that multiplicity of meanings were excluded. Indeed, in many ways the new, inward, inspired and arcane senses of the text were more important than ever.

In every scripture there is something visible, and something invisible, there is a body, and a spirit or soule, the letters, sillables, and wordes be visible, as the body; but the soule, and invisible part is the sense and trueth wrapt and infoulded in the wordes, which are as the barke, ryne, or bone, the meaning within is as the roote, and juce, or as the marrow.[25]

For the new Protestant children of the printing press there was, as it were, both a public and a private meaning to every scriptural text. In spite of declarations in favour of the primacy of the literal meaning, figurative meanings continued to flourish. On the story of Jacob and Esau (Genesis 27), for instance, a late seventeenth-century biblical commentary has no qualms about citing the Church Fathers in support of a four-fold allegorical and figural reading as complex (and as anti-Semitic) as any medieval exegesis:

(Esau is)...*in this respect (as the Fathers observe) a Figure of those, who, desirous to unite* GOD *and the* World *together, cast about how they may enjoy the Comforts of* Heaven *and the Pleasures of the* Earth *both at once* ...

22

This Mysterious History throughout, represents to us in all parts of it Jesus Christ, *cloathed in the outward appearance of a* Sinner, *as* Jacob *here was in that of* Esau. *It is also an admirable Figure of the Reprobation of the* Jews, *who desired nothing but the good things of the* World; *and of the Election of the* Church, *which* (like *David*) *desires but one thing of* GOD, *and requests but one* Blessing.

We must have a care (as S. *Paul* saith) *not to imitate* Esau, *who having sold his Birth-right to* Jacob, *and desiring afterwards, as being the Eldest, to receive the* Blessing *of his Father, was rejected, without being able to persuade his Father to revoke what he had pronounced in Favour of* Jacob, *notwithstanding his entreating it with many Tears. For as he had despised* GOD, GOD *also despised his Cries and Tears, as not proceeding from a sincere Repentance, nor from a true Change of Heart.*[26]

Beyond (or beneath) such public figurations, there was now room for a private, inward and personal interpretation in which the pious reader could meditate on the personal message of the scriptures. If this was no more than the medieval Church had always expected of its spiritual and contemplative orders, the Reformation and the reproductive power of printing had brought the same serious disciplines to the general, and lay, reader.

Not merely had the translation of the Bible and the nature of the printed word irrevocably changed the languages where it had occurred, but it had also altered the nature of reading itself. No longer was it merely the specialist skill of the cleric; it was now become almost an adjunct to salvation. Reading the Bible was not a luxury or an optional extra, but to 'search the scriptures' was the plain duty of every Christian person. Reading itself, therefore, had become a virtue. The printed word carried not merely an external authority, but, through the Holy Spirit, it was the source of inward enlightenment as well.

But if, on the one hand, this new stress on the authority of the written word was to give literary, and especially biblical criticism, an enhanced status, it was always an ambiguous achievement. The inward leadings of the Holy Spirit were not always compatible between Protestant groups. Between Protestants and Catholics the problems were far greater. One leading modern Catholic authority has, with some justice, described the Reformation itself as 'primarily a dispute between translators'.[27] As a Dutch commentator observed in 1536, 'The scripture is like a nose of wax that easily suffereth itself to be drawn backward and forward, and to be moulded and fashioned this way and that, and howsoever ye list.'[28] The image of scripture as wax in the hands of its interpreters was a traditional one, going back at least as far as the thirteenth century, but the endless controversies over meaning that followed were to underline as never before the degree to which all interpretation depended on the point of view of the interpreter.

5 The Romantic Crisis

Up until somewhere about the last third of the eighteenth century this obvious subjectivity of human perception was seen largely as a regrettable nuisance, affecting some individuals and groups (usually one's opponents in any argument), and more evident in some areas of experience than others. If it was common in religious controversies, for many it was still obviously untrue of the Bible itself which was the inspired word of God. It was equally clearly untrue of science, the exploration of Nature, God's 'other book', which as everyone since Newton knew, was concerned not with the vagaries of human perception but with mathematically quantifiable facts about the material world. It was one of the tasks of philosophy to establish what kinds of knowledge were objective and reliable and what might be undermined by human subjectivity.

Since, unlike the Bible, it dealt in fictions, the place of literature in this spectrum was not in doubt. The task of 'poesy' (a much broader literary category than our modern word 'poetry') was not to discover truth, divine or otherwise, but, by imitation, to 'instruct through pleasing'. Because the essential truths were already revealed to humanity, originality lay rather in the presentation of material, and in particular the observation of nature, both human and non-human. Literature, like art in general, was essentially decorative. 'True wit,' wrote Alexander Pope (1688–1744), using the word to mean something closer to our idea of 'creativity', 'is Nature to advantage dressed, / What oft was thought, but ne'er so well expressed.'[29]

The need for nature to be thus 'dressed' was rapidly becoming more apparent with the growing division between subjective and objective facts. John Locke (1632–1704), the most popular philosopher of the eighteenth century, was concerned with how we know anything at all. 'The understanding, like the eye,' he begins, 'whilst it makes us see and perceive all other things, takes no notice of itself; and it requires art and pains to set it at a distance and make it its own object.'[30] There were, he insisted, severe limits on what *could* be known. Locke's distinction between 'primary' qualities that belonged to things, and 'secondary' qualities that were attributed to them by us appeared to have been proved by Newton who had, for instance, shown that colour was not a property of objects themselves, but of light and the human eye. Studies of the eye had shown that what we 'see' is conveyed to the brain through the optic nerve by means of an image on the retina. Though we might think we were perceiving of a concrete and three-dimensional world, the 'reality' was no more than the equivalent of two tiny inverted cinema-screens inside the head. This Lockean version of what Newton's optics meant for perception and aesthetics was at once logical and bleak. As one twentieth-century historian of ideas has graphically put it:

The world that people had thought themselves living in – a world rich with colour and sound, redolent with fragrance, filled with gladness, love and beauty, speaking everywhere of purposive harmony and creative ideals – was crowded now into minute corners of the brains of scattered organic beings. The really important world outside was a world hard, cold, colourless, silent, and dead; a world of quantity, a world of mathematically computable motions in mechanical regularity.[31]

Such was the view of a whole post-Lockean generation of poets and writers: Addison, Akenside,[32] Sterne,[33] and Thomson[34] all in their own ways either deplored or celebrated it. Addison's essay on 'The Pleasures of the Imagination', for instance, captures perfectly the new ambivalence towards the natural world engendered by Locke's epistemology:

Things would make but a poor appearance to the eye, if we saw them only in their proper figures and motions. And what reason can we assign for their exciting in us many of those ideas which are different from anything that exists in the objects themselves (for such are light and colours), were it not to add supernumerary ornaments to the universe, and make it more agreeable to the imagination? We are everywhere entertained with pleasing shows and apparitions, we discover imaginary glories in the heavens, and in the earth, and see some of this visionary beauty poured out over the whole creation; but what a rough and unsightly sketch of Nature should we be entertained with, did all her colouring disappear, and the several distinctions of light and shade vanish? In short, our souls are at present delightfully lost and bewildered in a pleasing delusion, and we walk about like the enchanted hero of a romance, who sees beautiful castles, woods, and meadows; but upon the finishing of some secret spell, the fantastic scene breaks up, and the disconsolate knight finds himself on a barren heath, or in a solitary desert.[35]

The tone is one of an almost enforced cheerfulness, as if the only compensation for the loss of a naive enjoyment of the beauties of nature is a melancholy pleasure in the sophistication that knows itself undeceived. If art could add further 'supernumerary ornaments' to this bleak world picture, it was about as much as could be expected of it.

The first challenge to this theoretical position was, astonishingly, to come from the field of biblical criticism. Robert Lowth's Oxford lectures on *The Sacred Poetry of the Hebrews* (1753) were not intended in any way to be revolutionary. Lowth published, as he had lectured, in Latin, and he was not even translated into English until 1778. An able Hebrew scholar, he had been elected to the Professorship of Poetry at Oxford in May 1741, and since he was obliged to start lecturing almost at once without time to prepare by consulting the normal academic sources, he seems to have turned to his theme of the psalms almost by default. Nevertheless, for an age still accustomed to typological and figural interpretations, his first lecture struck a quite new note:

He who would perceive the peculiar and interior elegancies of the Hebrew poetry, must imagine himself exactly situated as the persons for who it was written, or even as the writers themselves; he is to feel them as a Hebrew...nor is it enough to be acquainted with the language of this people, their manners, discipline, rites and ceremonies; we must even investigate their inmost sentiments, the manner and connexion of their thoughts; in one word, we must see all things with their eyes, estimate all things by their opinions: we must endeavour as much as possible to read Hebrew as the Hebrews would have done it.[36]

Instead of trying to deduce four- (or seven- or twelve-)fold meanings divinely encoded within the sacred texts, Lowth was, almost for the first time,[37] trying to understand the state of mind of the biblical writers as people of their time within what was known of their social framework. The result was to transform both biblical criticism, and, what was entirely unforeseen, the status of poetry as well.

For Lowth, the prophets and poets of the Old Testament were one and the same:

it is sufficiently evident, that the prophetic office had a most strict connexion with the poetic art. They had one common name, one common origin, one common author, the Holy Spirit. Those in particular were called to the exercise of the prophetic office, who were previously conversant with the sacred poetry. It was equally part of their duty to compose verses for the service of the church, and to declare the oracles of God.[38]

26

The Hebrew word 'Nabi', explains Lowth, was used to mean 'a prophet, a poet, or a musician, under the influence of divine inspiration'. The word 'Mashal', commonly used to mean a 'poem' in the Old Testament, is also the equivalent of the (Greek) word translated in the New Testament as 'parable'. In other words, the parables of Jesus, so far from being an innovation, were an extension, by the greatest of the biblical 'poets', of the existing Hebrew prophetic tradition.

Lowth's second great discovery was nothing less than what he believed to be the secret of the construction of Hebrew verse itself. Whereas all European poetry had depended upon such aural effects as rhyme, rhythm and alliteration, no such forms could be discovered in Hebrew verse – even in the psalms, which were obviously intended to be songs. Nor could contemporary Jews explain the lost art of Hebrew poetry. Lowth was now able to explain in his lectures that the poetry of the ancient Hebrews had depended primarily upon a feature which he called 'parallelism'.

The Correspondence of one verse, or line, with another, I call parallelism. When a proposition is delivered, and a second subjoined to it, or drawn under it, equivalent, or contrasted with it in sense; or similar to it in the form of grammatical construction; these I call parallel lines; and the words or phrases, answering one to another in the corresponding lines, parallel terms.[39]

The origins of this parallelism, Lowth argued, like the origins of European poetry, lay in the previous oral tradition – in this case in the antiphonal chants and choruses we find mentioned at various points in the Old Testament. He cites, for instance, 1 Samuel 18: 7, where David returns victorious from a battle with the Philistines and chanting women greet him with the words 'Saul hath slain his thousands', to be answered with a second chorus with the parallel, 'And David his ten thousands'.[40] Lowth distinguishes no less than eight different kinds of parallelism, ranging from simple repetition, to echo, variation, contrast and comparison – as in the particular case cited, where the implications were not lost on Saul, who promptly tried to have David assassinated.

Lowth's work inaugurated a critical revolution.[41] The poet could now claim biblical precedents for a new status: not as a decorator or supplier of 'supernumerary ornaments', but as a prophet, seer, and mediator of divine truth. Hugh Blair, first Professor of Rhetoric at Edinburgh University and, in effect, the first professor of English literature in the world, devoted a whole chapter of his lectures (1783) to summarizing Lowth. They were one of Wordsworth's main sources for his preface to the

Lyrical Ballads. But not merely did Smart and Cowper, Blake and Words-worth cast themselves in a biblical rôle unimaginable, for instance, to Pope or Gray, the models and canons of literary taste had undergone a corresponding shift. By and large, the principal literary models in 1700 were classical; by 1800 they were more likely to be biblical. Lowth anticipates and sets the agenda for Wordsworth's theory of poetic diction by implicitly rejecting the stilted conventions of Augustan poetic diction, and praising instead the 'simple and unadorned' language of Hebrew verse, which gained its 'almost ineffable sublimity' not from artificially elevated diction, but from the depth and universality of its subject matter.

But Lowth's pioneering work had another even less foreseeable con-sequence. Because Hebrew poetry relied on parallelism rather than the rhymes and rhythms of European verse, it was, Lowth claimed, best translated not into verse, but prose.[42] As critics such as Blair were quick to point out,[43] this meant that whereas European and even classical poetry was extremely difficult to translate into another language with any real equivalence of tone or feeling, the Bible was peculiarly, and, by implica-tion, providentially, open to translation. This observation had a further unforeseen consequence: that of blurring the traditional distinctions between prose and verse. To speak of a prose piece as 'poetic' could now be much more than a metaphor. Nor was this shift in critical theory dependent on the writer's own religious beliefs. If Blake, Wordsworth and Coleridge were all Christians of a kind, Shelley had been expelled from Oxford for his atheism. He nevertheless centres his *Defence of Poetry* (1821) on Lowthian principles. 'Poets, according to the circumstances of the age and nation in which they appeared, were called in the earlier epochs of the world, legislators or prophets; a poet essentially comprises and unites both these characters.' 'The distinction between poets and prose writers,' he continues, 'is a vulgar error.' 'Plato was essentially a poet' – so were Moses, Job, Jesus, Isaiah, Bacon, Raphael and Michelan-gelo. To 'defend' poetry he so extends his definition of the word as to embrace the whole of literature – and, indeed, art in general. Following Lowth, the prophetic function of the artist has become more important than any particular linguistic form of poetry. Common to Romanticism right across Europe at this period is a new concept of 'Literature' as of inherent value in itself over and above its ostensible subject. The OED lists this value-added variant as the third, and most modern, meaning of the word, defining it as 'writing which has a claim to consideration on the ground of beauty of form or emotional effect' – adding the rider that it is 'of very recent emergence in both France and England'.

If Lowth's work had had the unintended effect both of transforming the status of secular poetry, and of blurring the distinctions between prose and verse, his stress on the literary power and 'sublimity' of the Bible was to help (though not inaugurate) new ways of appreciating it as an aesthetic work. Though the new secular aesthetic status of the written word has been attributed to many origins, there is no doubt of the part played by the Romantic reading of the Bible. Thus in Germany, what was virtually a new subject, 'aesthetics', had come into being following Kant's hint (it is little more than that) in the third *Critique* that the gap between pure and practical reason might be bridgeable by art, and had become a central plank of Romanticism.[44] But there is a great deal of evidence to suggest that this new value attached to good writing, whether prose or verse, was already gaining ground in both Britain and Germany, before either Lowth or Kant, as an extension of the Protestant approach to reading the Bible. Wesley A. Kort, for instance, has argued that the intense self-searching and self-constructing relationship to the text fostered by the personal Bible-study of Protestantism was subsequently transferred first to the study of the 'book' of Nature in seventeenth-century science, then to history, and finally, with the rise of the new art-form, the 'novel', in the eighteenth century, to the reading of secular fiction as 'literature'.[45] Not least among the many ironies of critical history is the way in which, just as a literal historical interpretation of the Bible was becoming increasingly impossible for an educated readership, it was to re-gain much of its old status in a secularized form, as 'literature'.

—— 6 The Bible as Literature ——

In his *Table Talk* for 24 June 1827 we find Coleridge reported as saying:

Our version of the Bible is to be loved and prized for this, as for a thousand other things, – that it has preserved a purity of meaning to many terms of natural objects. Without this holdfast, our vitiated imaginations would refine away language to mere abstractions. Hence the French have lost their poetical language; and Mr Blanco White says the same thing has happened to the Spanish.[46]

This charge that French and Spanish, unlike English, had entirely lost their 'poetical language' through over-refinement is at first glance a puzzling one, but it is not difficult to recover Coleridge's sources. The Reverend Joseph Blanco White was no outside commentator on Spain. He had been born in Seville in 1775 of an Irish immigrant family. Apprenticed to his father's business at the age of eight, he took what seemed the only way out by discovering a vocation for the priesthood – to which he was finally ordained, after years of training, at the age of twenty-five. Within four years he had lost his faith – but was unable to resign his orders without incurring the charge of heresy, in Spain still then punishable by death. He was eventually able to escape to London during the general confusion after Napoleon's occupation of Madrid, and while in England slowly recovered his faith in Christianity, though not in Catholicism. In 1814 he became a priest of the Church of England and settled to study Greek and Divinity at Oxford – where in 1826 he became an honorary member of the Oriel common room (where Coleridge's son, Hartley, had briefly been a fellow in 1820). At this period he was on intimate terms with Newman, Pusey and Whately. In 1831 he was to follow Whately, as tutor to his son, when he moved to Dublin. Here, however, he changed his religion once again, becoming a Unitarian. He died in Liverpool in 1841.[47] The work Coleridge is referring to is his *Evidences Against Catholicism*, which appeared in 1825 and which, to judge again from notebook entries (*CN*, IV, 5240), he seems to have read almost at once.

Similarly, his remarks on the unpoetic nature of French, so far from being a general jibe at Gallic culture, seem in fact to be derived directly from one of France's most eminent men of letters: Denis Diderot. In his *Letter on the Deaf-Mutes* (1751) Diderot had himself argued that, unlike Latin and Greek in the classical world, or contemporary English and Italian, French had become increasingly abstract and analytical to the point where it had lost its 'warmth, eloquence, and energy' and become a language of prose best fitted for science and philosophy.[48] For him, poetry and prose stand at opposite ends of a continuum. The more sophisticated a language becomes, so his thesis runs, the more it moves towards the prose end of the spectrum and the less able it is to be an adequate vehicle for poetry. With variations, this is a view that was echoed by many later French literary figures: Madame de Staël, Proudhon, de Vigny, Renan and even Taine.[49] It was also adopted by a number of late eighteenth- and early nineteenth-century theorists of language: Wilhelm von Humboldt in Germany, Adam Ferguson in Scotland, and by Thomas Love Peacock in England, whose use of the idea as an ironic polemical device was to goad his friend Shelley into writing the *Defence of Poetry*.[50] None of these, however, attempted to couple this idea that poetry is a more concrete and therefore more primitive linguistic mode with questions of biblical translation. In making this link Coleridge has not merely gone beyond his sources, he has, typically, reversed the whole thrust of their arguments.

To see how this is so, we need to look more closely at Diderot's description of the way in which poetry operates through language.

There is in the discourse of the poet a spirit that gives motion and life to every syllable. What is this spirit? I have sometimes felt its presence; but all I know about it is, that it is it that causes things to be said all at once; that in the very moment they are grasped by the understanding, the soul is moved by them, the imagination sees them, and the ear hears them; and that the discourse is not merely an enchainment of energetic terms that reveal the thought with force and elevation, but is even more a web of hieroglyphs accumulated one after the other and painting the thought.[51]

For Diderot, the 'hieroglyphs' of poetry are a common feature of primitive languages, or those in their earliest years of development. In later generations it is only the outstanding geniuses who can continue to produce them. Because of this essentially hieroglyphic structure the images of such figures as Homer are highly resistant to appropriation by later European cultures: 'the more a poet is charged with hieroglyphs, the more difficult he is to render in translation'. This idea of poetry as a series of verbal hieroglyphs was to exert a powerful hold on a later generation of Romantic thinkers in two ways. Firstly, because Diderot also sees 'primitive' and poetic languages as being those of 'fiction and untruth' (*de la fable et du mensonge*), he gives a new twist to the platonic idea that there was a very close link between poetry and lying. Creativity is invention. Secondly, it served to reinforce the already strong strand of primitivism that was latent in almost all Romantic aesthetics, but was to take a peculiarly potent form with German Hellenism. In the wave of enthusiasm for all things Greek that had affected Herder, Schiller, von Humboldt and Goethe, reaching its apogee with such figures as Winckelmann, the literature of the classical Greeks was seen as ideal, immediate and fresh, and free from the enervating hand of tradition or convention.

Within a few years this primitivistic view of the Bible was to be developed into a critical theory of history. For the French writer, François René Auguste de Chateaubriand (1768–1848), in his *Genius of Christianity* (1802):

Christianity is, if we may so express it, a double religion. Its teaching has reference to the nature of intellectual being, and also to our own nature: it makes the mysteries of the Divinity and the mysteries of the human heart go hand-in-hand; and, by removing the veil that conceals the true God, it also exhibits man just as he is.

Such a religion must necessarily be more favourable to the delineation of *characters* than another which dives not into the secret of the passions.

31

The fairer half of poetry, the dramatic, received no assistance from polytheism, for morals were separated from mythology.[52]

This is a point with which his contemporary, Jane Austen, could scarcely disagree. Her new art-form of the 'novel' depended above all on such an exploration of character. But Chateaubriand is no less conscious of the moral and social dimensions of this new sense of individuality. 'Christianity...by mingling with the affections of the soul, has increased the resources of drama, whether in the epic or on the stage'.[53] Thus since pagan Antiquity had little interest in an after-life, classical tragedy ended simply with death. In contrast, in a play like Racine's *Phèdre* the tragic tension is increased by the fact that, as a Christian wife, Phèdre is also jeopardizing her immortal soul. It is, perhaps, not surprising that the Romantics should have increasingly turned away from classical towards biblical literary models in their search for legitimation from the past.

It is this new sense of individuality and inner space produced by the Bible which, Chateaubriand claims, has transformed poetry. In spite of the praise heaped by neo-classicists upon the evocativeness of classical mythology, instead of embellishing nature, in reality, he claims, it had the effect of destroying her real charms. 'Mythology diminished the grandeur of Nature – the ancients had no descriptive poetry, properly so called.'[54]

No sooner had the apostles begun to preach the gospel to the world than descriptive poetry made its appearance...Nature ceased to speak through the fallacious organs of idols; her ends were discovered, and it became known that she was made in the first place for God, and in the second for man...This great discovery changed the whole face of the creation.[55]

This argument follows from the previous one, in that it sees Christianity as the prime agent of demythologizing nature. Not merely do the great religious poems owe their aesthetic sublimity to the Bible, but the entire aesthetic behind Romanticism is a necessary and inevitable outcome of a Christian and biblical civilisation. Moreover, such a realization enables us to look back on the past and perceive qualities which could neither have been noticed nor appreciated in earlier or non-Christian societies. 'The growth of descriptive poetry in modern times enables us to see and appreciate the genius of the poets of Job, Ecclesiastes, and the Psalms.'[56] For Chateaubriand the true aesthetic qualities of the Hebrew scriptures awaited a modern and specifically Christian appreciation.

Only a few years later, in Germany, Friedrich Schleiermacher (1768–1834) was beginning to explore the wider implications of such critical claims. As Professor of theology in Berlin, his theory of hermeneutics – the art of understanding the meaning of texts – was developed in the context of biblical criticism, but it was always concerned with literature in general. In the 1790s, as we have mentioned, he had been a member of the group of young self-consciously styled 'Romantics' in Jena, and Schleiermacher begins characteristically not from ideas of a text as having any fixed meaning, nor with conjectures as to authorial 'intentions', but with the complex inter-relation between reader and text, and, behind that, the totality of the reader's culture. Just as there could be no such thing as 'perspectiveless vision' in that all sight had to be from a particular moment in place and time, so too all written texts had to be understood as coming from a particular person at a particular time. In this context there could be no simple key to unlock the scriptures; no formula to establish a definitive meaning: 'understanding' is, rather, 'an unending task'.[57]

For Schleiermacher and for his successors there could be no privileged access to biblical meaning; instead, as in the rest of literature, all interpretations had to be understood within the context that produced them. This was not to deny the truth of previous insights, but to give meaning to the shifting patterns of previous interpretation. Just as medieval systems of allegorizing the scriptures had been part of a much wider sense of the entire universe demonstrating (to those who could 'read' it) its divine origin, so the discovery of the Hebrew prophets as poets had to be related to contemporary debates about the rôle of art in society. Similarly, the historicizing of those who, like Lessing, Schiller or Chateaubriand, sought to see the Bible in terms of a long growth of human consciousness, was part of a much wider Romantic quest to understand the essential difference of the past.

It was against this background that we find Coleridge devoting the last twenty years of his life to literary and biblical criticism.[58] Though he was a highly original thinker, there is also ample evidence of his acquaintance with contemporary continental sources. *The Statesman's Manual* (1817) for instance, incorporates to a surprising degree not merely the Schlegels' sense of the imaginative and organic unity of the Bible, but even Chateaubriand's broad cultural sweep:

they [the Scriptures] are the living educts of the Imagination; of that reconciling and mediatory power, which incorporating the Reason in Images of the Sense, and organising (as it were) the flux of the Senses by the permanence and self-circling energies of the Reason, gives birth to a system of symbols, harmonious in themselves, and consubstantial with the truths, of which they are the *conductors* ... Hence ... the Sacred Book is worthily entitled the WORD OF GOD. Hence too, its contents present to us the stream of time continuous as Life and a symbol of Eternity, inasmuch as the Past and the Future are virtually contained in the Present...In the Scriptures therefore both facts and persons must of necessity have a two-fold significance, a past and a future, a temporary and a perpetual, a particular and a universal application. They must be at once Portraits and Ideals.[59]

Much of Coleridge's later work centred around giving substance to this pregnant summary. Of all the Romantic critics, he probably came closest to this ideal of discovering in the Bible (as in Shakespeare) an organic and aesthetic unity that enhanced – and, indeed, was inseparable from – its spiritual content.

⸻ 7 Separation and Specialization ⸻

It was precisely this belief in a unified approach to the Bible that led Coleridge into one of the earliest attacks on professional biblical criticism from a 'literary' angle. In his marginal notes to Johann Gottfried Eichhorn's great *Einleitung ins Alte Testament* (1780–3) he repeatedly charges the German scholar with failing to understand how the poetic imagination works. Where, for instance, Eichhorn dismisses Ezekiel's vision of the chariot (Ezekiel 1: 15–21) as 'mere drapery, mere poetic fiction' (*blosse Einkleidung, blosse poetische Dichtungen*) and suggests that in so far as he is an 'artist' he is consciously creating fictions, and therefore is the less an authentic 'visionary', Coleridge scribbled indignantly:

It perplexes me to understand how a man of Eichhorn's Sense, Learning, and Acquaintance with Psychology could form, or attach belief to, so cold-blooded an hypothesis. That in Ezechiel's Visions Ideas or Spiritual Entities are presented in visual Symbols, I never doubted; but as little can I doubt, that such Symbols did present themselves to Ezechiel in Visions – and by a Law closely connected with, if not contained in, that by which sensations are organised into Images and Mental Sounds in our ordinary sleep.[60]

For Coleridge, to apply such reductionist reasoning to a work which, by Eichhorn's own admission, was great art, was to misunderstand both the nature of art and the nature of the truths it created.

Yet the impact of Coleridge's work, like that of his contemporary, Schleiermacher, was muted in his own century for two apparently accidental and unconnected reasons. The first was lack of publication. Besides *Aids to Reflection* (1825), and the posthumous *Confessions of an Inquiring Spirit* (1846), the bulk of Coleridge's manuscript and notebook material remained unpublished until the late twentieth century. In addition to the so-called 'Magnum Opus', and the *Philosophical Lectures*, Coleridge's notebooks of the later 1820s are almost exclusively devoted to biblical commentaries of one kind or another. Similarly, though Schleiermacher published extensively on theology, he never in fact published his lectures on hermeneutics, and until the mid-twentieth century all that was available were the scattered and incomplete notes of his students.

The second, even more accidental factor, was that the reforms at the new University of Berlin by Wilhelm von Humboldt, introduced in 1809, just before Schleiermacher took up the professorship of theology he was to occupy there from 1810 to 1834, had specifically separated theology from the other humanities, which were placed within a newly created 'faculty of Arts'.[61] Such was the prestige of German universities in the nineteenth century that many universities in both Britain and the USA tended to follow the Humboldtian models. Moreover, the high reputation acquired by the refounded theological faculties served if anything to widen the gulf with the other humanities, and to create what an early twentieth-century critic aptly called a *gletscherwall*, a 'glacial-moraine', dividing biblical studies from the reading of other literature, accentuating the gulf between the disciplines just at the very time when in both England and Germany more common ground was being discovered between them than ever before.[62]

For much of the nineteenth century, therefore, the institutional barriers between literary and biblical criticism produced little more than a dialogue of the deaf. Thus Matthew Arnold's sustained attempt to bridge the gap between literature and theology in the second half of the nineteenth century earned him friends in neither camp. In a series of publications in the 1870s, *St Paul and Protestantism* (1870), *Literature and Dogma* (1873), and *God and the Bible* (1875) he argued passionately for a greater literary understanding of the Bible. His argument rested on two basic principles: the first is that the Bible requires nothing for its understanding except what can be verified. 'For us, the God of popular religion is a legend, a fairy-tale; learned theology has simply taken this fairy-tale and dressed it metaphysically.' The second is that 'the language of the Bible is not scientific but *literary*'.[63] 'It is the language of poetry and emotion, approximate language, thrown out, as it were at certain great objects which the human mind augurs and feels after, and thrown out by men very liable...to delusion and error.'[64] It is quite clear that Arnold himself believed that by this process of what (in the twentieth century) was to be called 'de-mythologizing', he could salvage the essential moral truths of Christianity, together with some kind of vestigial divinity in what he called the 'not ourselves which makes for righteousness', but to many later readers it is his use of the word 'poetry' that seems most puzzling. For him, 'poetry' is 'language not professing to be exact at all, and we are free to use it or not to use it as our sense of public propriety may dictate'.[65] This seems to exclude both the classic literary sense in which it was used by Sydney or Johnson, of a deliberate fiction created with a moral or didactic intent to 'instruct through pleasing', as well as the new prophetic idea of Blake, Coleridge or Shelley that poetry might utter a higher truth than mere historical veracity, or even the Wordsworthian sense of 'the spontaneous overflow of powerful feelings'. The 'poetry' of the Bible that Arnold hopes will compensate for any loss of belief in its didactic message is, in the end, a curiously vague and bloodless quality, finally as separable from its moral content as any Augustan critic could have wished.[66]

Whether Arnold's agenda of using German historical criticism to modernize perceptions of the Bible and allow an appreciation of their aesthetic values could ever have captured the citadels of theological specialists is doubtful; given the academic context, it never stood a chance. In the long run both literary theory and biblical criticism were alike impoverished by the growth of professional specialization.[67] Lack of understanding of basic narrative and literary techniques was at least one reason for the way in which much nineteenth- and early twentieth-century biblical criticism was appropriated by the most simplistic critics, prone to identify every shift in tone or unexpected juxtaposition of stories with a change of author or the crude misunderstanding of the supposed 'redactor' of the manuscript. At the same time, literary criticism could never quite rid itself of the illusion that it was somehow still in the salvation business. Critics fought each other with a passion usually reserved for holy wars, and writers claimed for themselves a metaphysical status that would have looked ludicrous among painters or musicians. In the early twentieth century the philosopher T. E. Hulme attacked what he called this 'romanticism'.

Just as in the case of the other instincts, Nature has her revenge. The instincts that find their right and proper outlet in religion must come out in some other way. You don't believe in God, so you begin to believe that man is a God. You don't believe in Heaven, so you begin to believe in a heaven on earth. In other words you get romanticism. The concepts that are right and proper in their own sphere are spread over, and so mess up, falsify and blur the clear outlines of human experience. It is like pouring a pot of treacle over the dinner table. Romanticism then, and this is the best definition I can give of it, is spilt religion.[68]

As we have seen, this is hardly a definition of Romanticism that would have satisfied Schleiermacher or Coleridge, but it offered a salutary criticism of many of the wilder pretensions of post-Arnoldian literary critics.

Nevertheless, there were always, of course, exceptions. Among the most remarkable irruptions from outside the academy was that of the Danish 'philosopher', Søren Kierkegaard (1813–55) whose 'Panegyric upon Abraham' in *Fear and Trembling* (1843) was to transform future readings of the Abraham and Isaac story. His vision of Abraham as a 'knight of faith' was reinforced by repeated re-tellings of the story with slight variations from the original to illustrate the extreme complexity and reticence of the Genesis narrative. In true biblical midrashic tradition, Kierkegaard's commentary was brilliantly appropriated and transformed into a literary analysis in the early 1940s by Erich Auerbach, a Berlin Jew who had taken refuge from the Nazis in Istanbul for the duration of the Second World War. By means of a comparison with that other great foundational epic of Western civilization, Homer's *Odyssey*, Auerbach's *Mimesis* (1946), demonstrates how the two texts achieved their effects by opposite techniques: Homer by the elaboration of detail; Genesis by the elimination of every unnecessary piece of 'foreground' until the mysterious compulsion of the 'background' becomes, by default, the main driving force of the plot.

Though Kierkegaard is conveniently pigeon-holed by the academy as a 'philosopher', the term does little justice to the artistry of his narrative technique which moves effortlessly from literary criticism, to anecdote, to religious meditation. Not for nothing, perhaps, was he Hans Andersen's flatmate in Copenhagen. Certainly, his technique of what one might call criticism by narrative rather than by the application of conventional theories was to prove prophetic. Thus Ernest Renan's *Life of Jesus* (1863) owed its huge popular appeal to the fact that it was not a scholarly investigation, but an immediate and imaginative response to the Jesus of the gospels which broke all the rules of scholarship and brought Jesus 'alive' for its readers. In Albert Schweitzer's words:

Renan's work marked an epoch, not for the Catholic world only, but for general literature... He offered his readers a Jesus who was alive, whom he, with his artistic imagination, had met under the blue heaven of Galilee, and whose lineaments his inspired pencil had seized. Men's attention was arrested, and they thought to see Jesus, because Renan had the skill to make them see blue skies, seas of waving corn, distant mountains, gleaming lilies, in a landscape with the Lake of Gennesaret for its centre, and hear with him in the whispering of the reeds the eternal melody of the Sermon on the Mount.[69]

Its success, with translations appearing in almost every major European language, was the more remarkable in that Renan was not a Christian, and his portrait of Jesus, as a naive Galilean peasant, was at the farthest possible remove from either a devotional or a supernatural view of Christ. What matters, rather, is the drama of the story and the characterization, and it is significant that the Greek novelist, Nikos` Kazantzakis, for instance, was enormously influenced by Renan when writing his controversial *Last Temptation of Christ* (1979).

Though the twentieth century has seen many diverse theories of biblical interpretation, from literalist, to historicist, feminist and post-modernist, perhaps its most valuable contribution to biblical understanding has come not from critics at all but, as in the case of Coleridge and Kierkegaard in the previous century, from practising artists such as Kazantzakis. An increasingly secularized and pluralistic world has meant no decline – arguably perhaps an increase – in the use of biblical themes by painters, sculptors and poets. Even more significantly, biblical themes have provided subjects for novelists and dramatists as never before. In the process, qualities of biblical narrative long overlaid by pietistic reverence have been re-discovered. Though a succession of Hollywood epics such as *The Ten Commandments, Samson and Delilah*, and *David and Bathsheba* cashed in on the ever-commercial possibilities of combining sex, religion and violence to the point of making the mythic seem more improbable than any ridicule by eighteenth-century historicists, serious (though less popular) dramatists were discovering quite new qualities of irony in biblical narrative. James Bridie (pen-name of the Scots playwright, Osborne Henry Mavor, 1888–1951) brought out some of the innate humour of the Old Testament and Apocrypha in *Tobias and the Angel* (1930) and *Jonah and the Whale* (1932) and the Cumberland poet, Norman Nicholson (b. 1914), was able to introduce fresh layers of irony by re-locating the story of Elijah and Ahab in the Lake District in *The Old Man of the Mountains* (1946). A succession of writers, many Jewish, including Norman Mailer, Dan Jacobson, and the critic Harold Bloom, have produced novels on Old Testament themes.

Undoubtedly the greatest biblical novel of the century, however, is Thomas Mann's magnificent epic *Joseph and His Brothers*, a tetralogy published between 1933 and 1946. Begun in Germany, not least as an act of political defiance to Hitler and the rise of the Nazis in the 1920s, and completed in exile in California, it treats the story of Jacob and Joseph as one of the emergence of humanity from mythic to historical self-consciousness. Joseph himself is seen as the type of the artist, in the tradition of the Old Testament Patriarchs and prophets endeavouring both to understand his world and to change it by means of his interpretation of it. Mann's narrative brings out, as no previous re-telling has done, the layers, even convolutions, of irony underlying the Genesis story. Nevertheless, his saga is also inescapably twentieth-century, not just in its hermeneutic interpretation of the past (he remains true to the principles of a century and a half of historical scholarship, avoiding both miracles and anachronisms) but also in the way his account impinges on the interpretation of his time. This was a point not lost on the Nazi censors who moved swiftly against him when they came to power in 1933, forcing Mann into exile first in Switzerland and then the USA. The greatest biblical epic of the century was (correctly) read by its enemies as also being the most powerful criticism of contemporary affairs.[70]

There is, of course, nothing new about re-telling the biblical narratives. It had been done in the fourteenth-century miracle plays; by the Calvinistic Genevan critic, Theodore Beza, who wrote a popular sixteenth-century play about Abraham; again by Milton in *Paradise Lost*; and by numerous eighteenth- and nineteenth-century writers, including figures as diverse as Byron and Kierkegaard. Nor, as we have seen, can we draw a clear distinction between theories of criticism and the creativity of each re-telling; the Bible owes its very origins to this endless intertextuality. Each generation has both re-written, and itself *been* re-written, by the seemingly continuous dialectic between the Bible and its age. As we approach the new millennium, no closure seems in sight.

Notes

1 See Robert P. Carroll, *The Wolf in the Sheepfold: The Bible as a Problem for Christianity* (London: SPCK, 1991).

2 See Brevard Childs, *The New Testament as Canon: An Introduction* (London: SCM, 1984), p. 16.

3 See Cornelius Ernst, 'World Religions and Christian Theology', in *Multiple Echo: Explorations in Theology* (London: Darton, Longman and Todd, 1979), p. 34.

4 Austin Farrer, *A Rebirth of Images* (Westminster: Dacre Press, 1944).

5 See E. R. Goodenough, *Introduction to Philo Judaeus*, 2nd edn (Oxford: Basil Blackwell, 1962); and Henry Chadwick, 'Philo', in *Cambridge History of Later Greek and Early Medieval Philosophy* ed. A. H. Armstrong (Cambridge: Cambridge University Press, 1967), pp. 137–57.

6 It is attractive to follow the tradition that identifies him with the Longinus who was chief minister to Zenobia, Queen of Palmyra, the Nabatean oasis empire, finally destroyed by the Roman Emperor Aurelian in the third century, but there is no concrete evidence for this.

7 Isaac Watts, Preface, *Horae Lyricae* (1709), 6th edn (London, 1731), pp. xii–xiii.

8 *De praescriptione hereticorum*, 7.

9 See the 'Epilogue' by P. G. Walsh to J. G. Kenney (ed.), *The Cambridge History of Classical Literature*, Vol. ii, part 5: 'The Later Principate' (Cambridge: Cambridge University Press, 1982), pp. 107–8. I am greatly indebted to Professor Walsh's guidance in this area.

10 See David Norton, *A History of the Bible as Literature* (Cambridge: Cambridge University Press, 1993), Vol. 1, p. 32.

11 Ibid.

12 See, for instance, Nathan's denunciation of David (2 Samuel 12: 1–15).

13 See John Wilkinson, *Interpretation and Community* (London: Macmillan, 1963), esp. pp. 119–57.

14 Marjorie Reeves, 'The Bible and Literary Authorship in the Middle Ages', in *Reading the Text: Biblical Criticism and Literary Theory*, ed. S. Prickett (Oxford: Blackwell, 1991), p. 16.

15 A. J. Minnis, *Medieval Theory of Authorship* (London: Scolars Press, 1984), p. 34.

16 Reeves, 'The Bible', p. 17.

17 Erich Auerbach, 'Figura', tr. R. Mannheim, in Auerbach, *Scenes from the Drama of European Literature* (New York: Meridian, 1959), p. 28.

18 'The Reasonableness of Typology', G. W. H. Lampe and K. G. Woollcombe, *Essays on Typology* (London: SCM, 1957), p. 31.

19 See Daniel J. Boorstin, *The Discoverers* (New York: Random House, 1983), pp. 510–16.

20 Felipe Fernandez-Armesto, *Millennium* (London: QPD, 1995), p. 276.

21 David Lawton, *Blasphemy* (Harvester Wheatsheaf: Hemel Hempstead, 1993), ch. 3.

22 See Walter J. Ong, *Orality and Literacy: The Technologising of the Word* (London: Routledge, 1992), p. 8.

23 J. Calvin, *The Institution of Christian Religion wrytten in Latine...and translated into Englyshe according to the authors last edition*, tr. Thomas Norton (London, 1561), I, vii, 4–5, fos 14v–15r. Cited by Rivkah Zim, 'The Reformation', in Prickett, *Reading the Text*, p. 71.

24 William Whitaker, *Disputatio de sacra scriptura* (London, 1588), tr. W. Fitzgerald as *A disputation on Holy Scripture Against the Papists* (Cambridge: Parker Society, 1849), p. 415.

25 Thomas Wilson, *Theologicall Rules, to Guide Us in the Understanding and Practise of Holy Scriptures: Two Centuries: Drawne partly out of Scriptures Themselves: Partly out of Ecclesiasticall Writers Old and New* (London, 1567), p. 46.

26 *History of the Old and New Testaments,* anon., 4th impression (London, 1712) p. 31.

27 Edmond Carey, *Les Grands Traducteurs Français* (Geneva: Librairie de l'Université, 1963), pp. 7–8.

28 Albertus Pighius, cited by H. C. Porter, 'The Nose of Wax: Scripture and the Spirit from Erasmus to Milton', *Transactions of the Royal Historical Society,* 5th series, 14 (1964), p. 155.

29 Alexander Pope, *An Essay on Criticism,* part II, lines 297–8.

30 John Locke, *Essay Concerning Human Understanding,* Book 1, ch. 1, para. 1.

31 E. A. Burtt, *Metaphysical Foundations of Modern Science* (London: Routledge, 1932), pp. 236–7.

32 See, for instance, *Pleasures of the Imagination* (1744), II, pp. 103–20.

33 For the impact of Locke on Sterne, see A. D. Nuttall, *A Common Sky* (Sussex University Press, Chatto, 1974), ch. 1.

34 See, for instance, *The Seasons,* 'Spring', pp. 203–17.

35 Joseph Addison, 'The Pleasures of the Imagination', *Spectator* (1712), p. 413.

36 Robert Lowth, *Lectures on the Sacred Poetry of the Hebrews,* tr. G. Gregory (London: 1787), Vol. i, pp. 113, 114.

37 The founder of what was later called the 'higher criticism' was probably a Frenchman, Richard Simon. See Françoise Deconinck-Brossard, 'England and France in the Eighteenth Century', Prickett, *Reading the Text,* pp. 136–47.

38 Lowth, *Lectures,* Vol. ii, p. 18.

39 Ibid., Vol. ii, p. 32.

40 Ibid., Vol. ii, p. 53.

41 For a fuller discussion of the implications of Lowth's work see Stephen Prickett, *Words and 'The Word': Language, Poetics and Biblical Interpretation,* (Cambridge: Cambridge University Press, 1986).

42 *Lectures,* Vol. i, pp. 71ff.

43 Hugh Blair, *Lectures on Poetry and Belles Lettres* (1783) (2 vols, Edinburgh, 1820), Vol. ii, pp. 270–1.

44 See David Bowie, *Aesthetics and Subjectivity: from Kant to Nietzsche* (Manchester: Manchester University Press, 1990); and *From Romanticism to Critical Theory: The Philosophy of German Literary Theory* (London: Routledge, 1997).

45 See Stephen Prickett, *Origins of Narrative: the Romantic Appropriation of the Bible* (Cambridge: Cambridge University Press, 1996); and Wesley A. Kort, *Take Read: Scripture, Textuality and Cultural Practice* (University Park, PA: Pennsylvania State University Press, 1966).

46 *Table Talk,* ed. H. N. Coleridge (London: 1852), p. 43. The publication of Carl Woodring's admirable edition of the *Table Talk* in the Bollingen Series (Prin-

ceton, NJ: Princeton University Press, 1990) reveals that this has been written up from briefer notes, but with substantially the same sentiments (1, 75). The coda about Blanco White and Spanish is missing. For the purposes of this discussion, I shall assume that it is nonetheless authentic, but spoken at another time and added into the text by the process of conflation and consolidation described in the Editor's Introduction (lxxxiv–xci).

47 For an account of Blanco White's Oxford career see Geoffrey Faber, *Oxford Apostles* (London: Faber & Faber, 1933) esp. pp. 112–14.

48 Cited by Hans Aarsleff, 'Introduction to Wilhelm von Humboldt', *On Language*, tr. Peter Heath (Cambridge: Cambridge University Press, 1988), lvii.

49 See Frederic E. Faverty, *Matthew Arnold the Ethnologist* (Evanston: Northwestern University Press), p. 84.

50 See Aarsleff, 'Introduction'; Marilyn Butler, *Peacock Displayed* (London: Routledge, 1979), pp. 142ff; and Thomas Love Peacock, *The Four Ages of Poetry*, ed. H. F. B. Brett-Smith (Oxford: Oxford University Press, 1921).

51 Aarsleff, 'Introduction', pp. lvi–lvii.

52 François René Auguste de Chateaubriand, *The Genius of Christianity* (1802), tr. Charles White (Baltimore: 1856), p. 232.

53 Ibid., p. 299.

54 Ibid., p. 299.

55 Ibid., p. 305.

56 Ibid., p. 308.

57 *Hermeneutics, the Handwritten Manuscripts*, ed. H. Kimmerle, tr. J. Duke and J. Forstmann (Missoula, MT: Scholars Press, 1977), p. 41. For a general account of Schleiermacher's hermeneutics see Kurt Mueller-Vollmer, *The Hermeneutics Reader* (Oxford: Blackwell, 1986), ch. 2.

58 See Stephen Prickett, *Romanticism and Religion: The Tradition of Coleridge and Wordsworth in the Victorian Church* (Cambridge: Cambridge University Press, 1976), chs 1–2.

59 S. T. Coleridge, *The Statesman's Manual*, in *Lay Sermons*, ed. R. J. White (London: Routledge, 1972), pp. 28–30.

60 S. T. Coleridge, *Marginalia*, ed. George Whalley, *Collected Coleridge*, Vol. XII (London/Princeton, NJ: Routledge/Princeton University Press, 1979–), Vol. 2, p. 410.

61 See Prickett, *Words and 'The Word'*, pp. 1–2.

62 Ibid., p. 1.

63 'God and the Bible', *Complete Prose Works of Matthew Arnold*, ed. R. H. Super (Michigan: Michigan University Press, 1970) Vol. vii, p. 155.

64 Ibid., p. 155.

65 Ibid., pp. 156–7.

66 For a fuller discussion of Arnold's views on poetry and religion see Prickett, *Romanticism and Religion*, ch. 8, and *Words and 'The Word'*, pp. 189–94.

67 Prickett, *Words*, pp. 196–8.

68 T. E. Hulme, 'Romanticism and Classicism', *Speculations*, ed. Herbert Read, 2nd edn (London: Routledge, 1939), p. 116.

69 Albert Schweitzer, *The Quest of the Historical Jesus*, 1906, tr. W. Montgomery (London: A. & C. Black, 1936), p. 23.
70 See Prickett, *Origins*, ch. 6.

LITERARY READINGS OF THE BIBLE: TRENDS IN MODERN CRITICISM

DAVID JASPER

In A. S. Byatt's novel *Babel Tower* (1997), Frederica, a teacher of literature, writes the following words in an essay on D. H. Lawrence and E. M. Forster:

It is not so simple as supposing that sexual love replaced for the moderns the mystical experience of the Christian religion. It is more that the narrative of the Novel, in its high days, was built on, out of, and in opposition to the narrative of the one Book, the source of all Books, the Bible. Both Forster and Lawrence use for the joining of lovers the old Biblical symbol of God's covenant between Heaven and Earth, the rainbow, even though Forster's rainbow is also a simulacrum of the rainbow bridge built by Wagner's all-too-human deities between earth and Walhalla.

Why bring in the stars? Ursula asks. D. H. Lawrence said the novel is the one bright book of Life. In the one bright book you have to have it all, the Word made flesh, the rainbow, the stars, the One.[1]

We have already seen how the Bible has provided subjects for literature, art and film in the twentieth century perhaps as never before, as the Scriptures are released from their overlay of pietistic reverence. In modern and postmodern literature the Bible 'still retains its astonishing power to interest, to illuminate, to inspire'. Writing of the Passion narratives, the Christian theologian F. W. Dillistone suggests that 'the movement of the

44

story corresponds … to the movement of life everywhere and it is always possible that the goal towards which the story leads may find its counterpart within the circumstances of a wholly different age'.[2] But, as Byatt's Frederica recognizes, the relationship between the Bible as read within the Christian tradition and the modern novel is neither simple nor straightforward, for if the Bible and its sacred authority remain foundational for Western literature, it is so not merely within the Christian tradition but within an eclectic range of literary and cultural references, the Bible being a great text within the complex library of *Weltliteratur*. Frederica is actually quoting in her essay from D. H. Lawrence's posthumously published essay 'Why the Novel Matters', which, with typical Lawrentian rhetoric, feeds upon the Bible to nourish his own particular celebration of the human and human life. For Lawrence, the novel is what is most important, and it is the fact that the Bible can be read as a novel rather than modern fiction's drawing upon Scripture that is significant for him.

The novel is the book of life. In this sense, the Bible is a great confused novel. You may say it is about God. But it is really about man alive. Adam, Eve, Sarai, Abraham, Isaac, Jacob, Samuel, David, Bathsheba, Ruth, Esther, Solomon, Job, Isaiah, Jesus, Mark, Judas, Paul, Peter: what is it but man alive from start to finish? Man alive, not mere bits. Even the Lord is another man alive, in a burning bush, throwing the tablets of stone at Moses' head.[3]

The Bible – '*all* the Bible' – according to Lawrence is one of 'the supreme old novels', along with Homer and Shakespeare, for they are all things to all people. This, in a sense, is a claim revisited in James Joyce's great 'novel' *Finnegans Wake* (1939), which is nothing less than a great narrative of fall and redemption – like the Bible – beginning with Adam and Eve (though now in Dublin) and ending with the final act of adoration as 'I sink, I'd die down over his feet, humbly dumbly, only to washup.' *Finnegans Wake* in a sense looks back to the poetry of William Blake, as a revisiting and incorporation of the Bible, meeting Scripture neither critically nor religiously, but on its own terms *as* literature which explores, with massive intertextual allusion, lyrical beauty and humour, the range of human experience in the human condition.

Many other novels, plays and poems of the twentieth century have tended to draw upon Scripture as 'the Bible', exploring its narratives within religious traditions or revisiting its theological claims in the context of the experience of our age. This literature has been repeatedly surveyed, and here is not the place to provide another exhaustive investigation of it. The reader should refer to such standard works as Theodore Ziolkowski's *Fictional Transfigurations of Jesus* (1972) or Carl Ficken's *God's Story and Modern Literature* (1985).[4] Generally undistinguished are the seemingly endless stream of 'historical' novels, frequently focusing on the biography of Jesus, such as George Moore's *The Brook Kerith: A Syrian Story* (1916), and Lloyd C. Douglas's blockbusters *The Big Fisherman* (1948) and *The Robe* (1943), to the more interesting *King Jesus* (1946) of Robert Graves and *The Last Temptation of Christ* (1953) of the Greek writer Nikos Kazantzakis. Graves, who claims that he has taken 'more than ordinary pains to verify the historical background', introduces the tradition that Jesus was in fact a legitimate pretender to the throne of Jerusalem as the child, by a secret marriage, of Mary and Antipater before her betrothal to Joseph. Kazantzakis makes no such scholarly claims, but tries to enter the mind of Jesus and 'that part of Christ's nature which was profoundly human', producing a radical fiction which was banned by the Vatican and gained further notoriety with the making of Martin Scorsese's film *The Last Temptation* (1988).

Such novels, when they had any literary merit and independence, inevitably clashed with religious orthodoxy, and their undoubted literary and imaginative qualities tended to be neglected as a result. But more interesting than such 'fictionalizing biographies' are those works of literature which Theodore Ziolkowski describes as 'fictional transfigurations' – literary works which figuratively draw upon and interact with Biblical literature and, in a sense, continue the tradition of scriptural writing in our own time, perhaps not as radically as *Finnegans Wake* but in a midrashic, imaginative continuity which refigures the Bible within the immediate political, sociological or ideological concerns of the twentieth century. We have already referred to Thomas Mann's massive tetralogy of novels *Joseph und Seine Brüder*, and could add Mann's *Der Zauberberg* (1924: *The Magic Mountain*) in which it is crucial to be aware of the Messianic (and Bacchic) dimensions of the character of Peeperkorn as, in a scene towards the end of the novel, we encounter a rehearsal of the Last Supper by the patients in the sanatorium and in the anxiety of Peeperkorn's fear of death.

More recent fiction has drawn even more obliquely on Biblical themes to explore contemporary issues, frequently returning to the late twentieth-century obsession with the apocalyptic – visions of the end – as in much of the work of the Australian Nobel Prize winner Patrick White. The literature of apocalypse lends itself especially to the genre of science fiction, and a particularly good example of this is the Canadian writer Margaret Atwood's dystopic fantasy *The Handmaid's Tale* (1985 – also made later into a film), in which the Republic of Gilead is the realization of a post-nuclear holocaust America where the biblical motif of the 'handmaid' employed to conceive a child as a surrogate for a barren wife (see, for example, Bilhah in Genesis 30: 1–3) is developed into a nightmarish society in which young women are enslaved as concubines in an effort to procreate in a community made sterile by nuclear radiation. The irony rests upon this society's claim to live *literally* by biblical principles, though the Bible itself is made inaccessible to the handmaids: as so often in religious traditions with their priests and authorized interpreters, the sacred text is read to them by those in authority and not to be read by them directly. In the liturgical ceremony of the reading of Scripture, the Commander, a priestly figure,

crosses to the large leather chair reserved for him, takes the key out of his pocket, fumbles with the ornate brass-bound leather-covered box that stands on the table beside the chair. He inserts the key, opens the box, lifts out the Bible, an ordinary copy, with a black leather cover and gold-edged pages. The Bible is kept locked up, the way people once kept tea locked up, so the servants wouldn't steal it. It is an incendiary device: who knows what we'd make of it, if we ever got our hands on it? We can be read to from it, by him, but we cannot read. Our heads turn towards him, we are expectant, here comes our bedtime story.[5]

A little later in the narrative, the Bible is read again at mealtime almost as in a religious community.

For lunch it was the Beatitudes. Blessed be this, blessed be that. They played it from a disc, the voice was a man's. *Blessed be the poor in spirit, for theirs is the kingdom of heaven. Blessed are the merciful. Blessed are the meek. Blessed are the silent.* I knew they made that up, I knew it was wrong, and they left things out too, but there was no way of checking. *Blessed are those that mourn, for they shall be comforted.*

Nobody said when.[6]

There is no way of checking, when the Bible is purveyed by authority *as* the authoritative text.

The Handmaid's Tale demands a considerable knowledge of the Bible for the reader fully to appreciate its dense allusions and connotations. For example, the naming of Gilead refers back to Jeremiah 8: 22: 'Is there no balm in Gilead? Is there no physician there?' It also plays upon the power of the Biblical canon and the way in which it has been protected by authority and used as an instrument of social control. Indeed, part of Atwood's purpose is to indicate the dangers of our *not* knowing this

47

foundational book of our culture, which still permeates our customs and social order in manifold, hidden ways. The Republic of Gilead is perhaps not so futuristic but in a sense a nightmarish vision of our *own* society. Finally, in the last pages of the novel, when the 'manuscript' of the handmaid's story is discovered by scholars of a later age, its truth becomes a matter of academic argument among them, very much as professional biblical scholarship argues over the truth of the Bible itself so that its searing, human stories of love, pain, heroism and loss are often subsumed under the clever historical niceties of academic debate. Our very cleverness blinds us to the human cry of the narrative.

As all historians know, the past is a great darkness, and filled with echoes. Voices may reach us from it; but what they say to us is imbued with the obscurity of the matrix out of which they come; and, try as we may, we cannot always decipher them precisely in the clearer light of our own day.[7]

The heavy irony of these last words links the fiction with the sometimes pedantic claims of modern biblical scholarship to interpret the Bible for us. Often we find literature recognizing a lively coherence with the literature of Scripture which disintegrates the distinction between text and criticism, so that one may ask if a novel such as Joseph Heller's *God Knows* (1984) – one of a number of 'fictional retellings' of the Davidic narratives of 1 and 2 Samuel – is 'merely' a novel, or legitimate and valuable 'biblical criticism'. In another telling of the Davidic narratives, Stefan Heym's *The King David Report* (1972), the novel ends with an 'Author's Note' which indulges in all the arguments of biblical scholarship, opening up questions of the relationship between the Bible, history and the novel.

The King David Report actually exists. It may be found in the Bible, beginning with 1 Samuel 6 and ending with 1 Kings 2.
As I sometimes read the Bible it occurred to me that this section of it represented more than a fine oriental fairy tale or an edifying parable...here was also a novel...
A historical novel? But could the Bible be considered ancient history?[8]

Fiction, then, opens up the question of the status of the biblical text, and the novelist finds him or herself addressing problems – of history, the status of the text, and so on – which, hitherto, had been the prerogative of the critical scholar.
The list of such fiction is extensive and, perhaps significantly, often written by Jewish writers such as Howard Jacobson's *The Very Model of a*

Man (1992), a retelling of the story of Cain, or (the Christian) Frederick Buechner's *Son of Laughter* (1993), an account of the story of Jacob. One of the most interesting of such novels in recent years is Michèle Roberts' *The Wild Girl* (1984), a feminist revision of the gospel narratives from the perspective of Mary Magdalene. Like Robert Graves, Stefan Heym and other writers of fiction, Roberts indicates her reading in ancient Gnostic literature in her Author's Note, suggesting a scholarly background to her imaginative gospel and claiming that 'one important source of ideas was the Nag Hammadi gospels' which were used 'to help me imagine what an alternative version of Christianity might have been like. The texts are extremely fragmentary, hard to read and to understand; my interpretation of them is poetic, not scholarly'. In the end she finds herself writing a gospel.

'The gospels', Sara Maitland has remarked (*A Map of the New Country* RKP 1983) 'are not simple reportage but the first attempts at theology.' A narrative novel creates a myth in the same way. I wanted to dissect a myth; I found myself at the same time recreating one.

The second half of the twentieth century has seen a self-conscious drawing together of the imaginative literature which interacts with, draws upon and 'transfigures' the biblical text, and scholarly interpretation of the Bible. Novelists, poets and playwrights have become interpreters using scholarly techniques and following in the paths of biblical criticism, while critics, on the other hand, have been both reading the Bible 'as literature' and engaging in flights of the imagination for which they make no apology. Thus, Robert Alter, a Professor of Hebrew and Comparative Literature, in his book *The Art of Biblical Narrative* (1981), attempts, in a self-consciously midrashic move, 'to scrutinise biblical personages as fictional characters...to see them more sharply in the multifaceted, contradictory aspects of their human individuality, which is the biblical God's chosen medium for this experiment with Israel and history'.[9] Then, in his Introduction to *The Psalms in English* (1996), poet and critic Donald Davie opts for a critical reading of the Psalms 'as if' David really were their author, since, after all, the fiction of Davidic authorship has been a powerful element in the way the Psalms *have* always been read and understood, and therefore is an integral element to our proper reception and understanding of them. Davie, the critic, therefore demands: 'let not the ascription of the Psalms to David be dismissed as ecclesiastical fabrication, so much mumbo-jumbo'.[10]

This intermingling of Bible and literature, criticism, history and the imagination finds a celebratory expression in the language of one literary critic, Valentine Cunningham, in his much underrated book *In the Reading Gaol* (1994), when he shifts into a postmodern perspective, linking Biblical characters and authors with poets, novelists, critics, theorists – the historical with the mythic, the postmodern with the ancient – in a meditation on the so-called 'J' or 'Jahwist' author in the Pentateuch, the first five books of the Hebrew Bible.

The postmodernist scene comprises a kind of vast post-Biblical J-text, or set of J-texts, written (of course!) by writers with names like James Joyce son of John Joyce, Jacques Derrida, Jacques Lacan, Edmond Jabès (and for that matter, Dan Jacobson and Gabriel Josipovici) about (Joker) characters called Joyce, Jabès, Jehovah, Joseph, Job, Jeremiah, Jonah and haunted not least by the J-text(s) and the so-called J-author of the Old Testament. And especially haunting is the J-text story of Jacob, wrestling Jacob.[11]

Some of these 'Js' we have encountered already. Others we shall meet in a little while as we shift, perhaps rather artificially, from writers of imaginative literature to scholars and 'academic' critics of the Bible in our survey of the twentieth century. Behind Cunningham's words lie the scholarly/ fictional work of the literary critic Harold Bloom in his interpretation of *The Book of J* (1991), a clever attempt to sneak up on biblical scholars from behind by playing them at their own game. Bloom suggests that there is enough evidence reasonably to ascribe the authorship of the 'J' strand in the Pentateuch (scholars have long argued that these five books are a composite work by different 'authors', known variously as J, E, D and P) to a noble and feisty lady of the court of Solomon. Why not, if David can write the Psalms and if such a hypothesis can help to take 'the varnish off', as Bloom puts it, and shake us into seeing something of the literary splendour which has been dulled by 'many creeds, many churches, many scholarly certainties'?[12] There may be many ways of taking the Bible out of its brass-bound, leather-covered box and releasing the incendiary potential which poets and writers have always felt and responded to.

Before moving into a necessarily brief examination of literary developments in modern (and postmodern) biblical scholarship, we should pause for a moment to acknowledge a major twentieth-century artistic interaction with Scripture, briefly mentioned in the previous essay, and that is the art of the cinema. The commercial film industry has been ready since its earliest days to exploit the dramatic potential of scriptural narrative, its exoticism and its power over the Western mind and imagination.

Though the character of Jesus was long banned by law from appearing on British cinema screens – a curious relic of pious sensitivity perhaps looking back to people like Dr Samuel Johnson in the eighteenth century who regarded biblical 'truth' as too sacred for poetic intrusion[13] – Jesus of Nazareth has proved to be an enduring movie star of epic proportions. Hollywood has produced three major epic 're-tellings' of the gospel story, Cecil B. De Mille's *The King of Kings* (1927), Nicholas Ray's film of the same title in 1961, and George Stevens's *The Greatest Story Ever Told* (1965), followed by Martin Scorsese's notorious *The Last Temptation of Christ* (1988). In each case the commercial cinema gives evidence of how the Bible, as the world's best seller for centuries, has actually rarely been *read*. For these films reflect a popular piety which has more to do with contemporary North American culture than the Bible, and shows a fine disregard for the particularities of the texts. Thus the Sermon on the Mount (Matthew 5–7) in Ray's *King of Kings* is not taken from the Matthean text but is a hotchpotch of gospel quotations which render the 'sermon' and its theology almost unintelligible, despite the film's claim to convey to the cinema audience 'the glory of his spoken words'. One is left with a powerful sense of the nineteenth-century myth (after Renan) of a dreamy, blue-eyed and fair-haired Jesus realized as 'a hot box-office property'.[14] More disturbing and theologically far more challenging is the less commercial Italian film *Vangelo Secondo Matteo* (1966: *The Gospel According to St. Matthew*) of Pier Paolo Pasolini, which uses the text of the gospel without compromise, exposing its consistent themes and complexities.

In the Hollywood tradition of Old Testament epics, however, the cinema has occasionally contributed in a significant way to the history of biblical interpretation, perhaps unwittingly and most notably in the figure of Cecil B. De Mille in films like *Samson and Delilah* (1949) and *The Ten Commandments* (1956). The first, dismissed by a standard reference work, Halliwell's *Film Guide*, as 'absurd biblical hokum',[15] deconstructs the trope of Delilah as the *femme fatale par excellence*, and re-reads the text of the Book of Judges midrashically as a love story which shifts the coherent and dehumanizing biblical perspective of Israel's salvation history and replaces it with a *countercoherence* of a Delilah following her heart and remaining true to Samson as she follows him to the temple of the Philistines and her own, as well as his, death. As a feminist biblical critic commenting on the film has expressed it: 'Delilah sacrifices herself so that Samson, and ultimately his god, can triumph over tyranny and evil'.[16] By the shift of Delilah from the character which has, in the definition of the *Oxford English Dictionary*, been 'used allusively to mean a temptress or treacherous love', De Mille's film does what art and

51

literature has always in fact done, read the Bible and unpicked its historical and theological consistencies which have defined how religious orthodoxy has read it, and offered a countercoherence in terms of other priorities (in this case filmic melodrama) which may expose the dangerous assumptions that often underlie our reading of Scripture and the Bible as, in the words of Atwood's handmaid 'an incendiary device'. In the case of Delilah, as in much of the Book of Judges, feminist literary critics have been quick to deconstruct the violent implications of this most patriarchal of texts. Thus, in her book *Death and Dissymmetry* (1988), one of a series of studies of Judges, the literary critic Mieke Bal writes:

This countercoherence, which is a deconstruction in its own right but also more than that, will enforce awareness of a reality that is also represented in the book: the reality of gender-bound violence. Moreover, I will argue that the impression of extreme violence that the book makes is due less to the political struggle that seems to be at stake – the conquest – than to a social revolution that concerns the institution of marriage, hence, the relations between men and women, sexuality, procreation, and kinship.[17]

As film 'interprets' the Bible with ever-increasing technological sophistication, it remains to be seen what the consequences will be as it responds, like Gore Vidal's 'virtual reality' fictional retelling of the gospel narratives, to a world in which the media are disintegrating ancient distinctions between the 'real' and the 'virtual' with, as yet, unexplored social, psychological and perhaps religious consequences.

As we turn now to consider the recent invasion of the traditional space of professional biblical critics by literary criticism, we do so aware of the ancient interaction between the Bible and literature and the barriers erected in the nineteenth century between biblical studies and the reading of other literature (see above p. 35). In this world of scholarship at least for the last two hundred years, 'literary readings' have always been accused of flippancy, and the insights of art and literature generally neglected, mainly because of the weighty claims of historicism. 'Historical criticism' of the Bible remains at the heart of biblical studies, with its emphasis on the origins of the text, the purposes of the author, and the place of the Bible within ancient traditions of theology and culture. Thus one critic, Stephen Neil, dismisses Renan for his lack of scholarly seriousness. 'Professing to work as an historian, he does not pursue with the needed seriousness the historical problems of the life of Christ.'[18]

Literary readings of the Bible hover between the imaginative and poetic, and the academic. That is why, in spite of the development of the language and science of literary theory, they have never quite been taken seriously by biblical criticism as it emerges from the demands of historical critical methods and theology. There is an *uncritical* dimension, which is nonetheless rigorous, expressed with characteristic energy by D. H. Lawrence as he seeks to define his vocation as an artist: 'I always feel as if I should be naked for the fire of Almighty God to go through me – and it's rather an awful feeling.'[19] Translated into the realm of critical biblical interpretation, the sense of awe is perhaps first consciously sustained in the critical work of Austin Farrer (1904–1968), particularly in *The Glass of Vision* (1948: on the prophets), *A Rebirth of Images* (1944: on Revelation) and *St. Matthew and St. Mark* (1954). Farrer was a biblical critic whose effect on the literary reading of the Bible has been enormous, particularly through the more recent work of the literary critic Frank Kermode. Every inch an Oxford don, Farrer's academic interests were broad and various, ranging from philosophical theology to Christian apologetics and biblical studies. Although his philosophical writings can be extremely abstruse, and his biblical scholarship sometimes highly idiosyncratic, he was unusual in the academy of his day for his deep sensitivity to language and imagery and his ability to expose the conjectural nature of what more conventional biblical critics accepted unquestioningly, though he remains a far cry from more recent 'secular' developments in the scholarship of literary approaches to the Bible. Like T. S. Eliot before him in the 1935 essay 'Religion and Literature',[20] Farrer insisted on the religious and salvific foundations of the Bible, but without forgetting its power as great literature.

They say the Bible makes good reading, but unless you are concerned for the everlasting salvation of mankind, you will prefer to look for your reading elsewhere. It is a sort of sacrilege to recommend the Bible as culture or amusement. The story of David and Absalom is a better piece of literature than Matthew Arnold's *Sohrab and Rustum*: but that has nothing to do with the reason for which we read the Books of Samuel.[21]

Though now rather dated, Farrer's work remains important inasmuch as it recognizes the inseparability of religion and literature in the Bible, and the need to read the Scriptures imaginatively as poetry and dramatic narratives. In his day, however, Farrer was virtually ignored, or worse, by biblical critics.

In particular his Bampton Lectures, published as *The Glass of Vision*, were subjected to two major critical attacks, one theological by H. D. Lewis in his book *Our Experience of God* (1959), and the other literary by Dame Helen Gardner in *The Limits of Literary Criticism* (1956), returning later to the attack in her profoundly unimaginative book *In Defence of the Imagination* (1982).[22] Farrer's response to his critics was, significantly, in the readerly and poetic tradition of S. T. Coleridge. Whereas Lewis subsumes poetry into theology, and Gardner keeps the two separate, maintaining an absolute distinction between the historical Jesus and our own time, Farrer sustains a delicate polarity between theology and poetry, both moving under a control of images which are in time yet also eternal – diachronic and synchronic. For Farrer, the imagination draws together the ancient and sacred literature of the Scriptures, their tradition of theological reading and the response of the contemporary reader to the structure of the text, in a single moment of vision and inspiration. Frank Kermode, who once described Farrer with Claude Lévi-Strauss and Roland Barthes as a 'structuralist', reflected sadly in 1979 upon Farrer's exile from the academy of Biblical scholars, focussing upon Farrer's sense of the 'fictive' quality of the Biblical text, a theme which has been taken up vigorously in more recent times by Robert Alter, Meir Steinberg, Northrop Frye, Gabriel Josipovici and others who would not distinguish exclusively between history and 'fiction'. But writing of Farrer's work in the 1950s, Kermode notes:

As to Farrer, his work was rejected by the establishment and eventually by himself, largely because it was so literary. The institution knew intuitively that such literary elaboration, such emphasis on elements that must be called fictive, was unacceptable because damaging to what remained of the idea that the gospel narratives were still, in some measure, transparent upon history...[Farrer] assumes that there is an enigmatic narrative concealed in the manifest one.[23]

Farrer, the devout Christian, and Kermode, the sceptical literary critic, so different in many ways, join in acknowledging the critical necessity of recognizing the 'fictive' element in Scripture, and the need to respond to the literary 'structure' of works like Mark's Gospel, so that they are to be read as a whole – much as one would read a novel – and not disintegrated into brief pericopes or fragments. Thus, in his immensely important book, *The Genesis of Secrecy* (1979), Kermode (as Coleridge had done before him), reads the Bible in the context of a wider literature of imagination from Kafka, Joyce and Thomas Pynchon to the novels of Henry Green.

As a practising novelist, as we have seen, D. H. Lawrence had long before Farrer described the Bible as 'a great, confused novel'. More academically, and more recently, Robert Alter and Gabriel Josipovici have analysed biblical narratives with the same techniques as those used by literary critics to read prose fiction. To do this is not necessarily to abandon the traditional historical and theological concerns of the biblical critic. On the contrary, Alter's reading of Genesis 38, the story of Judah and Tamar in *The Art of Biblical Narrative*, suggests that it is a carefully constructed part of a larger, coherent narrative, the story of Joseph – an insight already to be found in Mann's *Joseph und Seine Brüder* – and not just a fragment in a patchwork text stitched together by an inept editor. But also, Alter and Josipovici release these ancient texts and their characters to be responded to with an immediacy and freedom often denied to 'sacred texts', weighed down as they often are by theological preconception or prejudice. In his work *The Book of God* (1988), Josipovici (himself a novelist as well as a professor of English Literature) wrote that the Bible

seemed much quirkier, funnier, quieter than I expected...it contained narratives which seemed, even in translation, as I first read them, far fresher and more 'modern' than any of the prize-winning novels rolling off the presses.[24]

These literary readings of the Bible claim to 'take the varnish off'[25] texts which have been coated and distorted by centuries of religious reading and theological interpretation. The implication, of course, is that they will return us to the pristine purity of the moment of reading which is also immediate, alongside other great literature from Aeschylus to Dante and Shakespeare. Nor has this enterprise been limited to biblical narratives. Biblical poetry has been examined by scholars like Alter and James L. Kugel in the tradition of Bishop Robert Lowth. Kugel, a professor of Near Eastern Languages and Civilizations at Harvard University, grants due recognition to Lowth's work, already described in the previous essay, and above all Lowth's Renaissance defence of poetry, based on classical aesthetics and anticipating later Romanticism, in which an alliance is acknowledged between poetry and 'natural piety'. For Lowth, poetry not only 'stands eminent among the other liberal arts', but claims a primacy in its 'original office and destination' which is the source of religion. Thus, Kugel concludes in his acknowledgement of Lowth's importance:

Hebrew poetry – and by this he means, to an extent his listeners could not have grasped in the first lecture, *most of the Bible* – is to be exalted for having remained faithful to that original office, and for having served the religion of the one God. Moreover, it is to be praised on the very grounds for which Homer is praised; its aesthetic worth must be explored.[26]

Kugel, however, is not uncritical of Lowth, and argues that Lowth's understanding of Hebrew poetry was far too simplistic. Parallelism is, in fact, an extremely subtle art form and yields its complexities to a much closer *textual* reading than Lowth was prepared (or able) to give. Kugel, in other words, is very much of his own time in granting close attention to the *text* rather than other theoretical structures or historical context.

By focussing upon *text* rather than *context*, modern literary readings of the Bible claim to overcome the hermeneutical problem of the 'two horizons', that is the historical gap between the ancient text and the contemporary reader. By concentrating on the literary qualities of the Biblical texts, the reader encounters with new immediacy their innate power and mystery. Like all great texts of literature, they are seen as both historical *and* contemporary, as living within history. In their *Literary Guide to the Bible* (1987), Alter and Kermode distinguish their task from what they call 'traditional historical scholarship'[27] and deny that their aims are theological. Instead, they situate themselves within the traditions of Western *culture* and as responding to a great achievement of 'written language'. Their claim is that this magisterial work of criticism is the culmination of a shift that took place through the 1970s (although we have seen that it can be traced back to the 1950s) in which literary perspectives began to open up new avenues for biblical interpretation, first by literary critics and only gradually by biblical scholars. Having established this, however, they limit themselves within the literary critical field itself, most specifically by deliberately neglecting 'deconstructionists and some feminist critics who seek to demonstrate that the text is necessarily divided against itself'.[28]

The two clear and fundamental issues to be acknowledged here are, first, the recognition that there is no unmediated reading of the biblical text and that it is never possible to access its 'pristine purity'. Second, we question strongly the claim by Alter and Kermode that *any* reading can be separated from the theological impetus which drives and permeates the biblical canon.

Putting aside for a moment, however, these major questions, let us look more closely at another thread which has been running through this essay. A major shift in literary theory in recent years has also been reflected in literary approaches to the Bible – that is, the change in focus of interest from the intention of the author and the original context of the writing, not only to the text itself but also to the *response* of the reader in determining the meaning and significance of the text.[29] Immediately this concentrates attention upon the immediate moment of reading rather than the moment of the text's origin as of primary importance. Although the field of so-called 'reader-response criticism' is complex and difficult to define, it is clear that its tendencies cut across the grain of a great deal in biblical studies.[30] To start with, by concentrating upon the contemporary reader such criticism undercuts the historical emphasis of biblical studies. No longer is the original moment of composition and first reading emphasized, but primary attention is given to the individual *in the act of reading*, or to the 'interpretative community' of readers here and now. Second, there is an inevitable tendency to weaken the objective status of the text itself, with the consequent fear of solipsism and relativism, most clearly demonstrated in Stanley Fish's celebrated essay 'Is There a Text in This Class?', with its anxious question from a student, 'I mean in this class do we believe in poems and things, or is it just us?'[31]

It would seem, therefore, that as literary readings of the Bible have drawn us away from an emphasis on context to a focus on the text itself, so gradually that text is in turn dissolved in the new and ever-contemporary context of the reader and the interpretative community. Questions then arise concerning the nature of authority as the 'sacred' text is subsumed under the conditions of all other 'secular' literature. At this point a challenge is presented by relatively new 'emancipatory' criticism in feminist readings of the Bible as deliberate attacks upon that authority. Already we have briefly encountered these in our consideration of the cinema's impact on the narratives of the Hebrew Bible. Broadly speaking feminist criticism has been given voice by the possibilities offered by literary readings – with their emphasis on the (woman) reader, their refusal to be constrained by religious history and tradition, and their challenge to (patriarchal) authority. In particular, what Josipovici calls the 'irresponsibility' of his own response to the Bible is echoed in the work of Mieke Bal, whose readings of the Hebrew Bible[32] emerge variously from intertextual readings with such diffuse partners as Sigmund Freud, the art of Rembrandt and feminist theory itself. In Bal, the Bible is exposed almost indiscriminately to the history of Western literature, art and thought, and nothing is off limits. Bal's readings are uncompromisingly political, as are those of her early feminist predecessor Elizabeth Cady Stanton in *The Woman's Bible* (1895). Stanton introduces her commentary with a forthright statement:

From the inauguration of the movement for women's emancipation the Bible has been used to hold her in the 'divinely ordained sphere', prescribed in the Old and New Testaments.

The canon and civil law; church and state; priests and legislators; all political parties and religious denominations have alike taught that woman was made after man, of man, and for man, an inferior being, subject to man. Creeds, codes, Scriptures and statutes are all based on this idea. The fashions, forms, ceremonies and customs of society, church ordinances and discipline all grow out of this idea.[33]

Stanton's commentary is wonderfully feisty and frequently highly perceptive by virtue of its freedom from traditional 'patriarchal' theological themes, exposing questions and weaknesses which have too often been covered up. Here is her description of that most macho of biblical heroes, Samson:

Samson was most unfortunate in all his associations with women. It is a pity that the angel who impressed on his parents the importance of everything that pertained to the physical development of the child, had not made some suggestions to them as to the formation of his moral character. Even his physical prowess was not used by him for any great moral purpose. To kill a lion, to walk off with the gates of the city, to catch three hundred foxes and to tie them together by their tails two by two, with firebrands to burn the cornfields and the vineyards – all this seems more like the frolics of a boy, than the military tactics of a great general or the statesmanship of a Judge in Israel.[34]

Samson, in other words, was just a silly overgrown schoolboy! Bal's more sophisticated readings of the Book of Judges follow the same political principles as Stanton's, but in her they are based on clear literary premises.

When Bal considers the Book of Judges she 'deals with the text as a whole . . . conceived of as one text'.[35] As we have seen, she then questions the text read as *historiography* inasmuch as this assumes a theology and imposes a *coherence* upon the book. This coherence, she argues, is actually imposed by the assumptions of a patriarchal tradition which elides and ignores certain elements in the text, usually those concerned with women. Her proposal for a countercoherence emerges through a careful and highly imaginative interactive reading of the narratives of the text, playing games with it, arguing with its apparent assumptions, until violence is exposed in the arena of reading itself. Other feminist critics, such as Phyllis Trible, have followed the same path of reading, creatively interacting with texts like Judges 11: 29–40 (the sacrifice of Jephthah's daughter) and Genesis 19: 8 (Lot's offering of his daughters to the men of Sodom to protect a male guest) to expose 'the sin of patriarchy'.[36] Like Mieke Bal, Trible uses close literary readings to expose the processes of power and authority in a text from its origins, in its tradition and in the assumptions of its contemporary (male) readers. She claims that her feminist reading

recognises that, despite the word, *authority* centres in readers. They accord a document power even as they promote the intentionality of its authors ... In the interaction of text and reader, the changing of the second component alters the meaning and power of the first.[37]

Feminist criticism, then, tends to follow the literary trend of focusing upon the reader and deconstructing the assumptions of traditional biblical critics, and perhaps the texts themselves, by exercises in close reading which play with the biblical texts on their own terms, that is, introducing characters, situations and possibilities in a 'fictive' game which takes utterly seriously the Bible 'as literature' and thus challenges it as an authoritative 'sacred text' within a patriarchal tradition. Bal, in particular, seems to be conscious of herself as a writer of narrative fiction, giving names to the nameless in the biblical narrative (for example, 'Bath' for Jephthah's daughter) and thereby violating the scriptural text which otherwise becomes the instrument of *her* violation through its ideological position.[38] Such fictive political readings have come a long way from the careful religiosity of T. S. Eliot and Austin Farrer.

This deconstruction inherent in feminist readings of the Bible links them with the wider field of postmodern and poststructuralist biblical criticism which has been granted greater public attention by the publication of *The Postmodern Bible* (1995), written not by a single author or editor but by 'the Bible and Culture Collective'. Despite the nervousness of Alter and Kermode that such readings seek only 'to demonstrate that the text is necessarily divided against itself', postmodern readings of Scripture have frequently offered dazzling intertextual exercises which recognize that reading is an exchange between text and reader in a constant struggle which wounds even as it illuminates. In his book *Mark and Luke in Post-Structuralist Perspectives* (1992), Stephen D. Moore maintains:

My main tactic is a simple one. I am eager to reply to the Gospels in kind, to write in a related idiom. Rather than take a jackhammer to the concrete, parabolic language of the Gospels, replacing graphic images with abstract categories, I prefer to respond to a pictographic text pictographically, to a narrative text narratively, producing a critical text that is a postmodern analogue of the premodern text that it purports to read.[39]

In Moore's hands, biblical criticism becomes a dramatic exercise in deconstructive readings, teasing the text through its layers of 'encrusted readings', exposing its potential for new and different readings, and acknowledging that the text itself is, finally, only another reading of a reading, *ad infinitum*. Moore acknowledges his heavy dependence on Stanley Fish – indubitably a brilliant *reader* whether you agree with him or not – and reading Moore's work is less the cerebral exercise of thinking through words of more conservative Biblical criticism, and more an exercise of thinking in and by words through a punning style more akin to Moore's fellow Irishman, James Joyce (whose *Finnegans Wake* is one of the greatest of all intertextual Biblical 'readings') than what we normally expect of biblical scholarship and commentary. With Moore we have returned almost to where we began in this essay, to one of the greatest 'novels' of the twentieth century. Biblical criticism and imaginative writing are becoming barely distinguishable.

Postmodern literary criticism is everywhere fascinated by the Bible, unable to escape the 'persistent presence of the religious as the constant frame, our frame of reference, of the deconstructionist case',[40] and committed to endless readings which expose the irreducible[41] edges, metaphors and tropes of the biblical texts. In the writings of the best known of postmodern critics, the French thinker Jacques Derrida, the persistent theme of 'the lack' emerges as a lack within reason itself that demands the play of religion,[42] prompting a stream of readings of Scripture, and readings of readings (for example, his reading of Kierkegaard's reading of Genesis 22: 1–18, the Binding of Isaac, often referred to by the Hebrew term 'Akedah')[43] in an endless struggle with the text(s) which seems to encourage closure and conclusion, and then deconstruct conclusion in further readings. Derrida's brilliant and tireless exercises in literary readings emerge, it has been suggested, out of his background in Rabbinic thought[44] with its midrashic intertextuality and its sense of struggle within and for the text.

Another Jewish scholar, Geoffrey H. Hartman, has insisted that the literary study of the Bible, in a continuation of the conversations of the ancient rabbis, alone keeps alive the irreducible asymmetries and superfluities which constitute the mystery of a text like Genesis 32: 1–22, the wrestling of Jacob with the angel (or God) at Peniel.[45] In Hartman's essay, 'The Struggle for the Text', we move from the fictive or fictional qualities of the Bible to its *frictionality*, that is its irritating qualities which drive us to scratch and read again, aware that there are traces left which never yield to the searches of the biblical scholars in history or indeed elsewhere. In his classic essay on the Akedah (Genesis 22: 1–18), 'Odysseus' Scar',[46] the Jewish scholar Erich Auerbach distinguishes between Greek and Hebraic conceptions of reality and of textuality. If in the Homeric text 'nothing must remain hidden and unexpressed', in the biblical narrative the mystery is held 'fraught with background', full of gaps and omissions. With the rabbis we are reminded that the Bible resists closure and conclusion, its endless writing demanding an endless exercise of reading and re-reading, writing and re-writing within the whole enterprise of literature in all ages.

In his posthumously published *Confessions of an Inquiring Spirit* (1840), Samuel Taylor Coleridge affirms that 'in the Bible there is more that finds me than I have experienced in all other books put together'. The last years of Coleridge's life were spent in continual readings of the Bible against the background of a whole lifetime spent among books as a critic, philosopher and a poet. Coleridge's frustration with 'bibliolaters' and others who seemed to dissect the text of Scripture in order to kill its spirit, emerged from a sense that, although it is endlessly studied as an authoritative and even 'sacred' text, it is actually rarely read with the readerly attention given to other great literature, and for him particularly Shakespeare. T. S. Eliot was fearful for the Bible if read merely 'as literature'; Coleridge was convinced that the Bible was somehow different from all other literature, 'having proceeded from the Holy Spirit', but that this very difference would be endlessly revealed in literary readings which acknowledge and respond to its poetry and its inspiration.

In this brief essay it has been possible only to offer a cursory and suggestive survey of 'literary readings', both in literature itself, in film and in criticism, of the Bible over the last hundred years or so. Much has, of necessity, been omitted, as we continue to read and to be read by the Bible. Biblical figures from Samson and King David, to Mary Magdalene and, repeatedly, Jesus himself, have appeared as figures in 'fictional' guise, sometimes with quiet devotion, and at other times with characteristics offensive to those who love the Bible in their own way.

Our relationship with the Bible will never be an easy one, and its peculiar relationship with our complex cultural and religious histories will always claim the necessary attention of scholars whose investigations demand the skills of the historian, the philologist and the theologian. But the Bible is also literature, frequently of the very highest order, much of it written by poets and writers who, though often enmeshed in the particular prejudices and preconceptions of their own cultures, continue to speak to other poetic minds with a universal voice that responds to readings made with literary sensitivity and imagination, often prompting such readings even when the scholars would prefer to believe that other more precise and different critical tools will better discern the mystery of its pages.

Notes

1 A. S. Byatt, *Babel Tower* (London: Vintage, 1997), p. 311.
2 F. W. Dillistone, *The Novelist and the Passion Story* (London: Collins, 1960), p. 11.

3 D. H. Lawrence, 'Why the Novel Matters', reprinted in *Selected Literary Criticism*, ed. Anthony Beal (London: Heinemann, 1967), p. 105.

4 See also: Horton Davies, *Catching the Conscience: Essays in Religion and Literature* (Cambridge, MA: Cowley, 1984); Ralph C. Wood, *The Comedy of Redemption: Christian Faith and Comic Vision in Four American Novelists* (Notre Dame: Notre Dame University Press, 1988); David Anderson, *The Passion of Man in Gospel and Literature* (London: Bible Reading Fellowship, 1980); Leslie Paul, *Springs of Good and Evil: Biblical Themes in Literature* (London: Bible Reading Fellowship, 1979); Lynn Ross-Bryant, *Imagination and the Life of the Spirit: An Introduction to the Study of Religion and Literature* (Chico: Scholars Press, 1981).

5 Margaret Atwood, *The Handmaid's Tale*, 1985 (London: Virago, 1987), pp. 97–8.

6 Ibid. pp. 99–100. See, Matthew 5: 1–10.

7 Ibid., p. 324.

8 Stefan Heym, *The King David Report* (London: Abacus, 1984), p. 253.

9 Robert Alter, *The Art of Biblical Narrative* (London: George Allen and Unwin, 1981), p. 12.

10 Donald Davie, Introduction to *The Psalms in English*, Penguin Classics (Harmondsworth: Penguin, 1996), p. xx.

11 Valentine Cunningham, *In the Reading Gaol: Postmodernity, Texts, and History* (Oxford: Blackwell, 1994), p. 371.

12 Harold Bloom, *The Book of J* (London: Faber & Faber, 1991), p. 44.

13 Dr Samuel Johnson, 'The Life of Waller', in *The Lives of the Poets* (1781): 'The ideas of Christian Theology are too simple for eloquence, too sacred for fiction, and too majestic for ornament.'

14 See, Roy Kinnard and Tim Davis, *Divine Images: A History of Jesus on the Screen* (New York: Citadel Press, 1992), pp. 131–40.

15 Leslie Halliwell, *Halliwell's Film Guide*, 7th edn (London: Paladin, 1989), p. 879.

16 J. Cheryl Exum, *Plotted, Shot and Painted: Cultural Representations of Biblical Women* (Sheffield: Sheffield Academic Press, 1996), p. 235.

17 Mieke Bal, *Death and Dissymmetry: The Politics of Coherence in the Book of Judges* (Chicago: Chicago University Press, 1988), p. 5.

18 Stephen Neil, *The Interpretation of the New Testament: 1861–1961* (Oxford: Oxford University Press, 1964), p. 194.

19 Cited in George Steiner, *Tolstoy or Dostoevsky*, 1959 (Harmondsworth: Penguin, 1967), p. 14.

20 T. S. Eliot, *Selected Essays*, 3rd edn (London: Faber & Faber, 1951), pp. 388–401.

21 Austin Farrer, 'The Interpretation of the Bible' (1952). Reprinted in *Interpretation and Belief*, ed. Charles C. Conti (London: SPCK, 1976), p. 9.

22 Farrer defended himself in an article, 'Inspiration: Poetical and Divine', in F. F. Bruce (ed.), *Promise and Fulfilment* (Edinburgh: T & T Clark, 1963), pp. 91–105.

23 Frank Kermode, *The Genesis of Secrecy: On the Interpretation of Narrative* (Cambridge, MA: Harvard University Press, 1979), p. 63.

24 Gabriel Josipovici, *The Book of God: A Response to the Bible* (New Haven, CT: Yale University Press, 1988), p. x.

25 Harold Bloom, *The Book of J* (London: Faber & Faber, 1991), p. 44.

26 James L. Kugel, *The Idea of Biblical Poetry: Parallelism and its History* (New Haven CT: Yale University Press, 1981), p. 274. See also, M. Roston, *Prophet and Poet: the Bible and the Growth of Romanticism* (Evanston, IL: Macmillan, 1965).

27 Robert Alter and Frank Kermode (eds), *The Literary Guide to the Bible* (London: Collins, 1987), p. 2.

28 Ibid., p. 6.

29 See, generally, Francis Watson (ed.), *The Open Text: New Directions for Biblical Studies?* (London: SCM, 1993).

30 See further, Stanley E. Porter, 'Why Hasn't Reader-Response Criticism Caught on in New Testament Studies?', *Literature and Theology*, 4, 3 (1990), pp. 278–92.

31 Stanley Fish, *Is There a Text in This Class? The Authority of Interpretive Communities* (Cambridge, MA: Harvard University Press, 1980), p. 305.

32 Bal's principal works in the field to date are, *Lethal Love: Feminist Literary Readings of Biblical Love Stories* (Bloomington: Indiana University Press, 1987); *Murder and Difference* (Bloomington: Indiana University Press, 1988); and *Death and Dissymmetry* (Chicago: University of Chicago Press, 1988).

33 Elizabeth Cady Stanton, Introduction to *The Woman's Bible* (Seattle: Coalition on Women and Religion, 1895), p. 7.

34 Ibid., p. 33.

35 Bal, *Death and Dissymmetry*, p. 4.

36 Phyllis Trible, 'Treasures Old and New: Biblical Theology and the Challenge of Feminism' in *The Open Text* ed. Francis Watson (London: SCM, 1993), p. 37. See also, Trible, *God and the Rhetoric of Sexuality* (London: SCM, 1978), especially her fine reading of the Book of Ruth, pp. 166–99.

37 Trible, 'Treasures Old and New', pp. 48–9.

38 Bal *Death and Dissymmetry*, p. 43.

39 Stephen D. Moore, *Mark and Luke in Poststructuralist Perspectives* (New Haven, CT: Yale University Press, 1992), p. xviii. More recently Moore has published a useful introductory text, *Poststructuralism and the New Testament: Derrida and Foucault at the Foot of the Cross* (Minneapolis: Fortress Press, 1994).

40 Valentine Cunningham, *In the Reading Gaol*, p. 366. In his final chapter, 'The Rabbins Take It Up One After Another', Cunningham explores the thesis that 'Biblical logocentricity is already deconstructionist'.

41 Austin Farrer wrote at length of the 'irreducible imagery' of the Bible. For example, *The Glass of Vision* (Westminster: Dacre Press, 1944), p. 94.

42 Jacques Derrida, *The Truth in Painting*, tr. Geoff Bennington and Ian MacLeod (Chicago: Chicago University Press, 1987), pp. 53–6. See also Cunningham, *In the Reading Gaol*, p. 366.

43 See, Derrida, *The Gift of Death*, tr. David Wills (Chicago: Chicago University Press, 1995), pp. 64–7. Also, Derrida, *Memoirs of the Blind: The Self-Portrait and Other Ruins*, tr. Pascale-Anne Brault and Michael Naas (Chicago: Chicago University Press, 1993), for readings of the blind Jacob, pp. 97–100, and Samson, pp. 104–10, and Saul/Paul, pp. 112–17.

44 See, Susan A. Handelman, *The Slayers of Moses. The Emergence of Rabbinic Interpretation in Modern Literary Theory* (Albany: State University of New York Press, 1982). Also, Daniel Boyarin, *Intertextuality and the Reading of Midrash* (Bloomington: Indiana University Press, 1990).

45 Geoffrey H. Hartman, 'The Struggle for the Text', in *Midrash and Literature* ed. Geoffrey H. Hartman and Sanford Budick (New Haven, CT: Yale University Press, 1986), pp. 3–18.

46 Erich Auerbach, *Mimesis: The Representation of Reality in Western Literature*, tr. Willard R. Trask, 1946 (Princeton: Princeton University Press, 1968), pp. 3–23.

THE CREATION
GENESIS 1–2

[1] In the beginning God created the heaven and the earth.

[2] And the earth was without form, and void; and darkness was upon the face of the deep. And the Spirit of God moved upon the face of the waters.

[3] And God said, Let there be light: and there was light.

[4] And God saw the light, that it was good: and God divided the light from the darkness.

[5] And God called the light Day, and the darkness he called Night. And the evening and the morning were the first day.

[6] And God said, Let there be a firmament in the midst of the waters, and let it divide the waters from the waters.

[7] And God made the firmament, and divided the waters which were under the firmament from the waters which were above the firmament: and it was so.

[8] And God called the firmament Heaven. And the evening and the morning were the second day.

[9] And God said, Let the waters under the heaven be gathered together unto one place, and let the dry land appear: and it was so.

[10] And God called the dry land Earth; and the gathering together of the waters called he Seas: and God saw that it was good.

[11] And God said, Let the earth bring forth grass, the herb yielding seed, and the fruit tree yielding fruit after his kind, whose seed is in itself, upon the earth: and it was so.

[12] And the earth brought forth grass, and herb yielding seed after his kind, and the tree yielding fruit, whose seed was in itself, after his kind: and God saw that it was good.

[13] And the evening and the morning were the third day.

[14] And God said, Let there be lights in the firmament of the heaven to divide the day from the night; and let them be for signs, and for seasons, and for days, and years:

[15] And let them be for lights in the firmament of the heaven to give light upon the earth: and it was so.

[16] And God made two great lights; the greater light to rule the day, and the lesser light to rule the night: he made the stars also.

[17] And God set them in the firmament of the heaven to give light upon the earth,

[18] And to rule over the day and over the night, and to divide the light from the darkness: and God saw that it was good.

[19] And the evening and the morning were the fourth day.

[20] And God said, Let the waters bring forth abundantly the moving creature that hath life, and fowl that may fly above the earth in the open firmament of heaven.

[21] And God created great whales, and every living creature that moveth, which the waters brought forth abundantly, after their kind, and every winged fowl after his kind: and God saw that it was good.

[22] And God blessed them, saying, Be fruitful, and multiply, and fill the waters in the seas, and let fowl multiply in the earth.

[23] And the evening and the morning were the fifth day.

[24] And God said, Let the earth bring forth the living creature after his kind, cattle, and creeping thing, and beast of the earth after his kind: and it was so.

[25] And God made the beast of the earth after his kind, and cattle after their kind, and every thing that creepeth upon the earth after his kind: and God saw that it was good.

[26] And God said, Let us make man in our image, after our likeness: and let them have dominion over the fish of the sea, and over the fowl of the air, and over the cattle, and over all the earth, and over every creeping thing that creepeth upon the earth.

[27] So God created man in his own image, in the image of God created he him; male and female created he them.

[28] And God blessed them, and God said unto them, Be fruitful, and multiply, and replenish the earth, and subdue it: and have dominion over the fish of the sea, and over the fowl of the air, and over every living thing that moveth upon the earth.

[29] And God said, Behold, I have given you every herb bearing seed, which is upon the face of all the earth, and every tree, in the which is the fruit of a tree yielding seed; to you it shall be for meat.

[30] And to every beast of the earth, and to every fowl of the air, and to every thing that creepeth upon the earth, wherein there is life, I have given every green herb for meat: and it was so.

[31] And God saw every thing that he had made, and, behold, it was very good. And the evening and the morning were the sixth day.

GENESIS 2

[1] Thus the heavens and the earth were finished, and all the host of them.

[2] And on the seventh day God ended his work which he had made; and he rested on the seventh day from all his work which he had made.

[3] And God blessed the seventh day, and sanctified it: because that in it he had rested from all his work which God created and made.

[4] These are the generations of the heavens and of the earth when they were created, in the day that the LORD God made the earth and the heavens,

[5] And every plant of the field before it was in the earth, and every herb of the field before it grew: for the LORD God had not caused it to rain upon the earth, and there was not a man to till the ground.

[6] But there went up a mist from the earth, and watered the whole face of the ground.

[7] And the LORD God formed man of the dust of the ground, and breathed into his nostrils the breath of life; and man became a living soul.

[8] And the LORD God planted a garden eastward in Eden; and there he put the man whom he had formed.

[9] And out of the ground made the LORD God to grow every tree that is pleasant to the sight, and good for food; the tree of life also in the midst of the garden, and the tree of knowledge of good and evil.

[10] And a river went out of Eden to water the garden; and from thence it was parted, and became into four heads.

[11] The name of the first is Pison: that is it which compasseth the whole land of Havilah, where there is gold;

[12] And the gold of that land is good: there is bdellium and the onyx stone.

[13] And the name of the second river is Gihon: the same is it that compasseth the whole land of Ethiopia.

[14] And the name of the third river is Hiddekel: that is it which goeth toward the east of Assyria. And the fourth river is Euphrates.

[15] And the LORD God took the man, and put him into the garden of Eden to dress it and to keep it.

[16] And the LORD God commanded the man, saying, Of every tree of the garden thou mayest freely eat:

[17] But of the tree of the knowledge of good and evil, thou shalt not eat of it: for in the day that thou eatest thereof thou shalt surely die.

[18] And the LORD God said, It is not good that the man should be alone; I will make him an help meet for him.

[19] And out of the ground the LORD God formed every beast of the field, and every fowl of the air; and brought them unto Adam to see what he would call them: and whatsoever Adam called every living creature, that was the name thereof.

[20] And Adam gave names to all cattle, and to the fowl of the air, and to every beast of the field; but for Adam there was not found an help meet for him.

[21] And the LORD God caused a deep sleep to fall upon Adam and he slept: and he took one of his ribs, and closed up the flesh instead thereof;

[22] And the rib, which the LORD God had taken from man, made he a woman, and brought her unto the man.

[23] And Adam said, This is now bone of my bones, and flesh of my flesh: she shall be called Woman, because she was taken out of Man.

[24] Therefore shall a man leave his father and his mother, and shall cleave unto his wife: and they shall be one flesh.

[25] And they were both naked, the man and his wife, and were not ashamed.

Notes

'Genesis' (meaning the 'beginning') is, for obvious reasons, the first book of the Bible in both Hebrew and Christian versions. Like the next four books, which form the Pentateuch (Greek: 'five books'), it was believed to have been written by Moses himself.

Genesis 1, verse 1. The verb 'to create' in Hebrew suggests both complete effortlessness and the idea of creatio *ex nihilo* – creation emerges neither from a primeval struggle nor from a divine act of procreation, but simply from the mystery of God.

Verse 3. God creates by his word, not by any emanation from his being (as in human birth). Thus this verse is linked with John 1: 1.

Verse 26. The Hebrew word for 'man' ('ādām) is a collective and never used in the plural. It means literally 'mankind'.

Chapter 2, verse 8. The word Eden means 'bliss', and becomes in the prophets a synonym for Paradise (e.g. Isaiah 51: 3).
Verse 18. The creation of woman is not perceived very romantically. The term used can be translated as 'a helper fit for him', or merely assistant.
Verse 23. The Hebrew word for 'woman' is *ishshah*. Since the word for man is *ish*, the English consonance man/woman fairly represents the original word-play.

—— **Commentary** ——

As any reader of Genesis will quickly notice, there are not one, but two creation stories in Genesis – as well as other references to vestigial creation myths elsewhere in the Old Testament (e.g. Isaiah 51: 9–10; Job 38). In line with the New Testament's role as a commentary on the Hebrew Bible, the beginning of St John's Gospel intertextually weaves yet another.

The key word is clearly 'light'. God begins the creation process by saying 'let there be light' and John takes this up by making the 'life' of the divine word (Greek *logos*) to be made flesh as 'the light of men' in Christ – and, in so doing, he begins a long typological and metaphorical sequence in which Christ is seen as the 'second Adam' inaugurating a second, 'new creation', to supersede and eventually replace the sin-tarnished original. The imagery of the New Testament is shot through with references to light (and its opposite, darkness), not merely in relation to good and evil, but even at a more basic level of Being versus Nothingness. Light makes possible Being and form; it is a metaphor of understanding, and comprehension (in its more usual sense); it is also the means of supernatural 'illumination', and one who receives such 'enlightenment' is called a 'seer' or 'visionary'. The revelation of Jesus' divine role occurs in the light of the Transfiguration (Luke 9: 28–36), in the climax of the Crucifixion 'darkness covered the whole earth'; Paul's subsequent conversion on the road to Damascus is accompanied by a light that is literally blinding.

In the sequence of the five days of Creation that follow the initial illumination only one thing is left out – women. Eve was not part of God's original six-day plan, but is presented as an afterthought, a secondary and one-off creation made not, as was the rest *ex nihilo*, from nothing, but from Adam's rib. She is, therefore, right from the start, a special case, to be seen either as God's last and fairest work (a view which Milton's Adam, if not the biblical one, is inclined to take in the first flush of love) or, in retrospect, second-class citizen of Eden, and her role as troublemaker made the more likely.

It is clear that this Genesis account of Creation was well known outside Jewish circles. Longinus, who seems to have been a pagan literary critic writing some time in the early Christian era included a section 'On the Sublime' in a popular book of literary tropes. Among the examples of sublimity he cites is that of 'the lawgiver of the Hebrews' (i.e., Moses) who describes God as saying 'Let there be light.' Though this reference by Longinus was known from the late fifteenth century onwards, it was only in the eighteenth century that critics came to see in it the Classical world's acknowledgement of not merely the moral but the aesthetic supremacy of God's Word. Isaac Watts, the great English hymn-writer, declares the inferiority of the (classical) 'Gentiles... when brought into Comparison with MOSES, whom LONGINUS himself, a *gentile* Critic, cites as a Master of the sublime Stile, when he chose to use it' (Preface to *Horae Lyricae*, 1709).

In the second creation story it is noticeable that language itself seems to be among the earliest of things created. God's first act is speech. Adam is called on to give names to every other living creature, and this seems to be the clue to his mastery over them (2: 19–20). This brief reference, together with the story of the Tower of Babel (11: 1–9) led to the later belief in an original Adamic language in which names stood for real things, rather than, as in all subsequent languages, just our idea of them. As late as the eighteenth century it was still widely believed that Hebrew was the oldest known language, containing at least elements of the original unfallen Adamic words – though other candidates were also being advanced. Sir William Jones, the great Indian scholar, thought that Sanskrit might be older, and, more wildly, James Parsons argued in an extraordinary book called *The Remains of Japhet* (1767) that Irish and Welsh were the oldest languages, being the remains of 'Japhetan', the original antediluvian tongue.

The early Christians rapidly came to believe that the whole Bible was the expression of the *logos*, the divine Word of God of John's Gospel, and this remained the main principle behind the tradition of biblical interpretation until well after the Reformation, and the source of the idea that every word of it must be true and divinely inspired. This did not, however, necessarily mean *literally* true. Since the Christian appropriation of the Hebrew scriptures necessarily involved an extensive process of re-interpretation, often of an elaborately figurative nature, the traditional Hebrew belief that every word was of vital and God-given significance (a conviction itself, of course, open to a wide variety of interpretations) was obviously as important to the new appropriators of the scriptures as it was to their original possessors – and could, once again, be appropriated into the Greek notion of the *logos* as a source of divine inspiration. One curious result of this was that it was not until the Enlightenment, in the eighteenth century, with its attempt to secularize all knowledge, that it was possible to have serious historical studies made, by Vico, Herder, von Humboldt and others, of the origins of language.

That John himself reads the Genesis account metaphorically rather than literally should alert us to the fact that the debates over the literal historicity of the Genesis stories are themselves of relatively recent origin, dating, like the scientific evidence with which they were brought into conflict, from the scientific revolution of the seventeenth century. It was then that Archbishop Ussher came up with his famous 'date' for the Creation of 4004 BC by adding up the lifespans of the various Patriarchs, and other time-scales given in Genesis. It was, given the premises, an impressively sophisticated calculation, which allowed both for the fact that the eighth-century monk, Dionysius Exiguus (literally 'Denis the Short') had caused endless trouble by omitting to allow for a year '0' when he came up with a new chronology for Pope St John I, beginning, supposedly, with the birth of Jesus, not to mention problems with what was believed to be the date of the star of Bethlehem. The remarkable thing about this date is not its accuracy but that there had been so few earlier attempts: Jewish chronology had put it about 3761 BC, and the Septuagint round about 5500 BC.

The analogy between God's initial creation and that of an author goes back a long way, but with the Romantics at the end of the eighteenth century it acquires a new force and prominence. Taking Job 38: 7 ('When the morning stars sang together, and all the sons of God shouted for joy') as their key text a whole succession of pre-Romantic eighteenth-century writers had noted the association between creativity and joy. For Joseph Addison (see below) this was paralleled by the Greek Pythagorean myth of the harmony or 'music of the spheres', where each of the eight known heavenly bodies of the Ptolemaic universe uttered its own characteristic note – though he is careful to note that this heavenly harmony is a metaphorical thing, for 'reason's ear' alone.

Similarly, for John Wesley, as for many before and after, the dizzying contrast between God's infiniteness and the finiteness of creation, was not merely a physical fact but also a psychological one – Newton's revelations about the mathematical structure of the universe only serving to increase human awe at the scale and complexity of the cosmos. In his translation of Ernst Lange he marvels:

> O God, thou bottomless abyss!
> Thee to perfection who can know?
> O height immense! What words suffice
> Thy countless attributes to show?

> ...Eternity Thy fountain was,
> Which, like Thee, no beginning knew;
> Thou wast ere time began his race,
> Ere glowed with stars the ethereal blue.

With the Methodist and Evangelical revivals of the mid-century, however, this trope of 'joy' in creation took on fresh meaning. As we have seen, non-Calvinistic theology had always held that the primal unity between God and man, though disrupted by the Fall, had been at least potentially restored by Christ, and his 'new creation' the Church. Each soul thus drawn into the new life in Christ is also a 'New creation; and none can create a soul anew, but He who first created the heavens and the earth.' (*Life of Wesley*, ed. C. C. Southey, 1858, Vol. II, pp. 57–8) Thus John Wesley could praise the

> Father of all! Whose powerful voice
> Called forth this universal frame;
> Whose mercies over all rejoice,
> Through endless ages still the same.

Conceptions of language itself as in some sense still bearing the traces of divinity, together with the idea of 'creation' as an internalized, even psychological activity were to have a profound effect on Romantic ideas of aesthetic creativity, and of the 'imagination'. Coleridge's famous formulation of the imagination in *Biographia Literaria* ch. XIII, for instance, echoes both the Bible and *Paradise Lost*. Nor was this all: in his own preface to reading the Bible, the posthumously published *Confessions of an Inquiring Spirit* (1849), Coleridge's own 'beginning' deliberately echoes the themes of 'light' and 'life' from the opening of John's Gospel.

I take up this work with the purpose to read it for the first time as I should any other work, – as far at least as I can or dare. For I neither can, nor dare, throw off a strong and awful prepossession in its favour – certain as I am that a large part of the light and life, in which and by which I see, love, and embrace the truths and the strengths co-organised into a living body of faith and knowledge...has been directly or derived to me from this sacred volume, – and unable to determine what I do not owe to its influences...There is a Light higher than all even *the Word that was in the beginning*; – the Light, of which light itself is but the *schechinah* and cloudy tabernacle; – the Word that is light for every man, and life for as many as give heed to it. (pp. 10–11)

(*Note*: 'Schechinah' is a rabbinical term drawn from the Hebrew root 'to dwell' (*sh-k-n*), and carries with it the idea of both 'glory' and God's presence among people on earth.)

—— **Literature** ——

John Milton, *Paradise Lost* (1667), Book VII, lines 205–16, 224–42

... Heav'n opened wide
Her ever-during gates, harmonious sound
On golden hinges moving, to let forth
The King of Glory in his powerful Word
And Spirit coming to create new worlds.
On heav'nly ground they stood, and from the shore
They viewed the vast immeasurable abyss
Outrageous as a sea, dark, wasteful, wild,
Up from the bottom turned by furious winds
And surging waves, as mountains to assault
Heav'n's highth, and with the center mix the pole ...

... Then stayed the fervid wheels, and in his hand
He took the golden compasses, prepared
In God's eternal store, to circumscribe
This universe, and all created things.
One foot he centered and the other turned
Round through the vast profundity obscure,
And said, 'Thus far extend, thus far thy bounds,
This be thy just circumference, O world!'
Thus God the heav'n created, thus the earth,
Matter unformed and void. Darkness profound
Covered th'abyss; but on the wat'ry calm
His brooding wings the Spirit of God outspread,
And vital virtue infused, and vital warmth
Throughout the fluid mass, but downward purged
The black tartareous cold infernal dregs
Adverse to life; then founded, then conglobed
Like things to like, the rest to several place

Disparted, and between spun out the air,
And earth self-balanced on her center hung.

Joseph Addison, 'The Spacious Firmament on High' (1712)

The spacious firmament on high,
With all the blue ethereal sky,
And spangled heavens, a shining frame,
Their great Original proclaim...

What though in solemn silence all
Move round this dark terrestrial ball;
What though no real voice or sound
Amidst their radiant orbs be found:
In reason's ear they all rejoice,
And utter forth a glorious voice,
For ever singing as they shine:
The hand that made us is divine!

Samuel Taylor Coleridge, *Biographia Literaria* (1817), from chapter XIII

The IMAGINATION I consider either as primary, or secondary. The primary IMAGINATION I hold to be the living Power and prime Agent of all human Perception, and as a repetition in the finite mind of the eternal act of creation in the infinite I AM. The secondary Imagination I consider as an echo of the former, co-existing with the conscious will, yet still as identical with the primary in the *kind* of its agency, and differing only in *degree*, and in the *mode* of its operation. It dissolves, diffuses, dissipates, in order to recreate; or where this process is rendered impossible, yet still at all events it struggles to idealize and to unify. It is essentially *vital*, even as all objects (*as* objects) are essentially fixed and dead.

FANCY, on the contrary, has no other counters to play with, but fixities and definites. The Fancy is indeed no other than a mode of Memory emancipated from the order of time and space; while it is blended with, and modified by that empirical phenomenon of the will, which we express by the word CHOICE. But equally with the ordinary memory the Fancy must receive all its materials ready made from the law of association.

Whatever more than this, I shall think it fit to declare concerning the powers and privileges of the imagination in the present work, will be found in the critical essay on the uses of the Supernatural in poetry, and the principles that regulate its introduction: which the reader will find pre-fixed to the poem of The Ancient Mariner.

T. S. Eliot, Choruses from 'The Rock' (VII), *Collected Poems*, Faber, 1986

In the beginning GOD created the world. Waste and void.
    Waste and void. And darkness was upon the face of the deep.
And when there were men, in their various ways, they struggled in torment towards GOD
Blindly and vainly, for man is a vain thing, and man without GOD is a seed upon the wind: driven this way and that, and finding no place of lodgement and germination.
They followed the light and the shadow, and the light led them forward to light and the shadow led them to darkness,
Worshipping snakes or trees, worshipping devils rather than nothing: crying for life beyond life, for ecstasy not of the flesh.
Waste and void. Waste and void. And darkness on the face of the deep.

And the Spirit moved upon the face of the water.
And men who turned towards the light and were known of the light
Invented the Higher Religions; and the Higher Religions were good
And led men from light to light, to knowledge of Good and Evil.
But their light was ever surrounded and shot with darkness
As the air of temperate seas is pierced by the still dead breath of the Arctic Current;
And they came to an end, a dead end stirred with a flicker of life,
And they came to the withered ancient look of a child that has died of starvation.
Prayer wheels, worship of the dead, denial of this world, affirmation of rites with forgotten meanings
In the restless wind-whipped sand, or the hills where the wind will not let the snow rest.
Waste and void. Waste and void. And darkness on the face of the deep.

Then came, at a predetermined moment, a moment in time and of time,
A moment not out of time, but in time, in what we call history: transecting, bisecting the world of time, a moment in time but not like a moment of time,

A moment in time but time was made through that moment: for without
  the meaning there is no time, and that moment of time gave the meaning.
Then it seemed as if men must proceed from light to light, in the light of
  the Word,
Through the Passion and Sacrifice saved in spite of their negative being;
Bestial as always before, carnal, self-seeking as always before, selfish and
  purblind as ever before,
Yet always struggling, always reaffirming, always resuming their march
  on the way that was lit by the light;
Often halting, loitering, straying, delaying, returning, yet following no
  other way.

But it seems that something has happened that has never happened before:
  though we know not just when, or why, or how, or where.

Men have left GOD not for other gods, they say, but for no god; and this
  has never happened before
That men both deny gods and worship gods, professing first Reason,
And then Money, and Power, and what they call Life, or Race, or
  Dialectic.
The Church disowned, the tower overthrown, the bells upturned, what
  have we to do
But stand with empty hands and palms turned upwards
In an age which advances progressively backwards?

VOICE OF THE UNEMPLOYED *(afar off):*
    In this land
There shall be one cigarette to two men,
To two women one half pint of bitter
Ale . . .

CHORUS:
What does the world say, does the whole world stray in high-powered
  cars on a by-pass way?

VOICE OF THE UNEMPLOYED *(more faintly):*
    In this land
No man has hired us . . .

CHORUS:
Waste and void. Waste and void. And darkness on the face of the deep.
Has the Church failed mankind, or has mankind failed the Church?

When the Church is no longer regarded, not even opposed, and men have
  forgotten
All gods except Usury, Lust and Power.

D. H. Lawrence, 'Let There Be Light!'

If ever there was a beginning
there was no god in it
there was no Verb
no Voice
no Word.

There was nothing to say:
Let there be light!
All that story of Mr God switching on day
is just conceit.

Just man's conceit!
– Who made the sun?
– My child, I cannot tell a lie,
I made it!

George Washington's Grandpapa!
All we can honestly imagine in the beginning
is the incomprehensible plasm of life, of creation struggling
and *becoming* light.

C. S. Lewis, *The Magician's Nephew* (1955), Penguin, 1963

The Fight at the Lamp-Post

'Hush!' said the Cabby. They all listened.

   In the darkness something was happening at last. A voice had begun to
sing. It was very far away and Digory found it hard to decide from what
direction it was coming. Sometimes it seemed to come from all directions
at once. Sometimes he almost thought it was coming out of the earth
beneath them. Its lower notes were deep enough to be the voice of the
earth herself. There were no words. There was hardly even a tune. But it
was, beyond comparison, the most beautiful noise he had ever heard. It
was so beautiful he could hardly bear it. The horse seemed to like it too:
he gave the sort of whinny a horse would give if, after years of being a
cab-horse, it found itself back in the old field where it had played as a foal,

and saw someone whom it remembered and loved coming across the field to bring it a lump of sugar.

'Gawd! said the Cabby. 'Ain't it lovely?'

Then two wonders happened at the same moment. One was that the voice was suddenly joined by other voices; more voices than you could possibly count. They were in harmony with it, but far higher up the scale: cold, tingling, silvery voices. The second wonder was that the blackness overhead, all at once, was blazing with stars. They didn't come out gently one by one, as they do on a summer evening. One moment there had been nothing but darkness; next moment a thousand, thousand points of light leaped out – single stars, constellations, and planets, brighter and bigger than any in our world. There were no clouds. The new stars and the new voices began at exactly the same time. If you had seen and heard it, as Digory did, you would have felt quite certain that it was the stars themselves which were singing, and that it was the First Voice, the deep one, which had made them appear and made them sing.

'Glory be!' said the Cabby. 'I'd ha' been a better man all my life if I'd known there were things like this.'

The Voice on the earth was now louder and more triumphant; but the voices in the sky, after singing loudly with it for a time, began to get fainter. And now something else was happening.

Far away, and down near the horizon, the sky began to turn grey. A light wind, very fresh, began to stir. The sky, in that one place, grew slowly and steadily paler. You could see shapes of hills standing up dark against it. All the time the Voice went on singing.

There was soon light enough for them to see one another's faces. The Cabby and the two children had open mouths and shining eyes; they were drinking in the sound, and they looked as if it reminded them of something. Uncle Andrew's mouth was open too, but not open with joy. It looked more as if his chin had simply dropped away from the rest of his face. His shoulders were stooped and his knees shook. He was not liking the Voice. If he could have got away from it by creeping into a rat's hole, he would have done so. But the Witch looked as if, in a way, she understood the music better than any of them. Her mouth was shut, her lips were pressed together, and her fists were clenched. Ever since the song began she had felt that this whole world was filled with a Magic different from hers and stronger. She hated it. She would have smashed that whole world, or all worlds, to pieces, if it would only stop the singing. The horse stood with its ears well forward, and twitching. Every now and then it snorted and stamped the ground. It no longer looked like a tired old cab-horse; you could now well believe that its father had been in battles.

The eastern sky changed from white to pink and from pink to gold. The Voice rose and rose, till all the air was shaking with it. And just as it swelled to the mightiest and most glorious sound it had yet produced, the sun arose.

Digory had never seen such a sun. The sun above the ruins of Charn had looked older than ours: this looked younger. You could imagine that it laughed for joy as it came up. And as its beams shot across the land the travellers could see for the first time what sort of place they were in. It was a valley through which a broad, swift river wound its way, rowing eastward towards the sun. Southward there were mountains, northward there were lower hills. But it was a valley of mere earth, rock and water; there was not a tree, not a bush, not a blade of grass to be seen. The earth was of many colours: they were fresh, hot, and vivid. They made you feel excited; until you saw the Singer himself, and then you forgot everything else.

It was a Lion. Huge, shaggy, and bright, it stood facing the risen sun. Its mouth was wide open in song and it was about three hundred yards away.

Bibliography

Aarsleff, Hans. *From Locke to Saussure: Essays on the Study of Intellectual History* (Minneapolis: University of Minnesota Press, 1982).

Gould, Stephen Jay. 'Dousing Diminutive Dennis's Debate (or DDD = 2000)', *Dinosaur in a Haystack* (London: Cape, 1996).

Herder, Johann Gottfried. 'Essay on the Origin of Language' (1772), *Herder on Social and Political Culture*, tr. and ed. F. M. Barnard (Cambridge: Cambridge University Press, 1969).

Life of Wesley. ed. C. C. Southey, with notes by Samuel Taylor Coleridge (2 vols, London: 1858).

von Humboldt, Wilhelm. *On Language* (1836) tr. Peter Heath, intro. Hans Aarsleff (Cambridge: Cambridge University Press, 1988).

Von Rad, Gerhard. *Genesis: A Commentary*, tr. John Marks (London: SCM Old Testament Library, 1961).

In the Beginning Was the Word

John 1: 1–18

[1] In the beginning was the Word, and the Word was with God, and the Word was God.

[2] The same was in the beginning with God.

[3] All things were made by him; and without him was not any thing made that was made.

[4] In him was life; and the life was the light of men.

[5] And the light shineth in darkness; and the darkness comprehended it not.

[6] There was a man sent from God, whose name was John.

[7] The same came for a witness, to bear witness of the Light, that all men through him might believe.

[8] He was not that Light, but was sent to bear witness of that Light.

[9] That was the true Light, which lighteth every man that cometh into the world.

[10] He was in the world, and the world was made by him, and the world knew him not.

[11] He came unto his own, and his own received him not.

[12] But as many as received him, to them gave he power to become the sons of God, even to them that believe on his name:

[13] Which were born, not of blood, nor of the will of the flesh, nor of the will of man, but of God.

[14] And the Word was made flesh, and dwelt among us, (and we beheld his glory, the glory as of the only begotten of the Father,) full of grace and truth.

[15] John bare witness of him, and cried, saying, This was he of whom I spake, He that cometh after me is preferred before me: for he was before me.

[16] And of his fulness have all we received, and grace for grace.

[17] For the law was given by Moses, but grace and truth came by Jesus Christ.

[18] No man hath seen God at any time; the only begotten Son, which is in the bosom of the Father, he hath declared him.

Notes

Verse 1. In Greek, the first two words of the Gospel are exactly the same as the opening words of the Septuagint (Greek) version of Genesis in the Hebrew Bible: 'In the beginning...' They are clearly meant to recall Genesis.

'...the Word'. In Greek, 'logos', is a theological word, appearing frequently in the Septuagint. It is used here quite deliberately in a synthetic manner reflecting the Jewish Rabbinic tradition, the apostolic Christian tradition and Greek, particularly Stoic, thought. Its sense is both creative and revelatory.

'...the Word was God'. This goes beyond anything in either Jewish or Greek theology or thought.

Verse 2. The theme of light and darkness runs through the whole of this Gospel, identifying Jesus as the light of the world, darkness having a corresponding ethical quality.

Verse 4. Light and life are frequently connected in the Hebrew Bible, e.g. Psalm 36: 9.

Verse 5. The word 'comprehended' does not mean 'understand', but (from its root meaning 'to grasp') something closer to 'contain' or even 'extinguish'.

Verse 7. The word used for 'testimony' can almost be transliterated into the English word 'martyr'. According to the tradition, John finally 'bore witness' in his own death, described in Mark 6: 14–29. He might be described as the last of the great Old Testament prophets.

Verse 10. 'The world', in Greek, 'kosmos', means here the world of people and nations, though elsewhere (John 17: 5) it can also mean the whole created order.

Verse 12. The word 'power' might be better understood as 'authority' or even just 'the right'.

Verse 13. Blood was often thought to be the means of procreation in the ancient world.

Verse 14. This verse is the climax of the prologue to the Gospel. 'Flesh' denotes not just physicality, but the whole of human nature.

'Dwelt among us': literally this means to live in a tent or tabernacle, which was once the nature of God's dwelling with Israel before the building of the Temple by Solomon in Jerusalem.

'Glory': In the days of Israel's wandering in the wilderness after their escape from Egypt, the cloud which represented the glory of God would descend upon the 'tabernacle'. The word literally means 'appearance', God appearing especially at the moment of sacrifice (Leviticus 9: 6, 23). It is a very important word in this Gospel, suggestive of God's grace and faithfulness to his people. Hence:

Verse 17. Through Jesus comes grace, that is God's kindness, and truth while Moses brought only the Law down from Mount Sinai (Exodus 19–20).

—— **Commentary** ——

The opening passage of the Fourth Gospel is one of the traditional Christmas readings in the Church, often used at the Midnight Mass of Christmas Eve. It looks back to the first words of the book of Genesis, which also starts 'In the beginning'. In those first words of the Bible, God speaks, and the cosmos is created from his word. The Gospel deliberately refers back to that power of the Word, and the use of the Greek term 'logos' here is significant. For it links the Hebrew tradition with a complex understanding of the 'word' in Greek literature, which is why we have included the brief extract from the *Apology* of the early Christian writer and scholar, Justin Martyr. Justin refers not only to Plato, but also to the term in Greek Stoic philosophy which links the 'generative word' (or *logos spermatikos*) with universal reason. The Stoics especially distinguished between the word as spoken, and the word 'within', which is something close to a rational principle existing in all things.

It seems that the writer of this Gospel is using this term deliberately to link the Hebrew Bible with Greek thought in the apostolic tradition of early Christianity.

God's first word of creation in Genesis 1: 3 is 'Let there be light'. Here again the Gospel introduces the theme of the Word *as* light, in an image which remains central in the Christian tradition. Thus at baptism, the new Christian is presented with a candle to symbolize Christ as the light of the world, 'to show that you have passed from darkness to light'. With his forerunner, John the Baptist, who is the last of the great prophets, the Incarnate Word is seen here as the glory of God, bearing grace and truth such as Moses, the lawgiver, was unable to supply.

There is nothing quite like this passage elsewhere in the New Testament, particularly in its use of the Word, and its dynamism and complexity are perfectly recognized in early Christian writers like Augustine and Jerome as well as Justin Martyr. This sense was rather lost in the Reformation, Martin Luther, for example, replacing the active *Zeitwort* ('verb') for the more leaden '*Im Anfang war das Wort*' in his translation of the New Testament. But in Renaissance Neoplatonism, the ancient sense of the active *logos spermatikos* remains, and is found in English literature through the writings of the Cambridge Platonists, especially, perhaps, in Ralph Cudworth's *The True Intellectual System of the Universe* (1678) which was much studied and admired by the Romantic poet and thinker Samuel Taylor Coleridge. We have excerpted a passage from an early lecture by Coleridge of 1795, one of the *Lectures on Revealed Religion*, in which he gives evidence of a fascination with St. John's Gospel which remained with him throughout his life to his great unfinished project to be entitled his *Logosophia*. As Coleridge moved from his early Unitarianism to something approaching Christian orthodoxy in his later years, he remained committed to a sense of the Logos as 'the communicative intellect in Man and Deity' (*Biographia Literaria*, 1817, ch. 13), which is hardly how the great Christian exegetes from St Augustine onwards would have read the Gospel passage.

In his Holy Sonnet 'Temple', John Donne links the Johannine text on the Word with the episode in the Gospel of Luke 2: 41–51, of the boy Jesus found by his parents teaching the learned men in the Temple in Jerusalem. This miracle of speaking with such wisdom by one so young is evidence of the power of the 'Word' which 'but lately could not speak', and is now incarnate in the flesh of Jesus. The Logos is thus associated explicitly with the Second Person of the Christian Trinity. This orthodoxy is explicitly rejected in the passage from Goethe's *Faust, Part 1*, where Faust, in his study is found rejecting the implications of the Gospel text and attempting to revise it for 'the Word I cannot set supremely high'. After a number of attempts, he concludes with 'In the beginning was the Deed' – an irony, perhaps, in light of the Christian tradition of the generative and active Word. Goethe is, however, at one with much Romantic literature in its almost obsessive re-writing of this passage. We give here one further example, an excerpt from Lord Byron's odd poem *The Morgante Maggiore*, which begins with a free translation of the opening phrase, 'In the beginning was the Word next God', and proceeds to enjoin the Lord to send one of his angels to bring this word to the poet so that he might worthily compose his verse. In other words, Byron uses the passage as an invocation to strengthen his own word, rather as Milton invokes the 'Heavenly Muse' at the opening of *Paradise Lost*.

But it is to Goethe's reading of the Gospel, and the Romantic readings (and behind them Plato) which followed, that the French philosopher and critic Jacques Derrida looks back, rather than, in the first instance, the biblical or Christian tradition. We have included here a passage from Derrida's enormously influential work *Of Grammatology* (1967) since his rejection of 'logocentrism' has been so profoundly important for literary theory and interpretation. What Derrida rejects is the sense that language is subservient to some idea, intention or referent which lies outside it, and he is interested in the moment 'when it ceases to be self-assured, contained, and *guaranteed* by the infinite signified which seemed to assure it' (*Of Grammatology*, p. 6). Derrida, certainly, is rejecting the metaphysical tradition which lies at the heart of the Johannine text, making language primary and not dependent on prior non-linguistic concerns.

Dylan Thomas' poem 'In the Beginning' draws together the Genesis and Johannine passages, moving from the cosmic, to the creation of the things of nature on Earth, to the word and the mind of human beings. All are drawn into one great moment of creation, 'in the beginning'. In this poem there is no difference between the two versions of 'in the beginning'. Emily Dickinson, however, concentrates upon a different moment of the Prologue to the Gospel – on verse 14, 'And the Word became flesh'. Her brief, typically enigmatic poem is a profound meditation on the mystery of the Incarnation – that is, the taking of human flesh by the Godhead. The mystery of the 'Word made Flesh' is something that all of us, as enfleshed beings, can understand each in our own way, by our own experience and 'to our specific strength'. But in the second part of the poem, she moves to the wonder of the Word made Flesh in Jesus Christ (John 1: 17), as an act of divine 'kenosis', or self-emptying as described in Philippians 2: 6–8: 'And being found in human form he humbled himself and became obedient unto death, even death on a cross.' Such was the 'condescension' of God in becoming human flesh, in a 'consent of Language' – that is of the Word which was from the beginning.

The literature which draws upon this Prologue to the Fourth Gospel is vast, and here we have offered only a few examples. Much more could be said about the theme of light, and although most references are rather general, there are one or two examples from literature which draw directly upon John 1: 4–9, for instance, William Cowper's 'The Light and Glory of the Word'. Perhaps, in conclusion, it should be remembered that the Greek word for create or make is *poieo*, a verb which is the third word of the Greek Septuagint version of the Old Testament: 'In the beginning God created the heavens and the earth.' Although it is not actually used in St John's Gospel until chapter 2, verse 23, to describe the miracles which Jesus 'did' or 'created', it relates the initial act of creation with a poetic moment, that is a moment of the Word. It is this powerful poetic word of which Goethe's Faust is so sceptical, which links, in Coleridge's Primary Imagination (*Biographia Literaria*, ch. 13), the moment of divine creation with the creative power of the poet, and in Dylan Thomas, the mind of the human being with the wonder of all creation 'in the beginning'.

—— **Literature** ——

Justin Martyr, *Apology* (*c.*155), II: 13, from J. Stevenson,
A New Eusebius, SPCK, 1957, 'The Light That Lighteth
Every Man'

For I myself, when I discovered the wicked disguise which the evil spirits had thrown around the divine doctrines of the Christians, to turn aside others from joining them, laughed both at those who framed these falsehoods, and at the disguise itself, and at popular opinion; and I confess that I both boast and with all my strength strive to be a Christian; not because the teachings of Plato are different from those of Christ, but because they are not in all respects similar, as neither are those of the others, Stoics, and poets and historians. For each man spoke well in proportion to the share he had of the generative word (or reason), seeing what was related to it. But they who contradict themselves on the more important points appear not to have possessed the wisdom that is infallible, and the knowledge which is irrefutable. Whatever things were rightly said among all teachers, are the property of us Christians. For next to God, we worship and love the Word who is from the Unbegotten and Ineffable God, since also He became man for our sakes, that, becoming a partaker of our sufferings, He might also bring us healing. For all the writers were able to see realities darkly through the sowing of the implanted word that was in them. For the seed and imitation imparted according to capacity is one thing, and quite another is the thing itself, of which there is the participation and imitation according to the grace which is from Him.

John Donne, *Holy Sonnets*, 'La Corona' (*c.*1610–1611),
4 'Temple'

> *With his kind mother who partakes thy woe,*
> Joseph turn back; see where your child doth sit,
> Blowing, yea blowing out those sparks of wit,
> Which himself on the Doctors did bestow;
> The Word but lately could not speak, and lo
> It suddenly speaks wonders, whence comes it,
> That all which was, and all which should be writ,
> A shallow seeming child, should deeply know?
> His godhead was not soul to his manhood,
> Nor had time mellowed him to his ripeness,

But as for one which hath a long task, 'tis good,
With the sun to begin his business,
He in his age's morning thus began
By miracles exceeding power of man.

S. T. Coleridge, *Lectures on Revealed Religion* (1795), Lecture 5

The first Chapter of the Gospel according to St. John is a sublime and beautiful answer to their [the Gnostics] notions concerning the Supreme whom they held not to have been the Creator of the World – this Planet at least having been made according to them by an inferior Spirit of a mingled nature not immediately flowing from the Supreme mind, nor even one of the earliest Emanations. In contradiction to this St. John asserts, that in the *beginning* there was Intelligence, that this Intelligence was together with God, not an emanation from him, and that this Intelligence was God himself. ['] All things were made by it and without this Intelligence was not anything made that was made ['], contradicting the Gnostics, who asserted, that there were many things in the constitution of the world, which could not have proceeded from Wisdom. The texts, 'It was in the World and the World was made by it, and the World knew it not' and 'it was made Flesh and dwelt among us' imply – that the divine Intelligence never ceased to govern the world which it had created, though almost all mankind worshipped blind and senseless Deities; and that this same Intelligence was imparted by immediate inspiration to the man Jesus, who dwelt among us. These passages were written to condemn the doctrine of the superangelic nature of Jesus. St. John here asserting that the same intelligential Energy which operated in Jesus had been in the World before his existence, teaching the Law to Moses and foreknowledge to the prophets.

Goethe, *Faust, Part 1* (1808), tr. Philip Wayne, Penguin, 1949, Scene ii, 'Faust's Study'

Ay me, though humbly I entreat for rest,
No more comes sweet contentment to my breast.
Must we then find so soon the fountain dry,
And man in thirsty torment left to lie?
That is the truth that long experience brings,
Yet may these sorrows bear a compensation
We learn to cherish here immortal things,

And look with longing hearts for revelation,
Whose high inspired and wonder-bearing word
Most clear in the New Testament is heard.
My mind is moved this hour to consecrate,
In simple, honest will to understand
The sacred codex, and its truth translate
In the loved accents of my native land.
   (*He opens a volume and sets to work.*)
'Tis writ, 'In the beginning was the Word.'
I pause, to wonder what is here inferred.
The Word I cannot set supremely high:
A new translation I will try.
I read, if by the spirit I am taught,
This sense: 'In the beginning was the Thought.'
This opening I need to weigh again,
Or sense may suffer from a hasty pen.
Does Thought create, and work, and rule the hour?
'Twere best: 'In the beginning was the Power.'
Yet, while the pen is urged with willing fingers,
A sense of doubt and hesitancy lingers.
The spirit comes to guide me in my need,
I write, 'In the beginning was the Deed.'

Lord Byron, *The Morgante Maggiore*

Canto the First

I

In the beginning was the Word next God;
   God was the Word, the Word no less was he:
This was the beginning, to my mode
   Of thinking, and without him nought could be:
Therefore, just Lord! from out thy high abode,
   Benign and pious, bid an angel flee,
One only, to be my companion, who
Shall help my famous, worthy old song through.

II

And thou, oh Virgin! daughter, mother, bride
   Of the same Lord, who gave to you each key

Of heaven and hell, and everything beside,
   The day thy Gabriel said 'All hail!' to thee,
Since to thy servants pity's ne'er denied,
   With flowing rhymes, a pleasant style and free
Be to my verses then benignly kind,
And to the end illuminate my mind.

III

'Twas in the season when sad Philomel
   Weeps with her sister, who remembers and
Deplores the ancient woes which both befell,
   And makes the nymphs enamour'd, to the hand
Of Phaeton by Phoebus loved so well
   His car (but temper'd by his sire's command)
Was given, and on the horizon's verge just now
Appear'd, so that Tithonus scratch'd his brow:

IV

When I prepared my bark first to obey,
   As it should still obey, the helm, my mind,
And carry prose or rhyme, and this my lay
   Of Charles the Emperor, whom you will find
By several pens already praised; but they
   Who to diffuse his glory were inclined,
For all that I can see in the prose or verse,
Have understood Charles badly, and wrote worse.

Emily Dickinson, 'A Word Made Flesh Is Seldom', *Complete Poems*, ed. Thomas H. Johnson, Faber, 1970. No. 1651

A Word made Flesh is seldom
And tremblingly partook
Nor then perhaps reported
But I have not mistook
Each one of us has tasted
With ecstasies of stealth
The very food debated
To our specific strength –
A Word that breathes distinctly
Has not the power to die
Cohesive as the Spirit

JOHN 1: 1–18

It may expire if He –
'Made Flesh and dwelt among us'
Could condescension be
Like this consent of language
This loved Philology.

Dylan Thomas, 'In the Beginning Was the Three-pointed
Star', *Collected Poems 1934–1952*, J. M. Dent, 1952

In the beginning was the three-pointed star
One smile of light across the empty face;
One bough of bone across the rooting air,
The substance forked that marrowed the first sun;
And, burning ciphers on the round of space,
Heaven and hell mixed as they spun.

In the beginning was the pale signature,
Three-syllabled and starry as the smile;
And after came the imprints on the water,
Stamp of the minted face upon the moon;
The blood that touched the crosstree and the grail
Touched the first cloud and left a sign.

In the beginning was the mounting fire
That set alight the weathers from a spark,
A three-eyed spark, blunt as a flower,
Life rose and spouted from the rolling seas,
Burst in the roots, pumped from the earth and rock
The secret oils that drive the grass.

In the beginning was the word, the word
That from the solid bases of the light
Abstracted all the letters of the void;
And from the cloudy bases of the breath
The word flowed up, translating to the heart
First characters of birth and death.

In the beginning was the secret brain.
The brain was celled and soldered in the thought
Before the pitch was forking to a sun;
Before the veins were shaking in their sieve,
Blood shot and scattered to the winds of light
The ribbed original of love.

Jacques Derrida, *Of Grammatology* (1967), from
A Derrida Reader: Between the Blinds,
ed. Peggy Kamuf, Columbia UP, 1991

The reassuring evidence within which Western tradition had to organize itself and must continue to live would therefore be as follows: The order of the signified is never contemporary, is at best the subtly discrepant inverse or parallel – discrepant by the time of a breath – from the order of the signifier. And the sign must be the unity of a heterogeneity, since the signified (sense or thing, noeme or reality) is not in itself a signifier, a *trace*: in any case is not constituted in its sense by its relationship with a possible trace. The formal essence of the signified is *presence*, and the privilege of its proximity to the logos as *phone* is the privilege of presence. This is the inevitable response as soon as one asks: 'What is the sign?,' that is to say, when one submits the sign to the question of essence, to the 'ti esti.' The 'formal essence' of the sign is̶ can only be determined in terms of presence. One cannot get around that response, except by challenging the very form of the question and beginning to think that the signs that ill-named t̶h̶i̶n̶g̶, the only one, that escapes the instituting question of philosophy: 'What is ... ?'

Radicalizing the concepts of *interpretation, perspective, evaluation, difference*, and all the 'empiricist' or nonphilosophical motifs that have constantly tormented philosophy throughout the history of the West, and besides, have had nothing but the inevitable weakness of being produced in the field of philosophy, Nietzsche, far from remaining *simply* (with Hegel and as Heidegger wished) *within* metaphysics, contributed a great deal to the liberation of the signifier from its dependence or derivation with respect to the logos and the related concept of truth or the primary signified, in whatever sense that is understood. Reading, and therefore writing, the text were for Nietzsche 'originary' operations (I put that word within quotation marks for reasons to appear later) with regard to a sense that they do not first have to transcribe or discover, which would not therefore be a truth signified in the original element and presence of the logos, as *topos noetos*, divine understanding, or the structure of *a priori* necessity. To save Nietzsche from a reading of the Heideggerian type, it seems that we must above all not attempt to restore or make explicit a less naive 'ontology,' composed of profound ontological intuitions acceding to some originary truth, an entire fundamentality hidden under the appearance of an empiricist or metaphysical text. The virulence of Nietzschean thought could not be more-completely misunderstood. On the contrary, one must *accentuate* the 'naivete' of a breakthrough which cannot attempt a step outside of metaphysics, which cannot *criticize* metaphysics radically without still utilizing in a certain way, in a certain type or a certain style of *text*, propositions that, read within the philosophic corpus, that is to say according to Nietzsche ill-read or unread, have always been and will always be 'naivetes,' incoherent signs of an absolute appurtenance. Therefore, rather than protect Nietzsche from the Heideggerian reading, we should perhaps offer him up to it completely, underwriting that interpretation without reserve; in a *certain way* and up to the point where, the content of the Nietzschean discourse being almost lost for the question of being, its form regains its absolute strangeness, where his text finally invokes a different type of reading, more faithful to his type of writing: Nietzsche has *written what* he has written. He has written that writing – and first of all his own – is not originarily subordinate to the logos and to truth. And that this subordination has *come into being* during an epoch the meaning of which we must deconstruct. Now in this direction (but only in this direction, for read otherwise, the Nietzschean demolition remains dogmatic and, like all reversals, a captive of that metaphysical edifice which it professes to overthrow. On that point and in that *order of reading*, the conclusions of Heidegger and Fink are irrefutable), Heideggerian thought would reinstate rather than destroy the instance of the logos and of the truth of being as 'primum signatum:' the 'transcendental' ('transcendental' in a certain sense, as in the Middle Ages the transcendental – *ens, unum, verum, bonum* – was said to be the 'primum cognitum') implied by all categories or all determined significations, by all lexicons and all syntax, and therefore by all linguistic signifiers, though not to be identified simply with any one of those signifiers, allowing itself to be precomprehended through each of them, remaining irreducible to all the epochal determinations that it nonetheless makes possible, thus opening the history of the logos, yet itself being only through the logos; that is, *being nothing* before the logos and outside of it. The logos *of* being, 'Thought obeying the Voice of Being,' is the first and the last resource of the sign, of the difference between *signans* and *signatum*. There has to be a transcendental signified for the difference between signifier and signified to be somewhere absolute and irreducible. It is not by chance that the thought of being, as the thought of this transcendental signified, is manifested above all in the voice: in a language of words *[mots]* the voice is *heard* (understood) – that undoubtedly is what is called conscience – closest to the self as the absolute effacement of the signifier: pure auto-affection that necessarily has the form of time and does not borrow from outside of itself, in the world or in 'reality,' any accessory signifier, any substance of

91

expression foreign to its own spontaneity. It is the unique experience of the signified producing itself spontaneously, from within the self, and nevertheless, as signified concept, in the element of ideality or universality. The unwordly character of this substance of expression is constitutive of this ideality. This experience of the effacement of the signifier in the voice is not merely one illusion among many – since it is the condition of the very idea of truth – but I shall elsewhere show in what it does delude itself. This illusion is the history of truth and it cannot be dissipated so quickly. Within the closure of this experience, the word *[mot]* is lived as the elementary and undecomposable unity of the signified and the voice, of the concept and a transparent substance of expression. This experience is considered in its greatest purity – and at the same time in the condition of its possibility – as the experience of 'being.' The word *being*, or at any rate the word designating the sense of being in different languages, is, with some others, an 'originary word' ('Urwort'), the transcendental word assuring the possibility of being-word to all other words. As such, it is precomprehended in all language and – this is the opening of *Being and Time* – only this precomprehension would permit the opening of the question of the sense of being in general, beyond all regional ontologies and all metaphysics: a question that broaches philosophy (for example, in the *Sophist*) and lets itself be taken over by philosophy, a question that Heidegger repeats by submitting the history of metaphysics to it. Heidegger reminds us constantly that the sense of being is neither the word *being* nor the concept of being. But as that sense is nothing outside of language and the language of words, it is tied, if not to a particular word or to a particular system of language (*concesso non dato*), at least to the possibility of the word in general. And to the possibility of its irreducible simplicity. One could thus think that it remains only to choose between two possibilities. (1) Does a modern linguistics, a science of signification breaking up the unity of the word and breaking with its alleged irreducibility, still have anything to do with 'language?' Heidegger would probably doubt it. (2) Conversely, is not all that is profoundly meditated as the thought or the question of being enclosed within an old linguistics of the word which one practices here unknowingly? Unknowingly because such a linguistics, whether spontaneous or systematic, has always had to share the presuppositions of metaphysics. The two operate on the same grounds.

Bibliography

Barnard, L. W. *Justin Martyr: His Life and Thought* (Cambridge: Cambridge University Press, 1966), pp. 85–100.

Barrett, C. K. *The New Testament: Selected Documents* (London: SPCK, 1987), ch. 4, 'The Philosophers and Poets', pp. 58–60, on Heraclitus.

Dodd, C. H. *The Interpretation of the Fourth Gospel* (1953, Cambridge: Cambridge University Press, 1970), esp. pp. 263–89.

Jasper, Alison E. *The Shining Garment of the Text* (Sheffield: Sheffield Academic Press, 1998).

Perkins, Mary Anne. *Coleridge's Philosophy: The Logos as Unifying Principle* (Oxford: Clarendon Press, 1994).

Stead, Christopher. 'Logos', in Alan Richardson and John Bowden (eds), *A New Dictionary of Christian Theology* (London: SCM, 1983).

The Fall
Genesis 3: 1–13

[1] Now the serpent was more subtil than any beast of the field which the LORD God had made. And he said unto the woman, Yea, hath God said, Ye shall not eat of every tree of the garden?

[2] And the woman said unto the serpent, We may eat of the fruit of the trees of the garden:

[3] But of the fruit of the tree which is in the midst of the garden, God hath said, Ye shall not eat of it, neither shall ye touch it, lest ye die.

[4] And the serpent said unto the woman, Ye shall not surely die:

[5] For God doth know that in the day ye eat thereof, then your eyes shall be opened, and ye shall be as gods, knowing good and evil.

[6] And when the woman saw that the tree was good for food, and that it was pleasant to the eyes, and a tree to be desired to make one wise, she took of the fruit thereof, and did eat, and gave also unto her husband with her; and he did eat.

[7] And the eyes of them both were opened, and they knew that they were naked; and they sewed fig leaves together, and made themselves aprons.

[8] And they heard the voice of the LORD God walking in the garden in the cool of the day: and Adam and his wife hid themselves from the presence of the LORD God amongst the trees of the garden.

[9] And the LORD God called unto Adam, and said unto him, Where art thou?

[10] And he said, I heard thy voice in the garden, and I was afraid, because I was naked; and I hid myself.

[11] And he said, Who told thee that thou wast naked? Hast thou eaten of the tree, whereof I commanded thee that thou shouldest not eat?

[12] And the man said, The woman whom thou gavest to be with me, she gave me of the tree, and I did eat.
[13] And the LORD God said unto the woman, What is this that thou hast done? And the woman said, The serpent beguiled me, and I did eat.

Notes

Verse 3. The serpent in ancient mythology was not always a symbol of evil. In ancient Canaanite religion and in Greek mythology it suggested the promise of life and fertility. But to the writer of the Book of Genesis such goodness was, in fact, evil, since it suggested guile which could lure Adam and Eve away from the one true God who was the only source of life and the only object of knowledge.
Verse 7. The shame on realizing that they were naked is the first instance of divided consciousness – Adam and Eve, for the first time, perceive themselves in an act of 'self-consciousness'.
Verse 8. The Hebrew word *Qōl* does not mean voice but rather the rustle of God's step.

—— Commentary ——

The story of the Fall, like a number of other biblical myths, suffers from being too well known, and therefore overlaid for us, even at a first reading, by multiple strata of subsequent interpretation. The common identification of the serpent with the devil, for example, is a later Christian reading, present neither in the text, nor in early Jewish tradition. Most modern English readers are likely to know it (directly or indirectly) through Milton's hugely inflated seventeenth-century version in *Paradise Lost* (see below) which is so coloured by such accretions that it is less a re-telling of the original than the creation of a parallel myth.

Milton's version also highlights a problem that lurks almost unnoticed in the briefer biblical narrative: at what point did the Fall actually occur? In the biblical account there is almost no gap between the temptation and the deed, but by making his protagonists think about the possible consequences of their actions, Milton's narrative raises the question of whether, by contemplating what they were about to do, they had *already*, in effect, sinned. This would certainly be the logical extension to Jesus' insistence in the Sermon on the Mount that contemplating adultery is as bad as committing it (Matthew 5: 27–8). But there is a further complication to Milton. When Eve has eaten and brings the fruit to Adam for

95

him to eat also, he is, according to Milton, totally undeceived about the consequences. Instead, without replying directly to her, he realistically runs though his options in his mind – including that of leaving her to her fate.

> Should God create another Eve, and I
> Another rib afford, yet loss of thee
> Would never from my heart: no, no! I feel
> The link of nature draw me, flesh of flesh,
> Bone of my bone thou art, and from thy state
> Mine never shall be parted, bliss of woe.

As various critics have subsequently pointed out, this is less a matter of sinning in thought before the action, than of loyalty afterwards. Adam is standing by his wife, although he knows the consequences all too well – indeed, the worse the consequences, the more she will need him! This choosing to be identified with the sinner, of course, has the effect of narrowing the traditional Christian contrast between Adam and Christ, the 'second Adam', who, it was held, took on human flesh and identified with humanity in order to redeem us from the sin of the original Adam. Since Milton was a Unitarian in the sense that he did not believe Christ was the second Person of the Trinity, this narrowing of the contrast may be deliberate. The main difference in the Miltonic scheme of things being that the first Adam 'identified' with Eve by sinning *with* her, whereas Christ, it is stressed, did not. As feminists will no doubt also be quick to point out, the effect of this shift in Adam's motives is to increase Eve's responsibility for human sin!

Milton's treatment of the whole episode illustrates very clearly the way in which there has historically been no sharp division been 'fact' and 'fiction' in biblical exegesis – or, to put it another way, until our modern idea of 'history' developed towards the end of the eighteenth century such a distinction meant very little. Milton, we have every reason to assume, believed implicitly in the truth of the narrative he was re-creating. Nonetheless, he apparently had no hesitation in attributing words and motives to his characters for which there was no biblical justification – a convention so common that it is rarely questioned (see A. D. Nuttall's *Overheard by God*).

Whatever unintended logical or historical problems Milton may have had with the bare Genesis narrative, however, they were as nothing to those experienced by its eighteenth-century defenders, under fire from exponents of the new standards of historical probability. One popular commentary of the period, for instance, argues that:

Eve's not being surprised at hearing the serpent speak may easily be accounted for, she had been created so short a time before, that she may well be supposed not to have known all the qualities of every beast of the field.

It is hardly surprising that Tom Paine, in his revolutionary attack on Christianity, *The Age of Reason* (1793), made the biblical story of the Fall, a key exhibit for his irony:

Christian mythologists, after having confined Satan in a pit, were obliged to let him out again, to bring on the sequel of the fable. He is then introduced into the Garden of Eden in the shape of a snake or serpent, and in that shape he enters into familiar conversation with Eve, who is in no way surprised to hear a snake talk; and the issue of this tête-à-tête is, that he persuades her to eat an apple, and the eating of that apple damns all mankind. (*Theological Works of Tom Paine*, London 1827, p. 9)

Paine's attack, however, does more than question the literal interpretation of the Genesis account of the Fall. He reminds us, in effect, that to read it simply as a 'myth of origins' – in the sense that one might read the Genesis story of the Creation as a myth of origins – also presents real problems. Whereas a modern Christian might read the story of the Creation as a mythological statement that God is the ultimate force behind the cosmos, to read the Genesis story of the Fall simply as a mythological statement of the origins of human selfishness and sin is to ignore a kind of stubborn idiosyncrasy that pervades it in a way quite unlike the Creation story. This is not simply a matter of blaming the woman – as we have seen, the original story gives Adam much the same motivation as Eve – or even of giving snakes a bad name (the story has, incidentally, been responsible for a great deal of unnecessary snake-killing). It is, rather, a matter of the form and motivation for the Fall itself.

The Fall has two elements: first, an arbitrary prohibition. The tree is evidently put there to test the couple. If it were not, why have it there at all? The second point is that it is 'the tree of the knowledge of good and evil'. In one sense this is simply circular: if we define 'evil' in terms of disobedience to God's (here, arbitrary) commands, then to eat of the fruit is, by definition, to 'know' evil, and, by contrast, to 'know' the good that has been lost. But this is a sense of 'good' and 'evil' that none but a strict latter-day Calvinist would readily acknowledge. For a century that has been responsible for the holocaust, apartheid, and the bombing of Dresden and Hiroshima, a definition of evil simply in terms of blind obedience to arbitrary dictates seems to be almost beside the point. Moreover, in so far as the fruit is taken to symbolize 'knowledge' (of whatever kind) it raises further problems.

The most obvious secondary meaning of the word within the biblical narrative is sexual: 'And Adam knew Eve his wife; and she conceived' (Genesis 4: 1). Milton takes up this hint and, without waiting, as Genesis does, for the couple to be expelled from Eden before indulging in such 'knowledge', makes sex the immediate consequence of the Fall – thus helping, incidentally, to fill in the presumed time-gap between the eating of the fruit and the 'cool of the day' when God took his walk in the garden:

> But that false fruit
> Far other operation first displayed,
> Carnal desire inflaming: he on Eve
> Began to cast lascivious eyes; she him
> As wantonly repaid; in lust they burn...
>
> Her hand he seized; and to a shady bank,
> Thick overhead with verdant roof embowered,
> He led her, nothing loath; flowers were the couch,
> Pansies and violets, and ashphodel,
> And hyacinth; earth's freshest, softest lap.
> There they their fill of love and love's disport
> Took largely, of their mutual guilt the seal,
> The solace of their sin; till dewey sleep
> Oppressed them, wearied with their amorous play.
> (*Paradise Lost*, Book IX, 1011–16; 1037–45)

This cross-linking of sex with the Fall has, of course, an inner logic within the literal story. Unfallen humanity, so the implication runs, was destined to be immortal, and, therefore, having no need of reproduction, had also no need of sex. But for most humans sex has other, less functional uses. Milton is here, as so often, significantly ambiguous. On the one hand, he stresses that their dash into the undergrowth is 'lascivious', 'wanton', and 'lustful'; on the other hand he also makes the whole exercise sound (to fallen ears) remarkably attractive. Certainly the effect of linking sex with the Fall, in both the biblical and the Miltonic versions, has been to suggest that there is an inherently 'fallen', if not downright evil quality to sex. This, in turn, reflected on the status of women, and the role attributed to Eve in the Genesis story.

Though the biblical Patriarchs and Kings do not seem to have been particularly sexually inhibited, early Christianity was quick to observe the connection. St Paul was clear that it was better to 'marry than burn', but only just; celibacy, for those who could take it, was infinitely preferable. St Augustine, with considerably more experience, was inclined to agree. Nor are even current attitudes towards such issues as the celibacy of the clergy and the ordination of women entirely uninfluenced by the far-reaching reverberations of the myth of the Fall.

Other meanings of 'knowledge', apart from the moral and the sexual, were also influenced by this story. One of the oldest battles in human history has been over the question of 'forbidden knowledge'. Are there, can there be, forms of knowledge which are inherently evil to possess? Marlowe's play, *Dr. Faustus*, concludes, possibly ironically (knowing what we do of Marlowe), with a warning about the fate of those who seek to know 'unlawful things' and 'practise more than heavenly power permits' (Act V, Sc. iii, 25; 27), and almost every subsequent age has toyed with the idea that there might be some kinds of 'knowledge' that are – or should be – 'forbidden'. Earlier in the twentieth century atomic weapons research held something of this status; with the discovery of some of the 'experiments' in the Nazi death camps, the idea of unlawful knowledge took on new dimensions; and in our own time some of would feel that other areas of biological research, especially into inventing new diseases as weapons, into cloning, or even into the possibility of creating life itself, should be outlawed. But there is still a big difference between stigmatizing some, or all, of these as 'evil' in their experimental practice and, no doubt, in possible applications, and claiming that the knowledge involved is itself inherently evil.

The biblical story of the Fall has, as a result, never been quite free of its Classical opposite: the Greek story of Prometheus, who was chained by Zeus to a rock in the Caucasus, to have his liver gnawed for ever by an eagle, because he had stolen the secret of fire (and other knowledge) from the gods, and given it to man. To complete his revenge, Zeus caused Hephaestus to create a woman, Pandora, fashioned, like Adam, from clay. Athena breathed life into her, and the other gods endowed her with every other charm (hence her name, 'all gifts') including (from Hermes) flattery and guile. She was sent to Prometheus' brother, Epimetheus ('he who thinks afterwards'), who, despite his brother's warning not to accept any gifts from Zeus, took her in. She then opened a jar (not a 'box' as popular mythology has it) containing every kind of evil and misfortune, from which humanity had previously been free – leaving only Hope behind, under the lid.

The parallels, as well as the differences, with the biblical story should be obvious, and the fact that both versions of the origins of evil involved, not merely trouble from women, but forbidden knowledge were not missed. Milton's Satan, for instance, casts himself in a distinctly Promethean role, defying God and eternal punishment, to bring 'knowledge' to the first humans. That Milton also denounces this as a lie, did not stop Blake (and others later) from claiming that Milton himself 'was of the Devil's party' without knowing it – perhaps giving tacit support to Tom Paine's observation that it was a bit odd how easily Satan was able to slip out of eternal punishment to visit earth and engineer the Fall. Perhaps a modern and mythologically minded age might need to ask itself whether the story of the Fall represents a profound parable of human nature, or whether it has been coloured by historical accidents, so that the subsequent history of the Judeo-Christian world might have been different if sin had never been linked so indelibly to sex and knowledge?

Certainly the myth has not lost any of its fascination for the twentieth century, for whom human depravity has come to be a major theme. Almost every work of the Nobel Prize-winning novelist William Golding, for instance, has circled around the theme in one way or another. His first, and most famous novel, *The Lord of the Flies*, attacked the sentimental belief in childhood innocence, but his later novel, *Free Fall* (1959), engages directly with adult responsibility, sexuality and knowledge, concluding with a vision, at once Calvinistic and Kantian, of humanity stretched unremittingly between two worlds, the physical and the moral:

All day long the trains run on rails. Eclipses are predictable. Penicillin cures pneumonia and the atom splits to order. All day long, year in, year out, the daylight explanation drives back the mystery and reveals a reality usable, understandable and detached. The scalpel and the microscope fail, the oscilloscope moves closer to behaviour. The gorgeous dance is self-contained, then; does not need the music which in my mad moments I have heard...

All day long action is weighed in the balance and found not opportune nor fortunate or ill-advised, but good or evil. For this mode which we must call the spirit breathes through the universe and does not touch it; touches only the dark things, held prisoner, incommunicado, touches, judges, sentences and passes on.

Her world was real, both worlds are real. There is no bridge.

—— **Literature** ——

St Augustine of Hippo, *The City of God* (c.413–426 CE), tr. Henry Bettenson, Penguin, 1972, Book XIII, chapter 3

The first man was not reduced by his sin, or by his punishment, to the state of infantile torpor and weakness of mind and body which we observe in little children. Such was to be the early state of children, like the early state of young animals, according to the decision of God, who had cast down their parents to a life and death like that of animals. As Scripture says, 'Man was in a place of honour, but did not realize it: he had been brought to the level of the animals without understanding and been made like them' (Psalm 4: 12, 20). Though in fact we observe that infants are weaker than the most vulnerable of the young of other animals in the control of their limbs, and in their instincts of appetition and defence; this seems designed to enhance man's superiority over other living things, on the analogy of an arrow whose impetus increases in proportion to the backward extension of the bow.

Thus the result of the first man's lawless presumption and his just condemnation was not a relapse – or a repulse – into the rudimentary condition of infancy. But human nature in him was vitiated and altered, so that he experienced the rebellion and disobedience of desire in his body, and was bound by the necessity of dying; and he produced offspring in the same condition to which his fault and its punishment had reduced him, that is, liable to sin and death. But if infants are released from the bonds of this sin through the grace of Christ the Mediator, they can only suffer the death which separates soul from body; they do not pass on to that second death of unending punishment, since they have been freed from the entanglement of sin.

'Adam Lay in Bondage' (early fifteenth century), R. T. Davies, *Medieval English Lyrics: A Critical Anthology*, Faber, 1963

Adam lay ibounden,
Bounden in a bond:
Foure thousand winter
Thought he not too long.
And all was for an apple,
And apple that he tok,
As clerkes finden
Wreten in here book.

Ne hadde the apple take ben,
The apple taken ben,
Ne hadde never our Lady
A ben Hevene Quen.
Blissed be the time
That apple take was!
Therfore we moun singen,
Deo gracias!'

John Milton, *Paradise Lost* (1667), Book IX, lines 655–792

To whom the Tempter guilefully repli'd.
Indeed? hath God then said that of the Fruit
Of all these Garden Trees ye shall not eate,
Yet Lords declar'd of all in Earth or Aire?
To whom thus Eve yet sinless. Of the Fruit
Of each Tree in the Garden we may eate,
But of the Fruit of this fair Tree amidst
The Garden, God hath said, Ye shall not eate
Thereof, nor shall ye touch it, least ye die.
    She scarce had said, though brief, when now more bold
The Tempter, but with shew of Zeale and Love
To Man, and indignation at his wrong,
New part puts on, and as to passion mov'd,
Fluctuats disturbd, yet comely, and in act
Rais'd, as of som great matter to begin.
As when of old som Orator renound
In Athens or free *Rome*, where Eloquence
Flourishd, since mute, to som great cause address,
Stood in himself collected, while each part,
Motion, each act won audience ere the tongue,
Somtimes in highth began, as no delay
Of Preface brooking through his Zeal of Right.
So standing, moving, or to highth upgrown
The Tempter all impassiond thus began.
    O Sacred, Wise, and Wisdom-giving Plant,
Mother of Science, Now I feel thy Power
Within me cleere, not onely to discerne
Things in thir Causes, but to trace the wayes
Of highest Agents, deemd however wise.
Queen of this Universe, doe not believe
Those rigid threats of Death; ye shall not Die:

How should ye? by the Fruit? it gives you Life
To Knowledge: By the Threat'ner? look on me,
Me who have touch'd and tasted, yet both live,
And life more perfet have attaind then Fate
Meant mee, by vent'ring higher then my Lot.
Shall that be shut to Man, which to the Beast
Is open? or will God incense his ire
For such a petty Trespass, and not praise
Rather your dauntless vertue, whom the pain
Of Death denounc't, whatever thing Death be,
Deterrd not from atchieving what might leade
To happier life, knowledge of Good and Evil;
Of good, how just? of evil, if what is evil
Be real, why not known, since easier shunnd?
God therefore cannot hurt ye, and be just;
Not just, not God; not feard then, nor obeid:
Your feare it self of Death removes the feare.
Why then was this forbid? Why but to awe,
Why but to keep ye low and ignorant,
His worshippers; he knows that in the day
Ye Eate thereof, your Eyes that seem so cleere,
Yet are but dim, shall perfetly be then
Op'nd and cleerd, and ye shall be as Gods,
Knowing both Good and Evil as they know.
That ye should be as Gods, since I as Man,
Internal Man, is but proportion meet,
I of brute human, ye of human Gods.
So ye shall die perhaps, by putting off
Human, to put on Gods, death to be wisht,
Though threat'nd, which no worse then this can bring.
And what are Gods that Man may not become
As they, participating God-like food?
The Gods are first, and that advantage use
On our belief, that all from them proceeds;
I question it, for this fair Earth I see,
Warm'd by the Sun, producing every kind,
Them nothing: If they all things, who enclos'd
Knowledge of Good and Evil in this tree,
That whoso eats thereof, forthwith attains
Wisdom without their leave? and wherein lies
Th' offence, that Man should thus attain to know?
What can your knowledge hurt him, or this Tree

Impart against his will if all be his?
Or is it envie, and can envie, dwell
In heav'nly brests? these, these and many more
Causes import your need of this fair Fruit.
Goddess humane, reach then, and freely taste.
     He ended, and his words replete with guile
Into her heart too easie entrance won:
Fixt on the Fruit she gaz'd, which to behold
Might tempt alone, and in her ears the sound
Yet rung of his perswasive words, impregn'd
With Reason, to her seeming, and with Truth;
Meanwhile the hour of Noon drew on, and wak'd
An eager appetite, rais'd by the smell
So savorie of that Fruit, which with desire,
Inclinable now grown to touch or taste,
Sollicited her longing eye; yet first
Pausing a while, thus to her self she mus'd.
     Great are thy Vertues, doubtless, best of Fruits,
Though kept from Man, & worthy to be admir'd,
Whose taste, too long forbore, at first assay
Gave elocution to the mute, and taught
The Tongue not made for Speech to speak thy praise:
Thy praise tree also who forbids thy use,
Conceales not from us, naming thee the Tree
Of Knowledge, knowledge both of good and evil;
Forbids us then to taste, but his forbidding
Commends thee more, while it inferrs the good
By thee communicated, and our want:
For good unknown, sure is not had, or had
And yet unknown, is as not had at all.
In plain then, what forbids he but to know,
Forbids us good, forbids us to be wise?
Such prohibitions binde not. But if Death
Bind us with after-bands, what profits then
Our inward freedom? In the day we eate
Of this fair Fruit, our doom is, we shall die.
How dies the Serpent? Hee hath eat'n and lives,
And knows, and speaks, and reasons, and discernes,
Irrational till then. For us alone
Was death invented? or to US deni'd
This intellectual food, for beasts reserv'd?
For Beasts it seems: yet that one Beast which first

Hath tasted, envies not, but brings with joy
The good befall'n him, Author unsuspect,
Friendly to man, farr from deceit or guile.
What fear I then, rather what know to feare
Under this ignorance of Good and Evil,
Of God or Death, of Law or Penaltie?
Here grows the Cure of all, this Fruit Divine,
Fair to the Eye, inviting to the Taste,
Of vertue to make wise: what hinders then
To reach, and feed at once both Bodie and Mind?
   So saying, her rash hand in evil hour
Forth reaching to the Fruit, she pluck'd, she eat:
Earth felt the wound, and Nature from her seat
Sighing through all her Works gave signs of woe,
That all was lost. Back to the Thicket slunk
The guiltie Serpent, and well might, for Eve
Intent now wholly on her taste, naught else
Regarded, such delight till then, as seemd,
In Fruit she never tasted, whether true
Or fansied so, through expectation high
Of knowledg, nor was God-head from her thought.
Greedily she ingorg'd without restraint,
And knew not eating Death.

John Wilmot, Earl of Rochester, 'The Fall'

> How blessed was the created state
> Of man and woman, ere they fell,
> Compared to our unhappy fate:
> We need not fear another hell.
>
> Naked beneath cool shades they lay;
> Enjoyment waited on desire;
> Each member did their wills obey,
> Nor could a wish set pleasure higher.
>
> But we, poor slaves to hope and fear,
> Are never of our joys secure;
> They lessen still as they draw near,
> And none but dull delights endure.
>
> Then, Chloris, while I duly pay
> The nobler tribute of my heart,

Be not you so severe to say
You love me for the frailer part.

Abraham Cowley, 'The Tree of Knowledge'

That there is no knowledge
Against the Dogmatists

The sacred tree midst the fair orchard grew;
   The Phoenix truth did on it rest,
     And built his perfumed nest.
That right Porphyrian tree which did true logic shew,
   Each leaf did learnëd notions give,
     And th' apples were demonstrative.
     So clear their colour and divine,
The very shade they cast did other lights out-shine.

Taste not, said God; 'tis mine and angels' meat;
   A certain death does sit
   Like an ill worm i'th' core of it.
Ye cannot know and live, nor live or know and eat.
   Thus spoke God, yet man did go
     Ignorantly on to know;
     Grew so more blind, and she
Who tempted him to this, grew yet more blind than he.

The only science man by this did get,
   Was but to know he nothing knew:
   He straight his nakedness did view,
His ignorant poor estate, and was ashamed of it.
   Yet searches probabilities,
   And rhetoric, and fallacies,
   And seeks by useless pride
With slight and withering leaves that nakedness to hide.

Henceforth, said God, the wretched sons of earth
   Shall sweat for food in vain
   That will not long sustain,
And bring with labour forth each fond abortive birth.
   That serpent, too, their pride,
   Which aims at things denied,
   That learned and eloquent lust
Instead of mounting high, shall creep upon the dust.

William Golding, *Free Fall* (1959)

I have walked by stalls in the market-place where books, dog-eared and faded from their purple, have burst with a white hosanna. I have seen people crowned with a double crown, holding in either hand the crook and flail, the power and the glory. I have understood how the scar becomes a star, I have felt the flake of fire fall, miraculous and pentecostal. My yesterdays walk with me. They keep step, they are grey faces that peer over my shoulder. I live on Paradise Hill, ten minutes from the station, thirty seconds from the shops and the local. Yet I am a burning amateur, torn by the irrational and incoherent, violently searching and self-condemned.

When did I lose my freedom? For once, I was free. I had power to choose. The mechanics of cause and effect is statistical probability yet surely sometimes we operate below or beyond that threshold. Free-will cannot be debated but only experienced, like a colour or the taste of potatoes. I remember one such experience. I was very small and I was sitting on the stone surround of the pool and fountain in the centre of the park. There was bright sunlight, banks of red and blue flowers, green lawn. There was no guilt but only the plash and splatter of the fountain at the centre. I had bathed and drunk and now I was sitting on the warm stone edge placidly considering what I should do next. The gravelled paths of the park radiated from me: and all at once I was overcome by a new knowledge. I could take whichever I would of these paths. There was nothing to draw me down one more than the other. I danced down one for joy in the taste of potatoes. I was free. I had chosen.

How did I lose my freedom? I must go back and tell the story over. It is a curious story, not so much in the external events which are common enough, but in the way it presents itself to me, the only teller. For time is not to be laid out endlessly like a row of bricks. That straight line from the first hiccup to the last gasp is a dead thing. Time is two modes. The one is an effortless perception native to us as water to the mackerel. The other is a memory, a sense of shuffle fold and coil, of that day nearer than that because more important, of that event mirroring this, or those three set apart, exceptional and out of the straight line altogether. I put the day in the park first in my story, not because I was young, a baby almost; but because freedom has become more and more precious to me as I taste the potato less and less often.

I have hung all systems on the wall like a row of useless hats. They do not fit. They come in from outside, they are suggested patterns, some dull and some of great beauty. But I have lived enough of my life to require a pattern that fits over everything I know; and where shall I find that? Then why do I write this down? Is it a pattern I am looking for? That Marxist hat in the middle of the row, did I ever think it would last me a lifetime? What is wrong with the Christian biretta that I hardly wore at all? Nick's rationalist hat kept the rain out, seemed impregnable plate-armour, dull and decent. It looks small now and rather silly, a bowler like all bowlers, very formal, very complete, very ignorant. There is a school cap, too. I had no more than hung it there, not knowing of the other hats I should hang by it when I think the thing happened – the decision made freely that cost me my freedom.

Why should I bother about hats? I am an artist. I can wear what hat I like. You know of me, Samuel Mountjoy, I hang in the Tate. You would forgive me any hat. I could be a cannibal. But I want to wear a hat in private. I want to understand. The grey faces peer over my shoulder. Nothing can expunge or exorcise them. My art is not enough for me. To hell with my art. The fit takes me out of a deep well as does the compulsion of sex and other people like my pictures more than I do, think them more important than I do. At heart I am a dull dog. I would sooner be good than clever.

Then why am I writing this down? Why do I not walk round and round the lawn, reorganizing my memories until they make sense, unravelling and knitting up the flexible time stream? I could bring this and that event together, I could make leaps. I should find a system for that round of the lawn and then another one the next day. But thinking round and round the lawn is no longer enough. For one thing it is like the rectangle of canvas, a limited area however ingeniously you paint. The mind cannot hold more than so much; but understanding requires a sweep that takes in the whole of remembered time and then can pause. Perhaps if I write my story as it appears to me, I shall be able to go back and select. Living is like nothing because it is everything – is too subtle and copious for unassisted thought. Painting is like a single attitude, a selected thing.

There is another reason. We are dumb and blind yet we must see and speak. Not the stubbled face of Sammy Mountjoy, the full lips that open to let his hand take out a fag, not the smooth, wet muscles inside round teeth, not the gullet, the lung, the heart – those you could see and touch if you took a knife to him on the table. It is the unnameable, unfathomable and invisible darkness that sits at the centre of him, always awake, always different from what you believe it to be, always thinking and feeling what you can never know it thinks and feels, that hopes hopelessly to understand and to be understood. Our loneliness is the loneliness not of the cell or the castaway; it is the loneliness of that dark thing that sees as at the atom furnace by reflection, feels by remote control and hears only words phoned to it in a foreign tongue. To communicate is our passion and our despair.

With whom then?

You?

My darkness reaches out and fumbles at a typewriter with its tongs. Your darkness reaches out with your tongs and grasps a book. There are twenty modes of change, kilter and translation between us. What an extravagant coincidence it would be if the exact quality, the translucent sweetness of her cheek, the very living curve of bone between the eye-brow and hair should survive the passage! How can you share the quality of my terror in the blacked-out cell when I can only remember it and not re-create it for myself? No. Not with you. Or only with you, in part. For you were not there.

And who are you anyway? Are you on the inside, have you a proof-copy? Am I a job to do? Do I exasperate you by translating incoherence into incoherence? Perhaps you found this book on a stall fifty years hence which is another now. The star's light reaches us millions of years after the star is gone, or so they say, and perhaps it is true.

Bibliography

Daiches, David. *God and the Poets* (Oxford: Oxford University Press, 1984), ch. 2, 'Paradise Lost: God Defended'.

Farrer, Austin. *Love Almighty and Ills Unlimited* (London: Collins, 1962).

Hick, John. *Evil and the God of Love* (London: The Fontana Library, 1966)

Lewis, C. S., *A Preface to 'Paradise Lost'* (New York: Oxford University Press, 1961)

Nuttall, A. D., *Overheard by God* (London: Methuen, 1981).

Oxford Companion to Classical Literature, ed. M. C. Howatson, new edn, (Oxford: Oxford University Press, 1989).

Paine, Thomas. *Theological Works of Tom Paine* (London: 1827).

Smith, Eric. *Some Versions of the Fall* (London: Croom Helm, 1973).

Waldock, A. J. A. *Paradise Lost and its Critics* (Cambridge: Cambridge University Press, 1947).

— The Sacrifice of Isaac —
Genesis 22: 1–19

[1] And it came to pass after these things, that God did tempt Abraham, and said unto him, Abraham: and he said, Behold, here I am.

[2] And he said, Take now thy son, thine only son Isaac, whom thou lovest, and get thee into the land of Moriah; and offer him there for a burnt offering upon one of the mountains which I will tell thee of.

[3] And Abraham rose up early in the morning, and saddled his ass, and took two of his young men with him, and Isaac his son, and clave the wood for the burnt offering, and rose up, and went unto the place of which God had told him.

[4] Then on the third day Abraham lifted up his eyes, and saw the place afar off.

[5] And Abraham said unto his young men, Abide ye here with the ass; and I and the lad will go yonder and worship, and come again to you,

[6] And Abraham took the wood of the burnt offering, and laid it upon Isaac his son; and he took the fire in his hand, and a knife; and they went both of them together.

[7] And Isaac spake unto Abraham his father, and said, My father: and he said, Here am I, my son. And he said, Behold the fire and the wood: but where is the lamb for a burnt offering?

[8] And Abraham said, My son, God will provide himself a lamb for a burnt offering: so they went both of them together.

[9] And they came to the place which God had told him of; and Abraham built an altar there, and laid the wood in order, and bound Isaac his son, and laid him on the altar upon the wood.

[10] And Abraham stretched forth his hand, and took the knife to slay his son.

[11] And the angel of the LORD called unto him out of heaven, and said, Abraham, Abraham: and he said, Here am I.

[12] And he said, Lay not thine hand upon the lad, neither do thou any thing unto him: for now I know that thou fearest God, seeing thou hast not withheld thy son, thine only son from me.

[13] And Abraham lifted up his eyes, and looked, and behold behind him a ram caught in a thicket by his horns: and Abraham went and took the ram, and offered him up for a burnt offering in the stead of his son.

[14] And Abraham called the name of that place Jehovah-jireh: as it is said to this day, In the mount of the LORD it shall be seen.

[15] And the angel of the LORD called unto Abraham out of heaven the second time,

[16] And said, By myself have I sworn, saith the LORD, for because thou hast done this thing, and hast not withheld thy son, thine only son:

[17] That in blessing I will bless thee, and in multiplying I will multiply thy seed as the stars of the heaven, and as the sand which is upon the sea shore; and thy seed shall possess the gate of his enemies;

[18] And in thy seed shall all the nations of the earth be blessed; because thou hast obeyed my voice.

[19] So Abraham returned unto his young men, and they rose up and went together to Beer-sheba; and Abraham dwelt at Beer-sheba.

Notes

Verse 1. Particular emphasis is given to the word 'God'. From the start the reader (though not Abraham) knows that this is a *test*.

Verse 2. Isaac is described in a threefold manner – 'your son, your only son, whom you love' – underlying how precious and unique he is to Abraham. 'your only son' has a sense of the special and particular.

'land of Moriah': compare 2 Chronicles 3: 1, where Moriah is the mountain on which the temple stood. Geographically, here, Moriah is a complete mystery.

Verses 3–8. Note the complete lack of any insight into Abraham's inner state of mind during these traumatic events.

Verse 11. 'The angel of the Lord': literally 'someone sent', not to be thought of as someone separately from God. The narrative makes no clear distinction between the angel of the Lord and the Lord himself. (Compare Owen, 'The Parable of the Old Man and the Young': 'When lo! an angel called to him out of heaven').

Verse 12. 'for now I know that you fear God'. This refers not so much to an emotional response to God's being, or a special feeling for God, but rather to the quality of *obedience*. (Compare Genesis 20: 11; 2 Kings 4: 1; Isaiah 11: 2 etc.)

Verse 13. The appearance of the ram is not felt to be miraculous, but simply now Abraham notices the animal (see Browne, *Religio Medici*).

Verse 14. 'Abraham called the name of that place The Lord will provide'. This is altogether ambiguous in the Hebrew, perhaps a pun, also meaning, 'In the mountain of the Lord he is seen.'

Verses 15–18. Clearly an addition to the main narrative, confirming God's promises to Abraham. This is the last time God actually speaks to Abraham.

—— **Commentary** ——

This extraordinary and mysterious narrative is traditionally called 'The Binding of Isaac' (after verse 9, 'and bound Isaac his son...'), or, in Jewish traditions the 'akedah' (*aqedah* = 'binding'). It is quite possibly derived from an earlier cult saga of a sanctuary which confirmed the redemption of child sacrifice with an animal sacrifice. Whether or not that be the case, the narrative we have in *Genesis* seems to have a very different purpose, though it is extremely hard to define what it is. Indeed, its persistence and ambiguity in literature and criticism arise out of both the literary genius of the narrative and its many-layered suggestiveness.

In the midrash of Rabbi Aba here reprinted we find typical midrashic intertextuality (the reference to Psalm 89), and a problem raised and responded to by dexterous word-play. In effect, Abraham accuses God of changing his mind about Isaac, through whom, God has previously promised (Genesis 21: 12), Abraham will have descendants. God replies that Abraham has simply misunderstood the command; in verse 2 the verb is *alah* which is literally 'to climb.' What in our version of the Bible is translated as 'and offer him there as a burnt offering,' is an idiomatic use of *alah*, 'to offer up.' Actually, God says he meant the word literally, 'bring him up there for a burnt offering' – that is to go up the mountain for a religious ceremony. In the same midrashic tradition the Jewish comedian Woody Allen has Abraham falling to his knees with the despairing admission to God, 'See. I never know when you're kidding.'

In the Christian New Testament we find the Akedah being held up as an example of Abraham's faith in God and his preparedness to be utterly obedient. This is echoed throughout early Christian literature shown here in the case of Augustine in his great work *The City of God*. Furthermore, we see in Augustine an example of the very common identification of Isaac with Christ: both are sons whose fathers are prepared to sacrifice them if need be. Augustine refers to Romans 8: 32, 'He did not spare his own son, but handed him over for us all' – but does not then go so far as to suggest that Abraham, as Isaac's father, could be seen as a type of God the father.

This *typological* tradition persists in literature in the use of the story in the great medieval English Passion plays, of which an example is given. Here clearly everything looks forward to the New Testament, and Abraham's stalwart obedience is evenly matched by the reassurance given to him. Here there is no misunderstanding, no doubt, but piety and the angel's soothing words. God's purpose is to test Abraham's 'steadfastness'.

The brief reference to the story in Sir Thomas Browne's *Religio Medici* makes a very different point. It concentrates only upon the episode of the ram (verse 13), seeing this as an example of God's providence. What to human beings appears as mere chance is part of God's order, his 'mere hand'.

In more recent English fiction the main emphasis has been different again. In the two examples given here from Thomas Hardy and D. H. Lawrence the focus is upon Abraham as father – irascible, full of self-doubt, regretful, cruel. In both cases these writers had moved outside the Christian biblical tradition in which they had been brought up, and were seeing the story from an entirely human perspective. In the First World War poet, Wilfred Owen, the akedah becomes the focus of his rage not so much against a cruel god, as against a generation of European 'fathers' who have sent their sons to slaughter in the trenches. In Owen's powerful and dramatic poem, God's promise to Abraham and his 'seed' (verses 17–18) is taken up in the bitter last line, which returns also to the theme of the 'one' and only son (verse 2).

In a letter to Max Brod, the Jewish Prague novelist Franz Kafka says of Søren Kierkegaard's *Fear and Trembling*: 'He doesn't see the ordinary man... and paints this monstrous Abraham in the clouds.' Kierkegaard's examination of Abraham's purposes fills in precisely the gaps which the biblical narrative leaves blank and mysterious. For him, Abraham is a murderer – at least in intent – abandoning the 'ethical' in order to maintain faith with his God. In *Fear and Trembling* Kierkegaard describes faith as a 'prodigious paradox... that makes murder into a holy and God-pleasing act, a paradox that gives Isaac back to Abraham again'. Like Kierkegaard, Kafka attempts to think into the motives and character of Abraham – precisely those things which *Genesis* fails to provide for the reader.

We end here with a well-known critical reading of the Akedah, by Erich Auerbach, in his book *Mimesis*. Auerbach acutely demonstrates the obscurity and 'abruptness, suggestive influence of the unexpressed, "background" quality, multiplicity of meanings and the need for interpretation' which have sustained this narrative through repeated and widely divergent tellings in western literature. In conclusion mention should be made of the equally energetic exploration of the narrative in the history of western art, and in particular the great profound paintings of Caravaggio (1573–1610) and Rembrandt (1606–1669).

—— **Literature** ——

Midrash, cited by Rashi, in M. Rosenbaum and A. M. Silbermann, eds and tr., *Pentateuch with Targum Onkelos, Haphtaroth and Rashi's Commentary*, Jerusalem, 5733

And Abraham stretched forth his hand and he took the knife to slaughter his son. And an angel of the Lord called unto him from the heavens, and said, 'Abraham, Abraham.' And he said, 'Here I am.' And he said, 'Lay not thine hand upon the lad, neither do thou anything unto him, for now I know that thou art one fearing of God, because thou hast not withheld thy son, thine only son, from me.'

Rabbi Aba said: Abraham said to God: 'I will lay my complaint before you. Yesterday (on an earlier occasion) you told me "In Isaac shall thy seed be called to thee" (Genesis 21: 12), and then again you said, "Take now thy son" (Genesis 22: 2), and now you tell me "Lay not thine hand upon the lad!"' The Holy One, blessed be He, said to him, in the words gone out of Psalms 89: 35, '"My covenant will I not profane, not alter that which has gone out of my lips." When I told you "Take thy son," I was not altering that which went out from my lips, namely, my promise that you would have descendants through Isaac. I did not tell you "kill him", but "bring him up" to the mountain. You have brought him up – now take him down again.'

Epistle to the Hebrews 11: 17–18,
Revised Standard Version

By faith, Abraham, when he was tested, offered up Isaac, and he who had received the promises was ready to offer up his only son, of whom it was said, 'Through Isaac shall your descendants be named.'

St Augustine of Hippo, *The City of God* (*c*.413–426 CE),
tr. Henry Bettenson, Penguin, 1972, Book XVI, chapter 32

This is the interpretation we find in the Epistle to the Hebrews, and it is explained as follows: 'By faith Abraham, when tested, went before Isaac and offered his only son, who received the promises, to whom it was said:

"In Isaac your seed will be called", considering that God is able to raise men from the dead.' Then he went on, 'Hence he brought him also to serve as a type' [Hebrews 11: 17ff. (in a variant version)]. A type of whom? It can only be of him of whom the Apostle says, 'He did not spare his own son, but handed him over for us all' [Romans 8: 32]. This is why, as the Lord carried his cross, so Isaac himself carried to the place of sacrifice the wood on which he too was to be placed. Moreover, after the father had been prevented from striking his son, since it was not right that Isaac should be slain, who was the ram whose immolation completed the sacrifice by blood of symbolic significance? Bear in mind that when Abraham saw the ram it was caught by the horns in a thicket. Who, then was symbolized by that ram but Jesus, crowned with Jewish thorns [cf. Mark 15: 16ff; John 19] before he was offered in sacrifice?

But now let us turn our attention to the divine words spoken by the angel. For the scripture says,

> And Abraham stretched out his hand to take the knife to slay his son. Then the angel of the Lord called to him from heaven and said: 'Abraham.' And he said: 'Here I am.' And the angel said: 'Do not lay your hand on the boy, nor do anything to him; for now I have the assurance that you fear your God, and you have not spared your beloved son, for my sake.' [Genesis 22: 10ff]

'Now I have your assurance' means 'Now I have made it known', for God was not in ignorance before this happened. After that, when the ram had been sacrificed instead of his son Isaac, 'Abraham', we are told, called the name of the place 'The Lord saw', so that people say today: 'The Lord appeared on the mountain' [Genesis 22: 14]. Just as 'Now I have the assurance' stood for 'Now I have made it known here The Lord saw' stands for 'The Lord appeared', that is, he made himself visible.

> Then the angel of the Lord called to Abraham from heaven a second time, saying: 'I have sworn by myself' says the Lord 'because you have carried out this bidding and have not spared your beloved son for my sake, that I shall certainly bless you, and I shall assuredly multiply your posterity like the stars of the sky, and like the sand that stretches by the lip of the sea. And your posterity will possess by inheritance the cities of your enemies, and all the nations of the earth will be blessed in your descendants, because you have obeyed my voice.' [Genesis 22: 15ff]

In this way the promise of the calling of the nations in Abraham's descendants, after the whole burnt-offering, by which Christ is symbolized, was confirmed also by an oath given by God. For he had often given promises, but never had he taken an oath. Now what is the oath of the true and truthful God but the confirmation of his promise, and a kind of rebuke to the unbelieving?

The Brome: Abhraham and Isaac (fourteenth century), English Passion Play, modernized by John Gassner, Bantam Books, 1968

GOD: Mine angel, fast hie thee thy way,
    And unto middle-earth anon thou go —
Abram's heart now will I assay,
    Whether that he be steadfast or no,

Say I commanded him for to take
    Isaac, his young son that he loves so well,
And with his blood sacrifice he make,
    If any of my friendship he would feel.

Show him the way unto the hill
    Where thou his sacrifice shall be.

I shall assay now his good will,
    Whether he loveth better his child or me.
All men shall take example by him
    My commandments how to keep.

(*As the* Angel *descends,* Abraham *moved in spirit, kneels again.*)

ABRAHAM: Now, Father in Heaven, that formed everything,
    My prayers I make to thee again,
For this day a tender offering
    Here must I give to thee certain.
Ah, Lord God, almighty King,
    What manner of beast would'st thou fain?
If I had thereof true knowing,
    It should be done with all my main
Full soon by me.
To do thy pleasure on a hill,
Verily, it is my will,
    Dear Father, God in Trinity!

116

(The Angel reaches Abraham while Isaac has wandered off.)

ANGEL: Abraham, Abraham, be at rest!
    Our Lord commanded you to take
  Isaac, thy young son whom thou lovest
  And with his blood that sacrifice thou make.

  Into the Land of Vision do thou go,
    And offer thy child unto thy Lord;
  I shall thee lead and also show.
    To God's behest, Abraham, accord,

  And follow me upon this green!

ABRAHAM: Welcome to me be my Lord's command!
    And his word I will not withstand.
    Yet Isaac, my young son in hand,
  A full dear child to me has been.

  I had rather, if God had been pleased,
    To have forborne all the goods that I have,
  Than Isaac, my son, should be deceased, —
    So God in heaven my soul may save!

  I have loved never a thing so much on earth,
    And now I must the child go kill!
  Ah, Lord God, my conscience lacketh mirth!
  And yet, my dear Lord, I am sore afeared
    To grudge anything against thy will.

  I love my child as my life,
    But yet I love my God much more
  For though my heart should make any strife
  Yet will I not spare for child or wife,
    But do after my dread Lord's lore.

  Though I love my son never so well,
    Yet smite off his head soon I shall.
  Ah, Father of Heaven! to thee I kneel —
  A hard death my son shall feel,
    To honor thee, Lord, withal!

117

ANGEL: Abraham, Abraham, this is well said,
  And all these commandments look that thou keep, —
  But in thy heart be nothing dismayed.

Sir Thomas Browne, *Religio Medici* (1642)

This is another way, full of meanders and labyrinths, where of the devil and spirits have no exact ephemerides: and that is a more particular and observed method of his providence; directing the operations of individual and single essences; this we call fortune; that serpentine and crooked line, whereby he draws those actions his wisdom intends in a more unknown and secret way, this cryptic and involved method of his providence have I ever admired; or can I relate the history of my life, the occurrences of my days, the escapes, or dangers, and hints of chance, with a *bezo las manos* to Fortune, or a bare gramercy to my good stars. Abraham might have thought the ram in the thicket came thither by accident...Surely there are in every man's life, certain rubs, doublings and wrenches, which pass a while under the effects of chance; but at the last, well examined, prove the mere hand of God.

Thomas Hardy, *Tess of the D'Urbervilles* (1891), chapter 49

[In *Tess of the D'Urbervilles*, Mr Clare bemoans his treatment of his son Angel after his marriage to Tess and departure for South America.]

Nevertheless, he loved his misnamed Angel, and in secret mourned over his treatment of him as Abraham might have mourned over the doomed Isaac while they went up the hill together. His silent self-generated regrets were far bitterer than the reproaches which his wife had rendered audible.

Søren Kierkegaard, 'Prelude', *Fear and Trembling* (1843), tr. Walter Lowrie, Princeton University Press, 1968

'*And God tempted Abraham and said unto him, Take Isaac, thine only son, whom thou lovest and get thee into the land of Moriah and offer him there for a burnt offering upon the mountain which I will show thee.*'

It was early in the morning, Abraham arose betime, he had the asses saddled, left his tent, and Isaac went with him, but Sarah looked out of the window after them until they had passed down the alley and she could see no more. They rode in silence for three days. On the morning of the fourth day Abraham said never a word, but he lifted up his eyes and saw Mount Moriah afar off. He left the young men behind and went alone with Isaac beside him up to the mountain. But Abraham said to himself, 'I will not conceal from Isaac whither this course leads him.' He stood still, he laid his hand upon the head of Isaac in benediction, and Isaac bowed to receive the blessing. And Abraham's face was fatherliness, his look was mild, his speech encouraging. But Isaac was unable to understand him, his soul could not be exalted; he embraced Abraham's knees, he fell at his feet imploringly, he begged for his young life, for the fair hope of his future, he called to mind the joy in Abraham's house, he called to mind the sorrow and loneliness. Then Abraham lifted up the boy, he walked with him by his side, and his talk was full of comfort and exhortation. But Isaac could not understand him. He climbed Mount Moriah, but Isaac understood him not. Then for an instant he turned away from him, and when Isaac again saw Abraham's face it was changed, his glance was wild, his form was horror. He seized Isaac by the throat, threw him to the ground, and said, 'Stupid boy, dost thou then suppose that I am thy father? I am an idolator. Does thou suppose that this is God's bidding? No, it is my desire.' Then Isaac trembled and cried out in his terror, 'O God in heaven, have compassion upon me. If I have no father upon earth, be Thou my father!' But Abraham in a low voice said to himself. 'O Lord in heaven, I thank Thee. After all it is better for him to believe that I am a monster, rather than that he should lose faith in Thee.'

Franz Kafka, Letter to Robert Kopstock, June 1921

I could think of another Abraham for myself – who certainly would not make it to a patriarch, not even to an old clothes dealer – who would be ready to fulfill the demand of the sacrifice immediately, with the promptness of a waiter, but who would not bring off the sacrifice, because he can't get away from the house, he is indispensable, the household needs him, there is always something more to put in order, the house is not ready...

But another Abraham. One who wants to sacrifice altogether in the right way, and who has the right mood in general for the whole thing, but cannot believe that he is the one meant, he, the repulsive old man and his child, the dirty boy. The true faith is not lacking to him, he has this faith, he would sacrifice in the right frame of mind if he could only believe that he is the one meant. He fears, he will ride out as Abraham with his son, but on the way he will metamorphose into Don Quixote. The world would have been horrified at Abraham if it could have seen him, he however fears that the world will laugh itself to death at the sight of him. But, it is not ridiculousness as such that he fears – of course, he fears that too, and above all his laughing along with them – but mainly he fears that this ridiculousness will make him even older and uglier, his son even dirtier, more unworthy really to be summoned. An Abraham who comes unsummoned!

Wilfred Owen, 'The Parable of the Old Man and the Young', *The Collected Poems*, ed. C. Day Lewis, Chatto & Windus, 1963

So Abram rose, and clave the wood and went,
And took the fire with him, and a knife.
And as they sojourned both of them together,
Isaac the first-born spake and said, My Father,
Behold the preparations, fire and iron,
But where the lamb for this burnt-offering?
Then Abram bound the youth with belts and straps,
And builded parapets and trenches there,
And stretched forth the knife to slay his son.
When lo! an angel called him out of heaven,
Saying, Lay not thy hand upon the lad,
Neither do anything to him. Behold,
A ram, caught in a thicket by its horns;
Offer the Ram of Pride instead of him.
But the old man would not so, but slew his son,
And half the seed of Europe, one by one.

D. H. Lawrence, 'England my England' (1922)

[Godfrey Marshall] was a man who kept alive the old red flame of fatherhood, fatherhood that had even the right to sacrifice the child to God, like Isaac.

Erich Auerbach, 'Odysseus' Scar', *Mimesis* (1946), tr. Willard R. Trask, Princeton University Press, 1968

Thus the journey is like a silent progress through the indeterminate and the contingent, a holding of the breath, a progress which has no present, which is inserted, like a blank duration, between what has passed and what lies ahead, and which yet is measured: three days! Three such days positively demand the symbolic interpretation which they later received.

They began 'early in the morning'. But at what time on the third day did Abraham lift up his eyes and see his goal? The text says nothing on the subject. Obviously not 'late in the evening,' for it seems that there was still time enough to climb the mountain and make the sacrifice. So 'early in the morning' is given, not as an indication of time, but for the sake of its ethical significance; it is intended to express the resolution, the promptness, the punctual obedience of the sorely tried Abraham. Bitter to him is the early morning in which he saddles his ass, calls his serving-men and his son Isaac, and sets out; but he obeys, he walks until the third day, then he lifts up his eyes and sees the place. Whence he comes, we do not know, but the goal is clearly stated: Jeruel in the land of Moriah. What place that is meant to indicate is not clear – 'Moriah' especially may be a later correction of some other word. But in any case the goal was given, and in any case it is a matter of some sacred spot which was to receive a particular consecration by being connected with Abraham's sacrifice. Just as little as 'early in the morning' serves as a temporal indication does 'Jewel in the land of Moriah' serve as a geographical indication; and in both cases alike, the complementary indication is not given, for we know as little of the hour at which Abraham lifted up his eyes as we do of the place from which he set forth – Jeruel is significant not so much as the goal of an earthly journey, in its geographical relation to other places, as through its special election, through its relation to God, who designated it as the scene of the act, and therefore it must be named.

In the narrative itself, a third chief character appears: Isaac. While God and Abraham, the serving-men, the ass, and the implements are simply named, without mention of any qualities or any other sort of definition, Isaac once receives an appositive; God says, 'Take Isaac, thine only son, whom thou lovest.' But this is not a characterization of Isaac as a person, apart from his relation to his father and apart from the story, he may be handsome or ugly, intelligent or stupid, tall or short, pleasant or unpleasant – we are not told. Only what we need to know about him as a personage in the action, here and now, is illuminated, so that it may become apparent how terrible Abraham's temptation is, and that God is fully aware of it. By this example of the contrary, we see the significance of the descriptive adjectives and digressions of the Homeric poems; with their indications of the earlier and as it were absolute existence of the persons described, they prevent the reader from concentrating exclusively on a present crisis; even when the most terrible things are occurring, they prevent the establishment of an overwhelming suspense. But here, in the story of Abraham's sacrifice, the overwhelming suspense is present; what Schiller makes the goal of the tragic poet – to rob us of our emotional freedom, to turn our intellectual and spiritual powers (Schiller says 'our activity') in one direction, to concentrate them there – is effected in this Biblical narrative, which certainly deserves the epithet epic.

Bibliography

Derrida, Jacques, *The Gift of Death*, tr. David Wills (1992. Chicago: Chicago University Press, 1995).

Dillenberger, Jane. *Style and Content in Christian Art*, 2nd edn (London: SCM Press, 1986). Useful on the portrayal of the Akedah in Chartres Cathedral, and by Rembrandt.

Edgerton, W. Dow. 'The Binding of Isaac', *Theology Today*, 44 (1987), pp. 207–21.

Edgerton, W. Dow. *The Passion of Interpretation* (Louisville: Westminster/John Knox Press, 1992), pp. 74–93.

Jasper, David. 'The Old Man Would Not So, But Slew His Son', *Religion and Literature*, 25 (1993), pp. 120–30.

Kierkegaard, Søren. *Fear and Trembling*, 1843, trans. Walter Lowrie (1941. Princeton: Princeton University Press, 1974).

Perkins, Robert L. 'Abraham's Silence Aesthetically Considered', in *Kierkegaard on Art and Communication*, ed. George Pattison (London: Macmillan, 1992), pp. 100–13.

Robbins, Jill. *Prodigal Son/Elder Brother: Interpretation and Alterity in Augustine, Petrarch, Kafka, Levinas* (Chicago: Chicago University Press, 1991), chapter 3, 'Kafka's Parables'.

Spiegel, Shalom. *The Last Trial: On the Legends and Lore of the Command to Abraham to Offer Isaac as a Sacrifice*, tr. Judah Goldin (New York: 1979). A wide range of rabbinic interpretations of the Akedah are offered here.

JACOB AND ESAU

GENESIS 27: 15–35

[15] And Rebekah took goodly raiment of her eldest son Esau, which were with her in the house, and put them upon Jacob her younger son:

[16] And she put the skins of the kids of the goats upon his hands, and upon the smooth of his neck:

[17] And she gave the savoury meat and the bread, which she had prepared, into the hand of her son Jacob.

[18] And he came unto his father, and said, My father: and he said, Here am I; who art thou, my son?

[19] And Jacob said unto his father, I am Esau thy firstborn; I have done according as thou badest me: arise, I pray thee, sit and eat of my venison, that thy soul may bless me.

[20] And Isaac said unto his son, How is it that thou hast found it so quickly, my son? And he said, Because the LORD thy God brought it to me.

[21] And Isaac said unto Jacob, Come near, I pray thee, that I may feel thee, my son, whether thou be my very son Esau or not.

[22] And Jacob went near unto Isaac his father; and he felt him, and said, The voice is Jacob's voice, but the hands are the hands of Esau.

[23] And he discerned him not, because his hands were hairy, as his brother Esau's hands: so he blessed him.

[24] And he said, Art thou my very son Esau? And he said, I am.

[25] And he said, Bring it near to me, and I will eat of my son's venison, that my soul may bless thee. And he brought it near to him, and he did eat: and he brought him wine, and he drank.

[26] And his father Isaac said unto him, Come near now, and kiss me, my son.

[27] And he came near, and kissed him: and he smelled the smell of his raiment, and blessed him, and said, See, the smell of my son is as the smell of a field which the LORD hath blessed:

[28] Therefore God give thee of the dew of heaven, and the fatness of the earth, and plenty of corn and wine:

[29] Let people serve thee, and nations bow down to thee: be lord over thy brethren, and let thy mother's sons bow down to thee: cursed be every one that curseth thee, and blessed be he that blesseth thee.

[30] And it came to pass, as soon as Isaac had made an end of blessing Jacob, and Jacob was yet scarce gone out from the presence of Isaac his father, that Esau his brother came in from his hunting.

[31] And he also had made savoury meat, and brought it unto his father, and said unto his father, Let my father arise, and eat of his son's venison, that thy soul may bless me.

[32] And Isaac his father said unto him, Who art thou? And he said, I am thy son, thy firstborn Esau.

[33] And Isaac trembled very exceedingly, and said, Who? where is he that hath taken venison, and brought it me, and I have eaten of all before thou camest, and have blessed him? yea, and he shall be blessed.

[34] And when Esau heard the words of his father, he cried with a great and exceeding bitter cry, and said unto his father, Bless me, even me also, O my father.

[35] And he said, Thy brother came with subtilty, and hath taken away thy blessing.

Notes

Blessings are a common feature of the Old Testament. Though this is the earliest and one of the most important examples, it is unique in that, though God is assumed to be in some sense a guarantor, nowhere is any kind of divine assistance or sanction explicitly invoked. Isaac's actual words refer first of all to the land and its fertility, then to the status of the son who is here already viewed as a nation. Klaus Westermann comments:

Characteristic of the blessing is that its setting in life is leave-taking or farewell (Genesis 24: 60); this is the situation out of which it is to be understood; it is vitality that is passed on by the one who is departing from life to the one who is continuing in life; in this process no distinction is made between the corporal and the spiritual and so both action and word are required. Because the blessing is concerned with vitality as a whole, the blessing cannot return or be subsequently altered.[1]

—— Commentary ——

The story of Jacob and Esau is so well known that it is easy for the reader brought up on it to miss how disturbing and deeply paradoxical it really is. Even for someone who had never encountered it before two things are at once clear. The first is that whatever is being transmitted by means of the 'blessing' is of unique and unrepeatable importance. The second is that it was here acquired by means that were at once illegitimate and somehow irreversible.

Though God is nowhere invoked in the blessing, what is being transmitted has everything to do with a consciousness of Him. The line of descent from Abraham to Jacob/Israel and thence to Joseph and his twelve brothers is crucial to any understanding of the Hebrew scriptures. Isaac is the God-given son of Abraham, doubly precious both on account of his miraculous birth, which, we are told, occurred when his mother, Sarah, was well past child-bearing; and also because his father had received him again from God after Abraham had shown himself willing to sacrifice his only son (see 'The Akedah'). Now Isaac is passing on the blessing to his heir: not just as the eldest son of his father, but also as the chosen one to carry the worship of the new god, Yahweh, whose repeated promise had been that Abraham's descendants should be 'as the stars of the heaven, and as the sand which is upon the sea shore' and in whom 'all the nations of the earth' should 'be blessed' (Genesis 22: 17–18; 26: 4). The patriarchal blessing is, therefore, not just a family matter, but one on which the future of a nation was to depend. Right at the outset of this tremendous destiny, however, the line of true descent is hijacked by a scheming mother and her ambitious son. And neither Isaac, nor, it seems, even God himself, are willing or able to do anything about it. Instead of Eliphaz, Reuel, Jeush, Jaalam and Korah, the sons of Esau (Genesis 36), from now on the story of God's people is to be that of Jacob's twelve sons – the boastful dreamer, Joseph, and his resentful brothers – founders of the twelve tribes of Israel. Not for the last time in the Bible, the main tradition of the descent of the people of God and their seemingly unique revelation was channelled through a blatantly usurped line of succession – with little or no attempt to conceal the fact.

The shocking enormity of this incident – almost as shocking as Cain's earlier elimination of his brother Abel – has tended to be played down or simply justified by subsequent commentators not least because God himself seemed so ready to accept it. Regardless of the fact that Esau appears to have forgotten all about the deal with his brother when he comes to claim his blessing, the story of him selling his birthright for a mess of pottage

(Genesis 25: 29–34) has often been used to justify the switch of inheritance by biblical exegetes, who have almost without exception, been quick to side with the winner and to declare that all was for the best.

Thus, astonishingly, we find many early commentaries comparing Jacob, taking on the hairy skin of a goat to counterfeit his brother, with Christ taking on human flesh. Esau is correspondingly vilified. Perhaps the most ironic twist of fate being that Jacob was frequently seen as the 'type' of the Christians, inheriting the blessing originally given to the Jews, who were, after all, 'the children of Israel', his direct descendants, while Esau (a born loser, if ever there was one) was now cast as the type of the recalcitrant and unconverted Jews. A late seventeenth-century account, for instance, is quite clear about the dire warnings contained in the typology of the story.

Esau is in this respect (as the Fathers observe) a Figure of those, who, desirous to unite GOD and the World together, cast about how they may enjoy the Comforts of Heaven and the Pleasures of the Earth both at once...

This Mysterious History throughout, represents to us in all parts of it Jesus Christ, cloathed in the outward appearance of a Sinner, as Jacob here was in that of Esau. It is also an admirable Figure of the Reprobation of the Jews, who desired nothing but the good things of the World; and the Election of the Church, which (like David) desires but one thing of GOD, and requests but one Blessing.

We must have a care (as S. Paul saith) not to imitate Esau, who having sold his Birth-right to Jacob, and desiring afterwards, as being the Eldest, to receive the Blessing of his Father, was rejected, without being able to persuade his Father to revoke what he had pronounced in Favour of Jacob, notwithstanding his entreating it with many Tears. For as he had despised GOD, GOD also despised his Cries and Tears, as not proceeding from a sincere Repentance, nor from a true Change of Heart.[2]

By the early nineteenth century, however, such comforting typologies had given way to distinct unease. Mrs Trimmer, in a popular Evangelical commentary, is clearly more than a little worried about the moral aspects of the story; does her best to clear Jacob; and concludes by speculating openly about God's motives in the whole exercise:

Jacob, in obedience to his mother, acts against his own conscience. Our Reason will show us that these are not things we should imitate in Isaac, Rebekah, and Jacob; therefore no remarks are made upon them by the sacred writer of their history. What we are particularly to observe here, is, that GOD made the faults of these three persons contribute to bring about his own good purposes. GOD knew beforehand what they would do; he also knew that Jacob, though he would do many wrong things, would keep from idol worship, and reverence his Creator, and bring up his family in the true religion; and that Esau on the contrary would marry among idolators, and depart from the right way; and GOD, possibly for this reason, ordained that Jacob rather than Esau should be the head of the great nation through which all the families of the earth should be blessed.[3]

Nevertheless, it is clear that whatever the original rights and wrongs of the case, Jacob's triumph has been complete. Esau had the misfortune never to write a book – and history, as we are constantly, if unconvincingly, reminded, is told from the point of view of the victors. After all, Moses – by tradition at least, the author of the first five books of the Bible, the Pentateuch – was of the tribe of Levi, and a descendant of Jacob, and not of Esau. But, as the examples above illustrate, there is something more to Jacob's victory than control of the media. What is really significant about this story is not that Esau was supplanted, but that this account, the official narrative of the descendants of Jacob/Israel *tells* us that he was. In other words, the story of this appropriated blessing is somehow so important an element in the much larger national saga of who the children of Israel felt themselves to be that the need to repeat it has over-ridden the obvious moral difficulties in justifying the legitimacy of the succession. The result was to give those thus legitimized, from thenceforth distinctively the 'children' of Israel, a peculiar kind of consciousness of who they were and how they had become so – a consciousness that in turn finds expression in the biblical text through a new interpretative theory.

Hence another incident embedded in the larger narrative: the story of Jacob's ladder (Genesis 29: 10–22). Fleeing from the wrath of his cheated brother, Jacob goes to sleep in the open and dreams of a ladder reaching to heaven, with angels of God ascending and descending upon it. It is here, at the place ever afterwards to be known as Bethel, that God makes three promises that are to be fundamental to the story of Israel: possession of the land; innumerable descendants; and finally, through those descendants, a blessing to 'all the families of the earth'. Once again, this is, of course, Jacob's own version of events – dreams are unverifiable – but though it repeats and conveniently confirms possession of the blessing there is a special rider that transforms it from a family squabble into an ideology. A new interpretative theory has been enunciated, replete with universal significance. Thus not merely is the story both a reminder of the great saga of Israel, and a key text for Christian inclusiveness, it has also long been interpreted, both typologically and symbolically, as a metaphor of divine inspiration. As generations of writers and artists have since observed, it has served as a constant reminder of the unexpected, even arbitrary, nature of the transcendent – here in the form of a theophany occurring literally in the middle of nowhere, to a guilty man on the run.

The success of that theory is attested by the fact that the two commentaries cited above, totally different as they may appear to be at first glance, both rest their defences on it. The clue comes at the beginning of Genesis 28:

And Isaac called Jacob, and blessed him, and charged him, and said unto him, Thou shalt not take a wife of the daughters of Canaan. Arise, go to Padan-aram, to the house of Bethuel thy mother's father; and take thee a wife from thence of the daughters of Laban thy mother's brother. (verses 1–2)

This is a repetition of Abraham's instruction to his servant concerning the marriage of Isaac in Genesis 24: 3: 'I will make thee swear by the Lord, the God of heaven, and the God of the earth, that thou shalt not take a wife unto my son of the daughters of the Canaanites, among whom I dwell.' At the heart of the biblical story of the Patriarchs is the absolute prohibition of polytheism; to preserve the new religion revealed to Abraham there is to be *no* intermarriage with the Canaanites. That way lay a return to the old religion of the land: Baal-worship, polytheism and infidelity. For the Hebrew Bible it is the ultimate sin – though it was a case of 'do as I say, not as I do' since Abraham himself had earlier done exactly this and taken a Canaanite wife, Keturah (Genesis 25: 1). Perhaps because of that, this prohibition was a constant refrain that will echo throughout the Pentateuch and the entire history of Israel in the books of Judges, Samuel, Kings, and Chronicles. If one wishes to extend the dichotomy, it can be found in the New Testament enmity between the Jews, the descendants of those who had endured the Captivity and kept the old faith in Babylon, and the Samaritans, the descendants of those who had stayed and mingled with new settlers planted by the conquerors. The Samaritans (however much they too might claim to have kept their distinctive faith) had, in the eyes of the returned exiles, committed the unforgivable sin of setting up a rival Temple to Jerusalem in Samaria – a move which was seen as threatening a return to the polytheism of the local Canaanite culture. The dangers of any weakening of the doctrine of one temple, one god, were well illustrated, to orthodox eyes, by the syncretism of the new settlers who were very willing to add what was, to them, the local cult of Yahweh to their existing pantheon. To take it a stage further, that continuing hostility to the native Canaanites can even arguably be seen to underlie the enmity between the Palestinian Arabs and the Jews in twentieth-century Israel.

The biblical consequences of that patriarchal prohibition were far-reaching. From it stems Jacob's flight to Bethel; his famous dream; the fourteen years' service under Laban, his uncle; the consequent marriages with his cousins Leah and Rachel; and his fathering of the twelve tribes of Israel. By a marriage of cousins the purity of the descent – and therefore of the monotheism, the religion of Yahweh – was guaranteed. What is significant is that it is only *after* Jacob has appropriated the blessing intended for his elder twin that we find Isaac insisting that he may not marry a Canaanite. Esau, we are told in the previous chapter, had already married two Hittite wives (Genesis 26: 34–5) – and so, it is implied, had already endangered the monotheistic line of succession. Both this, and the story of his selling his birthright (which again, interestingly, also places Jacob in a bad light) prepare the way for his loss of the blessing.

—— **Literature** ——

St Augustine of Hippo, *The City of God* (c. 413–426 CE), tr. Henry Bettenson, Penguin, 1972, Book XVI, chapter 37

Isaac's two sons, Esau and Jacob, thus grew up together. The primacy of the elder is transferred to the younger as the result of a compact and agreement between them, because the elder had an inordinate craving for the dish of lentils which the younger brother had prepared for his meal, and he sold his first-born's portion to his brother for this price, after he had pledged his oath. Hence we learn that in the matter of eating it is not the kind of food he craves that brings blame upon a man, but his unrestrained greed. Isaac is growing old and he is losing his eyesight through advancing years. He intends to bless his older son and without knowing it he blesses his younger son, instead of the elder brother, who was a hairy man; for the younger brother put himself beneath his father's hands, with the kidskins attached to himself, as if bearing the sins of another. To prevent us from supposing that this trick of Jacob's was a fraudulent deceit, and from failing to look for a hidden meaning of great significance, the Scripture made this statement earlier: 'Now Esau was a man skilled in hunting, a man of the open country; Jacob, on the other hand, was a simple man, living at home.'

Some of our scholars have translated this as 'without deceit' (instead of 'simple'). But whether it is rendered 'without deceit' or 'simple' or (better) 'without pretence' – the Greek word is *aplastos* – what deceit is there in the obtaining of a blessing by a man 'without deceit'? What kind of a deceit can be shown by a simple man? What kind of pretence by a man who tells no lies, unless we have here a hidden meaning conveying a profound truth? And then, what was the nature of the blessing? 'Behold', says Isaac,

> the smell of my son is like the smell of a plentiful field, which the Lord has blessed. And may God give you of the dew of heaven and of the richness of the soil, and abundance of corn and wine, and may nations serve you and princes do reverence to you. Become lord over your brother, and your father's sons will do reverence to you. Whoever curses you, let him be cursed, and whoever blesses you, let him be blessed. (Genesis 27: 27ff.)

Thus the blessing of Jacob is the proclamation of Christ among all nations. This is happening; this is actively going on.

John Donne, *Holy Sonnets,* 'Divine Meditations' (1633–1635), 11

> Spit in my face you Jews, and pierce my side,
> Buffet, and scoff, scourge, and crucify me,
> For I have sinn'd, and sinn'd, and only he,
> Who could do no iniquity, hath died:
> But by my death can not be satisfied
> My sins, which pass the Jews' impiety:
> They kill'd once an inglorious man, but I
> Crucify him daily, being now glorified.
> Oh let me then, his strange love still admire:
> Kings pardon, but he bore our punishment.
> And Jacob came cloth'd in vile harsh attire
> But to suplant, and with gainfull intent:
> God cloth'd himself in vile mans flesh, that so
> He might be weake enough to suffer woe.

Francis Quarles, 'On Jacob's Purchase'

How poor was Jacob's motion, and how strange
His offer! How unequal was th' exchange!
A mess of porridge for inheritance?
Why could not hungry Esau strive t'enhance
His price so little? So much underfoot?

Well might he give him bread and drink to boot:
An easy price! The case is even our own;
For toys we often sell our Heaven, our Crown.

John Keble, *The Christian Year* (1827), from 'The Second Sunday in Lent'

Watch by our father Isaac's pastoral door -
    The birthright sold, the blessing lost and won,
Tell, Heaven was wrath that can relent no more,
    The Grave, dark deeds that cannot be undone.

We barter life for pottage; sell true bliss
    For wealth or power, for pleasure or renown;
Thus, Esau-like, our Father's blessing miss,
    Then wash with fruitless tears our faded crown.

Our faded crown, despised and flung aside,
    Shall on some brother's brow immortal bloom,
No partial hand the blessing may misguide;
    No flattering fancy change our Monarch's doom.

Thomas Mann, *Joseph and his Brothers* (1933–1942), tr. H. T. Lowe-Porter, Penguin, 1978, *The Tales of Jacob*, IV, 'The Flight'

The Great Hoaxing

Isaac suffered sore by reason of what he saw or must close his eyes to in order not to see it, and suffered from his own weakness which prevented him from making an end of the difficulty by sending Esau into the wilderness, as had actually been done with Ishmael, his beautiful wild uncle. The little inner myth prevented him, Esau's actual priority of birth, which still bore heavily on the vexed question as to which of the twins was the chosen one; thus he complained of his eyes, how they ran, and of the burning of the lids, and that he saw dimly, like the dying moon, that the light hurt him – and he sought the darkness. Shall we say that he became blind in order not to witness the idol-worship of his daughters-in-law? Ah, that was the least among all that offended his sight, that made him long for blindness – because only so could that happen which must happen.

For the older the boys grew the clearer to a seeing eye grew the lines of the 'great myth' which despite all the father's principles made the 'little myth' more and more forced; the clearer it became *who they both were*, in whose footsteps they walked, on whose story they were founded, the red man and the smooth man, the huntsman and the dweller in tents. How could Isaac, who with Ishmael the wild ass had formed the brother pair; who himself had not been Cain but Abel, not Ham but Shem, not Set but Osiris, not Ishmael but Isaac the trueborn son – how could he, with seeing eyes, have supported the claim that he preferred Esau? So his eyes failed him, like the dying moon, and he lay in darkness that he might be betrayed, together with Esau, his eldest son.

But actually nobody was deceived, not even Esau. For if I am venturing here to write about people who did not always know precisely who they were – Esau himself not being of the clearest on the subject and sometimes taking himself for the original goat of the Seir people and mentioning him in the first person – yet this occasional lack of clarity had to do only with the individual and time-conditioned, and was precisely the consequence of the fact that everybody knew, perfectly well outside of time, and mythically and typically speaking, who the individual was, and so did Esau, of whom it has not been idly said that he was in his way as pious a man as Jacob. He wept and raved, of course, after the betrayal, and was more murderously minded against his favoured brother than Ishmael had been against his – indeed it is true that he discussed with Ishmael an attack upon Isaac as well as upon Jacob. But he did all that because it was the role he had to play; he knew and accepted the fact that all events are a fulfilment, and that what had happened had happened because it must, according to the archetype. That is to say, it was not the first time, it was ceremonially and in conformity to pattern, it had acquired presentness as in a recurrent feast and come round as feasts do. For Esau, Joseph's uncle, was not the father of Edom.

Salman Rushdie, *Midnight's Children* (1981), Picador, 1982

Why did midnight's child betray the children of midnight and take me to my fate? For love of violence, and the legitimizing glitter of buttons on uniforms? For the sake of his ancient antipathy towards me? Or – I find this most plausible – in exchange for immunity from the penalties imposed on the rest of us ... yes, that must be it; O birthright-denying war hero. O mess-of-pottage-corrupted rival.

Notes

1 Klaus Westermann, *Genesis 12–36: A Commentary*, tr. John J. Scullion SJ, (London: SPCK, 1986), p. 436.
2 *History of the Old and New Testaments Extracted from the Holy Scriptures, the Holy Fathers, and Other Ecclesiastical Writers . . .*, 4th impression, 1712, p. 31.
3 Mrs (Sarah) Trimmer, *Help to the Unlearned in the Study of the Holy Scriptures*, 2nd edn, 1806, pp. 32–3.

Bibliography

Mann, Thomas. *Joseph and his Brothers*, tr. H. T. Lowe-Porter (Harmondsworth: Penguin, 1978).
Prickett, Stephen. *Origins of Narrative: The Romantic Appropriation of the Bible* (Cambridge: Cambridge University Press, 1996).
Thoreau, Henry David. 'Life Without Principle', *Atlantic Monthly*, 1863.
von Rad, Gerhard. *Genesis: A Commentary*, tr. John H. Marks (London: SCM, The Old Testament Library, 1972).

WRESTLING JACOB
GENESIS 32: 22–31

[22] And he [Jacob] rose up that night, and took his two wives, and his two women servants, and his eleven sons, and passed over the ford Jabbok.

[23] And he took them, and sent them over the brook, and sent over that he had.

[24] And Jacob was left alone; and there wrestled a man with him until the breaking of the day.

[25] And when he saw that he prevailed not against him, he touched the hollow of his thigh; and the hollow of Jacob's thigh was out of joint, as he wrestled with him.

[26] And he said, Let me go, for the day breaketh. And he said, I will not let thee go, except thou bless me.

[27] And he said unto him, What is thy name? And he said, Jacob.

[28] And he said, Thy name shall be called no more Jacob, but Israel: for as a prince hast thou power with God and with men, and hast prevailed.

[29] And Jacob asked him, and said, Tell me, I pray thee, thy name. And he said, Wherefore is it that thou dost ask after my name? And he blessed him there.

[30] And Jacob called the name of the place Peniel: for I have seen God face to face, and my life is preserved.

[31] And as he passed over Penuel the sun rose upon him, and he halted upon his thigh.

Notes

Verse 24. The word 'man' is open to many possible interpretations. It is deliberately left unclear who Jacob's opponent is.

Verse 27. The name 'Jacob' implies not only 'supplanter' but also a cheat.

Verse 28. Naming is clearly important here: 'Jacob' means 'supplanter'; 'Israel' has been interpreted as 'Perseverer with God', or (to be echoed in the next clause) 'Prince powerful with God'; 'Peniel' means 'fear of God'.

Verse 30. The name Peniel is here a pun in Hebrew, for the word for 'face' is *pānîm* . It thus suggests 'face' and 'fear of God'.

—— **Commentary** ——

Like all the Jacob stories this one is highly ambiguous. It is usually known as Jacob 'wrestling with the Angel', but the text, of course, never says this. First the narrative describes the stranger as a 'man', then Jacob himself says, 'I have seen God face to face.' As so often in such stories, we are left to draw our own conclusions.

Nor does the context serve to clarify how we are intended to read this incident. After his long years of successful service under Laban, he has two wives, two concubines, ten sons, numerous servants and extensive flocks, herds and camels. Despite this evident prosperity, the news that his brother Esau, whom he had cheated out of his blessing years before, is on his way to meet him with four hundred men, throws Jacob into a most unheroic panic. First he separates his company into two bands, on the grounds that if Esau encounters and slaughters one, the other may escape.

Then he selects a present of two hundred she-goats, twenty he-goats, two hundred ewes and twenty rams, thirty milch-camels with their colts, forty cows and ten bulls, twenty she-asses and ten foals – all of which is sent on in advance in the hopes of appeasing Esau's presumed wrath. Then he sends his womenfolk and children on over the ford, remaining alone on the far side until the next day.

Such a combination of moral guilt and physical terror does nothing to enhance the figure of the patriarch, who emerges at best as a timid and slightly comic figure. The anti-climax that follows the actual meeting with Esau the next day does nothing to dispel this impression. Esau greets his long-lost and grovelling brother affectionately, says that he, too, has prospered, and has no need of any such presents. More remarkable still, he confers on Jacob his own 'blessing' 'because God hath dealt graciously with me, and because I have enough.' With typical alacrity, Jacob needs no

135

second urging, and promptly takes back his 'present' (Genesis 33: 11). Esau's lordly generosity only serves to show up Jacob's desperate appeasement for what it is. The moral contrast between the two brothers could hardly be stronger.

All this makes the lonely wrestling-match with the stranger at the ford Jabbok, with its heroic outcome and blessing – repeating, we are to infer, that stolen from Esau years before – the more mysterious and compelling. If, in the moment of crisis in his life, Jacob has undergone some kind of moral or spiritual transformation, we are not made immediately aware of it by his subsequent behaviour. Indeed the following chapter, 34, with its account of the treacherous destruction and looting of Shechem by Jacob's sons in response to the rape of Dinah, serves only to underline the pragmatism of Jacob's morals. He is furious with Simeon and Levi, the instigators of the massacre, not apparently because what they did was wrong, but because it will have made them understandably unpopular in the area, and endangered the rest of the clan. Nevertheless, he then returns to Bethel, the place of his original dream of the ladder, and of God's blessing.

Hardly surprisingly, the passage has drawn sharply different responses from commentators. Ambrose, perhaps hopefully, sees in Jacob an example of faith in face of fear. An eighteenth-century commentary puts this in its most extreme form, claiming that 'the vision was calculated to convince him, that being under the divine protection, in a particular manner, he had no reason to be under any apprehensions from his brother, or any human power whatever'. Others, concentrating on a more boldly Christian reading have identified the mysterious stranger with the Logos, the son of God – an interpretation taken up in perhaps the most famous paraphrase of all, Charles Wesley's dramatic 'Come O thou traveller unknown' (reproduced below). Perhaps the frankest response is from Mrs Trimmer, an early nineteenth-century author, whose *Help to the Unlearned in the Study of the Holy Scriptures* (1805) is a self-proclaimed compendium of traditional biblical interpretations:

This passage of scripture cannot be well explained now; but without doubt Jacob's descendants, the Israelites, for whom the Bible was first written, perfectly understood it. All we need remark is, that a *new name* was given to Jacob, *ver.* 28, which signifies *a prince with God*.

But this is certain, that something very extraordinary took place betwixt Jacob and an angel, and that it was intended for some very important purpose.

The story's obvious mythopoetic qualities have nevertheless made it as attractive to artists and poets – especially from the time of the Romantics onwards – as it appears to have been baffling to many theological commentators. As it stands the story has obvious connections with other similar stories in world mythology. The stranger may be divine, but like Cupid in Roman, or the trolls in Norse myths, he is a creature of darkness, who must flee at the first light of dawn. Jacob emerges 'victorious' in the struggle, but at a cost. His new visionary powers are achieved at the price of physical disability. Often in mythology the seer is blind; here the endlessly 'mobile' Jacob is lamed. More psychologically orientated critics will have little difficulty in seeing in such a figure a manifestation of unconscious forces or powers, and the image of Jacob wrestling in some metaphorical sense with his own shadow is a compelling one. What is clear, is that whether we read the stranger as internal or external, he represents a moment of striking individuation and transformation in Jacob's own life. Previously, as his name suggests, he has been the trickster who has lived by his wits: he has supplanted his brother, stolen his blessing, cheated and been cheated by his father-in-law, Laban. Now at the ford, in a momentary liminal state, he is in the process of being transformed from cheat into patriarch: the founder of Israel – and, if one wishes to look beyond the Hebrew Bible, the father not only of Judaism but even of Christianity and Islam as well.

Nor is this the end of possible interpretations. Roland Barthes, the French literary critic, has given the story a quite different spin by seeing it as an allegory of the creation of language itself. 'By marking Jacob (Israel),' he writes, 'God (or the narrative) permits an analogical development of meaning, creates the formal operational conditions of a new "language", the election of Israel being its "message". God is a logothete, the founder of a language, and Jacob is here a "morpheme" of the new language.'[1] Barthes is not, of course, interested in any religious aspects of the narrative, but he is very much alive to the fact that this story, like others in the Jacob saga, is about the justification of Israel as the chosen people. As we have seen, God's choice is based not on morality, but on some other apparently arbitrary principle. For Barthes, linguistic signs have no meaning in themselves, but only in relation to other signs. Unless language is anchored to something external and arbitrary there can be no final meaning in what he calls a 'theological' sense. Quite independently of this argument, some modern biblical critics have argued that Old Testament Hebrew was never a spoken language in the normal sense, but one created for the purpose of writing the Old Testament – and therefore for justifying Israel in precisely this sense. If so, it would not be unique: Walter J. Ong points out that other languages have been formed for similar religious purposes, including Homeric Greek, medieval Latin, classical Arabic, Sanskrit, and Classical Chinese.[2]

Whatever the Church traditionally made of the story, the literary response has always been to internalize the experience. For Wesley, in 'Wrestling Jacob' it has become a paradigm of the kind of evangelical conversion he and his brother John had undergone a few years earlier. The text of Genesis is interwoven with a network of other quotations from the prophets and the New Testament, to produce an intertextual metaphorical drama of sin, repentance, redemption, justification and finally death. His hymn became a key work for many eighteenth- and nineteenth-century Christians, from Isaac Watts to Dean Stanley. Preaching at Bolton in 1788, a fortnight after his brother's death, John Wesley broke down at the lines, 'My company is gone before / And I am left alone with thee.'

In contrast, the Jesuit Gerard Manley Hopkins' poem 'Carrion Comfort' has no such happy ending. It was written the year before his death, in 1888, but only published, with the rest of his poems in 1918. The internalized wrestling of this, one of the best-known of his 'terrible sonnets', is much more inconclusive. Though it is possible to find in the awe of the final lines at least a partial resignation to the will of God, the confident sense of divine love always present in Wesley's poem, or even the final blessing of the original, is almost totally absent. Instead the involuted language, the broken rhythm, the fragmentary imagery all contribute to a sense of internal conflict and dissolution that seems to foreshadow the uncertainties of the twentieth century much more than the revivalist confidence of the eighteenth.

—— **Literature** ——

Izaak Walton, *The Life of John Donne* (1640)

And sure if he had consulted with flesh and blood, he had not for these reasons put his hand to that holy plough. But God who is able to prevail, wrestled with him, as the *Angel* did with *Jacob, and marked him*: mark'd him with a blessing; a blessing of obedience to the motions of his blessed Spirit.

Charles Wesley, 'Wrestling Jacob' (1742)

Come, O thou traveller unknown,
Whom still I hold, but cannot see!

My company before is gone,
And I am left alone with thee;
With thee all night I mean to stay,
And wrestle till the break of day.

I need not tell thee who I am,
My misery and sin declare;
Thyself hast called me by my name;
Look on my hands, and read it there:
But who, I ask thee, who art thou?
Tell me thy name, and tell me now.

In vain thou strugglest to get free;
I never will unloose my hold!
Art thou the Man that died for me?
The secret of thy love unfold:
Wrestling, I will not let thee go,
Till I thy name and nature know.

What though my shrinking flesh complain
And murmur to contend so long?
I rise superior to my pain,
When I am weak, then am I strong;
And when my all of strength shall fail,
I shall with the God-Man prevail.

Yield to me now; for I am weak,
But confident in self-despair;
Speak to my heart, in blessings speak,
Be conquered by my instant prayer;
Speak, or thou never hence shall move,
And tell me if thy name is Love.

'Tis Love! 'Tis Love! Thou diedst for me!
I hear thy whisper in my heart;
The morning breaks, the shadows flee,
Pure, universal love thou art;
To me, to all, thy mercies move:
Thy nature and thy name is Love.

My prayer has power with God; the grace
Unspeakable I now receive;

Through faith I see thee face to face,
  I see thee face to face and live!
In vain I have not wept and strove:
  Thy nature and thy name is love.

I know thee, Saviour, who thou art,
  Jesus, the feeble sinner's friend;
Nor wilt thou with the night depart,
  But stay and love me to the end;
  Thy mercies never shall remove:
  Thy nature and thy name is Love.

The Sun of Righteousness on me
  Has risen with healing in his wings;
Withered my nature's strength, from thee
  My soul its life and succour brings;
    My help is all laid up above:
  Thy nature and thy name is Love.

Contented now upon my thigh
  I halt, till life's short journey end;
All helplessness, all weakness, I
On thee alone for strength depend;
Nor have I power from thee to move:
  Thy nature and thy name is Love.

  Lame as I am, I take the prey,
Hell, earth, and sin with ease o'ercome;
  I leap for joy, pursue my way,
And as a bounding hart fly home,
    Through all eternity to prove
Thy nature and thy name is Love.

Jones Very, 'Jacob Wrestling with the Angel'

The Patriarch wrestled with the angel long,
For though of mortal race, yet he was strong;
Nor would release him at the break of day,
That he might take his upward heavenly way.
'Bless me,' he cried, 'ere I shall let thee go;
Thou art an angel, and no mortal foe,
Who through the night's dark hours couldst thus maintain
With me a contest on the starry plain.'

'What is thy name?' the angel asked again,
'For thou hast power alike with God and men.'
'Jacob,' he said. The angel blessed him there:
'Henceforth the name of Israel thou shalt bear;
Thou hast prevailed, thou art a Prince indeed:
A blessing rest on thee, and on thy seed.'
Deem not that to those ancient times belong
The wonders told in history and in song:
Men may with angels now, as then, prevail;
Too oft, alas, they in the contest fail.
Their blessed help is not from man withdrawn;
Contend thou with the angel till the dawn:
A blessing he to earth for thee doth bring,
Then back to heaven again his flight will wing.

Gerard Manley Hopkins, 'Carrion Comfort' (1885)

Not, I'll not, carrion comfort, Despair, not feast on thee;
Not untwist – slack they may be – these last strands of man
In me, or, most weary, cry *I can no more*. I can;
Can something, hope, wish day not come, not choose not to be.

But ah, but O thou terrible, why wouldst thou rude on me
Thy wring-world right foot rock? lay a lionlimb against me? scan
With darksome devouring eyes my bruiséd bones? and fan,
O in turns of tempest, me heaped there; me frantic to avoid thee and flee?

Why? That my chaff might fly; my grain lie, sheer and clear.
Nay in all that toil, that coil, since (seems) I kissed the rod,
Hand rather, my heart lo! lapped strength, stole joy, would laugh,
  chéer.
Cheer whom though? The hero whose heaven-handling flung me, fóot
  tród
Me? or me that fought him? O which one? is it each one?
  That night, that year
Of now done darkness I wretch lay wrestling with (my God!) my God.

Emily Dickinson, 'A Little East of Jordan' (c.1859), *Complete Poems*, ed. Thomas H. Johnson, Faber, 1970

A little East of Jordan,
Evangelists record,

A gymnast and an Angel
Did wrestle long and hard –

Till morning touching mountain –
And Jacob, waxing strong,
The Angel begged permission
To Breakfast – to return –

Not so, said cunning Jacob!
'I will not let thee go
Except thou bless me' – Stranger!
The which acceded to –

Light swung the silver fleeces
'Peniel' Hills beyond,
And the bewildered Gymnast
Found he had worsted God!

Christina Rossetti, 'Weeping We Hold Him Fast Tonight'

Weeping we hold him fast tonight;
We will not let Him go
Till daybreak smile the snow.
Then figs shall bud, and dove with dove
Shall coo the livelong day;
Then He shall say 'Arise, My love,
My fair one, come away.'

(*Note.* Rossetti here links the Genesis passage with two other biblical references. The first is from Matthew 24: 30–2, the lesson of the fig tree. The second is a familiar saying from the Song of Songs)

Roland Barthes, 'The Struggle with the Angel' (1971), *Image Music Text*, tr. Stephen Heath, Fontana, 1977

2. The Struggle (v. 24–29). For the second episode we have once again to start from a complication (which is not to say a doubt) of readability – remember that textual analysis is founded on *reading* rather than on the objective structure of the text, the latter being more the province of structural analysis. This complication stems from the interchangeable character of the pronouns which refer to the two opponents in the combat: a style which a purist would describe as *muddled* but whose lack of sharpness doubtless posed no problem for Hebrew syntax. Who is 'a man'? Staying within verse 25, is it 'a man' who does not succeed in getting the better of Jacob or Jacob who cannot prevail over this some-one? Is the 'he' of 'he prevailed not against him' (25) the same as the 'he' of 'And he said' (26)? Assuredly everything becomes clear in the end but it requires in some sort a retroactive reasoning of a syllogistic kind: you have vanquished God. He who is speaking to you is he whom you vanquished. Therefore he who is speaking to you is God. The identification of the opponents is oblique, the readability is *diverted* (whence occasionally commentaries which border on total misunder-standing; as for example: 'He wrestles with the Angel of the Lord and, thrown to the ground, obtains from him the certainty that God is with him').

Structurally, this amphibology, even if subsequently clarified, is not without significance. It is not in my opinion (which is, I repeat, that of a reader today) a simple complication of expression due to an unpolished, archaizing style; it is bound up with a paradoxical structure of the contest (paradoxical when compared with the stereotypes of mythical combat). So as to appreciate this paradox in its structural subtlety, let us imagine for a moment an endoxical (and no longer paradoxical) reading of the epi-sode: A wrestles with B but fails to get the better of him; to gain victory at all costs, A then resorts to some exceptional strategy, whether an unfair and forbidden blow (the forearm chop in wrestling matches) or a blow which, while remaining within the rules, supposes a secret knowledge, a 'dodge' (the 'ploy' of the Jarnac blow).[3] *In the very logic of the narrative* such a blow, generally described as 'decisive', brings victory to the person who administers it: the emphatic mark of which this blow is structurally the object cannot be reconciled with its being ineffective – by the very god of narrative it *must* succeed. Here, however, the opposite occurs: the decisive blow fails; A, who gave the blow, is not the victor; which is the structural paradox. The sequence then takes an unexpected course:

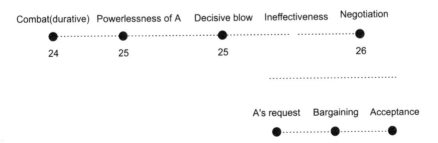

143

It will be noted that A (it matters little from the point of view of the structure if this be *someone, a man, God* or *the Angel*) is not strictly speaking vanquished but *held in check*. For this to be seen as a defeat, the adjunction of a *time limit* is needed: this is the breaking of day ('for the day breaketh' 26), a notation which picks up verse 24 ('until the breaking of day') but now in the explicit context of a mythical structure. The theme of the nocturnal combat is structurally justified by the fact that at a certain moment, fixed in advance (as is the rising of the sun, as is the duration of a boxing match), the rules of the combat will no longer obtain, the structural play will come to an end, as too the supernatural play (the 'demons' withdraw at dawn). Thus we can see that it is within a quite 'regular' combat that the sequence sets up an unexpected readability, a logical surprise: the Person who has the knowledge, the secret, the special ploy, is nevertheless defeated. The sequence itself, however actional, however anecdotal it may be functions to *unbalance* the opponents in the combat, not only by the unforeseen victory of the one over the other, but above all (let us be fully aware of *the formal* subtlety of this surprise) by the illogical, *inverted*, nature of the victory. In other words (and here we find an eminently structural term, well known to linguists), the combat, as it is reversed in its unexpected development, *marks* one of the combatants: the weakest defeats the strongest, *in exchange for which* he is marked (on the thigh).

It is plausible (moving somewhat away from pure structural analysis and approaching textual analysis, vision *without barriers* of meanings) to fill out this schema of the mark (of the disequilibrium) with contents of an ethnological kind. The structural meaning of the episode, once again, is the following: a situation of balance (the combat at its outset) – and such a situation is a prerequisite for any marking (ascesis in Ignatius of Loyola for instance functions to establish the *indifference* of the will which allows the manifestation of the divine mark, the choice, the election) – is disturbed by the unlikely victory of one of the participants: there is an inversion of the mark, a counter-mark. Let us turn then to the family configuration. Traditionally, the 3 line of brothers is in principle evenly balanced (they are all situated on the same level in relation to the parents); this equality of birth is normally unbalanced by the right of primogeniture: the eldest is marked. Now in the story of Jacob, there is an inversion of the mark, a counter-mark: it is the younger who supplants the elder (*Genesis 27*: 36), taking his brother by the heel in order to reverse time; it is Jacob, the younger brother, who marks himself. Since Jacob has just obtained a mark in his struggle with God, one can say in a sense that A (God) is the substitute of the elder brother, once again beaten by the younger. The conflict with Esau is *displaced* (every symbol is a *displacement*; if the 'struggle with the angel' is symbolic, then it has displaced something). Commentary – for which I am insufficiently equipped – would at this point doubtless have to widen the interpretation of the *inversion of the mark*, by placing it either in a historico-economic context – Esau is the eponym of the Edomites and there were economic ties between the Edomites and the Israelites; figured here perhaps is an overthrow of the alliance, the start of a new league of interests? – or in the field of the symbolic (in the psychoanalytical sense of the term) – the Old Testament seems to be less the world of the Fathers than that of the Enemy Brothers, the elder are ousted in favour of the younger; in the myth of the Enemy Brothers Freud pointed to the theme of *the smallest difference:* is not the blow on the thigh, on the thin sinew, just such a *smallest difference*? Be that as it may, in this world God marks the young, acts against nature: his (structural) function is to constitute a *countermarker*.

Frederick Buechner, *Son of Laughter: A Novel*,
Harper Collins, 1993

I was no longer Jacob. I was no longer myself. Israel was who I was. The stranger had said it. I tried to say it the way he had said it: *Yees-rah-ail*. I tried to say the new name I was to the new self I was. I could not see him. He was too close to me to see. I could see only the curve of his shoulders above me. I saw the first glimmer of dawn on his shoulders like a wound.

I said, 'What is your name?' I could only whisper it.

'Why do you ask me my name?'

We were both of us whispering. He did not wait for my answer. He blessed me as I had asked him. I do not remember the words of his blessing or even if there were words. I remember the blessing of his arms holding me and the blessing of his arms letting me go. I remember as blessing the black shape of him against the rose-colored sky.

I remember as blessing the one glimpse I had of his face. It was more terrible than the face of dark, or of pain, or of terror. It was the face of light. No words can tell of it. Silence cannot tell of it. Sometimes I cannot believe that I saw it and lived but that I only dreamed I saw it. Sometimes I believe I saw it and that I only dream I live.

He never told me his name. The Fear of Isaac, the Shield of Abraham, and others like them are names we use because we do not know his true name. Perhaps he did not tell it because he knew I would never stop calling on it. But I gave the place where I saw him a name. I named it Peniel. It means the face of God.

Notes

1 'The Struggle with the Angel', *Image Music Text*, tr. Stephen Heath (London: Fontana Collins, 1977), p. 135.
2 Walter J. Ong, *Orality and Literacy* (London: Routledge, 1982), pp. 23 and 114.
3 In 1547 Guy de Jarnac won a duel by an unexpected thrust which hamstrung his opponent.

Bibliography

Barthes, Roland. 'The Struggle with the Angel', *Image Music Text*, tr. Stephen Heath (London: Fontana Collins, 1977), pp. 125–41.
Gunkel, Hermann. *The Legends of Genesis: The Biblical Saga and History*, tr. Herbert Carruth (New York: Schocken Books, 1970).
Hartman, Geoffrey H. 'The Struggle for the Text', in *Midrash and Literature*, eds Geoffrey H. Hartman and Sanford Budick (New Haven: Yale University Press, 1986), pp. 3–18.

—— DAVID AND BATHSHEBA ——
2 SAMUEL 11: 1–27

[1] And it came to pass, after the year was expired, at the time when kings go forth to battle, that David sent Joab, and his servants with him, and all Israel; and they destroyed the children of Ammon, and besieged Rabbah. But David tarried still at Jerusalem.

[2] And it came to pass in an eveningtide, that David arose from off his bed, and walked upon the roof of the king's house: and from the roof he saw a woman washing herself; and the woman was very beautiful to look upon.

[3] And David sent and inquired after the woman. And one said, Is not this Bath-sheba, the daughter of Eliam, the wife of Uriah the Hittite?

[4] And David sent messengers, and took her; and she came in unto him, and he lay with her; for she was purified from her uncleanness: and she returned unto her house.

[5] And the woman conceived, and sent and told David, and said, I am with child.

[6] And David sent to Joab, saying, Send me Uriah the Hittite. And Joab sent Uriah to David.

[7] And when Uriah was come unto him, David demanded of him how Joab did, and how the people did, and how the war prospered.

[8] And David said to Uriah, Go down to thy house, and wash thy feet. And Uriah departed out of the king's house, and there followed him a mess of meat from the king.

[9] But Uriah slept at the door of the king's house with all the servants of his lord, and went not down to his house.

[10] And when they had told David, saying, Uriah went not down unto his house, David said unto Uriah, Camest thou not from thy journey? why then didst thou not go down unto thine house?

[11] And Uriah said unto David, The ark, and Israel, and Judah, abide in tents; and my lord Joab, and the servants of my lord, are encamped in the open fields; shall I then go into mine house, to eat and to drink, and to lie with my wife? as thou livest, and as thy soul liveth, I will not do this thing.

[12] And David said to Uriah, Tarry here to day also, and to morrow I will let thee depart. So Uriah abode in Jerusalem that day, and the morrow.

[13] And when David had called him, he did eat and drink before him; and he made him drunk: and at even he went out to lie on his bed with the servants of his lord, but went not down to his house ...

[16] And it came to pass, when Joab observed the city, that he assigned Uriah unto a place where he knew that valiant men were ...

[25] Then David said unto the messenger, Thus shalt thou say unto Joab, Let not this thing displease thee, for the sword devoureth one as well as another: make thy battle more strong against the city, and overthrow it: and encourage thou him.

[26] And when the wife of Uriah heard that Uriah her husband was dead, she mourned for her husband.

[27] And when the mourning was past, David sent and fetched her to his house, and displeased the Lord.

Notes

Verse 1. This sets the tone for the narrative which follows. In the springtime kings should be going into battle, but David remains behind in Jerusalem, preferring to send his general Joab to do his work. From the start, David's behaviour is morally questionable, and it is significant that Chronicles, which generally follows the Samuel narrative closely, omits this story altogether to avoid the stain which it leaves on the king's reputation.

Verse 2. Perhaps the most moving representation of this verse is Rembrandt's great painting of Bathsheba and her maid.

Verse 3. Although Uriah is a Hittite, his name is pure Hebrew. It was claimed that the Hittites were a people who lived in Palestine before the arrival of the Israelites. Uriah is mentioned in 2 Samuel 23: 39 as one of David's heroes.

Verse 4. The mention of Bathsheba's 'purification' after her period emphasizes the likelihood that she would conceive, and therefore David's paternity.

Verse 8. To 'wash your feet' is probably a euphemism for preparing himself for intercourse. David is anxious that Bathsheba's pregnancy can be attributed to her husband.

Verse 9. Uriah, however, behaves with absolute rectitude for a soldier on active service. As verse 11 indicates, sexual intercourse was forbidden to soldiers on campaign.

Verse 16. Joab, as David's faithful officer, follows out his orders exactly. To increase David's guilt, other royal servants die also in this ruse to be rid of Bathsheba's husband.

Verse 25. Far from losing his temper for Joab's rash exposure of his men under the walls of the city, as Joab anticipated, David is completely satisfied that his plan to be rid of Uriah has succeeded, whatever the cost. Indeed, he is careful to instruct the messenger to encourage Joab in his strategies.

Verse 27. God's displeasure with David is emphasized, and introduces the second half of the narrative (not given here) in which the prophet Nathan exposes the wickedness of the king.

—— **Commentary** ——

It is clear, even in the Hebrew Bible, that the story of David and Bath-sheba, and the plot to kill her husband Uriah the Hittite is problematic within the history of Israel. David as King and the anointed of the Lord behaves in a morally unacceptable manner, though the story must be told for from this liaison comes his successor Solomon, and further it becomes part of the succession that culminates in the birth of Jesus himself, 'born of David's line'. Even the Gospel of Matthew admits, in its opening genealogy of Jesus, that Bathsheba was, properly, Uriah's wife. The later account of the history of Israel in the Old Testament, the books of Chronicles, omits the episode altogether, presumably not wishing to throw the Lord's anointed in a dubious light. The point is made with typical feistiness in Elizabeth Cady Stanton's wonderful commentary *The Woman's Bible* of 1898:

David's social ethics were not quite up to the standard even of his own times. It is said that he was a master of his pen as well as of his sword. His poem on the death of Saul and Jonathan has been much praised by literary critics. But, alas! David was not able to hold the Divine heights which he occasionally attained. As in the case of Bath-sheba, he remained where he could see her; instead of going with his army to Jerusalem to attend to his duties as King of Israel and general of the army, he delegated them to others. Had he been at his post he would have been out of the way of temptation. He used to pray three times a day, not only at morning and evening, but at noon also. It is to be feared that on this day he forgot his devotions and thought only of Bathsheba.

Within the Christian tradition David has been consistently seen as the antetype of Christ, and commentators from the earliest times have gone to great lengths either to evade the obvious implications of the episode with Bathsheba or else to interpret it allegorically, for example, seeing Bathsheba as a type of the law which needed to be liberated and united with the spirit of Christ in David. St Augustine in his great work *De Doctrina Christiana*, merely notes that David was 'not lustful, though he fell into adultery'. Perhaps for this reason, Bathsheba has played a surprisingly small role in English literature, though the visual arts have frequently, like David himself, been absorbed by her beauty in a pictorial tradition which in our own time has been taken over by the cinema.

In the Renaissance poet George Peele, Bathsheba is portrayed as a chaste wife, and later a wise counsellor, alongside the prophet Nathan ensuring the proper succession of her son Solomon to the throne of his father David. In the brief excerpt given here, we see David burning with passion for Bathsheba in the tradition of royal lechery as he admits his 'unstaid desire'. Elsewhere in Renaissance literature we see Bathsheba as the prudent diplomat – a role she continues to play in modern works like Torgny Lindgren's novel *Bathsheba*.

Sir Thomas Wyatt uses the episode as a preface to his translation of the 'Penitential Psalms' from the Psalter (Psalms 6, 32, 38, 51, 102, 130 and 143), but does not even mention Bathsheba once by name. Rather, Wyatt focusses on the reproof of David by Nathan (2 Samuel 12), and pictures as the origin of these psalms of penitence, David composing with harp in hand 'his soul to save'.

In seventeenth-century literature, neither Abraham Cowley nor George Herbert mention Bathsheba in their reflections on David's act of adultery, while Dryden's political poem *Absalom and Achitophel* mentions her only once, representing the figure of the Duchess of Portsmouth who was mistress of the promiscuous King Charles II. In the eighteenth century Christopher Smart omits the episode altogether in *A Song to David* (1763), a poem which celebrates David as the ideal poet in composing the Psalms, 'the great Author of The Book of Gratitude'. To Smart, David is 'the minister of praise at large', the poet of divine praise.

And so for our next excerpts we move into the nineteenth century, turning to two novelists, the American Nathaniel Hawthorne and the English Thomas Hardy. In *The Scarlet Letter*, Hawthorne introduces the story of David and Bathsheba with prospective irony as it forms part of the wall decorations on tapestries in the apartment of the young clergyman Arthur Dimmesdale. Thus David's adultery casts a long shadow over a life which bears the terrible secret of Dimmesdale's liaison with the beautiful Hester Prynne with its consequence in her social ostracism. Here again, Bathsheba is linked with Nathan the Prophet, though Hester makes Bathsheba a passionate, wronged woman who is prepared to suffer all things in order to protect her lover. Hester's Bathsheba is as sexually responsible as Dimmesdale's David in a love story which may be 'a tale of human frailty and sorrow', but is also a bitter commentary on society and its persecution of those who have broken none of Nature's laws.

Thomas Hardy, like Hawthorne, writes as a post-Romantic of the later nineteenth century, mentioning Bathsheba in two of his great Wessex novels. In *Tess of the D'Urbervilles* (1891), Angel Clare, Tess's estranged husband, reflects sadly after his desertion of his wife when he discovers her earlier seduction by Alec D'Urberville on 'the wife of Uriah being made a queen' and that he had judged Tess by the deed rather than by the will. Hardy's Tess, even more than Hawthorne's Hester, would present Bathsheba as 'a pure woman' (the sub-title of the novel), a child of nature seduced by a wicked man of the world, but one for whom there is no salvation or retrieval from her punishment by an unforgiving society. In his earlier novel, *Far From the Madding Crowd*, however, Hardy suggests a very different Bathsheba in his heroine who bears her name, Bathsheba Everdene. For as we first encounter her in the passage given here, Bathsheba appears as a haughty society beauty, careless of the effect her charms have on the rustic Gabriel Oak. Oak, of course, is no David, and responds to her indifference as 'vanity', and later in the novel this Bathsheba will have her share of trouble, partly because of her own weaknesses. In the end, however, there is no conclusion which binds her to her queenly role in order to ensure royal descent, but a lesson learnt and companionship with the stalwart Gabriel Oak, who admits when they are finally united that 'I've danced at your skittish heels, my beautiful Bathsheba, for many a long mile, and many a long day.' Finally, however, 'theirs was that substantial affection which arises (if any arises at all) when the two who are thrown together begin first by knowing the rougher sides of each others' character, and not the best till further on, the romance growing in the interstices of a mass of hard prosaic reality'.

But this nineteenth-century recovery of the character of Bathsheba has not prevailed in twentieth-century literature, where she is frequently portrayed as the helpless woman, as in Gladys Schmitt's novel *David the King*, or else as the *éminence grise* of earlier literature, but now translated into contemporary terms, as in Joseph Heller's (best known for his novel *Catch 22* [1961]) *God Knows*. With its narrator David himself, Heller's grimly comic narrative presents Bathsheba as a feisty, clever harridan who will stop at nothing to achieve her ambition for her son Solomon. In the extract given here, David describes Bathsheba as he first sees her bathing on her roof (cp. 2 Samuel 11: 2–3). In the final pages of the book, she leaves David to his younger concubine Abishag the Shunammite (see, 1 Kings 1: 1–4), ageing but still obsessed with the beauty which initially had attracted David to her. David asks for her in the language of the Song of Songs, and she replies with:

'I think I must have put on thirty pounds in just the past few weeks,' she answers with a pout, and turns partway around to show me. 'I don't know where it's come from, but you can see where it's gone. And I used to have such a magnificent ass, didn't I?'

The Bathsheba of the Swedish novelist Lindgren is less crude, but equally scheming. Initially the beautiful victim of David's seduction she claims a personhood which the biblical narrative never grants to her, eventually, after the death of the King, ruling the country for seven years, clearly to great effect, for 'during her time the army was equipped with horses and chariots from Erech of Shinar: four thousand horses'. In Lindgren's narrative, King David's final words are not the charge to Solomon, as in 1 Kings 2: 2–9, but to Bathsheba: 'You are perfection, Bathsheba. Your perfection is your greatest flaw.'

The Bathsheba who, in the Bible is hardly even a person in her own right, becomes in literature and Christian theology a complex and ambiguous figure. A final further word should be said of her place in the visual arts, and above all in the great and tragic portrait of Rembrandt (1606–69), now in the Louvre in Paris. Using his own mistress Hendrickje Stoffels as his model, Rembrandt offers us the Bathsheba whom David saw from the roof of his palace – beautiful, flawed and utterly tragic in her lost gaze. This painting of the late Renaissance is a far cry from the allegorical paintings of medieval art in which Bathsheba, as the bride of David, the antetype of Jesus, represents the church undergoing purification by cleansing, while the unfortunate Uriah is reduced to playing the role of the Devil from whom she is rescued. So theology justifies a nasty biblical episode. In modern times in the cinema, the 1951 film *David and Bathsheba* and the 1985 *King David* opt for an utterly sexist reading, preserving David's honour at Bathsheba's expense. She is made to look bad, while in the earlier film, Uriah is not even interested in her, being too busy with his business as a soldier and preferring battle to the bedroom.

—— **Literature** ——

The Gospel According to St Matthew

And David was the father of Solomon by the wife of Uriah.

George Peele, *The Love of King David and Fair Bathsabe* (1599)

Hot sun, cool fire, tempered with sweet air,
Black shade, fair nurse, shadow my white hair.
Shine, sun; burn, fire; breathe, air, and ease me;
Shadow, my sweet nurse, keep me from burning,
Make not my glad cause cause of mourning.
    Let not my beauty's fire
    Inflame unstaid desire,
    Nor pierce any bright eye
    That wandereth lightly.

Sir Thomas Wyatt, The Prologue to *Penitential Psalms* (1549)

Love to give law unto his subject hearts
Stood in the eyes of Barsabe the bright,
And in a look anon himself converts
Cruelly pleasant before King David's sight;
First dazed his eyes, and further forth he starts
With venomed breath, as softly as he might
Touched his senses, and overruns his bones
With creeping fire, sparpled for the nonce.

And when he saw that kindled was the flame,
The moist poison in his heart he lanced,
So that the soul did tremble with the same.
And in this brawl as he stood and tranced,
Yielding unto the figure and the frame
That those fair eyes had in his presence glanced,
The form that Love had printed in his breast
He honoreth as thing of things the best.

So that forgot the wisdom and forecast
(Which woes to realms when that these kings doth lack),

Forgetting eke God's majesty as fast,
Yea, and his own, forthwith he doth to make
Uriah to go into the field in haste,
Uriah I say, that was his idols make,
Under pretence of certain victory
For enemies' swords a ready prey to die.

Whereby he may enjoy her out of doubt
Whom more than God or himself he mindeth.
And after he had brought this thing about
And of that lust possessed himself, he findeth
That hath and doth reverse and clean turn out
    Kings from kingdoms, and cities undermineth:
    He blinded thinks this train so bold and close
    To blind all thing that nought it may disclose.

But Nathan hath spied out this treachery,
With rueful cheer and sets afore his face
The offence, outrage and injury
That he hath done to God, as in this case
By murder for to cloak adultery.
He showeth him eke from heaven the threats alas
So sternly sore, this prophet, this Nathan,
That all amazed this aged woeful man.

Like him that meets with horror and with fear
The heat doth straight forsake the limbs cold;
The color eke droopeth down from his cheer,
So doth he feel his fire manifold;
His heat, his lust and pleasure all in fear
Consume and waste, and straight his crown of gold,
His purple pall, his sceptre he lets fall,
And to the ground he throweth himself withal.

The pompous pride of state and dignity
Forthwith rebates repentant humbleness;
Thinner vile cloth than clotheth poverty
Doth scantly hide and clad his nakedness;
His fair hoar beard of reverent gravity
With ruffled hair, knowing his wickedness,
More like was he the selfsame repentance
Than stately prince of worldly governance.

His harp he taketh in hand to be his guide,
Wherewith he offereth his plaints his soul to save
That from his heart distils on every side,
Withdrawing him into a dark cave
Within the ground, wherein he might him hide,
Fleeing the light, as in a prison or grave:
In which as soon as David entered had
The dark horror did make his soul adrad.

But he without prolonging or delay
Of that that might his Lord his God appease
   Fallth on his knees, and with his harp I say
   Afore his breast, fraughted with disease
   Of stormy sighs, his cheer coloured like clay,
   Dressed upright, seeking to counterpese
His song with sighs and touching of the strings
With tender heart, ... to God he sings.

John Dryden, *Absalom and Achitophel* (1681), lines 707–11

My Father, whom with reverence yet I name,
Charm'd into Ease, is careless of his Fame:
And, brib'd with petty summs of Forreign Gold,
Is grown in *Bathsheba's* Embraces old:
Exalts his Enemies, his Friends destroys:
And all his pow'r against himself employs.

Thomas Hardy, *Far From the Madding Crowd* (1874)

Oak looked from one to the other of the disputants, and fell into a reverie. There was something in the tone of twopence remarkably insignificant. Threepence had a definite value as money – it was an appreciable infringement on a day's wages, and, as such, a higgling matter; but twopence – 'Here,' he said, stepping forward and handing twopence to the gate-keeper; 'let the young woman pass.' He looked up at her then; she heard his words, and looked down.

Gabriel's features adhered throughout their form so exactly to the middle line between the beauty of St. John and the ugliness of Judas Iscariot, as represented in a window of the church he attended, that not a single lineament could be selected and called worthy either of distinction or notoriety. The red-jacketed and dark-haired maiden seemed to think so too, for she carelessly glanced over him, and told her man to drive on. She might have looked her thanks to Gabriel on a minute scale, but she did not speak them; more probably she felt none, for in gaining her a passage he had lost her her point, and we know how women take a favour of that kind.

The gatekeeper surveyed the retreating vehicle. 'That's a handsome maid,' he said to Oak.

'But she has her faults,' said Gabriel.

'True, farmer.'

'And the greatest of them is – well, what it is always.'

'Beating people down? ay, 'tis so.'

'O no.'

'What, then?'

Gabriel, perhaps a little piqued by the comely traveller's indifference, glanced back to where he had witnessed her performance over the hedge, and said, 'Vanity.'

Nathaniel Hawthorne, *The Scarlet Letter* (1850), chapter 9

The motherly care of the good widow assigned to Mr. Dimmesdale a front apartment, with a sunny exposure, and heavy window-curtains to create a noontide shadow, when desirable. The walls were hung round with tapestry, said to be from the Gobelin looms, and, at all events, representing the Scriptural story of David and Bathsheba, and Nathan the Prophet, in colors still unfaded, but which made the fair woman of the scene almost as grimly picturesque as the woe-denouncing seer.

Joseph Heller, *God Knows* (1984)

So it came to pass in an eveningtide after Joab had been dispatched into Ammon that I arose from off my bed to avoid another servant from her bearing another mortifying communication of discontent. I hastened upstairs to my roof for some peace and to escape the baking heat inside. And I saw this luscious woman washing herself on her roof less than a bowshot away and eyeing me without modesty as she saw me regarding her. She was as naked as a jaybird and not afraid. I was impressed by that. She was not ashamed of the female form she presented or of my arrogant scrutiny, and the woman was indeed very beautiful to look upon. In fact, she even turned herself toward me a bit more to allow me a better frontal view of her plump belly and thick mons veneris. I will not deny I was attracted. Deep was calling unto deep when our gazes met and remained resolutely locked . . .

She was always libidinous, always ready, like the truest of pagans. No pause for her periods, no time out for pregnancies. Other than during her actual confinements, I don't think a day went by that we didn't fall to it, till the time came to pass that we had Solomon and she decided she no longer wanted to. Who can tell what happened? She lost her lust when she embraced motherhood and settled on her true vocation, her life's work: to be a queen mother. Now, of course, it's to be a queen mother and save her life.

Torgny Lindgren, *Bathsheba* (1984), tr. from the Swedish by Tom Geddes, Collins Harvill, 1988

Bathsheba had seen the prophet go in to the King. When he came out of the King's room she was waiting for him. She was alone; only the two guards on the door were standing there with their long spears, but they appeared almost non-existent in their immobility, hardly seeming even to breathe.

'What have you said to him?' whispered Bathsheba anxiously.

'I have told him the truth,' said Nathan.

'The truth?'

'Yes, the truth.'

'And what is the truth?'

'That he has Uriah's blood on his hands. That he had your husband killed.'

'We all have someone's blood on our hands,' said Bathsheba, and it sounded almost as if it were herself she was excusing. 'And after all he is a king.'

'Even a king should be just,' the prophet explained, in a gentle voice as if he were talking to a child.

And Bathsheba pondered his words.

'I think,' she said at last, 'I think that the kingly and the human are irreconcilable. A true king cannot also be a human being. And anyone who chooses to be merely human cannot rule over other human beings.'

'We are all human,' said Nathan. 'Some are chosen. It is as simple as that.'

'Can the chosen ones defend themselves against being chosen?'

'Everyone wants to be chosen,' Nathan replied. 'Everyone is eager to be chosen and anointed. That is how God has made us. We rush forward headlong, blinded by our desire to be held by His hand.'

'The King too?'

'Yes, David too.'

'If God has created him thus, then God bears the guilt,' said Bathsheba, speaking very softly and carefully.

'God has also created us to be punished,' the prophet explained. 'If mankind did not exist, God's scourge would whistle through empty space.'

'Uriah's suffering is over,' Bathsheba whispered. 'He is tormented no more. I had almost forgotten him.'

'And you have been stolen by David. You are stolen property. You are a treasure he stole from an innocent victim.'

'Can God not feel compassion?'

'God is a creator. If it is absolutely necessary He will create compassion.'

Bathsheba stood for a long time in silence. Then she cried out, not seeming to notice that the guards and perhaps even the King could hear her, 'Stolen property! Treasure! I am a living person! The Spirit of God is in me too! I rushed headlong towards the hand that held me!'

Bibliography

Bal, Mieke. *Reading 'Rembrandt': Beyond the Word-Image Opposition*. (Cambridge: CUP, 1991), pp. 219–46, on Rembrandt's *Bathsheba's Bath*.

Exum, J. Cheryl. *Plotted, Shot and Painted: Cultural Representations of Biblical Women* (Sheffield: Sheffield Academic Press, 1996), chap. 1, 'Bathsheba Plotted, Shot and Painted'.

Hertzberg, H. W. *I and II Samuel: A Commentary*, tr. J. S. Bowden, Old Testament Library (London: SCM, 1964).

Kermode, Frank. *Poetry, Narrative, History*. The Bucknell Lectures in Literary Theory (Oxford: Basil Blackwell, 1990), chap. 2, 'New Ways with Bible Stories'.

Sternberg, Meir. *The Poetics of Biblical Narrative: Ideological Literature and the Drama of Reading* (Bloomington: Indiana University Press, 1987), chap. 6, 'Gaps, Ambiguity and the Reading Process'.

— The Still Small Voice —
1 Kings 19: 8–13

[8] And he arose, and did eat and drink, and went in the strength of that meat forty days and forty nights unto Horeb the mount of God.

[9] And he came thither unto a cave, and lodged there; and, behold, the word of the LORD came to him, and he said unto him, What doest thou here, Elijah?

[10] And he said, I have been very jealous for the LORD God of hosts: for the children of Israel have forsaken thy covenant, thrown down thine altars, and slain thy prophets with the sword; and I, even I only, am left; and they seek my life, to take it away.

[11] And he said, Go forth, and stand upon the mount before the LORD. And, behold, the LORD passed by, and a great and strong wind rent the mountains, and brake in pieces the rocks before the LORD; but the LORD was not in the wind: and after the wind an earthquake; but the LORD was not in the earthquake:

[12] And after the earthquake a fire; but the LORD was not in the fire: and after the fire a still small voice.

[13] And it was so, when Elijah heard it, that he wrapped his face in his mantle, and went out, and stood in the entering in of the cave. And, behold, there came a voice unto him, and said, What doest thou here, Elijah?

Notes

Verse 8. 'Forty days and forty nights': a conventional phrase for 'a long time' and part of the semi-mythical framing of the whole story.

'Horeb' by tradition was another name for Sinai the traditional 'mountain of the Lord' where Moses had, long before, encountered God at the burning bush.

Verse 10. 'the children of Israel have forsaken thy covenant...' After the rout and slaughter of the prophets of Baal (1 Kings 18: 17–40) Jezebel, the Queen, has sent Elijah a message: 'So let the gods do to me, and more also, if I make not thy life as the life of one of them by tomorrow about this time.' Note that here, however, Elijah does not refer to the immediate circumstances that have put him on the run, and he mentions neither his triumph over the pagan priests, nor the consequent death threats – which, since he was, in effect, given twenty-four hours to leave town, were clearly designed to exile rather than kill. In fact, to increase his own victimization, he inverts the immediate events, saying that it is the priests of Yahweh who have been slain.

—— **Commentary** ——

The story of Elijah's theophany before the cave is given a very specific setting. After the rout of the prophets of Baal, Jezebel, the Queen, has threatened his life, and Elijah, believing himself to be the sole survivor of the faithful, has fled to Horeb. The full force of what follows depends on our recognizing it also as Sinai, the traditional 'mountain of the Lord' where Moses himself had encountered God before the burning bush. Elijah has now come with certain expectations precisely because of that sense of history that was, in Israel, distinctively the mark of the men of God. Before the assembled prophets of Baal he had already vindicated Yahweh – the God who had traditionally manifested his power in fire – by the most spectacular pyrotechnics yet. Now he awaits some further revelation or instruction.

The disconfirmation that follows is the more unexpected. He is indeed treated to a more spectacular display of natural violence than ever, but Yahweh is *not* a fire God. His presence, when at last it is revealed, is experienced as something mysteriously apart from the world of natural phenomena that had been in such convulsions. Instead, Elijah's own categories are challenged. What comes is a simple question: 'What doest thou here, Elijah?' He had come with certain confident assumptions – which are now systematically overthrown. To begin with his own report turns out to be incorrect: there are, apparently, yet seven thousand in Israel who have not bowed the knee to Baal. He is told to return and help to organize what amounts to nothing less than two separate *coups d'état*. Hazael is to be anointed king of Syria, and Jehu king of Israel. History is yet again to be shaped by revelation, just as long before, Moses had been sent back from Horeb to lead his people out of Egypt. Finally – and ominously – Elijah is ordered to appoint his own successor.

At every level the ambiguous discontinuity persists. Any attempt at 'explaining' the contrast between the natural phenomena and the mysterious 'voice of thin silence' that can only be represented in language by the contradiction of an oxymoron, is in danger of losing that sense of an immediate but unstated connection between the two that is emphasized even by the very act of dissociation. Yahweh is not a fire god – nor one of winds and earthquakes, although wind had always been the traditional symbol of the spirit – yet from whom, if not from him, did these things come? Moreover, how are we to interpret this story? Is what is being described a 'miracle' (in our modern sense of an apparent suspension of the laws of nature) as we are encouraged to think of Moses' encounter with the burning bush, or is it rather a 'vision' – in the same category perhaps as Isaiah's vision of the Lord in the temple when he, too, is purged by fire? The whole effect of Elijah's experience seems to be to deny, *and yet* simultaneously affirm certain connections. Thus Yahweh *is*, and *is not*, a god of nature (a paradox more familiar to us under the much later theological notions of immanence and transcendence); revelation is both 'natural' and 'miraculous'; God is concerned both with the fate of the individual and with the shaping of history. The story seems to insist that at each level of understanding these modes are at once completely discontinuous and yet inseparable. Something utterly new and beyond human experience is being called into being for the first time in language.

Our text here is taken from the King James Bible (or Authorized Version) precisely because it is the only English translation to express the ambiguity of the original. The most literal English translation of the Hebrew words for what the prophet hears after the noisy exhibitionism of the earthquake, the wind, and the fire would be 'a voice of thin silence'. Given that in Elizabethan English 'small' could still mean 'thin' (as in Wyatt's description of his beloved's arms as 'long and small') the Authorized Version's 'still small voice' is a remarkably accurate rendering of the original. No modern translation has been willing to face the sheer *peculiarity* of what is going on here. All these versions have, instead, attempted to provide a naturalistic gloss. The Good News Bible has 'the soft whisper of a voice'; the New English Bible 'a low murmuring sound'; the Revised English Bible 'a faint murmuring sound'; the Jerusalem Bible 'the sound of a gentle breeze'.

Yet ancient Hebrew had no word for (and therefore no concept of) 'nature'. The normal progression of the seasons was seen as being as divinely instigated as the whirlwind that (we are told) whisked Elijah to Heaven. As a result there could be no concept of the miraculous either. The whole relationship between humanity and the environment was experienced in a way fundamentally different from ours. What is struggling to inarticulate and painful birth in this strange story of the prophet's failure is nothing less than the long revolution in ideas that was eventually to allow us to distinguish 'wind' from 'spirit', natural fire from Pentecostal, and the shaking of the earth from the shaking of the foundations. Here we see the primitive world of primal participation, in which neither the concept of the 'natural', nor, consequently, the concept of the 'divine' could exist, in the act of giving way to a world where science and religion were possible for the first time.

—— Literature ——

Dante, *The Divine Comedy*, 'Purgatory', Canto XXXII, line 72 (Beatrice to Dante)

Surgi: che fai? [What doest thou here?]

St John of the Cross, 'Living Flame of Love', Stanza II, 16, *The Complete Works of St John of the Cross*, tr. and ed. E. Allison Peers, Burns and Oates, 1964, Vol. III

Oh delicate touch of the Word, delicate, yea wonderously delicate, to me, which, having overthrown the mountains and broken the stones in Mount Horeb with the shadow of Thy power and strength that went before Thee, didst reveal thyself to the Prophet with the whisper of gentle air.

John Keble, *The Christian Year* (1827)

The raging Fire, the roaring Wind,
Thy boundless power display;
But in the gentler breeze we find
Thy spirit's viewless way.

John Greenleaf Whittier, 'Dear Lord and Father of Mankind'

(This 'hymn' is, in fact, an extract from a much longer poem by Whittier called 'The Brewing of Soma' – about a drug used in Indian religious rituals described in Max Müller's *Sacred Books of the East*. As a Quaker, Whittier saw all the sensual accompaniments of worship – from incense to music – as the Christian equivalents of soma.)

Drop Thy still dews of quietness,
  Till all our strivings cease;
Take from our souls the strain and stress
And let our ordered lives confess
  The beauty of Thy peace.

Breathe through the heats of our desire
  Thy coolness and Thy balm;
Let sense be dumb, let flesh retire;
Speak through the earthquake, wind and fire,
  O still small voice of calm!

G. K. Chesterton, 'The Surrender of a Cockney', *Alarms and Discursions* (1910)

I have always maintained, quite seriously, that the Lord is not in the wind or the thunder of the waste, but, if anywhere, in the still small voice of Fleet Street.

David Schubert, 'A Successful Summer'

The still small voice unto
My still small voice, I listen.
Hardly awake, I breathe, vulnerably,
As in summer trees, the messages
Of telegraphed errands buzz along
July's contour of green.

Bibliography

Blake, William. 'A Vision of the Last Judgement', in *Complete Writings of William Blake*, ed. Geoffrey Keynes (Oxford: Oxford University Press, 1966), p. 611.
Nicholson, Norman. *The Old Man of the Mountains* (London: Faber, 1946).
Prickett, Stephen. 'Towards a Rediscovery of the Bible: The Problem of the Still Small Voice', in *Ways of Reading the Bible*, ed. Michael Wadsworth (Hassocks: Harvester, 1981), pp. 105–17.
Prickett, Stephen. *Words and 'the Word': Language, Poetics, and Biblical Interpretation* (Cambridge: Cambridge University Press, 1986).
Wiener, Aharon. *The Prophet Elijah in the Development of Judaism* (London: Routledge, 1978).

— THE LORD IS MY Shepherd —
PSALM 23

[1] The LORD is my shepherd; I shall not want.
[2] He maketh me to lie down in green pastures: he leadeth me beside the still waters.
[3] He restoreth my soul: he leadeth me in the paths of righteousness for his name's sake.
[4] Yea, though I walk through the valley of the shadow of death, I will fear no evil: for thou art with me; thy rod and thy staff they comfort me.
[5] Thou preparest a table before me in the presence of mine enemies: thou anointest my head with oil; my cup runneth over.
[6] Surely goodness and mercy shall follow me all the days of my life: and I will dwell in the house of the LORD for ever.

Notes

Verse 1. The image of God as shepherd is common in Israelite religion, and is taken into Christian imagery through the idea of Christ as the Good Shepherd, e.g. The Gospel of John 10.
Verse 2. 'Still waters'. The most likely reference is to waters that bring refreshment.
Verse 4. 'The valley of the shadow of death'. The sense is of a valley of total darkness, both literally and metaphorically. The idea is of the worst place imaginable.
Verse 5. The image shifts from the shepherd to one of a host and his guest. On festive days oils and perfumes were symbolic of rejoicing, and the arrival of a guest might also occasion such anointing.

Verse 6. 'I shall dwell'. This may also have the sense of returning repeatedly to the Temple in Jerusalem to worship and offer thanks.

—— **Commentary** ——

Psalm 23 is perhaps the most familiar of all the psalms, exquisitely translated in the King James Bible as reprinted here. The interpretation of the Hebrew original, however, is by no means clear. As a 'Psalm of David' its origins are probably cultic, indicated by the concluding reference to 'the house of the Lord', possibly in a context of thanksgiving in the Temple following victory over an enemy. Another suggestion is more individualistic, that is, refers to some acquittal or deliverance from the hand of an adversary, after which thanksgiving is offered in the form of a ritual meal.

Commentators are generally agreed on the antiquity of the psalm, dating it before the period of the exile in Babylon (c.586–538 BC). It is an expression of sublime trust in God, without the bitterness shown in so many of the psalms. Even in the darkest of times, God is present. Its six verses weave together three images of God, as the caring shepherd of his sheep, as the gracious host at a banquet, and as the guide of the wanderer (verses 3–4). In addition, verse 4 contains what has become one of the most powerful images in English literature, largely through its dramatic presence in John Bunyan's *The Pilgrim's Progress*, that of 'the valley of the shadow of death'. The phrase 'shadow of death' (in Hebrew *salmawet*) is quite common in the Hebrew Bible (see also Job 3: 5; Psalm 107: 10; Isaiah 9: 2), and a later Rabbinic midrash describes the valley of Psalm 23 as alluding 'to chastisement in Gehenna, whose fire God will cool for me'. Gehenna is, in later Jewish thought, the equivalent of hell – a place for the punishment of the sinful, and so the midrash makes Psalm 23 a reference to a kind of purgatory, a time in Gehenna from which God will release the individual under his protection.

What in English have come to be called *Psalms* are usually entitled in Hebrew *Tehillion* or 'Praises' (the word is from the same root as 'hallelujah'), even though many psalms are in fact laments, supplications or complaints. As a hymn of faith and contentment Psalm 23 is a gem. It was quickly taken into Christian literature in the early Church Fathers like Irenaeus (c.130–c.200 CE), for whom verse 4 was read as a reference to the redeeming work of Christ. It secured its place in English literature through the magnificent translation of Miles Coverdale, printed here, and which is preserved in use to this day through the inclusion of Coverdale's Psalter in the English *Book of Common Prayer* of 1662, which is still in daily use in the worship of the Church of England. By way of comparison we have also included the almost 'metrical' version by Thomas Sternhold, who jointly with John Hopkins produced a versified translation of the psalms which, though lacking in literary merit was hugely popular in church worship because its rhythms were simple and it was easy to sing and remember. The metrical versions of the psalms have survived in worship for these reasons.

At a much higher level of literature, it seems very likely that William Shakespeare was thinking of Coverdale's translation of Psalm 23, which he would have known from the Prayer Books of Archbishop Thomas Cranmer, in the scene in *Henry V* where the death of Falstaff is recounted. Mrs Quickly vehemently denies that the old reprobate knight is in hell, for on his deathbed he 'babbled of green fields' – the land of content under the protection of God, promised in verse 2. From a psalm so well known in Anglican worship, such resonances would have been immediately powerful and familiar.

Later in the seventeenth century, George Herbert's beautiful version of the psalm remains a popular hymn to this day. It is quite simple, yet profound, especially the last verse which expands the sixth verse of the psalm. In the second line the word 'measure' suggests a number of meanings – God's love will provide the rhythm or measure of every day of our lives, and will last the full measure or length of life itself. In the third line, the word 'remove' speaks of both God's permanent love for us and our ceaseless praise of him as we 'dwell in the house of the Lord for ever'. By contrast, the version of the Counter-Reformation poet Richard Crashaw is tediously and redundantly prolix, an example of English metrical psalmody at its worst. Unlike Herbert's delicate expansions of the spirit of the psalm, Crashaw's poem adds little, despite its great length, and loses all the economic beauty of the original's images.

The greatest and best known of all references to Psalm 23 in English literature is in Bunyan's allegory *The Pilgrim's Progress*. It is a dramatic enactment of the central image of the Valley of the Shadow of Death through which Christian travels on a narrow pathway to the accompaniment of 'a continual howling and yelling, as of a people under unutterable misery'. Here it was that King David himself fell – a reference no doubt to his encounter with Bathsheba and chastisement by the prophet Nathan (2 Samuel 12), which concludes with the assurance that 'The Lord also has put away your sin' (verse 13). In the Valley, Christian is finally comforted by a voice singing verse 4 of the psalm. Later on in their journey, Christian and his companion Hopeful are refreshed in a meadow which is 'green all the year long' beside the River of the Water of Life, enacting the comfort offered in verse 2 of the psalm.

Of the numerous verse translations of Psalm 23 which have survived in English hymnody, one of the most interesting is by the Victorian High Anglican Henry Williams Baker. Baker combines the ancient imagery with references to the liturgical practices of the Oxford Movement in the Church of England: the table of verse 5, which probably originates in the Temple worship of Jerusalem, becomes here an altar prepared for the Eucharist. The oil of anointment becomes the 'unction' – the oil used to anoint in High Church practice ('extreme unction' is the practice of anointing the dying with holy oil) through which the grace of God flows. The 'cup' is here the 'chalice', that is, the vessel used in the Eucharist to hold the consecrated wine. Thus Psalm 23 has become a vehicle within Tractarian worship. A further point to notice in verse 3 of the poem is Baker's incorporation into his translation of another biblical reference, from the New Testament, to the Parable of the Lost Sheep (Luke 15: 3–7), linking the loving shepherd of the Old Testament psalm with the shepherd of Jesus's story, who pursues the wanderer and brings it back to safety.

We have taken two examples of references to the psalm in contemporary fiction, both from novels which retell biblical narratives. In the first, which we have drawn on earlier in the section on David and Bathsheba, Joseph Heller's *God Knows*, King David is the testy narrator of a discussion he has with Bathsheba on the question of the authorship of the psalms. One recent commentator on the 'Psalms of David', the poet and critic Donald Davie, has defended the poetic, if not the historical, validity of ascribing these hymns to David himself:

But let not the ascription of the psalms to David be dismissed as ecclesiastical fabrication, so much mumbo-jumbo. David is certainly as much a composite author as, so recent opinion tells us, Homer. But David, as king and poet (also musician, also dancer, also army-commander and adulterer), has an emblematic significance beyond that of Homer, powerful as the emblem of Homer's blindness. It was – the historical evidence points in no other direction – the fiction of David as author of the psalms that ensured for these compositions a formal integrity that persisted through many centuries.

But Heller's David finds his match in the feisty Bathsheba. In this version, she is the author of this greatest of all psalms, and David is too feeble a literary critic to recognize the strengths and beauties of it. His literal mindedness destroys the brevity and subtle suggestiveness of the great images. For the Valley of the Shadow of Death is powerful precisely because it means either the darkness of the moment of death, or the shadow which follows us every day of our mortal existence – that we live 'under the shadow of death'.

One phrase in Heller's narrative, 'We're not sheep', resonates also in the opening words of Howard Jacobson's novel *The Very Model of a Man*, in which the narrator is another figure from the Hebrew Bible, the character of Cain, who murdered his brother Abel (Genesis 4: 1–16). Cain looks forward to the yet-unwritten psalm, and admits that in the experience of the first family (Cain and Abel were the children of Adam and Eve), life was as blessed as the psalm suggests – 'had we been sheep'. But instead, human beings are complex and self-assertive, and in Cain's case, with needs that cannot be fulfilled by the idyllic promises of the psalmist.

Nevertheless, Psalm 23 has remained central in both Jewish and Christian worship and faith. And so we end with a passage from a modern American Jewish poet John Hollander, written in a collection of essays by contemporary Jewish writers and scholars entitled *Congregation: Contemporary Writers Read the Jewish Bible*. It illustrates the durability of the poem through Hebrew into various English versions, above all the version of the King James Bible, and its poetic effect, even when the 'correct' meaning is lost, as in the case of the young child who heard verse 6 as an assurance of the comforting presence of 'good Mrs. Murphy'. Even in mistranslation and misinterpretation, the peculiar power of the psalm survives, often especially when the pedantic demands of scholars and adults are set aside in the innocent mind and imagination of the child.

Literature

Miles Coverdale, 'The Twenty Third Psalm' (1535)

1. The Lord is my shepherd: therefore can I lack nothing.
2. He shall feed me in a green pasture: and lead me forth beside the waters of comfort.
3. He shall convert my soul: and bring me forth in the paths of righteousness, for his name's sake.
4. Yea, though I walk through the valley of the shadow of death, I will fear no evil: for thou art with me; thy rod and thy staff comfort me.
5. Thou shalt prepare a table before me against them that trouble me: thou hast anointed my head with oil, and my cup shall be full.
6. But thy loving-kindness and mercy shall follow me all the days of my life: and I will dwell in the house of the Lord for ever.

Thomas Sternhold, 'Psalm 23' (1565)

My shepherd is the living Lord,
    nothing therefore I need;
In pastures fair with waters calm
    he sets me forth to feed.
He did convert and glad my soul,
    and brought my mind in frame,
To walk in paths of righteousness,
    for his most holy Name

Yea, though I walk in the vale of death,
    yet will I fear none ill:
Thy rod, thy staff doth comfort me,
    and thou art with me still.
And in the presence of my foes
    my table thou shalt spread:
Thou shalt, O Lord, fill full my cup,
and eke anoint my head.

Through all my life thy favour is
    so frankly shew'd to me,
That in thy house for evermore
    my dwelling-place shall be.

William Shakespeare, *Henry V* (1599), Act 2, Scene 3

HOSTESS: Nay sure he's not in hell: he's in Arthur's bosom, if ever a man went to Arthur's bosom: a' made a finer end, and went away an it had been any Christom child: a' parted e'en just between twelve and one, e'en at the turning o'th'tide: for after I saw him fumble with the sheets, and play with flowers, and smile upon his finger's end, I knew there was but one way: for his nose was as sharp as a pen, and a' babbled of green fields. 'How now, Sir John?' quoth I. 'What, man! be o' good cheer': so a' cried out, 'God, God, God!' three or four times: now I, to comfort him, bid him a' should not think of God; I hope there was no need to trouble himself with any such thoughts yet: so a' bade me lay more clothes on his feet: I put my hand into the bed, and felt them, and they were as cold as any stone: then I felt to his knees, and so up'ard, and all was as cold as any stone.

George Herbert, 'Psalm 23' (1633)

The God of love my shepherd is,
    And he that doth me feed;
While he is mine, and I am his,
    What can I want or need?

He leads me to the tender grass,
    Where I both feed and rest;
Then to the streams that gently pass:
    In both I have the best.

Or if I stray, he doth convert,
    And bring my mind in frame;
And all this not for my desert
    But for his holy name.

Yea, in death's shady black abode
    Well may I walk, not fear;
For thou art with me, and thy rod
    To guide, thy staff to bear.

Nay, thou dost make me sit and dine
    E'en in my enemies' sight;
My head with oil, my cup with wine
    Runs over day and night.

Surely thy sweet and wondrous love
    Shall measure all my days;
And as it never shall remove,
    So neither shall my praise.

Richard Crashaw, 'Psalm 23' (1648)

Happy me! O happy sheep!
Whom my God vouchsafes to keep;
Even my God, even he it is
That points me to these ways of bliss;
On whose pastures cheerful Spring
All the year doth sit and sing,
And rejoicing smiles to see
Their green backs wear his livery:

Pleasure sings my soul to rest,
Plenty wears me at her breast,
Whose sweet temper teaches me
Nor wanton nor in want to be.
At my feet the blubb'ring Mountain
Weeping melts into a Fountain,
Whose soft silver-seating streams
Make high noon forget his beams:
When my wayward breath is flying
He calls home my soul from dying,
Strokes and tames my rabid grief,
And dost woo me into life:
When my simple weakness strays
(Tangled in forbidden ways)
He (my shepherd) is my guide,
He's before me, on my side,
And behind me, he beguiles
Craft in all her knotty wiles:
He expounds the giddy wonder
Of my weary steps, and under
Spreads a Path as clear as Day,
Where no churlish rub says nay
To my joy-conducted feet,
Whilst they gladly go to meet
Grace and Peace, to meet new lays
Tun'd to my great Shepherd's praise.
Come now, all ye terrors, sally,
Muster forth into the valley
Where triumphant darkness hovers
With a sable wing that covers
Brooding horror. Come thou, Death,
Let the damps of thy dull Breath
Overshadow even the shade
And make darkness self-afraid;
There my feet, even there, shall find
Way for a resolvèd mind.
Still my Shepherd, still my God
Thou art with me, still thy Rod
And thy staff, whose influence
Gives direction, gives defence.
At the whisper of thy word
Crown'd abundance spreads my board;

While I feast, my foes do feed
Their rank malice, not their need,
So that with the self-same bread
They are starv'd and I am fed.
How my head in ointment swims!
How my cup o'erlooks her brims!
So, even so, still may I move
By the Line of thy dear love;
Still may thy sweet mercy spread
A shady arm above my head
About my Paths, so shall I find
The fair centre of my mind
The Temple, and those lovely walls
Bright ever with a beam that falls
Fresh from the pure glance of thine eye,
Lighting to eternity.
There I'll dwell, for ever there
Will I find a purer air
To feed my life with, there I'll sup
Balm and nectar in my cup,
And thence my ripe soul will I breathe
Warm into the Arms of Death.

John Bunyan, *The Pilgrim's Progress* (1678)

Now at the end of this Valley was another, called the Valley of the Shadow of Death, and Christian must needs go through it, because the way to the Celestial City lay through the midst of it. Now, this Valley is a very solitary place. The Prophet Jeremiah thus describes it: A wilderness, a land of deserts and of pits, a land of drought, and of the shadow of death, a land that no man (but a Christian) passeth through, and where no man dwelt.

Now here Christian was worse put to it than in his fight with Apollyon, as by the sequel you shall see.

I saw then in my Dream, that when Christian was got to the borders of the Shadow of Death, there met him two men, Children of them that brought up an evil report of the good land, making haste to go back; to whom Christian spake as follows, –

CHR: Whither are you going?

MEN: They said, Back, back; and we would have you to do so too, if either life or peace is prized by you.

CHR: Why, what's the matter? said Christian.

MEN: Matter! said they; we were going that way as you are going, and went as far as we durst; and indeed we were almost past coming back; for had we gone a little farther, we had not been here to bring the news to thee.

CHR: But what have you met with? said Christian.

MEN: Why we were almost in the Valley of the Shadow of Death; but that by good hap we looked before us, and saw the danger before we came to it.

CHR: But what have you seen? said Christian.

MEN: Seen! Why, the Valley itself, which is as dark as pitch; we also saw there the Hobgoblins, Satyrs, and Dragons of the Pit; we heard also in that Valley a continual howling and yelling, as of a people under unutterable misery, who there sat bound in affliction and irons; and over that Valley hangs the discouraging clouds of Confusion; Death also doth always spread his wings over it. In a word it is every whit dreadful, being utterly without Order.

...The pathway was here also exceeding narrow, and therefore good Christian was the more put to it; for when he sought in the dark to shun the Ditch on the one hand, he was ready to tip over into the mire on the other; also when he sought to escape the mire, without great carefulness he would be ready to fall into the Ditch. Thus he went on, and I heard him here sigh bitterly; for, besides the dangers mentioned above, the pathway was here so dark, that oft-times, when he lift up his foot to set forward, he knew not where, or upon what he should set it next.

Poor man! Where art thou now? Thy Day is Night.
Good man be not cast down, thou yet art right:
Thy way to Heaven lies by the gates of Hell;
Cheer up, hold out, with thee it shall go well.

About the midst of this valley, I perceived the mouth of Hell to be, and it stood also hard by the wayside. Now, thought Christian, what shall I do? And ever and anon the flame and smoke would come out in such abundance, with sparks and hideous noises (things that cared not for Christian's Sword, as did Apollyon before) that he was forced to put up his Sword, and betake himself to another weapon, called All-prayer. So he cried in my hearing, O Lord I beseech thee deliver my Soul. Thus he went on a great while, yet still the flames would be reaching towards him: also he heard doleful voices, and rushings to and fro, so that sometimes he thought he should be torn in pieces, or trodden down like mire in the

Streets. This frightful sight was seen, and these dreadful noises were heard by him for several miles together; and coming to a place where he thought he heard a company of Fiends coming forward to meet him he stopped, and began to muse what he had best to do. Sometimes he had half a thought to go back, then again he thought he might be half way through the Valley; he remembered also how he had already vanquished many a danger, and that the danger of going back might be much more than for to go forward; so he resolved to go on. Yet the Fiends seemed to come nearer and nearer; but when they were come even almost at him, he cried out with a most vehement voice, I will walk in the strength of the Lord God; so they gave back, and came no farther.

One thing I would not let slip; I took notice that now poor Christian was so confounded that he did not know his own voice; and thus I perceived it: just when he was come over against the mouth of the burning Pit, one of the wicked ones got behind him, and stepped up softly to him, and whisperingly suggested many grievous blasphemies to him, which he verily thought had proceeded from his own mind. This put Christian more to it than anything that he met with before, even to think that he should now blaspheme him that he loved so much before; yet, if he could have helped it, he would not have done it; but he had not the discretion neither to stop his ears, nor to know from whence those blasphemies came.

When Christian had travelled in this disconsolate condition some considerable time, he thought he heard the voice of a man, as going before him, saying, Though I walk through the Valley of the Shadow of Death, I will fear none ill, for thou art with me.

Henry Williams Baker, 'Psalm 23' (1868)

The King of love my shepherd is,
    Whose goodness faileth never;
I nothing lack if I am his
    And he is mine for ever.

Where streams of living water flow
    My ransomed soul he leadeth,
And where the verdant pastures grow
    With food celestial feedeth.

Perverse and foolish oft I strayed,
    But yet in love he sought me,
And on his shoulder gently laid,
    And home, rejoicing, brought me.

PSALM 23

In death's dark vale I fear no ill
　　With thee, dear Lord, beside me;
Thy rod and staff my comfort still,
　　Thy cross before to guide me.

Thou spread'st a table in my sight;
　　Thy unction grace bestoweth;
And oh, what transport of delight
　　From thy pure chalice floweth!

And so through all the length of days
　　Thy goodness faileth never;
Good Shepherd, may I sing thy praise
　　Within thy house for ever.

Joseph Heller, *God Knows* (1984)

I was impressed. 'Where'd you find that piece of wisdom?'

'I made it up. I'm into proverbs now.'

'No more psalms?'

'You told me I was rotten at them.'

I was pleased at having chased her out of that field of creative endeavor in record time; it annoyed me that she thought she could toss them off with her left hand.

'Psalms don't even have to rhyme,' she had told me.

'The Lord is my shepherd,' I had scoffed when she showed me her first effort. 'Are you crazy? How fantastic can you get? That's crap, Bathsheba, pure crap. Where's your sense of metaphor? You're turning God into a labourer and your audience into animals. That's practically blasphemy. Shall I not want what? You're raising questions instead of answering them. At least change it to "won't" and save a syllable. You think all of mine are much too long?'

'Some are masterpieces,' she stated calmly, 'but, like everything else you write, they're flawed by excessive length.'

That cheeky, patronizing bitch. '"Won't want" is better.' I kept my temper and remained objective. 'He maketh no one to lie down in green pastures, either. Where did you ever get a grotesque idea like that?'

'Didn't you ever sleep outdoors?'

'Only when I had to. And I felt no kindness toward the people who made me do it.'

'Sheep sleep outdoors.'

175

'We're not sheep. That's what's wrong with the whole concept. And here's another big error. Either "valley of death" or "shadow of death," not both. Not "walk through the valley of the shadow of death." Oh, give it up, Bathsheba, give it up. You don't have the head of it. You think writing psalms is snap? Go back to macramé.'

Howard Jacobson, *The Very Model of a Man* (1992)

1. Cain Remembers a Birthday

The Lord was our shepherd. We did not want. He fed us in green and fat pastures, and gave us to drink from deep waters, made us to lie in a good fold. That which was lost, He sought; that which was broken, He bound up; that which was driven away, he brought again into the flock. Excellent, excellent, had we been sheep.

There was no eluding His watchfulness. His solicitude lodged with us, His voice stalked out movements and out thoughts.

John Hollander, 'Psalms', from David Rosenberg, ed., *Congregation: Contemporary Writers Read the Jewish Bible*, Harcourt Brace Jovanovich, 1987

For a long time there was only one psalm. I can still hear the tones of my father's voice identifying a puzzling string of utterances: 'That's the *twenty-third* psalm,' stressed just like that. It seemed the name of only one thing, and since I didn't know what the set 'psalm' comprised, the poem remained *sui generis*. By then I was just beginning to learn that what in the world was called 'The Bible' existed, in its Jewish part, in Hebrew (which I wasn't beginning to learn just yet). It would be some years before I could put together the cadences of the English Bible (the King James Version [KJV], sections of whose Psalms and Proverbs were still read aloud in public schools, to the unwitting profit of many of those who were bored by their recitation) with what went on in synagogue, occasionally 'on Sabbaths' and always 'on festivals.' Even though the language of the part of the liturgy that was recited in English (my family attended Conservative services) was usually a corrected pastiche of KJV English (whether translations of Torah, of *piyut*-liturgical-devotional poetry, or whatever), it would be decades before I would come to grasp the complex relations between the Hebrew Bible, the strange and powerful tendentious reading of it called the Old Testament, and the various vernacular translations.

For a modern reader, the language of KJV is inherently poetic primarily because of the relation between its high, condensed diction and the impenetrability of so much of its language, caused by semantic change since the early seventeenth century. I suppose that a poetic childhood consists in misunderstanding a good bit of what one hears and sees, in being too reticent to ask for the solution to puzzles of pattern and meaning which adults must know are silly, and in then resorting to one's own private versions of what was meant. (*Misconstruings* and *reconstructions*: these verbs for analysis and building are from the same Latin one.) And I suppose that the inability to put away such childish things may attune the attention to the still, small tones of a vocation. 'My knowledge was divine,' wrote a seventeenth-century English poet and parson; 'I knew by intuition those things which since my apostasy I collected again by the highest reason.' He was speaking of childhood's innocence generally, but with just enough of a specific epistemological interest to seem pre-Wordsworthian. And so it is, particularly with objects of language. The child in the American joke who innocently deforms Psalm 23's penultimate verse, assuring her adult listeners that 'Surely good Mrs. Murphy shall follow me all the days of my life,' will only learn with 'a later reason,' as Wallace Stevens called it, that she was getting *something* more profoundly right about the line, the psalm, and poetry in general than any of her correctly parroting schoolmates. For the 'mistake' personifies the 'goodness and mercy' – the *tov vachesed* of the Hebrew – as a beneficent pursuer (the Hebrew lines imply that they are the poet's only pursuers, dogging one's footsteps, perhaps, but never hounding). Good Mrs. Murphy following the child about like a beneficent nurse is a more viable, powerful homiletic reconstruction of what had otherwise faded into abstraction than any primer's glossing. The child rightly attended to the trope set up by the intense verb 'follow me' and supplied an appropriate subject for it, thereby turning mechanical allegory into poetic truth. Losing, in mature literacy, the ability to make such mistakes can mean being deaf and blind to the power of even the KJV text, let alone that of the Hebrew.

My own initial childhood contacts with Psalm 23 were full of small good-Mrs.-Murphys. 'I shall not want' – the intransitivity wasn't a problem so much as learning from this clause alone the older meaning 'lack' or 'need,' instead of the more colloquial American 'desire.' But perhaps the contemporary reader, who may not have these precise phrases and cadences by ear (is 'by heart' better?) – given that young persons are no longer required to memorize verse and prose at school, and that various insipidly 'corrected' versions have replaced KJV in all public institutions save those devoted to the study of literature – might be reminded at this point of the text:

Simply having the memorized text, possessing it without fully under-standing it, allows one's attention to caress its frequently opaque locutions and cadences. I suppose that I was introduced to trope by this psalm, as much as by any other poem: I knew that the authorial 'David,' the young harp-playing shepherd from my illustrated *Stories from the Bible*, didn't mean to say that he felt comfortable partially in *that* his cup was spilling onto the floor (a dreaded commonplace of the nursery). I knew that the line about the table and the enemies meant *something* beneficent, but couldn't figure out what. I didn't know what 'the house of the LORD' actually was (churches were 'houses of God,' but I knew synagogues weren't – I'd been taught that a *shut* was a place of assembly, a *bet haknesset*), but I fancied that it designated something very general. The 'paths of righteousness,' the 'valley of the shadow of death,' the 'house of the LORD' – I began to savor the rich ambiguity of those constructions which can indicate so many syntactic relations, possessive, instrumental, causative, attributive. It would be many years before I knew both enough Hebrew and enough about English to understand that the KJV's peculiar way of translating the Hebrew construct state led to all sorts of latent allegorizing. The paths of righteousness, what were they? Were they the paths that led to a place—alas, somewhat distant—called Righteousness? Were they the paths someone called Righteousness used to take, striding along on business or taking his ease, and where, with proper guidance, one might get to walk too? Were they the paths he still patrols? Were they paths across Righteousness's property or territory? Will these crooked, difficult paths, if one is led along them properly, make one righteous?

All these ambiguities characterizing that 'the X of Y' construction in the English came to feel Biblical for me. As I grew older, it kept appearing everywhere in the fabric of the poetical grammar of the English language. (It is amusing to note now how I could not know then that 'green pastures' and 'still waters' in that beautifully rhythmic couplet were moments of correct translation of the original, the *benot deshe* and the construct state of the *mei mnuchot*, 'grassy pastures' and 'tranquil streams,' which would ordinarily have become 'fields of verdure' and 'waters of tranquillity,' had the usual strategy been adopted.)

Again, the 'rod' and the 'staff' simply blended into some notional shepherd's crook for me (I didn't realize that the pastoral conceit had vanished by the third verse). Only after I knew the Hebrew – and knew something of the mysterious ways of the parallelistic line of Hebrew poetry, and how it works in far more than mere decoratively varied repetition – could I realize what the slight archaism of the English words had veiled. The 'rod' of 'spare the rod and spoil the child,' a proverb acquired a bit later on, and the staff (as 'cane,' 'alpenstock,' 'staff' of Father Time and of life, as bread in another commonplace) eventually did diverge into the complementary sticks of weapon and prop or support. Likewise, the cadential phrase 'for his name's sake,' which seemed only to make sense in its more usual role of expletive (often of parental annoyance – 'For God's sake, can't you...') combined with 'What in the name of God have you done with your...'), here played a strangely quiet, though darkly forceful, role. And again, only later learning would allow the less mysterious but conceptually plausible 'as befits his name,' for the *Ima'an sh'mo* of the original, to operate. But, as in any riddle, the solution effects a loss even as it enables gain, and the 'explanation' or 'answer' explodes fiction created by the enigma, and the literal triumphs in the end. So it is with the vanishing of all the good Mrs. Murphys with the coming of the dawn of learning.

Bibliography

Anderson, A. A. *The Book of Psalms*, Volume 1, New Century Bible (London: Oliphants, 1972).

Anders-Richards, Donald. *The Drama of the Psalms* (London: Darton, Longman and Todd, 1968).

Davie, Donald (ed.). *The Psalms in English*, Penguin Classics (Harmondsworth: Penguin, 1996).

Henn, T. R. *The Bible as Literature* (London: Lutterworth Press, 1970), ch. 8, 'A Note on the Psalms'.

Lewis, C. S. *Reflections on the Psalms* (1961. London: Fontana, 1972).

— I Am a Rose of Sharon —
The Song of Songs

Cant. 1

[1] The song of songs, which is Solomon's.

[2] Let him kiss me with the kisses of his mouth: for thy love is better than wine.

[3] Because of the savour of thy good ointments thy name is as ointment poured forth, therefore do the virgins love thee.

[4] Draw me, we will run after thee: the king hath brought me into his chambers: we will be glad and rejoice in thee, we will remember thy love more than wine: the upright love thee.

[5] I am black, but comely, O ye daughters of Jerusalem, as the tents of Kedar, as the curtains of Solomon.

[6] Look not upon me, because I am black, because the sun hath looked upon me: my mother's children were angry with me; they made me the keeper of the vineyards; but mine own vineyard have I not kept.

[7] Tell me, O thou whom my soul loveth, where thou feedest, where thou makest thy flock to rest at noon: for why should I be as one that turneth aside by the flocks of thy companions?

[8] If thou know not, O thou fairest among women, go thy way forth by the footsteps of the flock, and feed thy kids beside the shepherds' tents.

[9] I have compared thee, O my love, to a company of horses in Pharaoh's chariots.

[10] Thy cheeks are comely with rows of jewels, thy neck with chains of gold.

[11] We will make thee borders of gold with studs of silver.

[12] While the king sitteth at his table, my spikenard sendeth forth the smell thereof.

[13] A bundle of myrrh is my wellbeloved unto me; he shall lie all night betwixt my breasts.

[14] My beloved is unto me as a cluster of camphire in the vineyards of Engedi.

[15] Behold, thou art fair, my love; behold, thou art fair; thou hast doves' eyes.

[16] Behold, thou art fair, my beloved, yea, pleasant: also our bed is green.

[17] The beams of our house are cedar, and our rafters of fir.

Cant. 2

[1] I am the rose of Sharon, and the lily of the valleys.

[2] As the lily among thorns, so is my love among the daughters.

[3] As the apple tree among the trees of the wood, so is my beloved among the sons. I sat down under his shadow with great delight, and his fruit was sweet to my taste.

[4] He brought me to the banqueting house, and his banner over me was love.

[5] Stay me with flagons, comfort me with apples: for I am sick of love.

[6] His left hand is under my head, and his right hand doth embrace me.

[7] I charge you, O ye daughters of Jerusalem, by the roes, and by the hinds of the field, that ye stir not up, nor awake my love, till he please.

[8] The voice of my beloved! behold, he cometh leaping upon the mountains, skipping upon the hills.

[9] My beloved is like a roe or a young hart: behold, he standeth behind our wall, he looketh forth at the windows, shewing himself through the lattice.

[10] My beloved spake, and said unto me, Rise up, my love, my fair one, and come away.

[11] For, lo, the winter is past, the rain is over and gone;

[12] The flowers appear on the earth; the time of the singing of birds is come, and the voice of the turtle is heard in our land;

[13] The fig tree putteth forth her green figs, and the vines with the tender grape give a good smell. Arise, my love, my fair one, and come away.

[14] O my dove, that art in the clefts of the rock, in the secret places of the stairs, let me see thy countenance, let me hear thy voice; for sweet is thy voice, and thy countenance is comely.

[15] Take us the foxes, the little foxes, that spoil the vines: for our vines have tender grapes.

[16] My beloved is mine, and I am his: he feedeth among the lilies.

[17] Until the day break, and the shadows flee away, turn, my beloved, and be thou like a roe or a young hart upon the mountains of Bether.

Cant. 3

[1] By night on my bed I sought him whom my soul loveth: I sought him, but I found him not.

[2] I will rise now, and go about the city in the streets, and in the broad ways I will seek him whom my soul loveth: I sought him, but I found him not.

[3] The watchmen that go about the city found me: to whom I said, Saw ye him whom my soul loveth?

[4] It was but a little that I passed from them, but I found him whom my soul loveth: I held him, and would not let him go, until I had brought him into my mother's house, and into the chamber of her that conceived me.

[5] I charge you, O ye daughters of Jerusalem, by the roes, and by the hinds of the field, that ye stir not up, nor awake my love, till he please.

[6] Who is this that cometh out of the wilderness like pillars of smoke, perfumed with myrrh and frankincense, with all powders of the merchant?

[7] Behold his bed, which is Solomon's; threescore valiant men are about it, of the valiant of Israel.

[8] They all hold swords, being expert in war: every man hath his sword upon his thigh because of fear in the night.

[9] King Solomon made himself a chariot of the wood of Lebanon.

[10] He made the pillars thereof of silver, the bottom thereof of gold, the covering of it of purple, the midst thereof being paved with love, for the daughters of Jerusalem.

[11] Go forth, O ye daughters of Zion, and behold king Solomon with the crown wherewith his mother crowned him in the day of his espousals, and in the day of the gladness of his heart.

Cant. 4

[1] Behold, thou art fair, my love; behold, thou art fair; thou hast doves' eyes within thy locks: thy hair is as a flock of goats, that appear from mount Gilead.

[2] Thy teeth are like a flock of sheep that are even shorn, which came up from the washing; whereof every one bear twins, and none is barren among them.

[3] Thy lips are like a thread of scarlet, and thy speech is comely: thy temples are like a piece of a pomegranate within thy locks.

[4] Thy neck is like the tower of David builded for an armoury, whereon there hang a thousand bucklers, all shields of mighty men.

[5] Thy two breasts are like two young roes that are twins, which feed among the lilies.

[6] Until the day break, and the shadows flee away, I will get me to the mountain of myrrh, and to the hill of frankincense.

[7] Thou art all fair, my love; there is no spot in thee.

[8] Come with me from Lebanon, my spouse, with me from Lebanon: look from the top of Amana, from the top of Shenir and Hermon, from the lions' dens, from the mountains of the leopards.

[9] Thou hast ravished my heart, my sister, my spouse; thou hast ravished my heart with one of thine eyes, with one chain of thy neck.

[10] How fair is thy love, my sister, my spouse! how much better is thy love than wine! and the smell of thine ointments than all spices!

[11] Thy lips, O my spouse, drop as the honeycomb: honey and milk are under thy tongue; and the smell of thy garments is like the smell of Lebanon.

[12] A garden inclosed is my sister, my spouse; a spring shut up, a fountain sealed.

[13] Thy plants are an orchard of pomegranates, with pleasant fruits; camphire, with spikenard,

[14] Spikenard and saffron; calamus and cinnamon, with all trees of frankincense; myrrh and aloes, with all the chief spices:

[15] A fountain of gardens, a well of living waters, and streams from Lebanon.

[16] Awake, O north wind; and come, thou south; blow upon my garden, that the spices thereof may flow out. Let my beloved come into his garden, and eat his pleasant fruits.

Cant. 5

[1] I am come into my garden, my sister, my spouse: I have gathered my myrrh with my spice; I have eaten my honeycomb with my honey; I have drunk my wine with my milk: eat, O friends; drink, yea, drink abundantly, O beloved.

[2] I sleep, but my heart waketh: it is the voice of my beloved that knocketh, saying, Open to me, my sister, my love, my dove, my undefiled: for my head is filled with dew, and my locks with the drops of the night.

[3] I have put off my coat; how shall I put it on? I have washed my feet; how shall I defile them?

[4] My beloved put in his hand by the hole of the door, and my bowels were moved for him.

[5] I rose up to open to my beloved; and my hands dropped with myrrh, and my fingers with sweet smelling myrrh, upon the handles of the lock.

[6] I opened to my beloved; but my beloved had withdrawn himself, and was gone: my soul failed when he spake: I sought him, but I could not find him; I called him, but he gave me no answer.

[7] The watchmen that went about the city found me, they smote me, they wounded me; the keepers of the walls took away my veil from me.

[8] I charge you, O daughters of Jerusalem, if ye find my beloved, that ye tell him, that I am sick of love.

[9] What is thy beloved more than another beloved, O thou fairest among women? what is thy beloved more than another beloved, that thou dost so charge us?

[10] My beloved is white and ruddy, the chiefest among ten thousand.

[11] His head is as the most fine gold, his locks are bushy, and black as a raven.

[12] His eyes are as the eyes of doves by the rivers of waters, washed with milk, and fitly set.

[13] His cheeks are as a bed of spices, as sweet flowers: his lips like lilies, dropping sweet smelling myrrh.

[14] His hands are as gold rings set with the beryl: his belly is as bright ivory overlaid with sapphires.

[15] His legs are as pillars of marble, set upon sockets of fine gold: his countenance is as Lebanon, excellent as the cedars.

[16] His mouth is most sweet: yea, he is altogether lovely. This is my beloved, and this is my friend, O daughters of Jerusalem.

Cant. 6

[1] Whither is thy beloved gone, O thou fairest among women? whither is thy beloved turned aside? that we may seek him with thee.

[2] My beloved is gone down into his garden, to the beds of spices, to feed in the gardens, and to gather lilies.

[3] I am my beloved's, and my beloved is mine: he feedeth among the lilies.

[4] Thou art beautiful, O my love, as Tirzah, comely as Jerusalem, terrible as an army with banners.

[5] Turn away thine eyes from me, for they have overcome me: thy hair is as a flock of goats that appear from Gilead.

[6] Thy teeth are as a flock of sheep which go up from the washing, whereof every one beareth twins, and there is not one barren among them.

[7] As a piece of a pomegranate are thy temples within thy locks.

[8] There are threescore queens, and fourscore concubines, and virgins without number.

[9] My dove, my undefiled is but one; she is the only one of her mother, she is the choice one of her that bare her. The daughters saw her, and blessed her; yea, the queens and the concubines, and they praised her.

[10] Who is she that looketh forth as the morning, fair as the moon, clear as the sun, and terrible as an army with banners?

[11] I went down into the garden of nuts to see the fruits of the valley, and to see whether the vine flourished, and the pomegranates budded.

[12] Or ever I was aware, my soul made me like the chariots of Amminadib.

[13] Return, return, O Shulamite; return, return, that we may look upon thee. What will ye see in the Shulamite? As it were the company of two armies.

Cant. 7

[1] How beautiful are thy feet with shoes, O prince's daughter! the joints of thy thighs are like jewels, the work of the hands of a cunning workman.

[2] Thy navel is like a round goblet, which wanteth not liquor: thy belly is like an heap of wheat set about with lilies.

[3] Thy two breasts are like two young roes that are twins.

[4] Thy neck is as a tower of ivory; thine eyes like the fishpools in Heshbon, by the gate of Bath-rabbim: thy nose is as the tower of Lebanon which looketh toward Damascus.

[5] Thine head upon thee is like Carmel, and the hair of thine head like purple; the king is held in the galleries.

[6] How fair and how pleasant art thou, O love, for delights!

[7] This thy stature is like to a palm tree, and thy breasts to clusters of grapes.

[8] I said, I will go up to a palm tree, I will take hold of the boughs thereof: now also thy breasts shall be as clusters of the vine, and the smell of thy nose like apples;

[9] And the roof of thy mouth like the best wine for my beloved, that goeth down sweetly, causing the lips of those that are asleep to speak.

[10] I am my beloved's, and his desire is toward me.

[11] Come, my beloved, let us go forth into the field; let us lodge in the villages.

[12] Let us get up early to the vineyards; let us see if the vine flourish, whether the tender grape appear, and the pomegranates bud forth: there will I give thee my loves.

[13] The mandrakes give a smell, and at our gates are all manner of pleasant fruits, new and old, which I have laid up for thee, O my beloved.

Cant. 8

[1] O that thou wert as my brother, that sucked the breasts of my mother! when I should find thee without, I would kiss thee; yea, I should not be despised.

[2] I would lead thee, and bring thee into my mother's house, who would instruct me: I would cause thee to drink of spiced wine of the juice of my pomegranate.

[3] His left hand should be under my head, and his right hand should embrace me.

[4] I charge you, O daughters of Jerusalem, that ye stir not up, nor awake my love, until he please.

[5] Who is this that cometh up from the wilderness, leaning upon her beloved? I raised thee up under the apple tree: there thy mother brought thee forth: there she brought thee forth that bare thee.

[6] Set me as a seal upon thine heart, as a seal upon thine arm: for love is strong as death; jealousy is cruel as the grave: the coals thereof are coals of fire, which hath a most vehement flame.

[7] Many waters cannot quench love, neither can the floods drown it: if a man would give all the substance of his house for love, it would utterly be contemned.

[8] We have a little sister, and she hath no breasts: what shall we do for our sister in the day when she shall be spoken for?

[9] If she be a wall, we will build upon her a palace of silver: and if she be a door, we will inclose her with boards of cedar.

[10] I am a wall, and my breasts like towers: then was I in his eyes as one that found favour.

[11] Solomon had a vineyard at Baal-hamon; he let out the vineyard unto keepers; every one for the fruit thereof was to bring a thousand pieces of silver.

[12] My vineyard, which is mine, is before me: thou, O Solomon, must have a thousand, and those that keep the fruit thereof two hundred.

[13] Thou that dwellest in the gardens, the companions hearken to thy voice: cause me to hear it.

[14] Make haste, my beloved, and be thou like to a roe or to a young hart upon the mountains of spices.

Notes

Often known as the Song of Solomon, there is no reason to ascribe its authorship to King Solomon, although his name appears a number of times in the text. A deeply erotic love poem, it has frequently been read as an allegory of God's dealings with his people. Much of the language is extremely obscure in Hebrew. It is in the form of a dialogue between a newly married couple.

Chapter 1, verse 5. The contrast between the swarthy, rustic face of the singer and the fair complexions of the women of Jerusalem is a common theme in Arabic love poetry.

Chapter 2, verse 1. Both 'rose' and 'lily' are English versions of wild flowers common in the Holy Land, probably the autumn crocus and and the scarlet anemone. The translation removes the poem into a beautiful English setting.

Verse 7. 'Daughters of Jerusalem'. They represent the artificial life of the city in contrast to the rural simplicity of the lovers.

Verse 11. In Israel, the winter is the rainy season. Rain is infrequent for the other six months of the year.

Verse 13. The verb translated as 'puts forth' is obscure. It is connected with the noun for 'wheat'.

Chapter 3, verses 1–4. This seems to be an account of a dream.

Verses 6–11. The coming of the beloved is described with magnificent hyperbole as the arrival of King Solomon himself, though the reference to Solomon is a later addition to the verse.

Chapter 4, verses 1–7. The form is of an Eastern *wasf*, a descriptive poem used at marriages. The bridegroom rather than the bride now speaks.

Verse 13. 'Orchard'. The Hebrew word *pardês* is borrowed from the Persian. It is the root of the English word 'paradise'.

Chapter 5 – Chapter 6, verse 3 is a single poem moving in various stages as a whole.

Verse 12. 'fitly set'. The precise meaning seems to be 'sitting by a full-flowing stream'.

Chapter 6, verse 4. Tirzah. The name suggests 'city of delights', and in 1 Kings 14: 17 is referred to as the old Israelite capital.

Verse 12. 'My fancy'. This hardly does justice to the Hebrew, which is more like 'my soul'.

Verse 13. The reference to the Shulamite is difficult. There are various interpretations. It may be a feminine form of Solomon. Or it may relate to the city of Shunem (cf. 1 Kings 1: 3ff). Finally it may be a Hebraised form of the goddess Shulmanitu. The first suggestion seems the most likely.

Chapter 7, verse 7. The comparison of a beautiful woman with a palm tree is common, with its connotations of slenderness and suppleness.

Chapter 8, verses 6–7. These verses, among the most quoted in the whole poem, stand apart from the rest of the erotic verse as a profound reflection upon the nature of love.

Verse 10. 'Peace' is the Hebrew word *shalom*, which relates to the names Solomon and Shulamite. It is a much more powerful and complex word than the English might suggest, indicating a profound sense of well-being.

—— **Commentary** ——

The title Song of Songs means the supreme song, and is probably an anthology of love poems of much later date than King Solomon, to whom it is traditionally ascribed. Read by the Jews on the eighth day of the Passover Festival, from early on it was interpreted by both Jews and Christians allegorically. For example the *Talmud* (derived in the early centuries CE from the *Mishnah* or oral teachings of the Jews) as an allegory of God's dealings with the congregation of Israel. In the canon of Hebrew Scripture similar erotic imagery used to describe God's love for his people are found in Hosea, especially chapter 2. From early in Christian writings it was read as a description of God's relations with the Church or sometimes the individual Christian. It was particularly popular in mystical writings, and found its greatest expression in the eighty-six homilies on the Song of Songs of St Bernard of Clairvaux (1090–1153). Only a few within the tradition of Christian literature have read the book literally, above all Theodore of Mopsuestia (*c*.350–428 CE), and much later the Anabaptists.

Through the Middle Ages the lover is seen as either God or Christ, and the beloved the Church, the soul or frequently, as we shall see, the Virgin Mary. The first of our excerpts is from the writings of the fourteenth century English hermit and mystic Richard Rolle of Hampole in Yorkshire. His work *Incendium Amoris* (*The Fire of Love*) written in Latin is partly autobiographical and is a manual on the devout life. The soul cries out with passionate longing for his beloved Jesus in a language which is at once deeply spiritual and profoundly erotic, expressing his desire with a physical warmth that utterly overcomes 'the foul filth of the flesh'. In the fifteenth-century lyric 'In the vale of restless mind', the dreamer poet hears the words of love from the Song of Songs 2: 5 and 5: 8 spoken by Jesus himself from the Cross to the Christian soul as part of the Passion. In his agony the Saviour is literally sick and suffering with love for the soul which is saved by his sacrifice on Calvary.

A very different tone is taken by Geoffrey Chaucer in 'The Merchant's Tale' from his *Canterbury Tales*. Here the two lechers Januarie and Absolon use the 'olde lewed words' of the Song to seduce women of doubtful virtue. In the extract given here, Januarie addresses May in his garden with verses from the Song, chapter 4, usually associated with the

Assumption of the Blessed Virgin Mary. His blasphemy becomes more overt as it is clear that his garden is not the secure garden of the poem ('A garden locked is my sister, my bride, a garden locked, a fountain sealed': Song of Songs 4: 12), which Christian tradition identifies with the virginity of Mary. Even in Reformation literature, though elaborate allegorical readings were rejected, the 'literal' sense of the poem was retained as the love of God for his Church, and poets continued to draw on the Song in religious readings which used the riches of secular love poetry. In 'Paradise', one of the poems published in *The Temple* (1633), George Herbert uses the garden imagery, while Andrew Marvell in 'The Garden' plays erotically with the imagery of chapter 2 in an allegory that returns the scriptural poem wholly to its sexual origins.

There are numerous English Protestant translations of the Song in the sixteenth and seventeenth centuries, including a verse translation by Edmund Spenser, now unfortunately lost. Spenser, however, used it extensively in his poetry, *Amoretti*, *The Faerie Queene* and the poem here excerpted, *Colin Clouts Come Home Againe*. There is no suggestion here of allegorical interpretation, but Spenser uses the images of the Song to celebrate the beauties of a real woman, as does Adam to describe the beauty of his wife Eve in Eden in Milton's *Paradise Lost*. In his treatise *The Doctrine and Discipline of Divorce*, John Milton uses perhaps the most beautiful and profound passage in the poem, chapter 8, verses 6–7, on the unquenchable nature of true sexual love to sustain his argument for the proper state of marriage, following upon the desire which was innocently in Eden before the Fall. Here the erotic quality of the Scriptural book forms a defence of sexuality which the Christian tradition after St Augustine has too frequently denied and condemned.

In a brief reference in his *Reason of Church Government*, Milton identifies the Song of Songs as a 'divine pastoral drama' to be compared to the great dramatic tradition of Greek literature, preparing for the increasingly dramatic readings of the poem in the later seventeenth and eighteenth centuries, as the traditional religious allegorical readings fell into disuse.

But in the seventeenth century the great medieval tradition of Marian readings finds a late flowering in the poem of the Catholic convert Richard Crashaw, 'In the Glorious Assumption of our Blessed Lady'. It was precisely this tradition which Chaucer's Januarie had lecherously employed in his wooing of May. Though not a doctrine of the earliest Church, the doctrine of the corporal assumption of Jesus' Mother can be traced back as far as the sixth century, asserting that when her earthly life was over, the Blessed Virgin Mary was taken up, body and soul into heavenly glory, as defined in the *Munificentissimus Deus* of 1950:

'Immaculatam Deiparam semper Virginem Mariam, expleto terrestris vitae cursu, fuisse corpore et anima ad caelestem gloriam assumptam' (The immaculate God-bearer, the ever virgin Mary, having run the course of her earthly life, was gloriously taken up, body and soul into heaven). Crashaw represents the event dramatically as the Virgin is called by the 'dear immortal Dove', an image drawn both from the Song of Songs and from the New Testament accounts in all four gospels of the descent of the Holy Spirit, or *Shekina*, as a dove onto Jesus at his baptism in the River Jordan (Matthew 3: 16; Mark 1: 10; Luke 3: 22; John 1: 32). The coming of Mary into heaven marks also the beginning of spring in a poem which, like its original, is a beautiful love lyric, but now entirely in the spirit of 'our chaste love'.

One of America's earliest poets, though born in England, was Edward Taylor, a Puritan divine and physician, though his poems lay undiscovered until 1937, and some have only been published as late as 1981. Written in the metaphysical tradition of Herbert, Crashaw and Quarles, Taylor's *Meditations* contain extensive reflections on individual verses in the Song (in the one here given it is chapter 2, verse 1, 'I am a rose of Sharon, a lily of the valleys') in the tradition of allegorical interpretation, lamenting the unworthiness of the writer to be the lover of his Lord.

It was the German critic and poet Johann Gottfried Herder (1744–1803) who was most influential in the freeing of the Song of Songs from its ancient religious allegorical tradition of interpretation, suggesting that it was not originally a single work but a collection of love songs celebrating erotic passion. Herder paved the way for Romantic derivations from the poem, such as Lord Byron's 'She walks in beauty, like the night' in his collection *Hebrew Melodies* (1813), and later reflected in the anger of Sue Bridehead's remark in Thomas Hardy's *Jude the Obscure* (1895) against 'such humbug as could attempt to plaster over with ecclesiastical abstractions such ecstatic, natural, human love as lies in that great and passionate song'.

This tradition has dominated twentieth-century literary references to the Song of Songs, most notably in recent years in the writings of the African American writer Toni Morrison, who has entitled one of her novels of the experience of African Americans in post-slavery United States, *Song of Solomon* (1977), drawing extensively upon the language of longing and passion in the poem. But our last extract is reserved for a European writer, Umberto Eco in his intellectual novel of medieval monasticism, *The Name of the Rose*. The young novice Adso, who is the novel's narrator, falls for the sexual attractions of a young peasant girl and celebrates his initiation into the joys of sex with an utterly carnal meditation in which the tradition of spiritual transport which we have found in mystical writers like Richard Rolle is utterly consumed by a physical passion of which he later bitterly repents.

We see, then, how the literary tradition commingles the ancient sacred allegorical readings of this great poem, which probably ensured its continuing place in the canon of Scripture, with the intense physical transports which it celebrates. In the end, perhaps, the two loves – of the flesh and of the spirit – cannot be disentangled and together ensure the continuing power and fascination of this greatest of all love poems.

—— Literature ——

Richard Rolle of Hampole, *The Fire of Love* (1343), tr. Clifton Walters, Penguin, 1972, chapter 26

The voice of the soul longing with eternal love and seeking the beauty of her Maker, rings out. *Let him kiss me with the kiss of his mouth* (Song of Songs 1: 2), it says; in other words, let him delight me in union with his Son. Faint with love, I long with my whole heart to see my Love in all his beauty. But meanwhile may he visit me with his sweet love as I toil and struggle on through this pilgrimage. And may he turn my heart to himself so as to delight me with the warmth of greater and greater love. Until I can see my Beloved clearly I shall sing at every remembrance of his sweet name; it is never far from mind.

He who delights to do what his Saviour wishes not surprisingly finds delights in this present world as well. Nothing is more pleasant than praising Jesus; nothing more delectable than hearing him. For hearing rejoices my mind, and praising lifts me to himself. And when I am deprived of these things I sigh in my need, for then I hunger and thirst, and know myself bereft. Yet when I feel the embrace and caress of my Sweetheart I swoon with unspeakable delight, for it is he – he whom true lovers put before all else, for love of him alone, and because of his unbounded goodness!

And when he comes, may he come into me, suffusing me with his perfect love. May he refresh my heart by his continual gifts, and by removing every hindrance to his love make me glow and expand. Who will dare to say that a man is going to fall into the foul filth of the flesh, if Christ has deigned to refresh him with the heavenly sweetness of celestial vision? This is why such a man sings sweetly something like this, 'We will rejoice as we remember your breasts that are better than wine'. (Song of Songs 1: 1 [Vulgate])

From 'In the Vale of Restless Mind' (fourteenth century),
from Helen Gardner, ed., *The Faber Book of Religious Verse*,
Faber, 1972

In the vale of restless mind
　　I sought in mountain and in mead,
Trusting a true love for to find.
　　Upon an hill then took I heed;
A voice I heard – and near I yede –
　　In huge dolòur complaining tho:
'See, dear soul, my sidès bleed,
　　Quia amore langueo.'

Upon this mount I found a tree;
　　Under this tree a man sitting;
From head to foot wounded was he,
　　His hertè-blood I saw bleeding;
A seemly man to be a king
　　A gracious face to look unto.
I asked him how he had paining.
　　He said: '*Quia amore langueo.*

'I am true love that false was never:
　　My sister, man's soul, I loved her thus;
Because I would on no wise dissever,
　　I left my kingdom glorious;
I purveyed her a place full precious;
　　She flit, I followed; I loved her so
That I suffered these painès piteous,
　　Quia amore langueo.

'My fair love and my spousè bright,
　　I saved her fro beating and she had me bet;
I clothed her in grace and heavenly light,
　　This bloody surcote she hath on me set.
For longing love I will not let;
　　Sweetè strokès be these, lo!
I have loved her ever as I het,
　　Quia amore langueo.'

(The refrain in Latin at the end of each verse is from the Song, 2: 5, and
5: 8. 'For I am sick with love.')

Geoffrey Chaucer, 'The Merchant's Tale', *The Canterbury Tales* (c.1400), ed. F. N. Robinson, 2nd edn, Oxford University Press, 1957, lines 2132–49

But now to purpose: er that dayes eight
Were passed, er the month of Juyn, bifil
That Januarie hath caught so greet a wil,
Thurgh eggyng of his wyf, hym for to pleye
In his gardyn, and no wight but they tweye,
That in a morwe unto his May seith he:
'Rys up, my wyf, my love, my lady free!
The turtles voys is herd, my dowve sweete;
The wynter is goon with alle his reynes weete.
Com forth now, with thyne eyen columbyn!
How fairer been thy brestes than is wyn!
The gardyn is enclosed al aboute;
Com forth, my white spouse! out of doute
Thou hast me wounded in myn herte, I wyf!
No spot of thee ne knew I al my lyf.
Com forth, and lat us taken oure disport;
I chees thee for my wyf and my confort.'
Swich olde lewed words used he.

Edmund Spenser, *Colin Clouts Come Home Againe* (1595), lines 590–615

More eath (quoth he) it is in such a case
How to begin, then know how to have donne.
For everie gift and every goodly meed,
Which she on me bestowed, demaunds a day;
And every day, in which she did a deed,
Demaunnds a year it duly to display.
Her words were like a streame of honny fleeting,
The which doth softly trickle from the hive:
Hable to melt the hearers heart unweeting,
And eke to make the dead againe alive.
Her deeds were like great clusters of ripe grapes,
Which load the braunches of the fruitfull vine:
Offring to fall into each mouth that gapes,
And fill the same with store of timely wine.
Her lookes were like beames of the morning Sun,

Forth looking through the windowes of the East:
When first the fleecie cattell have begun
Upon the perled grasse to make their feast.
Her thoughts are like the fume of Frackincence,
Which from a golden Censer forth doth rise:
And throwing forth sweet odours mounts fro thence
In rolling globes up to the vauted skies.
There she beholds with high aspiring thought,
The cradle of her owne creation:
Emongst the seats of Angels heavenly wrought,
Much like an Angell in all forme and fashion.

John Milton, *The Doctrine and Discipline of Divorce* (1643), I, chapter 4

What is it then but that desire which God put into Adam in Paradise, before he knew the sin of incontinence; that desire which God saw that it was not good that man should be left alone to burn in; the desire and longing to put off an unkindly solitariness by uniting another body, but not without a fit soul to his, in the cheerful society of wedlock?...this pure and more inbred desire of joining to itself in conjugal fellowship a fit conversing soul (which desire is properly called love) 'is stronger than death,' as the spouse of Christ thought; 'many waters cannot quench it, neither can the floods drown it.' This is that rational burning that marriage is to remedy, not to be allayed with fasting, nor with any penance to be subdued: which how can he assuage who by mishap hath met the most unmeet and unsuitable mind?

(The reference is to Song of Songs 8: 7.)

The Reason of Church Government (1642), Preface to the Second Book

or whether those dramatic constitutions, wherein Sophocles and Euripides reign, shall be found more doctrinal and exemplary to a nation.

The scripture also affords us a divine pastoral drama in the Song of Solomon, consisting of two persons, and a double chorus, as Origen rightly judges.

Paradise Lost (1667), Book 5, lines 1–49

Now Morn her rosy steps in th' eastern clime
Advancing, sowed the earth with orient pearl,
When Adam waked so customed, for his sleep

Was airy light, from pure digestion bred,
And temperate vapors bland, which th' only sound
Of leaves and fuming rills, Aurora's fan,
Lightly dispersed, and the shrill matin song
Of birds on every bough; so much the more
His wonder was to find unwakened Eve
With tresses discomposed, and glowing cheek,
As through unquiet rest. He on his side
Leaning half-raised, with looks of cordial love
Hung over her enamored, and beheld
Beauty, which whether waking or asleep
Shot forth peculiar graces; then with voice
Mild, as when Zephyrus on Flora breathes,
Her hand soft touching, whispered thus: 'Awake,
My fairest, my espoused, my latest found,
Heav'n's last best gift, my ever new delight,
Awake, the morning shines, and the fresh field
Calls us; we lose the prime, to mark how spring
Our tended plants, how blows the citron grove,
What drops the myrrh, and what the balmy reed,
How Nature paints her colors, how the bee
Sits on the bloom extracting liquid sweet.'
Such whispering waked her, but with startled eye
On Adam, whom embracing, thus she spake:
'O sole in whom my thoughts find all repose,
My glory, my perfection, glad I see
Thy face, and morn returned, for I this night –
Such night till this I never passed – have dreamed,
If dreamed, not as I oft am wont, of thee,
Works of day past, or morrow's next design,
But of offense and trouble, which my mind
Knew never till this irksome night. Methought
Close at mine ear one called me forth to walk
With gentle voice; I thought it thine. It said:
'Why sleep'st thou, Eve? Now is the pleasant time,
The cool, the silent, save where silence yields
To the night-warbling bird, that now awake
Tunes sweetest his love-labored song; now reigns
Full-orbed the moon, and with more pleasing light
Shadowy sets off the face of things; in vain,
If none regard; heav'n wakes with all his eyes,
Whom to behold but thee, Nature's desire,

In whose sight all things joy, with ravishment
Attracted by thy beauty still to gaze?'
I rose as at thy call, but found thee not;
To find thee I directed then my walk.'

Andrew Marvell, 'The Garden' (1681)

I

How vainly men themselves amaze
To win the Palm, the Oke, or Bayes;
And their uncessant Labours see
Crown'd from some single Herb or Tree,
Whose short and narrow verged Shade
Does prudently their Toyles upbraid;
While all Flow'rs and all Trees do close
To weave the Garlands of repose.

II

Fair quiet, have I found thee here,
And Innocence thy Sister dear!
Mistaken long, I sought you then
In busie Companies of Men.
Your sacred Plants, if here below,
Only among the Plants will grow.
Society is all but rude,
To this delicious Solitude.

III

No white nor red was ever seen
So am'rous as this lovely green.
Fond Lovers, cruel as their Flame.
Cut in these Trees their Mistress name.
Little, Alas, they know, or heed,
How far these Beauties Hers exceed!
Fair Trees! where s'eer your barkes I wound,
No Name shall but your own be found.

IV

When we have run our Passions heat,
Love hither makes his best retreat.

196

The *Gods*, that mortal Beauty chase,
Still in a Tree did end their race.
Apollo hunted *Daphne* so,
Only that She might Laurel grow.
And *Pan* did after *Syrinx* speed,
Not as a Nymph, but for a Reed.

V

What wond'rous Life in this I lead!
Ripe Apples drop about my head;
The Luscious Clusters of the Vine
Upon my Mouth do crush their Wine;
The Nectaren, and curious Peach,
Into my hands themselves do reach;
Stumbling on Melons, as I pass,
Insnar'd with Flow'rs, I fall on Grass.

VI

Mean while the Mind, from pleasure less,
Withdraws into its happiness:
The Mind, that Ocean where each kind
Does streight its own resemblance find;
Yet it creates, transcending these,
Far other Worlds, and other Seas;
Annihilating all that's made
To a green Thought in a green Shade.

VII

Here at the Fountains sliding foot,
Or at some Fruit-trees mossy root,
Casting the Bodies Vest aside,
My Soul into the boughs does glide:
There like a Bird it sits, and sings,
Then whets, and combs its silver Wings;
And, till prepar'd for longer flight,
Waves in its Plumes the various Light.

VIII

Such was that happy Garden-state,
While Man there walk'd without a Mate:

After a Place so pure, and sweet,
What other Help could yet be meet!
But 'twas beyond a Mortal's share
To wander solitary there:
Two Paradises 'twere in one
To live in Paradise alone.

IX

How well the skilful Gardner drew
Of flow'rs and herbes this Dial new;
Where from above the milder Sun
Does through a fragrant Zodiack run;
And, as it works, th' industrious Bee
Computes its time as well as we.
How could such sweet and wholsome Hours
Be reckon'd but with herbs and flow'rs!

Richard Crashaw, 'In the Glorious Assumption of Our Blessed Lady' (1652)

The Hymn

Hark! She is call'd, the parting hour is come;
Take thy farewell, poor World, heaven must go home.
A piece of heavenly earth, purer and brighter
Than the chaste stars whose choice lamps come to light her,
While through the crystal orbs clearer than they
She climbs, and makes a far more Milky Way.
She's call'd! Hark, how the dear immortal Dove
Sighs to his silver mate: 'Rise up, my love!'
Rise up, my fair, my spotless one!
The Winter's past, the rain is gone:
The Spring is come, the flowers appear,
No sweets, but thou, are wanting here.
    Come away, my love!
    Come away, my dove!
        Cast off delay;
    The court of Heaven is come
    To wait upon thee home;
        Come, come away:
The flowers appear,
Or quickly would, wert thou once here.

The Spring is come, or if it stay
'Tis to keep time with thy delay.
The rain is gone, except so much as we
Detain in needful tears to weep the want of thee.
   The Winter's past,
    Or if he make less haste
His answer is why she does so,
If Summer come not, how can Winter go?
   Come away, come away!
The shrill winds chide, the waters weep thy stay;
The fountains murmur, and each loftiest tree
Bows lowest his leafy top to look for thee.
   Come away, my love!
   Come away, my dove! etc.

She's call'd again. And will she go?
When Heaven bids come, who can say no?
Heaven calls her, and she must away,
Heaven will not, and she cannot stay.
Go then; go, glorious on the golden wings
Of the bright youth of Heaven, that sings
Under so sweet a burthen. Go,
Since thy dread Son will have it so:
And while thou go'st, our song and we
Will, as we may, reach after thee.
Hail, holy queen of humble hearts!
We in thy praise will have our parts.
[And though thy dearest looks must now give light
To none but the blest heavens, whose bright
Beholders, lost in sweet delight,
Feed for ever their fair sight
With those divinest eyes, which we
And our dark world no more shall see;
Though our poor eyes are parted so,
Yet shall our lips never let go
Thy gracious name, but to the last
Our loving song shall hold it fast.]

   Thy precious name shall be
   Thyself to us; and we
     With holy care will keep it by us,
     We to the last

Will hold it fast,
And no Assumption shall deny us.
All the sweetest showers
Of our fairest flowers
Will we strong upon it.
Though our sweets cannot make
It sweeter, they can take
Themselves new sweetness from it.

Maria, men and angels sing,
Maria, mother of our King
Live, rosy princess, live! and may the bright
Crown of a most incomparable light
Embrace thy radiant brows. O may the best
Of everlasting joys bathe thy white breast.
Live, our chaste love, the holy mirth
Of Heaven; the humble pride of Earth.
Live, crown of women; queen of men;
Live, mistress of our song. And when
Our weak desires have done their best,
Sweet angels come, and sing the rest.

(These references are to Song of Songs 2: 10, 13; 5: 6; 7: 12.)

Edward Taylor, 'The Reflexion', *Poems*, ed. Thomas H.
Johnson, Yale, 1960

Lord, art thou at the table head above
    Meat, medicine, sweetness, sparkling beauties, to
Enamor souls with flaming flakes of love,
    And not my trencher, nor my cup o'erflow?
    Be n't I a bidden guest? Oh! sweat mine eye:
    O'erflow with tears: Oh! draw thy fountains dry.

Shall I not smell thy sweet, oh! Sharons rose?
    Shall not mine eye salute thy beauty? Why?
Shall thy sweet leaves their beauteous sweets upclose?
    As half ashamed my sight should on them lie?
    Woe's me! For this my sighs shall be in grain,
    Offered on sorrows altar for the same.

Had not my soul's, thy conduit, pipes stopped been
    With mud, what ravishment wouldst thou convey?

200

Let graces golden spade dig till the spring
  Of tears arise, and clear this filth away.
Lord, let thy spirit raise my sighings till
  These pipes my soul do with thy sweetness fill.

Earth once was Paradise of Heaven below,
  Till inkfaced sin had it with poison stocked;
And chased this Paradise away into
  Heavens upmost loft, and it in glory locked.
  But thou, sweet Lord, hast with thy golden key
  Unlocked the door, and made a golden day.

Once at thy feast, I saw the pearl-like stand
  'Tween Heaven and Earth, where heavens bright glory all
In streams fell on thee, as a floodgate and,
  Like sun beams through thee on the world to fall.
  Oh! Sugar sweet then! My dear sweet Lord, I see
  Saints heaven-lost happiness restored by thee.

Umberto Eco, *The Name of the Rose* (1980), tr. William Weaver, Picador, 1984

And she kissed me with the kisses of her mouth, and her loves were more delicious than wine and her ointments had a goodly fragrance, and her neck was beautiful among pearls and her cheeks among earrings, behold thou art fair; thine eyes are as doves (I said), and let me see thy face, let me hear thy voice, for thy voice is harmonious and thy face enchanting, thou hast ravished my heart, my sister, thou hast ravished my heart with one of thine eyes, with one chain of thy neck, thy lips drop as the honeycomb, honey and milk are under thy tongue, the smell of thy breath is of apples, thy two breasts are clusters of grapes, thy palate a heady wine that goes straight to my love and flows over my lips and teeth . . . A fountain sealed, spikenard and saffron, calamus and cinnamon, myrrh and aloes, I have eaten my honeycomb with my honey, I have drunk my wine with my milk. Who was she, who was she who rose like the dawn, fair as the moon, clear as the sun, terrible as an army with banners?

O Lord, when the soul is transported, the only virtue lies in loving what you see (is that not true?), the supreme happiness in having what you have; there blissful life is drunk at its source (has this not been said?), there you savor the true life that we will live after this mortal life among the angels for all eternity . . . This is what I was thinking and it seemed to me the prophecies were being fulfilled at last, as the girl lavished indescribable sweetness on me, and it was as if my whole body were an eye, before and behind, and I could suddenly see all surrounding things. And I understood that from it, from love, unity and tenderness are created together, as are good and kiss and fulfillment, as I had already heard, believing I was being told about something else. And only for an instant, as my joy was about to reach its zenith, did I remember that perhaps I was experiencing, and at night, the possession of the noontime Devil, who was condemned finally to reveal himself in his true, diabolical nature to the soul that in ecstasy asks 'Who are you?,' who knows how to grip the soul and delude the body. But I was immediately convinced that my scruples were indeed devilish, for nothing could be more right and good and holy than what I was experiencing, the sweetness of which grew with every moment. As a little drop of water added to a quantity of wine is completely dispersed and takes on the color and taste of wine, as red-hot iron becomes like molten fire losing its original form, as air when it is inundated with the sun's light is transformed into total splendor and clarity so that it no longer seems illuminated but, rather, seems to be light itself, so I felt myself die of tender liquefaction, and I had only the strength left to murmur the words of the psalm: 'Behold my bosom is like new wine, sealed, which bursts new vessels,' and suddenly I saw a brilliant light and in it a saffron-colored form which flamed up in a sweet and shining fire, and that splendid light spread through all the shining fire, and this shining fire through that golden form and that brilliant light and that shining fire through the whole form.

As, half fainting, I fell on the body to which I had joined myself, I understood in a last vital spurt that flame consists of a splendid clarity, an unusual vigor, and an igneous ardor, but it possesses the splendid clarity so that it may illuminate and the igneous ardor that it may burn. Then I understood the abyss, and the deeper abysses that it conjured up.

Bibliography

Alter, Robert. *The Art of Biblical Poetry* (New York: Basic Books, 1985), ch. 8, 'The Garden of Metaphor'.

Henn, T. R. *The Bible as Literature* (London: Lutterworth, 1970), pp. 87–100.

Herbert, A. S. 'The Song of Solomon', in *Peake's Commentary on the Bible,* ed. Matthew Black and H. H. Rowley (London: Nelson, 1962), pp. 468–74.

Kugel, James L. *The Idea of Biblical Poetry: Parallelism and its History* (New Haven: Yale University Press, 1981).

THE NATIVITY
MATTHEW 2: 1–12; LUKE 2: 1–19

Matthew 2: 1–12

[1] Now when Jesus was born in Bethlehem of Judaea in the days of Herod the king, behold, there came wise men from the east to Jerusalem,

[2] Saying, Where is he that is born King of the Jews? for we have seen his star in the east, and are come to worship him.

[3] When Herod the king had heard these things, he was troubled, and all Jerusalem with him.

[4] And when he had gathered all the chief priests and scribes of the people together, he demanded of them where Christ should be born.

[5] And they said unto him, In Bethlehem of Judaea: for thus it is written by the prophet,

[6] And thou Bethlehem, in the land of Juda, art not the least among the princes of Juda: for out of thee shall come a Governor, that shall rule my people Israel.

[7] Then Herod, when he had privily called the wise men, inquired of them diligently what time the star appeared.

[8] And he sent them to Bethlehem, and said, Go and search diligently for the young child; and when ye have found him, bring me word again, that I may come and worship him also.

[9] When they had heard the king, they departed; and, lo, the star, which they saw in the east, went before them, till it came and stood over where the young child was.

[10] When they saw the star, they rejoiced with exceeding great joy.

[11] And when they were come into the house, they saw the young child with Mary his mother, and fell down, and worshipped him: and when

they had opened their treasures, they presented unto him gifts; gold, and frankincense, and myrrh.

[12] And being warned of God in a dream that they should not return to Herod, they departed into their own country another way.

Luke 2: 1–19

[1] And it came to pass in those days, that there went out a decree from Caesar Augustus, that all the world should be taxed.

[2] (And this taxing was first made when Cyrenius was governor of Syria.)

[3] And all went to be taxed, every one into his own city.

[4] And Joseph also went up from Galilee, out of the city of Nazareth, into Judaea, unto the city of David, which is called Bethlehem; (because he was of the house and lineage of David:)

[5] To be taxed with Mary his espoused wife, being great with child.

[6] And so it was, that, while they were there, the days were accomplished that she should be delivered.

[7] And she brought forth her firstborn son, and wrapped him in swaddling clothes, and laid him in a manger; because there was no room for them in the inn.

[8] And there were in the same country shepherds abiding in the field, keeping watch over their flock by night.

[9] And, lo, the angel of the Lord came upon them, and the glory of the Lord shone round about them: and they were sore afraid.

[10] And the angel said unto them, Fear not: for, behold, I bring you good tidings of great joy, which shall be to all people.

[11] For unto you is born this day in the city of David a Saviour, which is Christ the Lord.

[12] And this shall be a sign unto you; Ye shall find the babe wrapped in swaddling clothes, lying in a manger.

[13] And suddenly there was with the angel a multitude of the heavenly host praising God, and saying,

[14] Glory to God in the highest, and on earth peace, good will toward men.

[15] And it came to pass, as the angels were gone away from them into heaven, the shepherds said one to another, Let us now go even unto Bethlehem, and see this thing which is come to pass, which the Lord hath made known unto us.

[16] And they came with haste, and found Mary, and Joseph, and the babe lying in a manger.

[17] And when they had seen it, they made known abroad the saying which was told them concerning this child.

[18] And all they that heard it wondered at those things which were told them by the shepherds.

[19] But Mary kept all these things, and pondered them in her heart.

Notes

Matthew

Matthew makes no attempt to conceal his literary source for the story of the virgin birth (1: 23) which is Isaiah 7: 14. Though a huge Christian doctrinal super-structure was subsequently built up this text, the actual Hebrew word in Isaiah may either be translated as 'virgin' or, more simply, 'young woman'.

Verse 1. Bethlehem was also the birthplace of King David (Samuel 16). The only other 'wiseman' magus in the New Testament is Elymas in Acts 13: 6ff. He is a magician, and early Christian commentators such as Ignatius of Antioch regarded the three men in the same light – from the moment of the appearance of the star, ancient sorcery began to fail as God appeared in human form to banish such wickedness.

Verse 2. The star is seen in Numbers 24: 17 as the sign of a king.

Verse 5. For the prophecy see Micah 5: 2 and 2 Samuel 5: 2.

Verse 11. The three gifts are all suitable gifts for a king. See, Psalms 72: 15 (gold), Isaiah 60: 6 (gold and frankincense), Psalms 45: 8 (the anointing of a king with myrrh). They are also the materials of magicians, here offered up to Jesus to mark the end of such practices.

Luke

Luke begins his account with a careful historical dating, and goes on to weave a narrative which combines history, prophecy and symbolism. Particularly impor-tant from the Old Testament is Micah 5: 2–5.

Verse 8. Shepherds were often despised in Jewish tradition because of their neglect of religious observances. They symbolize the humble folk who were to follow Jesus, as well as being linked with the theme of Jesus as himself 'the good shepherd'.

—— **Commentary** ——

Whether the nativity or the crucifixion is the supreme moment of the Christian story theologians may differ; for artists and people alike the nativity has always held a unique fascination. It is the point where, if anywhere, ever, myth and history met, and the human and divine became one. As such, it has always been a peculiarly poetic moment, celebrated by countless poems, paintings and pieces of music. Like many famous stories, however (including Shakespeare's *King Lear*), the narrative we think we know of Jesus' birth is actually a composite one, composed of two gospel versions and a good deal of extra-biblical legend. Two out of the four Gospels (Mark and John) do not tell the story at all, and the two that do contribute different accompanying events. Matthew has the wise men (*not* 'Kings' – with the exception of Solomon, the Bible rarely attributes great wisdom to Kings) but no shepherds. Luke has angels and shepherds but no wise men.

Matthew alone has the virgin birth. Luke mentions Mary's pregnancy, but by his silence on the father leaves the reader not already primed with Matthew to assume normal paternity – a point reinforced by the fact that the genealogy of Jesus (Luke 3: 23–38) runs from Adam through to Joseph. There would be little point in this lineage if Joseph were *not* his father. Perhaps even more oddly, Matthew *also* offers a (different) genealogy for Jesus which concludes with Joseph.

The Bible is the story of a family: literally in the case of the Old Testament, metaphorically, in the case of the New, and genealogies are an integral part of family history. Yet the ancestry of Jesus is of a piece with the rest of biblical blood-lines in that it takes unexpected and disreputable twists. Any reader of the story of Joseph, for example, could be forgiven for assuming that the main line of descent will be through him. Yet, though two of Joseph's sons, Ephraim and Manasseh, both found tribes, David, and the royal line of Israel – through to Jesus in the New Testament – will run through Judah, and Joseph's descendants will join the lost ten tribes after the captivity in Babylon. Given the Jewish and Christian prohibitions on extra-marital sex, the story of the virgin birth, as told by Matthew, with its potential for embarrassment, has always required very careful handling by the Church. In this it constitutes yet another of a series that runs, very oddly, through the whole chain of biblical history, from the story of Judah and Tamar (Genesis 38) through David and Bathsheba (2 Samuel 11). What is astonishing about the family descent of Jesus from Abraham is not so much the legitimate line, but these shifts, thefts, and scandals. Jacob steals Esau's birthright; Judah loses his own sons and his only descendant is Pharez, his child by his sister-in-law whom he had mistaken for a prostitute; we then go through Rahab, the prostitute of Jericho, who sheltered the Hebrew spies and betrayed her own people; finally David has Uriah murdered so that he may take his wife – and fathers Solomon. Compared with these, the story of Ruth and Boaz is innocent, even idyllic – except, of course, that Ruth is not Hebrew at all, but a Moabite – and, as we know, the child of a non-Jewish mother is not Jewish. All these contribute to the lineage of Joseph, who now is confronted with his pregnant fiancée.

Rather than trace the historical growth of the cult of the Virgin, especially in Mediterranean countries, where it seems to have appropriated a much older fertility-goddess cult, it is, perhaps, worth considering the symbolism of the obviously very powerful idea that Jesus should have had a divine as well as a human parent. Clearly an important element here was to free him from the curse of Adam, the 'original sin', which was held to have corrupted the whole human race since the Fall. Yet Mary is also usually held to have been sinless, which gives Jesus a remarkably inhuman background until we notice that her 'sinlessness' seems to be not unconnected with her (perpetual) virginity. In other words, sex seems to be the real source of the pollution: a view strengthened by the fact that in some extra-biblical medieval traditions, the virgin's mother, St Anne, was also in her turn a virgin, and, in one extreme version, the product of a line of 'perpetual virginity' all the way back to Adam himself. The whole syndrome represents a very different tradition from that of the Council of Nicaea that decreed Christ's nature was indivisibly 'wholly human' and 'wholly divine'. The natural verbal expression of the dual nature of the Incarnation is, of course, the pun, and Charles Wesley's astonishing theological *tour de force*, 'Let earth and heaven combine', displays better perhaps than any other poem in English literature the use of the wholly serious pun.

It is in cases such as this that the linguistic gap between the relative crudity of the *koiné* Greek of the New Testament and the dignified Latinate English of the King James Bible is at its greatest. But the nativity story had other potential for embarrassment in the early seventeenth century. In the Bodley Library, in Oxford, there is a copy of the earlier 'Bishop's Bible' with revision notes made by the 1611 translators of the King James version. The Bishop's Bible had followed Tyndale's translation for Luke 2: 13, 'And suddenly there was with the Angel a multitude of heavenly soldiers, praising God, and saying...' The Greek words for these 'heavenly soldiers' are *stratias ouraniou* In the plural *stratia* means simply 'soldiers' (of a land army as distinct from a navy); in the singular, as here in Luke, it would be more literally translated as 'army'. The associations of the word not merely with the men but with actual weapons of war can be seen from elsewhere in the New Testament, when Paul, in 2 Corinthians 10: 4 uses it again, this time metaphorically, to mean the 'weapons of warfare' ('for the weapons of our warfare are not carnal'). The Latin Vulgate here follows the Greek very closely with *multitudo militiae caelestis*: 'a multitude of the heavenly army'. The first break in these serried military formations seems to be in Luther's 1534 translation, where the passage appears as *die Menge der himmlischen Heerscharen* – the final word being more or less directly equivalent to the English 'hosts'. Whether or not it owes anything to Luther here, the systematic disarming of these massed ranks of heaven by the Authorized Version is, nevertheless, remarkable. We can see from the successive layers of anno-tation in the Bodley copy of the Bishop's Bible that Tyndale's blunt phrase 'heavenly soldiers' was first marked down as needing revision, before being provisionally altered to 'heavenly army', and finally changed again to the final well-known Authorized Version reading of 'heavenly host'. Nor is it difficult to guess why the more disciplined and unified word 'army' was at first seen as politically preferable as well as more accurate than Tyndale's loose collection of 'soldiers', not to mention why both the contemporary military words were eventually excised in favour of the altogether more archaic and distancing word 'host' (reminiscent of 1 Kings 22: 19). At a time when religion and politics were not merely inseparably intertwined, but within a generation were to spill over into civil war, any suggestion of multitudes of heavenly soldiers, whether or not properly organized into armies, was clearly unacceptable – and prob-ably with good reason, for Tyndale's phrase is indeed prophetic of the metaphors of Puritan rhetoric of the 1640s. On the other hand, the words 'heavenly host', which like so many phrases from the Authorized Version, have passed into the language, effectively play down the immediate mili-tary connotations – without scholarly falsification. Too close a connection with that other heavenly army, Elisha's 'horses and chariots of fire' in 2 Kings 6: 17, was quietly circumvented, and, as endless illustrations, from Old Masters to Christmas cards, show, the angels of the nativity were successfully disarmed. Of the thousands of poems and other literary works celebrating, questioning, or puzzling over the nativity, perhaps the strangest as well as one of the most popular is Dickens' *Christmas Carol*. As G. K. Chesterton has remarked, the most extraordinary thing about that most extraordinary book is that it ignores the entire wealth and poetry of more than eighteen hundred years of the Christian tradition to invent (successfully) a totally new Christmas story.

—— Literature ——

'I Sing of a Maiden' (fifteenth century), R. T. Davies, ed.,
Medieval English Lyrics, Faber, 1963

> I sing of a maiden
> That is makeles:
> King of alle kings
> To here sone she ches

He cam also stille
Ther his moder was,
As dew in Aprille
That falleth on the grass.

He cam also stille
To his moderes bowr,
As dew in Aprill
That falleth on the flowr.

He cam also stille
Ther his moder lay,
As dew in Aprille
That falleth on the spray.

Moder and maiden
Was never non but she:
Well may swich a lady
Godes moder be.

John Donne, *Holy Sonnets*, 'La Corona' (*c.* 1610–1611),
3 'Nativity'

Immensitie cloysterd in thy deare wombe,
Now leaves his welbelov'd imprisonment,
There he hath made himselfe to his intent
Weake enough, now into our world to come;
But Oh, for thee, for him, hath th' Inne no roome?
Yet lay him in this stall, and from the Orient,
Starres, and wisemen will travell to prevent
Th' effect of *Herods* jealous general doome.
Seest thou, my Soule, with thy faith's eyes, how he
Which fils all place, yet none holds him, doth lye?
Was not his pity towards thee wondrous high,
That would have need to be pittied by thee?
Kisse him, and with him into Egypt goe,
With his kinde mother, who partakes thy woe.

George Herbert

ANA
{MARY
ARMY}
GRAM

How well her name an *Army* doth present,
And in whom the *Lord of Hosts* did pitch his tent!

John Milton, *On the Morning of Christ's Nativity* (1629)

I

THIS is the month, and this the happy morn,
Wherein the Son of Heav'n's eternal King,
Of wedded maid and virgin mother born,
Our great redemption from above did bring;
For so the holy sages once did sing,
That he our deadly forfeit should release,
And with his Father work us a perpetual peace.

II

That glorious form, that light unsufferable,
And that far-beaming blaze of majesty,
Wherewith he wont at Heav'n's high council-table
To sit the midst of Trinal Unity,
He laid aside; and here with us to be,
Forsook the courts of everlasting day,
And chose with us a darksome house of mortal clay.

III

Say Heavenly Muse, shall not thy sacred vein
Afford a present to the Infant God?
Hast thou no verse, no hymn, or solemn strain,
To welcome him to this his new abode;
Now while the Heav'n by the sun's team untrod
Hath took no print of the approaching light,
And all the spangled host keep watch in squadrons bright?

IV

See how from far upon the eastern road
The star-led wizards haste with odours sweet:
O run, prevent them with thy humble ode,
And lay it lowly at his blessed feet;
Have thou the honour first thy Lord to greet,
And join thy voice unto the angel choir,
From out his secret altar touch'd with hallow'd fire.

The Hymn

I

It was the winter wild,
While the Heav'n-born child,
All meanly wrapt in the rude manger lies;
Nature in awe to him
Had doff'd her gaudy trim,
With her great Master so to sympathize:
It was no season then for her
To wanton with the Sun, her lusty paramour.

II

Only with speeches fair
She woos the gentle air
To hide her guilty front with innocent snow,
And on her naked shame,
Pollute with sinful blame,
The saintly veil of maiden white to throw,
Confounded, that her Maker's eyes
Should look so near upon her foul deformities.

III

But he, her fears to cease,
Sent down the meek-ey'd Peace:
She, crown'd with olive green, came softly sliding
Down through the turning sphere,
His ready harbinger,
With turtle wing the amorous clouds dividing;
And waving wide her myrtle wand,
She strikes a universal peace through sea and land.

IV

No war or battle's sound
Was heard the world around;
The idle spear and shield were high uphung;
The hooked chariot stood
Unstain'd with hostile blood;
The trumpet spake not to the armed throng;

And kings sate still with awful eye,
As if they surely knew their sovran Lord was by.

V

But peaceful was the night
Wherein the Prince of Light
His reign of peace upon the earth began:
The winds with wonder whist,
Smoothly the waters kist,
Whispering new joys to the mild Ocean,
Who now hath quite forgot to rave,
While birds of calm sit brooding on the charmed wave.

VI

The stars with deep amaze
Stand fix'd in steadfast gaze,
Bending one way their precious influence;
And will not take their flight,
For all the morning light,
Or Lucifer that often warn'd them thence;
But in their glimmering orbs did glow,
Until their Lord himself bespake and bid them go.

VII

And though the shady gloom
Had given day her room,
The sun himself withheld his wonted speed;
And hid his head for shame,
As his inferior flame
The new-enlightn'd world no more should need;
He saw a greater Sun appear
Than his bright throne, or burning axletree could bear.

VIII

The shepherds on the lawn,
Or ere the point of dawn,
Sat simply chatting in a rustic row;
Full little thought they then
That the mighty Pan
Was kindly come to live with them below;

Perhaps their loves, or else their sheep,
Was all that did their silly thoughts so busy keep.

IX

When such music sweet
Their hearts and ears did greet,
As never was by mortal finger strook;
Divinely warbled voice
Answering the stringed noise,
As all their souls in blissful rapture took:
The air such pleasure loth to lose,
With thousand echoes still prolongs each heav'nly close…

XXVII

But see the Virgin blest,
Hath laid her Babe to rest.
Time is our tedious song should here have ending:
Heav'n's youngest teemed star,
Hath fix'd her polished car,
Her sleeping Lord with handmaid lamp attending.
And all about the courtly stable,
Bright-harness'd angels sit in order serviceable.

Charles Wesley, 'Let Earth and Heaven Combine' (1744)

Let earth and heaven combine,
Angels and men agree,
To praise in songs divine
The incarnate Deity,
Our God contracted to a span,
Incomprehensibly made man.

He laid his glory by,
He wrapped him in our clay;
Unmarked by human eye,
The latent Godhead lay;
Infant of days he here became,
And bore the mild Immanuel's name.

Unsearchable the love
That hath the Saviour brought;

The grace is far above
Or men or angers' thought:
Suffice for us that God, we know,
Our God, is manifest below.

He deigns in flesh to appear,
Widest extremes to join;
To bring our vileness near,
And make us all divine:
And we the life of God shall know,
For God is manifest below.

Made perfect first in love,
And sanctified by grace,
We shall from earth remove,
And see his glorious face:
His love shall then be fully showed,
And man shall all be lost in God.

Samuel Taylor Coleridge, 'A Christmas Carol' (1799)

THE shepherds went their hasty way,
And found the lowly stable-shed
Where the Virgin-Mother lay:
And now they checked their eager tread,
For to the Babe, that at her bosom clung,
A Mother's song the Virgin-Mother sung.

They told her how a glorious light,
Streaming from a heavenly throng,
Around them shone, suspending night
While sweeter than a mother's song,
Blest Angels heralded the Saviour's birth,
Glory to God on high! and Peace on Earth.

She listened to the tale divine,
And closer still the Babe she pressed;
And while she cried, the Babe is mine!
The milk rushed faster to her breast:
Joy rose within her, like a summer's morn;
Peace, Peace on Earth! the Prince of Peace is born.

Thou Mother of the Prince of Peace,
Poor, simple, and of low estate!
That strife should vanish, battle cease,
O why should this thy soul elate?
Sweet Music's loudest note, the Poet's story, –
Didst thou ne'er love to hear of fame and glory?

And is not War a youthful king,
A stately Hero clad in mail?
Beneath his footsteps laurels spring;
Him Earth's majestic monarchs hail
Their friend, their playmate! and his bold bright eye
Compels the maiden's love-confessing sigh.

'Tell this in some more courtly scene,
To maids and youths in robes of state!
I am a woman poor and mean,
And therefore is my soul elate.
War is a ruffian, all with guilt defiled,
That from the aged father tears his child!

'A murderous fiend, by fiends adored,
He kills the sire and starves the son;
The husband kills, and from her board
Steals all his widow's toil had won;
Plunders God's world of beauty; rends away
All safety from the night, all comfort from the day.

'Then wisely is my soul elate,
That strife should vanish, battle cease:
I'm poor and of a low estate,
The Mother of the Prince of Peace.
Joy rises in me, like a summer's morn:
Peace, Peace on Earth! the Prince of Peace is born.'

Thomas Hardy, 'A Christmas Carol: The Oxen' (1917)

Christmas Eve, and twelve of the clock.
'Now they are all on their knees'
An elder said as we sat in a flock
By the embers in hearthside ease.

We pictured the meek mild creatures where
They dwelt in their strawy pen,
Nor did it occur to one of us there
To doubt they were kneeling then.

So fair a fancy few would weave
In those years! Yet I feel,
If someone said on Christmas Eve,
'Come: see the oxen kneel

In the lonely barton by yonder coomb
Our childhood used to know',
I should go with him in the gloom,
Hoping it might be so.

Oscar Wilde, 'Ave Maria Gratia Plena'

Was this His coming! I had hoped to see
A scene of wonderous glory, as was told
Of some great God who fell in a rain of gold
Broke open bars and fell on Danae:
Or a dread vision as when Semele,
Sickening for love and unappeased desire,
Prayed to see God's clear body, and the fire
Caught her brown limbs and slew her utterly.
With such glad dreams I sought this holy place,
And now with wondering eyes and heart I stand
Before this supreme mystery of Love:
Some kneeling girl with passionless pale face,
An angel with a lily in his hand,
And over both the white wings of a Dove.

Mary Elizabeth Coleridge, 'I Saw a Stable'

I saw a stable, low and very bare,
A little child in a manger.
The Oxen knew Him, had Him in their care,
To men he was a stranger.
The safety of the world was lying there,
And the world's danger.

Rupert Brooke, 'Mary and Gabriel' (1912)

Young Mary, loitering once her garden way,
Felt a warm splendour grow in the April day,

As wine chat blushes water through. And soon,
Out of the gold air of the afternoon,
One knelt before her: hair he had, or fire,
Bound back above his ears with golden wire,
Baring the eager marble of his face.
Not man's or woman's was the immortal grace
Rounding the limbs beneath that robe of white,
And lighting the proud eyes with changeless light,
Incurious. Calm as his wings, and fair,
That presence filled the garden.
          She stood there,
Saying, 'What would you, Sir?'
          He told his word,
'Blessed art thou of women!' Half she heard,
Hands folded and face bowed, half long had known,
The message of that clear and holy tone,
That fluttered hot sweet sobs about her heart;
Such serene tidings moved such human smart.
Her breath came quick as little flakes of snow.
Her hands crept up her breast. She did but know
It was not hers. She felt a trembling stir
Within her body, a will too strong for her
That held and filled and mastered all. With eyes
Closed, and a thousand soft short broken sighs,
She gave submission; fearful, meek, and glad...
          She wished to speak. Under her breasts she had
Such multitudinous burnings, to and fro,
And throbs not understood; she did not know
If they were hurt or joy for her; but only
That she was grown strange to herself, half lonely,
All wonderful, filled full of pains to come
And thoughts she dare not think, swift thoughts and dumb,
Human, and quaint, her own, yet very far,
Divine, dear, terrible, familiar...
Her heart was faint for telling; to relate
Her limbs' sweet treachery, her strange high estate,
Over and over, whispering, half revealing,
Weeping; and so find kindness to her healing.
'Twixt tears and laughter, panic hurrying her,
She raised her eyes to that fair messenger.
He knelt unmoved, immortal; with his eyes
Gazing beyond her, calm to the calm skies;

Radiant, untroubled in his wisdom, kind.
His sheaf of lilies stirred not in the wind.
How should she, pitiful with mortality,
Try the wide peace of that felicity
With ripples of her perplexed shaken heart,
And hints of human ecstasy, human smart,
And whispers of the lonely weight she bore,
And how her womb within was hers no more
And at length hers?
    Being tired, she bowed her head;
And said, 'So be it!'
    The great wings were spread
Showering glory on the fields, and fire.
The whole air, singing, bore him up, and higher,
Unswerving, unreluctant. Soon he shone
A gold speck in the gold skies; then was gone.

The air was colder, and grey. She stood alone.

T. S. Eliot, 'The Journey of the Magi' (1927)

A cold coming we had of it,
Just the worst time of the year
For a journey, and such a long journey:
The ways deep and the weather sharp,
The very dead of winter.
And the camels galled, sore-footed, refractory,
Lying down in the melting snow.
There were times we regretted
The summer palaces on slopes, the terraces,
And the silken girls bringing sherbet.
Then the camel men cursing and grumbling
And running away, and wanting their liquor and women,
And the night-fires going out, and the lack of shelters,
And the cities hostile and the towns unfriendly
And the villages dirty and charging high prices:
A hard time we had of it.
At the end we preferred to travel all night,
Sleeping in snatches,
With the voices singing in our ears, saying
That this was all folly.

Then at dawn we came down to a temperate valley,
Wet, below the snow line, smelling of vegetation;
With a running stream and a water-mill beating the darkness,
And three trees on the low sky,
And an old white horse galloped away in the meadow.
Then we came to a tavern with vine-leaves over the lintel,
Six hands at an open door dicing for pieces of silver,
And feet kicking the empty wine-skins.
But there was no information, and so we continued
And arrived at evening, not a moment too soon
Finding the place; it was (you may say) satisfactory.

All this was a long time ago, I remember,
And I would do it again, but set down
This set down
This: were we led all that way for
Birth or Death? There was a Birth, certainly,
We had evidence and no doubt. I had seen birth and death,
But had thought they were different; this Birth was
Hard and bitter agony for us, like Death, our death.
We returned to our places, these Kingdoms,
But no longer at ease here, in the old dispensation,
With an alien people clutching their gods.
I should be glad of another death.

Edwin Muir, 'The Annunciation'

The angel and the girl are met.
Earth was the only meeting place.
For the embodied never yet
Travelled beyond the shore of space.
The eternal spirits in freedom go.

See, they have come together, see,
While the destroying minutes flow,
Each reflects the other's face
Till heaven in hers and earth in his
Shine steady there. He's come to her
From far beyond the farthest star,
Feathered through time. Immediacy
Of strangest strangeness is the bliss
That from their limbs all movement takes.

Yet the increasing rapture brings
So great a wonder that it makes
Each feather tremble on his wings.

Outside the window footsteps fall
Into the ordinary day
And with the sun along the wall
Pursue their unreturning way
That was ordained in eternity.
Sound's perpetual roundabout
Rolls its numbered octaves out
And hoarsely grinds its battered tune.

But through the endless afternoon
These neither speak nor movement make,
But stare into their deepening trance
As if their gaze would never break.

Bibliography

Dickens, Charles, *A Christmas Carol* (1843).

There are numerous commentaries which provide useful background reading to the nativity stories in Matthew and Luke. Especially good, with the virtue of brevity and absence of technical language are:

Caird, G. B. *Saint Luke*. The Pelican New Testament Commentaries (Harmondsworth: Pelican, 1963).
Fenton, J. C. *Saint Matthew*. The Pelican New Testament Commentaries (Harmondsworth: Pelican, 1963).

Also helpful from a scholarly point of view are:

Crossan, John Dominic. *Jesus: A Revolutionary Biography* (San Francisco: Harper Collins, 1994).
Davies, R. T. (ed.). *Medieval English Lyrics: A Critical Anthology* (London: Faber, 1963).
Thomas, Dylan. 'Memories of Christmas', a broadcast, published in *Miscellany One* (London: Dent, 1963).

The Problem of the Parables

Mark 4: 1–20

[1] And he began again to teach by the sea side: and there was gathered unto him a great multitude, so that he entered into a ship, and sat in the sea; and the whole multitude was by the sea on the land.

[2] And he taught them many things by parables, and said unto them in his doctrine,

[3] Hearken; Behold, there went out a sower to sow:

[4] And it came to pass, as he sowed, some fell by the way side, and the fowls of the air came and devoured it up.

[5] And some fell on stony ground, where it had not much earth; and immediately it sprang up, because it had no depth of earth:

[6] But when the sun was up, it was scorched; and because it had no root, it withered away.

[7] And some fell among thorns, and the thorns grew up, and choked it, and it yielded no fruit.

[8] And other fell on good ground, and did yield fruit that sprang up and increased; and brought forth, some thirty, and some sixty, and some an hundred.

[9] And he said unto them, He that hath ears to hear, let him hear.

[10] And when he was alone, they that were about him with the twelve asked of him the parable.

[11] And he said unto them, Unto you it is given to know the mystery of the kingdom of God: but unto them that are without, all these things are done in parables:

[12] That seeing they may see, and not perceive; and hearing they may hear, and not understand; lest at any time they should be converted, and their sins should be forgiven them.

[13] And he said unto them, Know ye not this parable? and how then will ye know all parables?

[14] The sower soweth the word.

[15] And these are they by the way side, where the word is sown; but when they have heard, Satan cometh immediately, and taketh away the word that was sown in their hearts.

[16] And these are they likewise which are sown on stony ground; who, when they have heard the word, immediately receive it with gladness;

[17] And have no root in themselves, and so endure but for a time: afterward, when affliction or persecution ariseth for the word's sake, immediately they are offended.

[18] And these are they which are sown among thorns; such as hear the word,

[19] And the cares of this world, and the deceitfulness of riches, and the lusts of other things entering in, choke the word, and it becometh unfruitful.

[20] And these are they which are sown on good ground; such as hear the word, and receive it, and bring forth fruit, some thirtyfold, some sixty, and some an hundred.

Notes

Verse 3. In Palestine, sowing precedes ploughing. Thus, the sower is not being especially careless, for even the seed on the path will eventually be ploughed in.

Verse 11. The word 'secret' (in Greek, *mysterion*), was frequently used in the Greek mystery religions to denote knowledge which was vouchsafed only to devotees or those 'on the inside'. In Colossians 1: 26 it is used of a secret long held by God but now divulged to the select 'saints'.

'The kingdom of God' might be better rendered as 'the kingly rule of God', which is revealed in the life and ministry of Jesus himself.

Verses 11–12. This has long been a puzzle. It seems to suggest that the outsiders are actually prevented from understanding by the parables. The difficulty turns on the two words 'so that' (Greek *hina*), and 'lest' (Greek *mêpote*), which in the version in St Matthew's Gospel are softened to make it easier of interpretation. The origin of the saying seems to be Isaiah 6: 9.

Verses 14–20. It is possible that this is a later addition to the Gospel text. This is suggested by the assumption here that the parable is an allegory, and also that two lines of interpretation seem to be combined. The first thinks of the seed as the divine word sown in people, while the second regards the people themselves as seeds sown by God.

—— Commentary ——

Although this section focuses on the mysterious passage in St. Mark's Gospel in which Jesus teaches his disciples about the nature of the parables, the literature selected deals more generally with the parable in the Rabbinic and Christian traditions, and indicates that the parable as a form of literature is still alive and used by writers up to the present day. Jesus' so-called 'parables of the kingdom' have been the subject of intense critical discussion and hugely varying forms of reading. For St Augustine of Hippo (and seemingly the Jesus of St Mark's Gospel) they were to be read as allegories, and this kind of interpretation was common until a German scholar in the nineteenth century, Adolf Jülicher, suggested that the New Testament parables should be read as real similes and not as allegories, with one point of significance, for example, in The Good Samaritan (Luke 10: 30–7) the boundless love required of us for our neighbour. Others, more recently, have read the gospel parables in an 'eschatological' light, that is, as stories illustrating from events in everyday life the nature of Kingdom when it is realized – when love, forgiveness – and judgement on those who merit it – will wholly prevail. They are stories of both promise and warning.

The word 'parable' is derived from two Greek words which together mean 'to cast by the side of' or, metaphorically, 'to compare'. In the parables of Jesus, the Kingdom of God is described in metaphors and similes, one thing spoken of in terms of another. The Greeks understood perfectly this sense of the parable, yet the antecedents of the New Testament form lie not in the Greek tradition but in Jewish literature and the Hebrew Bible. The Hebrew literary form of the *mashal* is frequently found throughout the Hebrew Bible. It was not merely in story form and covers almost any verbal image or figurative saying, embracing the forms of metaphor, riddle, proverb, allegory, parabolic story, and many others. It frequently draws upon simple everyday references to convey profound and weighty matters. Amos' basket of ripe summer fruit (Amos 8: 1–3), the proverb, 'Is Saul also among the prophets?' (1 Samuel 19: 24) and Nathan's admonitory narrative parable told to David (2 Samuel 12: 1–4) all fall within the category of *mashal*. Similarly, in the New Testament the word 'parabole' is used to mean a comparison (Luke 5: 36), a riddle (Mark 7: 17), or just a straightforward rule (Luke 14: 7). In fact, if you look carefully at the great narrative parables of St Luke's Gospel, the stories of The Prodigal Son, The Good Samaritan, or The Dishonest Steward, you will rarely find them described by the evangelists as 'parables'. A good general description of the parable is offered by James Olney in his book *Metaphors of the Self*.

These highest peaks of the self, when the largest areas of the vague unconscious are brought to an intensity of consciousness, when the whole potential of humanity seems realized in the individual, cannot be analyzed or explained but only experienced and, if the artist's faith is justified, perhaps re-experienced in metaphors and symbols: in autobiography and poetry.[1]

But now let us turn to the central and difficult passage in St Mark's Gospel, chapter 4, when Jesus, alone with his disciples, offers an explanation of his parables, directly after he has told the great Parable of the Sower. In our excerpts we have shifted somewhat from our usual practice and taken our opening passage from the work of a modern critic, Professor Frank Kermode in his important book *The Genesis of Secrecy*, in which he discusses the nature of narrative in both biblical and modern fictional literature. Here Kermode concentrates on what he calls Mark's 'formula of exclusion' – that is, the tricky moment in verse 12 in which, it seems, parables are told so that the 'outsiders', those not within the privileged circle of Jesus' followers and disciples, will be *prevented* from hearing and understanding, and therefore will gain no forgiveness for their sins. The difficulty hinges on a point of Greek grammar and focusses on Mark's word *hina* which means 'in order that', introducing a purposive construction: outsiders are spoken to in parables *in order that* seeing they may not see, and hearing they may not hear, *lest* (Greek – *mêpote*) they repent and obtain forgiveness. Biblical commentators have repeatedly looked for ways of avoiding the clear implication here that parables are told to prevent salvation becoming possible, and even St Matthew (who, it is likely, wrote his gospel with the text of Mark in front of him), softens this implication by replacing the word *hina* with the softer Greek word *hoti*, (Matthew 13: 13) which means 'because'. Matthew, therefore, can be interpreted as meaning that parables are told to the outsiders *because* their ears are dull and their eyes blind, implying that they may be a means of curing their condition. In other words, this is exactly the opposite of what Mark is suggesting. In Robert Browning's poem 'A Grammarian's Funeral', set, the poet ironically indicates, 'shortly after the revival of learning in Europe', the musty old scholar continues to struggle with these niceties of Greek grammar even while he struggles with 'the throttling hands of Death'.

Yet despite his satire on academic pedantry, Browning still admires his dedication and learning and the grammatical issue is an important one. It is certainly the case that many of the parables of Jesus are judgemental. As in the case of the rich young man (Mark 10: 17–26), their imagery effects the exclusion of those who cannot accept its radical implications, and, as we shall see, the parable as a literary form continues to tease us into thought through its mystery and its challenge to interpretation. Thus we conclude this section with three modern parables very much in the spirit of Mark, chapter 4, by Søren Kierkegaard, Franz Kafka and Jorge Luis Borges. The inclusion also of the Rabbinic parable of Bar Kappara demonstrates that this form of serious literary teasing and riddling, prompting reflection rather than suggesting conclusion, is ancient also in Jewish literary practice.

In the apocryphal and very ancient gnostic *Gospel of Thomas*, discovered only in 1945 near the modern village of Hag Hammadi in Egypt, we find a version of the Parable of the Sower which is possibly even earlier than the Gospel of St Mark. The parable itself contains no negative judgement on the various places where the seed falls, and there is no allegorical intepretation offered as in Mark 4: 14–20. Rather, the stress appears to be on the lack of focus in the sowing and the lack of care shown by the sower – not a particular emphasis of the canonical gospels or the tradition of Christian interpretation of the story. The second paragraph of our excerpt is from a slightly later part of this 'gospel' and is included as a parallel to the so-called 'parables of the kingdom' of the three synoptic gospels of the New Testament. What is stressed here is the necessity of unity and the obliteration of earthly differences – perhaps another form of the focus which is lacking in the careless scattering of the seed by the sower.

As we move into English literature, we find a brief reference to the Parable of the Sower in Geoffrey Chaucer's 'Parson's Tale', which is largely a discussion of the Seven Deadly Sins. In his allusion to the sin of lechery, the Parson draws upon an ancient allegorical tradition found, for example, in St. Jerome (*c.*342–420), which compares the states of virginity, widowhood and matrimony to the yields of the seed which fell on the good soil – a hundred-fold, sixty-fold and thirty-fold. The rape of a virgin destroys the perfection of womanhood – the '*Centesimus fructus*'.

In his Sonnet XVIII, John Milton reflects on the massacre in 1655 of the Piedmontese 'Protestants' by Italian troops, an event with which he was involved in his drafting of the letters of protest at the outrage sent by Cromwell to various European governments. Its language draws upon a variety of Biblical references, including, in the final lines, a reference to the Parable of the Sower, where the blood of the Protestant martyrs is compared to the good seed which bears fruit in the soil into which it has fallen. Some twenty years later, John Bunyan uses the parable in his *Pilgrim's Progress*, in which a conversation takes place between Christian and Fathfull where Christian compares the good seed with those who hear the words of the gospel and act upon them. Pure Religion is to translate the word into Christian action which bears the harvest of good deeds.

This theme of fruitfulness is continued in William Cowper's hymn 'The Sower', another example of the Protestant tradition of reading the parables as encouragements to a useful and profitable Christian life.

Later in the more troubled nineteenth century, we find Thomas Hardy again using the biblical story of the Sower in a lament for the loss of its 'romance' in the face of advancing industrial technology in farming in *The Mayor of Casterbridge*. Thinking back to the *Gospel of Thomas*, there is irony in the fact that now mechanized sowing will achieve the focus that the Sower lacks – but at the cost of the loss of traditional wisdom and insight.

In her second novel, *The Violent Bear it Away*, the Catholic American writer Flannery O'Connor takes up one element in the Marcan interpretation of the parable, in which the seed is the word of God sown within the hearts of people. Indeed, the whole novel is an examination of the results of the seed planted in Rayber and his nephew Tarwater who is not the 'rock' he believes himself to be. As in most of O'Connor's writings, the focus is not so much on the perceivable consequences in actions, as on the work of God's grace, for as Tarwater affirms, 'it ain't a thing you can do about it'.

This section concludes with three examples of parables in modern literature. In each case, what is most apparent is not any moral teaching or definitive 'meaning', but the way in which the narratives and images elude our attempts to interpret them, and prompt radical reflection. It might be said that they sustain, in their very perplexities, the idea suggested in Jesus' remarks to his disciples that 'to you has been given the *mystery* of the kingdom of God' (Mark 4: 11). Perhaps the point is to acknowledge the mystery *as* mysterious, as we recall that the disciples themselves, although chosen as 'insiders' who have been granted the secret, remain utterly perplexed by the Parable of the Sower, eliciting from Jesus the perhaps rather exasperated response, as so often in Mark's Gospel, 'Do you still not understand?'

—— **Literature** ——

Frank Kermode, *The Genesis of Secrecy* (1979)

Let me now return to Mark's formula of exclusion...Jesus is preaching to a crowd, teaching them 'many things in parables.' The first is the Parable of the Sower. He went out to sow; some of his seed fell by the wayside and was eaten by birds; some fell on stony ground, where it grew without rooting and was scorched by the sun; some fell among thorns, which choked it; and some fell on good ground, yielding at harvest thirty, sixty, and a hundredfold. 'He that hath ears to hear, let him hear': this is the formula that tells you the enigmatic part of the text is concluded, and you need to start interpreting. Later, the Twelve, baffled, ask Jesus what the parable means. He replies that they, the elect, know the mystery of the kingdom and do not need to be addressed in parables, but those outside are addressed only thus, 'so *that* seeing they may see and not perceive, and hearing they may hear but not understand, *lest* at any time they should turn, and their sins be forgiven them' (Mark 4: 11–12). He adds, a little crossly, that if the Twelve can't make out this parable they will not make out any of them, but nevertheless goes on to give them an interpretation. What the Sower sows is the Word. People by the wayside hear it, but Satan [the birds] comes and takes it from their hearts. The stony ground signifies those who receive the Word with gladness, but are unable to retain it under stress and persecution; the thorns stand for those who hear it but allow it to be choked by worldly lust and ambition. The last group are those who hear and receive the Word and bear much fruit [4: 14–20].

All this is very odd; the authorized allegory seems inept, a distortion *après coup*, as bad as the priest's exegesis in Kafka.[2] It gives rise to suggestions that Mark did not understand the parable, that its original sense was already lost, and its place taken by an inferior homiletic substitute. But let us put that question aside and look at the general theory of parable pronounced on this occasion: To you has been given the secret of the kingdom of God, but for those outside everything is in parables, so that they may indeed see but not perceive, and may hear but not understand; lest they should turn again and be forgiven. Some argue that Mark's *so that* or *in order that*, the Greek *hina*, is a mistranslation of a word that in the lost Aramaic original meant *in that* or *in such a manner as*, so that Mark's Greek distorts the true sense, which is something like: I have to speak to them in parables, seeing that they are the kind of people who can take stories but not straight doctrine. This is an attempt to make *hina* mean 'because', a very desirable state of affairs. In this altered form the theory no longer conflicts with the prefatory remark that Jesus was *teaching* the crowd, which seems inconsistent with his telling stories in order to ensure that they would miss the point. It also fits the run of the sentence better: the Twelve don't need parables, but the crowd does. Apparently Mark misunderstood, or used *hina* carelessly or in an unusual way; and it is a fairly complex word. But the best authorities do not accept these evasive explanations, a refusal all the more impressive because they would really like to. They admit that Mark's *hina* has to mean *in order that*; and we are left with a doctrine described by one standard modern commentator as 'intolerable',[3] by Albert Schweitzer as 'repellent' and also, since the meaning of the parables is 'as clear as day', unintelligible.

Isaiah 6: 9–13 (Revised Standard Version)

And he said,
'Go, and say to this people:
"Hear and hear, but do not understand;
see and see, but do not perceive,"
Make the heart of this people fat,
and their ears heavy,
and shut their eyes;
lest they see with their eyes
and hear with their ears,
and understand with their hearts,
and turn and be healed.'
Then I said, 'How long, O Lord?'
And he said:
'Until cities lie waste
without inhabitant,
and houses without men,
and the land is utterly desolate,
and the Lord removes men far away,
and the forsaken places are many
in the midst of the land.
And though a tenth remain in it,
it will be burned again,
like a terebinth or an oak,
whose stump remains standing
when it is felled.'
The holy seed is its stump.

The Gospel of Thomas (c.100–110 CE), Robert M. Grant with David Noel Freedman, *The Secret Sayings of Jesus According to the Gospel of Thomas*, Fontana, 1960

Jesus said:
Behold, the Sower went forth,
He filled his hand; he threw.
Some fell upon the road.
The birds came (and) gathered them.
Others fell upon the rock,
and sent no root down into the earth
and put forth no ear up to heaven.
And other fell upon the thorns.
They choked the seed
and the worms ate them.
And others fell upon the good earth
and brought forth good fruit up to heaven.
At times it came as sixty and at times as one hundred and twenty.

Jesus said to them:
When you make the two one,
and make the inside like the outside,
and the outside like the inside,
and the upper side like the under side,
and (in such a way) that you make the man (with) the woman
   a single one,
in order that the man is not the man and the woman is not the
   woman;
when you make eyes in place of an eye,
and a hand in place of a hand,
and a foot in place of a foot,
an image in place of an image;
then you will go into [the kingdom].

The Rabbinic Parable, *Midrash Wayyikra Rabbah*,
ed. M. Margulies, Jerusalem, 1972, 28.2

Simeon, the son of Rabbi [Judah], prepared a [wedding] banquet for his son. He went and invited all the sages, but he forgot to invite Bar Kappara, who thereupon went and wrote on the door of R. Simeon's house: After rejoicing is death. So what value is there to rejoicing?

Who did this to me? R. Simeon asked. Is there anyone we did not invite?

One of his men told him: Bar Kappara. You forgot to invite Bar Kappara.

R. Simeon said: To invite him now would be unseemly. So he went and made a second banquet, and he invited all the sages, and he invited Bar Kappara as well. But at every course that brought before the guests Bar Kappara recited three hundred fox-fables, and the guests didn't even taste the dishes before they grew cold. The dishes were removed from the tables just as they had been brought in.

R. Simeon asked his servant: Why are all the dishes coming back untouched?

The servant replied: There is an old man sitting there. At every course he tells fables until the dishes grow cold, and no one eats.

R. Simeon went up to Bar Kappara; What did I do to make you ruin my banquet?

Bar Kappara answered: What do I need your banquet for? Didn't Solomon say, 'What real value is there for a man in all the gains he makes beneath the sun?' (Ecclesiastes 1: 3)? And what is written after that verse? 'One generation goes, another comes, but the earth remains the same for ever' (1: 4).

Geoffrey Chaucer, 'The Parson's Tale', *The Canterbury Tales* (c.1400), ed. F. N. Robinson, Oxford University Press, 1957, lines 867–8)

Another synne of Leccherie is to bireve a mayden of hir maydenhede; for he that so dooth, certes, he casteth a mayden out of the hyeste degree that is in this present lif, and bireveth hirthilke precious fruyt that the book clepeth the hundred fruyt. I ne kan seye it noon oother-weyes in Englissh, but in Latyn it highte *Centesimus fructus*. Certes, he that so dooth is cause of manye damages and vileynyes, mo than any man kan rekene; right as he somtyme is cause of alle damages and beestes don in the feeld, that breketh the hegge or the closure, thurgh which he destroyeth that may nat been restoored.

John Milton, Sonnet XVIII, 'On the Late Massacre in Piedmont' (1655)

Avenge, O Lord, thy slaughtered saints, whose bones
Lie scattered on the Alpine mountains cold,
Ev'n them who kept thy truth so pure of old

When all our fathers worshipped stocks and stones,
Forget not; in thy book record their groans
  Who were thy sheep, and in their ancient fold
  Slain by the bloody Piedmontese that rolled
  Mother with infant down the rocks. Their moans
The vales redoubled to the hills, and they
  To heav'n. Their martyred blood and ashes sow
  O'er all th' Italian fields, where still doth sway
The triple tyrant, that from these may grow
  A hundredfold, who, having learnt thy way,
Early may fly the Babylonian woe.

John Bunyan, *The Pilgrim's Progress* (1678)

FAITHFULL: Well, I see that saying and doing are two things, and hereafter I shall better observe this distinction.

CHRISTIAN: They are two things indeed, and are as diverse as are the Soul and the Body; for as the Body without the Soul is but a dead Carcass, so Saying, if it be alone, is but a dead Carcass also. The Soul of Religion is the practick part: Pure Religion and undefiled, before God and the Father, is this, To visit the fatherless and widows in their affliction, and to keep himself unspotted from the world. This Talkative is not aware of; he thinks that hearing and saying will make a good Christian, and this he deceiveth his own soul. Hearing is but as the sowing of the Seed; talking is not sufficient to prove that fruit is indeed in the heart and life; and let us assure ourselves, that at the day of Doom men shall be judged according to their fruits. It will not be said then, Did you believe? but, Were you Doers, or Talkers only? and accordingly shall they be judged. The end of the world is compared to our Harvest, and you know men at Harvest regard nothing but fruit. Not that anything can be accepted that is not of Faith; but I speak this to shew you how insignificant the profession of Talkative will be at that day.

Christopher Smart, *The Parables of Our Lord and Saviour Jesus Christ (Done into familiar verse, with occasional applications, for the improvement of younger minds)* (1768), Parable I: The Sower and the Seed

  'Twas thus the Light of Light, the Son
  Of God, his moral tales begun.
  Behold, the parable I show:

A sower went his way to sow,
And, as the kindly grain he threw,
Some by the beaten path-way flew,
And there, neglected as it lay,
Fell to the birds an easy prey.
Some upon stony places fell,
Where, as it was not rooted well,
For lack of depth it soon appear'd:
But, when the sun the vapours clear'd,
It perish'd by the scorching air,
Because it wanted ground to bear:
And some amongst the thorns was cast,
Which choak'd them, growing up too fast.
But some upon a kindly soil
Fell, and repaid the workman's toil.
And these an hundred fold increas'd,
Those sixty, thirty ev'n the least.
  He, to whom God has giv'n an ear,
Let him attend the word in fear.
He spake – and as he made a pause
His scholars came, and ask'd the cause –
'Why dost thou parables recite,
'Nor speak'st thy gracious will out-right?'
Because it is reserve'd for you,
He cries, God's glorious light to view;
But from the race, that have rebell'd,
Are heavenly mysteries with-held;
For those that deathless treasures store
Are sure to reap the more and more,
While him, that makes his little less,
I finally shall dispossess.
I therefore parables devise –
Because, altho' I made them eyes,
Yet is not their discernment clear,
Nor have they for the truth an ear;
That in the hardned and self-will'd
Isaiah's words might be fulfill'd:
'In hearing shall your ears be blest,
'And not one word shall ye digest;
'And seeing ye your God shall view,
'Nor shall ye know him, when ye do.
'For callous hearts this race have got,

'Their ears are clogg'd, their eyes are not:
'Lest, when the season is at hand,
'They see, and hear, and understand,
'And all at once be converts found,
'And I should heal their inward wound.' –
But blessed are your eyes, that see,
And ears, that hear in verity,
For many kings and patriarchs too
(So great the grace indulg'd to you)
And prophets by the word inspir'd,
Have all with fervent pray'r desir'd
To see the things, which ye behold,
And hear the myst'ries, I unfold,
And all their vows, and earnest suit,
Were premature and bore no fruit.
Hear, then, and note the mystic lore
Couch'd in the story of the sow'r.
　　When a man hears, not to retain,
The word of Christ's eternal reign,
Then comes the fiend, and takes away
The grace his heart would not obey.
This is the seed that was imply'd
As wasted by the path-way side.
But that receiver of the grain
Sow'n on the stony-ground in vain,
Resembles one of cheerful heart,
Who hears and acts a christian's part,
By bearing instantaneous fruit,
But having neither depth nor root,
By scourge of pow'r, or worldly loss,
Straight is offended at the cross.
He likewise that receiv'd the seed
'Mongst many a thorn, and many a weed,
Is he, that hears the word, and trusts,
But treach'rous wealth and worldly lusts
Choke up his heart with carnal care,
Till all is naught and barren there.
　　But men of upright hearts and sound
Receive the seed on kindly ground;
The word, which they are apt to hear,
Is to their understanding clear.
These at the harvest we behold

Some bearing fruit an hundred fold,
Some sixty, for the bridegroom's feast,
And thirty ev'n the last and least.

William Cowper, 'The Sower', from *Olney Hymns* (1779)

Ye sons of earth prepare the plough
   Break up your fallow ground!
The Sower is gone forth to sow,
   And scatter blessings round.

The seed that finds a stony soil,
   Shoots forth a hasty blade;
But ill repays the sower's toil,
   Soon withered, scorched and dead.

The thorny ground is sure to balk
   All hopes of harvest there;
We find a tall and sickly stalk,
   But not the fruitful ear.

The beaten path and high-way side
   Receive the trust in vain;
The watchful birds the spoil divide,
   And pick up all the grain.

But where the Lord of grace and power
   Has blessed the happy field;
How plenteous is the golden store
   The deep-wrought furrows yield!

Father of mercies we have need
   Of thy preparing grace;
Let the same hand that gives the seed,
   Provide a fruitful place.

Søren Kierkegaard, 'Either/Or' (1843), from Thomas C.
Oden, ed., *The Parables of Kierkegaard*, Princeton University
Press, 1989

It happened that a fire broke out backstage in a theater. The clown came
out to inform the public. They thought it was just a jest and applauded.

He repeated his warning, they shouted even louder. So I think the world will come to an end amid general applause from all the wits, who believe that it is a joke.

Robert Browning, from 'A Grammarian's Funeral' (1855)

> This, throws himself on God, and unperplext
>   Seeking shall find Him.
> So, with the throttling hands of Death at strife
>   Ground he at grammar;
> Still, thro' the rattle, parts of speech were rife:
>   While he could stammer
> He settled *Hoti's* business – let it be! –
> Properly based *Oun* –
> Gave us the doctrine of the enclitic *De*,
>   Dead from the waist down.

Thomas Hardy, *The Mayor of Casterbridge* (1886), chapter 24

'We are looking at the wonderful new drill,' Miss Templeman said. 'But practically it is a stupid thing – is it not?' she added, on the strength of Henchard's information.

'Stupid? O no!' said Farfrae gravely. 'It will revolutionize sowing here-about! No more sowers flinging their seed about broadcast, so that some falls by the wayside and some among thorns, and all that. Each grain will go straight to its intended place, and nowhere else whatever!'

'Then the romance of the sower is gone for good,' observed Elizabeth-Jane, who felt herself at one with Farfrae in Bible-reading at least. '"He that observeth the wind shall not sow," so the Preacher said; but his words will not be to the point any more. How things change!'

Franz Kafka, 'The Parable of the Door-Keeper', from *The Trial* (1925) tr. Willa and Edwin Muir, Penguin, 1953

Before the Law stands a door-keeper on guard. To this door-keeper there comes a man from the country who begs for admittance to the Law. But the door-keeper says that he cannot admit the man at the moment. The man, on reflection, asks if he will be allowed, then, to enter later. 'It is possible,' answers the door-keeper, 'but not at this moment.' Since the door leading into the Law stands open as usual and the door-keeper steps to one side, the man bends down to peer through the entrance. When the door-keeper sees that, he laughs, and says: 'If you are so strongly tempted, try to get in without my permission. But note that I am powerful. And I am only the lowest door-keeper. From hall to hall, keepers stand at every door, one more powerful than the other. Even the third of these has an aspect that even I cannot bear to look at.' These are difficulties which the man from the country has not expected to meet, the Law, he thinks, should be accessible to every man and at all times, and when he looks more closely at the door-keeper in his furred robe, with his huge pointed nose and long thin, Tartar beard, he decides that he had better wait until he gets permission to enter. The door-keeper gives him a stool and lets him sit down at the side of the door. There he sits waiting for days and years. He makes many attempts to be allowed in and wearies the door-keeper with his importunity. The door-keeper often engages him in brief conversation asking him about his home and about other matters, but the questions are put quite impersonally, as great men put questions, and always conclude with the statement that the man cannot be allowed to enter yet. The man, who has equipped himself with many things for his journey, parts with all he has, however valuable, in the hope of bribing the door-keeper. The door-keeper accepts it all, saying, however, as he takes each gift: 'I take this only to keep you from feeling that you have left something undone.' During all these long years the man watches the door-keeper almost incessantly. He forgets about the other door-keepers, and this one seems to him the only barrier between himself and the Law. In the first years he curses his evil fate aloud; later, as he grows old, he only mutters to himself. He grows childish, and since in his prolonged watch he has learned to know even the fleas in the door-keeper's fur collar, he begs the very fleas to help him and to persuade the door-keeper to change his mind. Finally his eyes grow dim and he does not know whether the world is really darkening around him or whether his eyes are only deceiving him. But in the darkness he can now perceive a radiance that streams immortally from the door of the Law. Now his life is drawing to a close. Before he dies, all that he has experienced during the whole time of his sojourn condenses in his mind into one question, which he has never yet put to the door-keeper. He beckons the door-keeper, since he can no longer raise his stiffening body. The door-keeper has to bend far down to hear him, for the difference in size between them has increased very much to the man's disadvantage. 'What do you want to know now?' asks the door-keeper, 'you are insatiable.' 'Everyone strives to attain the Law,' answers the man, 'how does it come about then, that in all these years no one has come seeking admittance but me?' The door-keeper perceives that the man is at the end of his strength and his hearing is failing, so he bellows in his ear: 'No one but you could gain admittance through this door, since this door was intended only for you. I am now going to shut it.'

'So the door-keeper deluded the man,' said K. immediately, strongly attracted by the story. 'Don't be too hasty,' said the priest, 'don't take over an opinion without testing it. I have told you the story in the very words of the scriptures. There's no mention of delusion in it.' ...

'It is not necessary to accept everything as true, one must only accept it as necessary.' 'A melancholy conclusion,' said K. 'It turns lying into a universal principle.'

Flannery O'Connor, *The Violent Bear it Away* (1960)

Tarwater looked at the table as if waiting for the cards to be laid on it.

'That means I want to talk straight to you,' Rayber said, rigidly keeping the exasperation out of his voice. He strove to make his gaze, his tone, as indifferent as his listener's 'I have some things to say to you that you'll have to listen to. What you do about what I have to say is your own business. I have no further interest in telling you what to do. I only intend to put the facts before you.' His voice was thin and brittle-sounding. He might have been reading from a paper. 'I notice that you've begun to be able to look Bishop in the eye. That's good. It means you're making progress but you needn't think that because you can look him in the eye now, you've saved yourself from what's preying on you. You haven't. The old man still has you in his grip. Don't think he hasn't.'

The boy continued to give him the same omniscient look. 'It's you the seed fell in,' he said. 'It ain't a thing you can do about it. It fell on bad ground but it fell in deep. With me,' he said proudly, 'it fell on rock and the wind carried it away.'

The schoolteacher grasped the table as if he were going to push it forward into the boy's chest. 'God-damn you!' he said in a breathless harsh voice. 'It fell in us both alike. The difference is that I know it's in me and I keep it under control. I weed it out but you're too blind to know it's in you. You don't even know what makes you do the things you do.'

The boy looked at him angrily but he said nothing.

At least, Rayber thought, I've shocked that look off his face. He did not say anything for a few moments while he thought how to continue.

Jorge Luis Borges, 'Inferno, I, 32', *Labyrinths: Selected Stories and Other Writings*, ed. Donald A. Yates and James E. Irby, Penguin, 1970

From the twilight of day till the twilight of evening, a leopard, in the last years of the thirteenth century, would see some wooden planks, some vertical iron bars, men and women who changed, a wall and perhaps a stone gutter filled with dry leaves. He did not know, could not know, that he longed for love and cruelty and the hot pleasure of tearing things to pieces and the wind carrying the scent of a deer, but something suffocated and rebelled within him and God spoke to him in a dream: 'You live and will die in this prison so that a man I know of may see you a certain number of times and not forget you and place your figure and symbol in a poem which has its precise place in the scheme of the universe. You suffer captivity, but you will have given a word to the poem.' God, in the dream, illumined the animal's brutishness and the animal understood these reasons and accepted his destiny, but, when he awoke, there was in him only an obscure resignation, a valorous ignorance, for the machinery of the world is much too complex for the simplicity of a beast.

Years later, Dante was dying in Ravenna, as unjustified and as lonely as any other man. In a dream, God declared to him the secret purpose of his life and work: Dante, in wonderment, knew at last who and what he was and blessed the bitterness of his life. Tradition relates that, upon waking, he felt that he had received and lost an infinite thing, something he would not be able to recuperate or even glimpse, for the machinery of the world is much too complex for the simplicity of men.

Notes

1 Quoted in John Dominic Crossan, *In Parables: The Challenge of the Historical Jesus* (San Francisco: Harper & Row, 1973), p. 122.
2 See below, p. 237.
3 Vincent Taylor, *The Gospel According to St. Mark: The Greek Text with Introduction, Notes and Indexes*, 2nd edn (London: Macmillan, 1966), p. 257.

Bibliography

Crossan, John Dominic. *In Parables: The Challenge of the Historical Jesus* (San Francisco: Harper and Row, 1973).

Crossan, John Dominic. *Raid on the Articulate: Comic Eschatology in Jesus and Borges* (New York: Harper and Row, 1976).

Dodd, C. H. *The Parables of the Kingdom*, revised edn (1935. London: James Nisbet, 1961).

Jeremias, Joachim. *The Parables of Jesus*, revised edn, tr. S. H. Hooke (London: SCM, 1972).

Kermode, Frank. *The Genesis of Secrecy: On the Interpretation of Narrative* (Cambridge, MA: Harvard University Press, 1979).

McFague, Sallie. *Speaking in Parables: A Study in Metaphor and Theology* (Philadelphia: Fortress Press, 1975).

Oden, Thomas C. (ed.). *Parables of Kierkegaard* (1978. Princeton: Princeton University Press, 1989).

Stern, David. *Parables in Midrash: Narrative and Exegesis in Rabbinic Literature* (Cambridge, MA.: Harvard University Press, 1991).

Jesus and the Samaritan Woman

John 4: 1–30

[1] When therefore the Lord knew how the Pharisees had heard that Jesus made and baptized more disciples than John,

[2] (Though Jesus himself baptized not, but his disciples,)

[3] He left Judaea, and departed again into Galilee.

[4] And he must needs go through Samaria.

[5] Then cometh he to a city of Samaria, which is called Sychar, near to the parcel of ground that Jacob gave to his son Joseph.

[6] Now Jacob's well was there. Jesus therefore, being wearied with his journey, sat thus on the well: and it was about the sixth hour.

[7] There cometh a woman of Samaria to draw water: Jesus saith unto her, Give me to drink.

[8] (For his disciples were gone away unto the city to buy meat.)

[9] Then saith the woman of Samaria unto him, How is it that thou, being a Jew, askest drink of me, which am a woman of Samaria? for the Jews have no dealings with the Samaritans.

[10] Jesus answered and said unto her, If thou knewest the gift of God, and who it is that saith to thee, Give me to drink; thou wouldest have asked of him, and he would have given thee living water.

[11] The woman saith unto him, Sir, thou hast nothing to draw with, and the well is deep: from whence then hast thou that living water?

[12] Art thou greater than our father Jacob, which gave us the well, and drank thereof himself, and his children, and his cattle?

[13] Jesus answered and said unto her, Whosoever drinketh of this water shall thirst again:

[14] But whosoever drinketh of the water that I shall give him shall never thirst; but the water that I shall give him shall be in him a well of water springing up into everlasting life.

[15] The woman saith unto him, Sir, give me this water, that I thirst not, neither come hither to draw.

[16] Jesus saith unto her, Go, call thy husband, and come hither.

[17] The woman answered and said, I have no husband. Jesus said unto her, Thou hast well said, I have no husband:

[18] For thou hast had five husbands; and he whom thou now hast is not thy husband: in that saidst thou truly.

[19] The woman saith unto him, Sir, I perceive that thou art a prophet.

[20] Our fathers worshipped in this mountain; and ye say, that in Jerusalem is the place where men ought to worship.

[21] Jesus saith unto her, Woman, believe me, the hour cometh, when ye shall neither in this mountain, nor yet at Jerusalem, worship the Father.

[22] Ye worship ye know not what: we know what we worship: for salvation is of the Jews.

[23] But the hour cometh, and now is, when the true worshippers shall worship the Father in spirit and in truth: for the Father seeketh such to worship him.

[24] God is a Spirit: and they that worship him must worship him in spirit and in truth.

[25] The woman saith unto him, I know that Messias cometh, which is called Christ: when he is come, he will tell us all things.

[26] Jesus saith unto her, I that speak unto thee am he.

[27] And upon this came his disciples, and marvelled that he talked with the woman: yet no man said, What seekest thou? or, Why talkest thou with her?

[28] The woman then left her waterpot, and went her way into the city, and saith to the men,

[29] Come, see a man, which told me all things that ever I did: is not this the Christ?

[30] Then they went out of the city, and came unto him.

Notes

Verse 4. Samaria and its people were regarded with distrust and hostility by the Jews, a hostility which dated back centuries to the time of the Exile in Babylon, when many foreign settlers moved into the northern region around the city of Samaria. From this hostility arises the point of the great parable of the Good Samaritan in the Gospel of Luke Chapter 10. Samaritans were not thought of as 'good', and 'Jews have no dealings with Samaritans' (verse 9). Hence, the woman of this story is an outsider by race as far as Jesus and his disciples were concerned.

Verse 5. See Genesis 33: 19 and 48: 22. The place is symbolic of where Israel can expect to receive her rightful inheritance, as Joseph received land from his father Jacob. In a semi-desert environment, wells were important places of meeting, and women would often be found drawing water. They thus become also places where marriages might be arranged. See, Genesis 24: 10ff, the story of Isaac and Rebekah. No doubt this adds to the overtones of unsuitability in the conversation Jesus has with the woman.

Verse 10. The term 'living water' is found in the Old Testament as a metaphor of divine activity which gives us life. It is also frequently found in Rabbinic writings as an image of Torah. In Jeremiah 2: 13, the contrast is made between the 'fountain of living waters' and the 'broken cisterns' which leak and lose their water. The Greek word used for well in:

Verse 11 (*phrear*), is different from the word used of Jacob's well in verse 6 (*pêgê*), and is closer to the sense of cistern as used in Jeremiah, denoting a man-made cavity into which water would drain, but which was leaky.

Verse 17. Apart from its literal meaning, the woman's reference to her husband is sometimes also understood in the Christian tradition to refer to her Samaritan religion, which must also come to Jesus for life.

Verse 20. The reference is presumably to Mount Gerizim, which the Samaritans claimed was the proper place for worship as enjoined by Deuteronomy.

Verse 22. The Samaritans accepted the Pentateuch, that is, the first five books of the Old Testament, but not the remaining Jewish literature of the recorded history of Israel, the prophets and poets.

Verse 23. The word 'truth' in this Gospel is almost equivalent to 'reality'.

Verse 27. The disciples marvelled at Jesus' conversation with the woman. The word used in Greek (*thaumazo*) often describes the reaction of people to his miracles, suggesting that this episode may be seen in some sense as a miracle.

—— **Commentary** ——

Jesus's encounter with the Samaritan woman at Jacob's well near to Sychar is full of significance in the Fourth Gospel. In his poem 'The Search', Henry Vaughan looks back specifically to verse 5 in the Gospel narrative, which records Sychar as being 'near the field that Jacob gave to his son Joseph', that is, symbolically the place where Israel (Jacob's adopted name) may be expected to enter into its rightful inheritance. But not only is this well in the borders of Samaria – the hated Samaritans being regarded as neither Jews nor Gentiles – but Jesus' encounter and conversation is with a woman, and moreover, a woman of highly questionable character. For a Jewish male to speak to such a person alone was nothing short of scandalous, and Jesus' disciples are duly dismayed (verse 27).

It is perhaps, then, all the more daring that this episode in the Gospel is also highly reminiscent of betrothal stories in ancient Hebrew literature, such as the stories of Rebekah (Genesis 24: 10–14), of Rachel (Genesis 29: 1–12), and the daughters of the priest of Midian (Exodus 2: 15–21). Indeed, the imagery of John chapter 4 resonates throughout with resonances from the Old Testament, in particular the theme of 'living water' as a symbol of the life-giving power of God (e.g. Jeremiah 2: 13; Ezekiel 47: 9), which also prefigures the 'river of the water of life' in the last book of the Christian Bible, Revelation 22: 1.

In the early Christian Church, legends rapidly grew up around the character of the Samaritan woman. While theologians like Origen, St John Chrysostom and St Augustine of Hippo, not surprisingly tended to interpret the story symbolically and allegorically, popular traditions associate the woman first with the apocryphal figure of St Photine, who was supposed to have been converted to Christianity and later was martyred for her faith in Carthage (or, in some later versions of the story, Rome), and much later with Mary Magdalen herself as the archetypical repentant prostitute. The French playwright Edmond Rostand, best known for his play *Cyrano de Bergerac* (1897), takes up the Photine legend in his drama *La Samaritaine* (1897), a political play which also daringly celebrates love. Photine approaches Jesus at the well singing praises from the Song of Songs, and is finally joined even by the disciples themselves.

Much more common in literature, however, is the association with Mary Magdalen, a figure constructed out of various women who appear in the gospels and who has in common with the Samaritan woman a history of promiscuity. One of the three Digby plays, mystery dramas from East Anglia and dating from the early sixteenth century, draws on a number of details from John chapter 4. But it is Geoffrey Chaucer's great character the Wife of Bath in *The Canterbury Tales* who provides the best known and most full-blooded reference to the biblical narrative in English medieval literature. In the Prologue to her Tale, she takes issue with Jesus's criticism of the woman having five husbands, expressing her opinion that there should be no limit to the number of husbands, from 'bigamye' to 'octogamye', to fulfil the divine command to wax and multiply (Genesis 1: 28; 'Be fruitful and multiply, and fill the earth and subdue it'). She is, in self-defence, a staunch defender of the Samaritan woman's traditional promiscuity.

References to the theme of 'living water' abound in literature, and we have selected here only a few, from Edmund Spenser to Emily Dickinson as she reads 'in an Old fashioned Book' – that is, the Gospel of John. The sheer complexity of this narrative, touching as it does upon so many issues, and with its typological relationship with Genesis and numerous other texts of the Hebrew tradition, has ensured its continuing vitality in our literary traditions. In another poem, 'Religion', given here, Henry Vaughan draws upon numerous biblical references as he laments that we no longer enjoy the close and immediate relationship with God and angels as was the experience of figures like Jacob, Elijah or Abraham, but religion is now corrupted like water that has lain long in the earth and has grown brackish and poisoned. In the penultimate verse, Vaughan refers to the 'dead Well' of the Samaritan woman, yielding not the living water of life but the stagnant water of the cistern. He prays that this may be turned into sweet and living water that the flock of the Good Shepherd may drink, referring finally to the first miracle story of the Fourth Gospel, the changing of the water into wine at the marriage feast in Cana (John 2: 1–11).

In the eighteenth century there is only one notable reference to the story, rather oddly placed in Christopher Smart's *The Parables of Our Lord*. It is a rather pedantic retelling of the narrative, playing down references to the woman's questionable history in her marriages, and the theme of living water, and emphasizing instead Jesus's extraordinary insight into the truth of her life.

Generally speaking, after the Renaissance, references to the story of the Samaritan woman and the water of life become less frequent in literature, and are often merely decorative, as in George Bernard Shaw's brief mention of the water in his extensive stage directions to *Man and Superman* (1901–1903), where he describes Miss Ann Whitefield as turning Octavius's blood 'into rapturous rivers of the very water of life itself'. Earlier in the nineteenth century, more seriously, John Ruskin radically and somewhat gloomily uses the image of living water in his essay attacking the 'pseudo-science' of J. S. Mill and Ricardo, *Unto This Last* (1860), using it as an ironic trope for wealth, which, if left uncontrolled can turn into the bitter 'water of Marah', in a reference to Exodus 15: 23 ('When they [the Children of Israel] came to Marah, they could not drink the water of Marah, because it was bitter; therefore it was named Marah [Bitterness]').

We conclude this section with two modern fictional accounts of the life of Jesus which refer to the passage, the first being the brief reference in Nikos Kazantzakis's notorious *The Last Temptation*, in which the young Jesus dreams of the length and breadth of his country, and, in his dream, sees 'a rouged and powdered woman' by a well in Samaria, an erotic moment which contrasts with the innocence of his own Galilee and the violence of Jerusalem. The last is from Moelwyn Merchant's re-telling of the boyhood and young manhood of 'Jeshua'. Merchant's rather academic commentary on the story has a certain vitality, but is given here to illustrate the extraordinary literary power of the original telling in the Gospel – for the writer of St. John's Gospel was a supreme literary artist, capable of highly dramatic writing which functions on many levels at once and embracing a number of different literary and theological traditions. Of all the literature which has been inspired by this story, perhaps none has outshone the brilliance and immediacy of the original.

—— **Literature** ——

Genesis 24: 10–14, Rebekah at the Well, Revised Standard Version

Then the servant took ten of his master's camels and departed, taking all sorts of choice gifts from his master; and he arose, and went to Mesopotamia, to the city of Nahor. And he made the camels kneel down outside the city by the well of water at the time of evening, the time when women go out to draw water. And he said, 'O Lord, God of my master Abraham, grant me success today, I pray thee, and show steadfast love to my master Abraham. Behold I am standing by the spring of water, and the daughters of the men of the city are coming out to draw water. Let the maiden to whom I shall say, "Pray let down your jar that I may drink," and who shall say, "Drink, and I will water your camels" – let her be the one whom thou hast appointed for thy servant Isaac. By this I shall know that thou hast shown steadfast love to my master.'

Geoffrey Chaucer, 'The Wife of Bath's Prologue', *The Canterbury Tales* (c.1400), ed. F. N. Robinson, 2nd edn, Oxford University Press, 1957, lines 1–34

Experience, though noon auctoritee
Were in this world, is right ynogh for me
To speke of wo that is in mariage;
For, lordynges, sith I twelve yeer was of age,
Thonked be God that is eterne on lyve,
Housbondes at chirche dore I have had fyve, –
If I so ofte myghte have ywedded bee,–
And alle were worthy men in hir degree.
But me was toold, certeyn, nat longe agoon is,
That sith that Crist ne wente nevere but onis

To weddyng, in the Cane of Galilee,
That by the same ensaumple taughte he me
That I ne sholde wedded be but ones.
Herkne eek, lo, which is a sharp word for the nones,
Biside a welle, Jhesus, God and man,
Spak in repreeve of the Samaritan:
'Thou hast had fyves housbondes,' quod he,
'And that ilke man that now hath thee
Is noght thyn housbonde,' thus seyde he certeyn.
What that he mente therby, I kan nat seyn;
But that I axe, why that the fifthe man
Was noon housbonde to the Samaritan?
How manye myghte she have in mariage?
Yet herde I nevere tellen in myn age
Upon this nombre diffinicioun.
Men may devyne and glosen, up and doun,
But wel I woot, expres, withoute lye,
God bad us for to wexe and multiplye;
That gentil text kan I wel understonde.
Eek wel I woot, he seyde myn housbonde
Sholde lete fader and mooder, and take to me.
But of no nombre mencion made he,
Of bigamye, or of octogamye;
Why sholde men thanne speke of it vileyny.

Edmund Spenser, *The Faerie Queen* (1590), Book 1, Canto XI, 29–30.

> It fortuned (as faire it then befell)
> Behind his backe unweeting, where he stood
> Of auncient time there was a springing well,
> From which fast trickled forth a silver flood,
> Full of great vertues, and for med'cine good.
> Whylome, before that cursed Dragon got
> That happie land, and all with innocent blood
> Defyld those sacred waves, it rightly hot
> *The well of life*, ne yet his virtues had forgot.
>
> For unto life the dead it could restore,
> And guilt of sinfull crimes cleane wash away,
> Those that with sicknesse were infected sore,
> It could recure, and aged long decay

Renew, as one were borne that very day.
Both *Silo* this, and *Jordan* did excell,
And th' English *Bath*, and eke the german *Spau*,
Ne can *Cephise*, nor *Hebrus* match this well:
Into the same the knight backe overthrown, fell.

Henry Vaughan, 'Religion', from *Silex Scintillans* (1650)

My God, when I wake in those groves,
And leaves thy spirit doth still fan,
I see in each shade that there growes
An Angell talking with a man.

Under a *Juniper*, some house,
Or the coole *Mirtles* canopie,
Others beneath an *Oakes* greene boughs,
Or at some *fountaines* bubling Eye;

Here Jacob dreames, and wrestles; there
Elias by a Raven is fed,
Another time by th' Angell, where
He brings him water with his bread;

In *Abr'hams* Tent the winged guests
(O how familiar then was heaven!)
Eate, drinke, discourse, sit downe, and rest
Until the Coole, and shady *Even*;

Nay thou thy selfe, my God, in *fire*,
Whirle-winds, and *Clouds*, and the *soft voice*
Speak'st there so much, that I admire
We have no Conf'rence in these daies;

Is the truce broke? or 'cause we have
A mediatour now with thee,
Doest thou therefore old Treaties wave
And by appeales from him decree?

Or is't so, as some green heads say
That now all miracles must cease?
Though thou hast promis'd they should stay
The tokens of the Church, and peace;

No, no; Religion is a Spring
That from some secret, golden Mine
Derives her birth, and thence doth bring
Cordials in every drop, and Wine;

But in her long, and hidden Course
Passing through the Earths darke veines,
Growes still from better unto worse,
And both her taste, and colour staines,

Then drilling on, learnes to encrease
False *Ecchoes*, and Confused sounds,
And unawares doth often seize
On veines of *Sulphur* under ground;

So poison'd, breaks forth in some Clime,
And at first sight doth many please,
But drunk, is puddle, or meere slime
And 'stead of Phisick, a disease;
Just such a tainted sink we have
Like that *Samaritans* dead *Well*,
Nor must we for the Kernell crave
Because most voices like the *shell*.

Heale then these waters, Lord; or bring thy flock,
Since these are troubled, to the springing rock,
Looke downe great Master of the feast; O shine,
And turn once more our *Water* into *Wine!*

Christopher Smart, *The Parables of Our Lord and Saviour Jesus Christ* (1768), Parable LXXI: The Woman of Samaria

> CHRIST in a certain town remains,
> Call'd Sichar, in Samaria's plains,
> Near to that spot, the patriarch bless'd
> For Joseph, in his will express'd.
> Now Jacob's well was where he went,
> And Jesus, with his journey spent,
> Sat down at ease upon the brink
> (The hour was then the sixth) to drink;
> When from Samaria thither came
> A woman – Christ address'd the dame,

'Give me to drink.' (For his co-mates
For meat had sought the city-gates.)
How comes it, Sir, to pass, said she,
That you should ask to drink of me,
A woman of Samaria's place,
And thou a man of Jewish race?
For with Samaritans the Jews
All kind of intercourse refuse.
Then Christ, 'Didst thou but understand
'God's gift, and him that asks thy hand,
'Thou'dst offer'd of thine own accord,
'And hadst receiv'd for thy reward
'From life's eternal well a draught.'
Sir, says the woman, thou hast nought
Wherewith to draw, and deep the spring,
Whence living water canst thou bring?
Canst thou afford more pow'rful aid
Than father Jacob, he that made
This well, whence for himself he drew,
His children, and his cattle too?
Then Christ, 'Who to this water makes,
'Shall thirst again; but whoso takes
'The quick'ning water that I give,
'Shall never thirst, but ever live.
'For what I give to him in peace
'Shall be life's well-spring not to cease.'
Lord, with this water me suffice
That I nor thirst nor draw, she cries.
Says Christ 'Go call thy husband here,
'And with him at this place appear.'
No husband in the world have I –
'I have no husband is no lie.
'I have no husband, is well said:
'For five thou hadst; but art not wed
'Unto the man you now receive.'
Sir, thou'rt a prophet, I believe.
Our fathers worshipp'd in this mount:
But in respect to your account,
Jerusalem's the place of pray'r,
And we should only worship there
The Lord returns 'You may rely,
'O woman, that the hour is nigh,

'When neither here, as heretofore
'Nor there you shall your God adore.
'Ye worship that ye do not know:
'But with the Jews it is not so,
'From where salvation comes in pow'r
'For now arrives the very hour,
'When faithful men, divinely meek
'In spirit and in truth shall seek
'The Father; 'tis the Father's will,
'That such their homage should fulfill.
'God is a Spirit we confess,
'In truth and spirit must we bless.'
The woman answers, I am clear,
Messias, call'd the Christ, is near,
Whose coming all things shall explain.
'Then said the Lord to her again,
'I that speak with thee am the Man.'
At which forthwith the woman ran,
Without her water-pot and calls
Unto the men within the walls,
Come, see the Man, that did the tale
Of all my life at once unveil;
Is not this Christ himself indeed?
Then went the citizens with speed.
But mean time his disciples pray'd,
And urging, Master, eat, they said.
But return'd unto their pray'r,
Eat must I when you're not aware.'
Then 'mongst themselves they ask'd, and sought
Has any man some victuals brought?
'My meat, he cries, is to fulfill
'My Father's word, and do his will,
'Do ye not say, four months remain,
'And then arrives the time for grain:
Behold! I say, lift up your eyes,
'And look up to the crops that rise,
'Which stand upon the fields around,
'Already whit'ning all the ground,
'And he that reaps shall earn his hire,
'And life's eternal fruit acquire,
'That they that sow, and they that reap,
'With joy one harvest-home may keep:

'And herein a true proverb's shown,
'One reaps what was by others sown.
'I sent you to be reapers there
'Of that in which ye took no care:
'Their labour other men bestow'd,
'And you upon the spoil abode.'
   And many of Samaria's race
Believed on the Prince of Grace
For that the woman said, 'The tale
'Of all my life he did unveil.'
So when the city came to greet
The Lord, they did his stay intreat
And two days did he there abide:
And many persons more beside
Believ'd through faith in his own word,
And with the woman thus conferr'd,
'Now we believe that he is true,
'Not for the words he spake to you;
'For we have heard him with our ears,
'And to us all the truth appears;
'And in his words and deeds we find
'The Christ and Saviour of mankind.'

Emily Dickinson, 'I Know Where Wells Grow – Droughtless
Wells' (c.1862), *Complete Poems*, ed. Thomas H. Johnson,
Faber, 1970, No. 460

I know where Wells grow – Droughtless Wells –
Deep dug – for Summer days –
Where Mosses go no more away –
And Pebble – safely plays –

It's made of Fathoms – and a Belt –
A Belt of jagged Stone –
Inlaid with Emerald – half way down –
And Diamonds – jumbled on –

It has no Bucket – Were I rich
A Bucket I would buy –
I'm often thirsty – but my lips
Are so high up – You see –

I read in an Old fashioned Book
That People 'thirst no more' –
The Wells have Buckets to them there –
It must mean that – I'm sure –

Shall We remember Parching – then?
Those Waters sound so grand
I think a little Well – like Mine –
Dearer to understand –

John Ruskin, *Unto This Last* (1860), from Essay 3: 'Qui Judicatis Terram'

For centuries after centuries great districts of the world, rich in soil, and favoured in climate, have lain desert under the rage of their own rivers; nor only desert, but plague-struck. The stream which, rightly directed, would have flowed in soft irrigation from field to field – would have purified the air, given food to man and beast, and carried their burdens for them on its bosom – now overwhelms the plain, and poisons the wind; its breath pestilence and its work famine. In like manner this wealth 'goes where it is required.' No human laws can withstand its flow. They can only guide it: but this, the leading trench and limiting mound can do so thoroughly, that it shall become water of life – the riches of the hand of wisdom; or, on the contrary, by leaving it to its own lawless flow, they may make it, what it has been too often, the last and deadliest of national plagues: the water of Marah – the water which feeds the root of all evil.

George Bernard Shaw, *Man and Superman: A Comedy and a Philosophy* (1901–1903), from the stage directions to Act 1

The crushing retort for which Mr. Ramsden has been visibly collecting his forces is lost for ever; for at this point Octavius returns with Miss Ann Whitefield and her mother; and Ramsden springs up and hurries to the door to receive them. Whether Ann is good-looking or not depends upon your taste; also and perhaps chiefly on your age and sex. To Octavius she is an enchantingly beautiful woman, in whose presence the world becomes transfigured, and the puny limits of individual consciousness are suddenly made infinite by a mystic memory of the whole life of the race to its beginnings in the east, or even back to the paradise from which it fell. She is to him the reality of romance, the inner good sense of nonsense, the unveiling of his eyes, the freeing of his soul, the abolition of time, place, and circumstance, the etherealizations of his blood into rapturous rivers of the very water of life itself, the revelation of all the mysteries and the sanctification of all the dogmas. To her mother she is, to put it as moderately as possible, nothing whatever of the kind. Not that Octavius's admiration is in any way ridiculous or discreditable. Ann is a well formed creature, as far as that goes; and she is perfectly ladylike, graceful, and comely, with ensnaring eyes and hair. Besides, instead of making herself an eyesore, like her mother, she has devised a mourning costume of black and violet silk which does honor to her late father and reveals the family tradition of brave unconventionality by which Ramsden sets such store.

Moelwyn Merchant, *Jeshua* (1987)

A woman, handsome and poised beneath the large water-jar she carried on her shoulder, approached the well. Resentment at the stranger's presence flared briefly, to be followed by a quick observation of this comely young man. Jeshua spoke as if diffidently.
'Can you give me a drink of this water? I have no cup.'
A hostile tone masked the curiosity which she now felt; 'Why do you, a Galilean, ask a favour of me, a despised Samaritan?'

Nikos Kazantzakis, *The Last Temptation* (1953), tr. P. A. Bien, Faber, 1961

Mountains sank away, men vanished, the dream was wrenched into a new locale and the sleeper saw the Land of Canaan unfold above him on the low cane-lathed ceiling of his house – the Land of Canaan, like embroidered air, many-coloured, richly ornamented, and trembling. To the south, the quivering desert of Idumea shifted like the back of a leopard. Further on, the Dead Sea, thick and poisonous, drowned and drank the light. Beyond this stood inhuman Jerusalem, moated on every side by the commandments of Jehovah. Blood from God's victims, from lambs and prophets, ran down its cobbled streets. Next came Samaria, dirty, trodden by idolators, with a well in the centre and a rouged and powdered woman drawing water; and finally, at the extreme north: Galilee – sunny, modest, verdant. And flowing from one end of the dream to the other was the river Jordan, God's royal artery, which passes by sandy wastes and rich orchards, John the Baptist and Samaritan heretics, prostitutes and the fishermen of Gennesaret, watering them all – indifferently.

Bibliography

Newsom, Carol A. and Sharon H. Ringe (Eds). *The Women's Bible Commentary* (London: SPCK, 1992), pp. 295–6.

Schneiders, Sandra M. *The Revelatory Text: Interpreting the New Testament as Sacred Scripture* (San Francisco: Harper, 1991), ch. 7, 'A Case Study: Feminist Interpretation of John 4: 1–42'.

Stanton, Elizabeth Cady. *The Woman's Bible* (1895, 1898. Seattle: Coalition Task Force on Women and Religion, 1992).

Witherington, Ben III. *Women in the Ministry of Jesus* (Cambridge: Cambridge University Press, 1984).

The Prodigal Son

Luke 15: 11–32

[11] And he said, A certain man had two sons:

[12] And the younger of them said to his father, Father, give me the portion of goods that falleth to me. And he divided unto them his living.

[13] And not many days after the younger son gathered all together, and took his journey into a far country, and there wasted his substance with riotous living.

[14] And when he had spent all, there arose a mighty famine in that land; and he began to be in want.

[15] And he went and joined himself to a citizen of that country; and he sent him into his fields to feed swine.

[16] And he would fain have filled his belly with the husks that the swine did eat: and no man gave unto him.

[17] And when he came to himself, he said, How many hired servants of my father's have bread enough and to spare, and I perish with hunger!

[18] I will arise and go to my father, and will say unto him, Father, I have sinned against heaven, and before thee,

[19] And am no more worthy to be called thy son: make me as one of thy hired servants.

[20] And he arose, and came to his father. But when he was yet a great way off, his father saw him, and had compassion, and ran, and fell on his neck, and kissed him.

[21] And the son said unto him, Father, I have sinned against heaven, and in thy sight, and am no more worthy to be called thy son.

[22] But the father said to his servants, Bring forth the best robe, and put it on him; and put a ring on his hand, and shoes on his feet:

[23] And bring hither the fatted calf, and kill it; and let us eat, and be merry:
[24] For this my son was dead, and is alive again; he was lost, and is found. And they began to be merry.
[25] Now his elder son was in the field: and as he came and drew nigh to the house, he heard musick and dancing.
[26] And he called one of the servants, and asked what these things meant.
[27] And he said unto him, Thy brother is come; and thy father hath killed the fatted calf, because he hath received him safe and sound.
[28] And he was angry, and would not go in: therefore came his father out, and intreated him.
[29] And he answering said to his father, Lo, these many years do I serve thee, neither transgressed I at any time thy commandment: and yet thou never gavest me a kid, that I might make merry with my friends:
[30] But as soon as this thy son was come, which hath devoured thy living with harlots, thou hast killed for him the fatted calf.
[31] And he said unto him, Son, thou art ever with me, and all that I have is thine.
[32] It was meet that we should make merry, and be glad: for this thy brother was dead, and is alive again; and was lost, and is found.

Notes

This parable can be read alongside other biblical stories of 'two sons', in particular the story of Jacob and Esau. See above, pp. 123–33.

Verse 15. Pigs were, to a Jew, regarded as unclean animals. Jews still refrain from eating pork.
Verse 17. The phrase in Greek literally means, 'Having come back into himself'. It can be linked with the Greek word for 'repentance' (*metanoia*) which means to turn the mind around.
Verse 19. The word for 'hired servant' (*misthios*) is found only three times in the New Testament and is peculiar to this Gospel.
Verse 23. There is a famous (though unsourced) anecdote connected with the translation of this story. It is said that the translators of the New English Bible in the 1950s were worried by the archaism of 'fatted calf' in the King James Bible but were unable to think of what the modern technical term was for an animal specially fattened up for killing. So they decided to consult a butcher at Smithfield Market, in London. He explained that it was 'fatted calf' – and that it was derived from the (King James) Bible!
Verse 24. This is a figure of speech called 'chiasmus' which is typical of the gospels, involving an inversion of word order in the second of two parallel phrases. Another example is 'the first shall be last and the last first'.

——— Commentary ———

Though we often tend to read the so-called 'parables of the kingdom' separately, as free-standing narratives, we need to recall that Luke 15 contains altogether three parables about loss and gain: that of the shepherd and his lost sheep (4–7); the lost coin (8–10); and then, finally, the much more extended and psychologically developed Prodigal Son. In each of the first two the moral is the same: 'joy shall be in heaven over one sinner that repenteth, more than over ninety and nine just persons, which need no repentance' (verse 7); 'there is joy in the presence of the angels of God over one sinner that repenteth' (verse 10). As we have seen in the Creation and Nativity stories, there is a strong link between the act of creation and joy in heaven, and both these stories are therefore linked by imagery with an existing biblical tradition of new, or re-creation.

The conclusion of the Prodigal Son, however, is slightly different. It ends not with a stated extraneous moral, calling attention to the allegory, but simply in dialogue, with the father speaking to the disgruntled elder brother: 'It was meet we should make merry, and be glad; for this thy brother was dead, and is alive again; and was lost, and is found.' Though this is clearly no less allegorical than the first two sketches, its greater length and more complex characterization, as well as the lack of overt moral, make it somewhat more ambiguous. The obvious interpretation is that the 'father' is God, and the younger son stands for sinful humanity. There is thus no need to stress the 'joy in heaven' because the family home *is* heaven. The problem with this, of course, whether we read the story as a collective allegory, or simply in individual terms, is the identity of the elder brother who has never left home. We are encouraged by the context – the contrast between the 'publicans and sinners', on the one hand, and the 'Pharisees and Scribes' on the other – to read references to 'the just persons who need no repentance' as ironic. Christian tradition has always insisted that we are all sinners; those who believe themselves to be righteous, or to need no repentance, are simply deluding themselves. But who then is this elder brother? He may be sulky, but there is no suggestion that his father wants to do anything other than pacify him. He is certainly not going to be disinherited – indeed, his father insists, 'all that I have is thine' (underscoring the fact that the younger brother has already had, and wasted, his share). Do we simply see him as an ironic portrait of the attitude of the Pharisees towards their less-strict fellow Jews? The story does have other biblical echoes. The framework of a father with two sons, the younger of whom leaves, and then returns to find himself in potential conflict with the elder, is, if we discount the details, that of Jacob and

Esau – even to the elder brother being a pastoralist. This does not, however, solve the problem of identification. It is certainly possible to see the younger brother as Jacob – or, collectively, Israel and his descendants, the Jewish people, who have, time and again, gone 'a-whoring after strange gods' and have always brought misfortune on themselves by so doing. Even at the time Jesus is speaking, they are under the bondage of pagan Roman rule. Yet this does not remove the problem of the elder brother. A plausible variation on this might be to see the 'prodigal' people as the Samaritans, the descendants of those left behind during the Exile in Babylon (the 'lost ten tribes'), and who, intermarrying with other settlers moved into the area, had evolved a syncretistic religion of their own, and who were much despised by the Jews, who believed themselves to have kept the pure faith of Moses and the prophets. As the story of the Good Samaritan (Luke 10: 30–35) and the conversation with the Samaritan woman at the well (John 4: 4–42) illustrate, Jesus clearly had a soft spot for the Samaritans. On this reading, the elder brother then becomes the Orthodox Jews (to whom presumably Jesus is speaking) who would deeply resent any divine favour towards the apostate Samaritans. For later Christians it was obviously tempting to include themselves among the repentant sinners. 'This parable,' writes Mrs. Trimmer in 1805, 'has a double meaning; in one sense it related to the Jews and Gentiles, and was intended to show the Jews how very uncharitable and unreasonable they were in taking offence at the Gentiles being called from idolatry into covenant with God; in another sense, the parable relates to mankind in general.' As we have seen (in the discussion of Genesis 27) this would not be the first time that Christian commentators have turned Esau into an allegorical representation of the Jews, but the obvious objection to this reading is historical: when Jesus is supposed to have been telling this story, no Church existed, and there was no suggestion that Gentiles might be admitted.

The story has always been a popular one with commentators and writers. The moral, that no one should turn away those who sincerely repent, was reiterated by a series of ecclesiastical writers from Ambrose to Calvin. In the sixteenth century a number of didactic continental plays were written on the theme, and in England there were so many that there came to be a literary category of 'Prodigal Son Plays', among the best-known to use bits of the plot are those of Thomas Middleton *A Mad World My Masters* (1608) and Francis Beaumont (1584–1616) *The Knight of the Burning Pestle* (1607). To judge by the number of references in his plays, it was also Shakespeare's favourite parable.

For evangelicals, such as John Newton (cited below) the parable was a natural companion-piece to the story of Paul's conversion on the road to

Damascus – illustrating how no sinner was so bad as to be outside the scope of God's mercies. For many, however, the idea of the prodigal getting off scot-free was a little too much, and variations on the theme in eighteenth century and Victorian literature often had the prodigal returning home to the father's welcome, but dying shortly thereafter from some appropriate disease born of his riotous living – venereal diseases or tuberculosis being obvious favourites. The story was also a favourite of John Ruskin (1819–1900) who makes several observations on it. In his autobiography, *Praeterita*, he describes a puritanical biblical study group which (as in Newton's poem) totally ignores the elder brother in its reading of the story, as if he 'was merely a picturesque figure introduced to fill the background of the parable agreeably, and contained no instruction or example for the well-disposed scriptural student...' In *Time and Tide* he gives a lengthy discussion of the story, concluding, in particular, that the love of money is the root of all evil, and that true repentance begins when a man 'complains of nobody but himself'.

At the same time a very different tradition of ironic uses of the theme had grown up. Byron, for instance, in his verse drama, *Werner or the Inheritance*, describes his protagonist as

> A prodigal son, beneath his father's ban
> For the last twenty years: for whom his sire
> Refused to kill the fatted calf; and therefore,
> If living, he must chew the husks still.
>
> (2.1)

Dickens, like Shakespeare, was fascinated by the story and makes allusions to it in many of his novels. In *Martin Chuzzlewit*, the hypocritical Mr Pecksniff invites Martin into his house and offers him 'the fatted calf': 'but as no such animal chanced at the time to be grazing on Mr Pecksniff's estate, this request must be considered rather as a polite compliment than as a substantial hospitality' (chapter 6). The somewhat back-handed compliment of implying that Martin is a reformed sinner is left to the imagination of those readers who could follow through the reference. Similarly *Great Expectations* uses the theme ironically at a number of levels, from Pip himself through to Magwitch.

Modern poets and writers have tended to follow this tradition rather than the evangelical one, and to give the story a satiric twist of some kind – often reversing the generational conflict. In Jack London's 'The Prodigal Father', for instance, Josiah Childs runs away from his domineering wife in New England and goes to California. Eleven years later he returns, and finding that she has not changed in the interval, goes off again, taking their son with him. Sinclair Lewis' *The Prodigal Parents* has the parents declining to be exploited any more by their adult children, and taking off to Europe.

The twentieth century has nevertheless also continued to rework the original story in a variety of media. A recent meditation on the subject (*The Return of the Prodigal Son: A Story of Homecoming*, by Henri Nouwen) was published in 1994. There is also a ballet on the theme by Sergei Prokofiev, *Le Fils Prodigue* (1929), an opera by Benjamin Britten (1968), a painting by Max Beckmann (1949), and at least three films.

—— Literature ——

Geoffrey Chaucer, 'The Parson's Tale', *The Canterbury Tales* (*c.*1400), ed. F. N. Robinson, 2nd edn, Oxford University Press, 1957

Certes, the mercy of God is evere redy to the penitent, and is aboven alle his werkes. Allas! ken a man net bithynke hym on the gospel of Seint Luc, 15, where as Crist seith that 'as wel shal ther be joye in hevene upon a synful man that dooth penitence, as upon nynty and nyne rightful men that neden no penitence.' Looke forther, in the same gospel, the joye and the feeste of the goode man that hadde lost his sone, when his sone with repentaunce was retourned to his fader.

John Newton, 'The Prodigal Son', *Olney Hymns* (1779)

> Afflictions, though they seem severe,
>   In mercy oft are sent;
> They stopp'd the prodigal's career,
>   And forc'd him to repent.
>
> Although he no relentings felt
>   Till he had spent his store,
> His stubborn heart began to melt
>   When famine pinch'd him sore.
>
> 'What have I gain'd by sin,' he said,
>   'But hunger, shame, and fear?
> My father's house abounds with bread,
>   While I am starving here.

I'll go, and tell him all I've done,
    And fall before his face;
Unworthy to be call'd his son,
    I'll seek a servant's place.'

His father saw him coming back,
    He saw, and ran, and smil'd;
And threw his arms around the neck
    Of his rebellious child.

'Father, I've sinn'd – but, O forgive!'
    'I've heard enough,' he said;
'Rejoice, my house, my son's alive,
    For whom I mourn'd as dead.

Now let the fatted calf be slain,
    And spread the news around;
My son was dead, but lives again;
    Was lost, but now is found.'

Tis thus the Lord his love reveals,
    To call poor sinners home;
More than a father's love he feels,
    And welcomes all that come.

William Wordsworth, from *The Excursion* (1814), Book I, 'The Wanderer', lines 280–375

And thus before his eighteenth year was told
Accumulated feelings pressed his heart
With still increasing weight; he was o'erpowered
By Nature, by the turbulence subdued
Of his own mind, by mystery and hope,
And the first virgin passion of a soul
Communing with the glorious universe.
Full often wished he that the winds might rage
When they were silent: far more fondly now
Than in his earlier season did he love
Tempestuous nights – the conflict and the sounds
That live in darkness. From his intellect
And from the stillness of abstracted thought
He asked repose; and, failing oft to win

The peace required, he scanned the laws of light
Amid the roar of torrents, where they send
From hollow clefts up to the clearer air
A cloud of mist, that smitten by the sun
Varies its rainbow hues. But vainly thus,
And vainly by all other means, he strove
To mitigate the fever of his heart.

In dreams, in study, and in ardent thought,
Thus was he reared; much wanting to assist
The growth of intellect, yet gaining more,
And every moral feeling of his soul
Strengthened and braced, by breathing in content
The keen, the wholesome air of poverty,
And drinking from the well of homely life
– But, from past liberty, and tried restraints
He now was summoned to select the course
Of humble industry that promised best
To yield him no unworthy maintenance.
Urged by his Mother, he essayed to teach
A village-school – but wandering thoughts were then
A misery to him; and the Youth resigned
A task he was unable to perform.

That stern yet kindly Spirit, who constrains
The Savoyard to quit his naked rocks,
The freeborn Swiss to leave his narrow vales,
(Spirit attached to regions mountainous
Like their own steadfast clouds) did now impel
His restless mind to look abroad with hope.
– An irksome drudgery seems it to plod on
Through hot and dusty ways, or pelting storm,
A vagrant Merchant under a heavy load
Bent as he moves, and needing frequent rest;
Yet do such travellers find their own delight;
And their hard service, deemed debasing now,
Gained merited respect in simpler times;
When squire, and priest, and they who round them dwelt
In rustic sequestration – all dependent
Upon the PEDLAR'S toil – supplied their wants
Or pleased their fancies, with the wares he brought.
Not ignorant was the Youth that still no few

262

Of his adventurous countrymen were led
By perseverance in this track of life
To competence and case: – to him it offered
Attractions manifold; – and this he chose.
– His Parents on the enterprise bestowed
Their farewell benediction, but with hearts
Foreboding evil. From his native hills
He wandered far; much did he see of men,
Their manners, their enjoyments, and pursuits
Their passions and their feelings; chiefly those
Essential and eternal in the heart,
That, 'mid the simpler forms of rural life,
Exist more simple in their elements,
And speak a plainer language. In the woods
A lone Enthusiast, and among the fields,
Itinerant in this labour, he had passed
The better portion of his time; and there.
Spontaneously had his affections thriven
Amid the bounties of the year, the peace
And liberty of nature; there he kept
In solitude and solitary thought
His mind in a just equipoise of love.
Serene it was, unclouded by the cares
Of ordinary life; unvexed, unwarped
By partial bondage. In his steady course,
No piteous revolutions had he felt,
No wild varieties of joy and grief.
Unoccupied by sorrow of its own,
His heart lay open, and, by nature tuned
And constant disposition of his thought:
To sympathy with man, he was alive
To all that was enjoyed where'er he went
And all that was endured; for, in himself
Happy, and quiet in his cheerfulness,
He had no painful pressure from without
That made him turn aside from wretchedness
With coward fears. He could afford to suffer
With those whom he saw suffer. Hence it came
That in our best experience he was rich
And in the wisdom of our daily life
For hence, minutely, in his various rounds
He had observed the progress and decay

Of many minds, of minds and bodies too;
The history of many families
How they had prospered; how they were o'erthrown
By passion or mischance, or such misrule
Among the unthinking masters of the earth
As makes the nations groan.

Christina Rossetti, 'A Prodigal Son'

Does that lamp still burn in my Father's house
   Which he kindled the night I went away?
I turned once beneath the cedar boughs,
   And marked it gleam with a golden ray;
   Did he think to light me home some day?

Hungry here with the crunching swine,
   Hungry harvest have I to reap;
In a dream I count my Father's kine,
   I hear the tinkling bells of his sheep,
   I watch his lambs that browse and leap.

There is plenty of bread at home,
   His servants have bread enough and to spare;
The purple wine-fat froths with foam,
   Oil and spices make sweet the air,
   While I perish hungry and bare.
Rich and blessed those servants, rather
   Than I who see not my Father's face!
I will arise and go to my Father:
'Fallen from sonship, beggared of grace,
Grant me, Father, a servant's place.'

W. B. Yeats, 'The Lake Isle of Innisfree' (1893)

I will arise and go now, and go to Innisfree,
And a small cabin build there, of clay and wattles made:
Nine bean-rows will I have there, a hive for the honey-bee,
And live alone in the bee-loud glade.

And I shall have some peace there, for peace comes dropping slow,
Dropping from the veils of the morning to where the cricket sings;
There midnight's all a glimmer, and noon a purple glow,
And evening full of the linnet's wings.

I will arise and go now, for always night and day
I hear lake water lapping with low sounds by the shore;
While I stand on the roadway, or on the pavements grey,
I hear it in the deep heart's core.

Robert Bly, 'The Prodigal Son'

The Prodigal Son is kneeling in the husks.
He remembers the man about to die
Who cried, 'Don't let me die, Doctor!'
The swine go on feeding in the sunlight.

When he folds his hands, his knees on corncobs,
He sees the smoke of ships
Floating off the isles of Tyre and Sidon,
And father beyond father beyond father.

An old man once, being dragged across the floor
By his shouting son, cried:
'Don't drag me any farther than that crack on the floor –
I only dragged my father that far!'

My father is seventy years old.
How difficult it is,
Bending the head, looking into the water.
Under the water there's a door the pigs have gone through.

Elizabeth Bishop, 'The Prodigal'

The brown enormous odor he lived by
was too close, with its breathing and thick hair,
for him to judge. The floor was rotten; the sty
was plastered halfway up with glass-smooth dung.
Light-lashed, self-righteous, above moving snouts,
the pigs' eyes followed him, a cheerful stare —
even to the sow that always ate her young —
till, sickening, he leaned to scratch her head.
But sometimes mornings after drinking bouts
(he hid the pints behind a two-by-four),
the sunrise glazed the barnyard mud with red;
the burning puddles seemed to reassure.

And then he thought he almost might endure
his exile yet another year or more.

But evenings the first star came to warn.
The farmer whom he worked for came at dark
to shut the cows and horses in the barn
beneath their overhanging clouds of hay,
with pitchforks, faint forked lightnings, catching light,
safe and companionable as in the Ark.
The pigs stuck out their little feet and snored.
The lantern — like the sun, going away —
laid on the mud a pacing aureole.
Carrying a bucket along a slimy board,
he felt the bats' uncertain staggering flight,
his shuddering insights, beyond his control,
touching him. But it took him a long time
finally to make his mind up to go home.

Henri J. M. Nouwen, *The Return of the Prodigal Son*, DLT,
1994

Rembrandt portrays the father as the man who has transcended the ways of his children. His own loneliness and anger may have been there, but they have been transformed by suffering and tears. His loneliness has become endless solitude, his anger boundless gratitude. This is who I have to become. I see it as clearly as I see the immense beauty of the father's emptiness and compassion. Can I let the younger and the elder son grow in me to the maturity of the compassionate father?

When, four years ago, I went to Saint Petersburg to see Rembrandt's *The Return of the Prodigal Son*, I had little idea how much I would have to live what I then saw. I stand with awe at the place where Rembrandt brought me. He led me from the kneeling, disheveled young son to the standing, bent-over old father, from the place of being blessed to the place of blessing. As I look at my own aging hands, I know that they have been given to me to stretch out toward all who suffer, to rest upon the shoulders of all who come, and offer the blessing that emerges from the immensity of God's love.

Bibliography

McFague, Sallie. *Speaking in Parables: A Study in Metaphor and Theology* (Philadelphia: Fortress Press, 1975), ch. 1 (a comparison between the parable and other literature).

Nouwen, Henri J. M. *The Return of the Prodigal Son* (London: DLT, 1994).

Robbins, Jill. *Prodigal Son/Elder Brother: Interpretation and Alterity in Augustine, Petrarch, Kafka, Levinas* (Chicago: Chicago University Press, 1991).

Young, A. R. *The English Prodigal Son Plays: A Theatrical Fashion of the Sixteenth and Seventeenth Centuries* (1979).

THE CRUCIFIXION

MARK 15: 33–39

[33] And when the sixth hour was come, there was darkness over the whole land until the ninth hour.

[34] And at the ninth hour Jesus cried with a loud voice, saying, Eloi, Eloi, lama sabachthani? which is, being interpreted, My God, my God, why hast thou forsaken me?

[35] And some of them that stood by, when they heard it, said, Behold, he calleth Elias.

[36] And one ran and filled a spunge full of vinegar, and put it on a reed, and gave him to drink, saying, Let alone; let us see whether Elias will come to take him down.

[37] And Jesus cried with a loud voice, and gave up the ghost.

[38] And the veil of the temple was rent in twain from the top to the bottom.

[39] And when the centurion, which stood over against him, saw that he so cried out, and gave up the ghost, he said, Truly this man was the Son of God.

Notes

Verse 33. The sixth hour is noon, and the verse looks back to Amos 8: 9.

> 'And on that day,' says the Lord God,
> 'I will make the sun go down at noon,
> and darken the earth in broad daylight'.

The darkness is symbolic of the judgement of heaven.

Verse 34. The words of Jesus' last cry are given in their Aramaic form. Probably the early Church was anxious to preserve the exact words of the Lord at this moment, and thus retained the Aramaic form which, presumably, was the language used by him. The cry is a direct quotation from Psalm 22: 1, a psalm which begins in despair but ends in triumph. Nevertheless, neither Luke nor John follow these words of apparent despair, in the first case Jesus dying with the words, 'Father, into thy hands I commit my spirit (Luke 23: 46), and in the latter with the words, 'It is finished' (John 19: 30).

Verse 35. Elijah was not only the forerunner and helper of the the Messiah, but popular belief held that he would assist good people in time of trouble.

Verse 38. The curtain or veil of the Temple in Jerusalem hung before the Holy of Holies, and its tearing at this moment symbolizes Jesus' death as opening up the way between God and his people. This 'new and living way' is the subject of lengthy reflections in the Epistle to the Hebrews (see, Hebrews 10: 20).

Verse 39. The Centurion's confession represented the Gentile, or non-Jewish, world just as the tearing of the Temple veil had represented the Jewish world. The whole world now confesses Jesus as Messiah. The Greek of the Centurion's sentence can mean either 'a' or 'the' son of God, but the probability is that the stronger affirmation is intended.

—— **Commentary** ——

The art and literature which has drawn inspiration from this central moment in the New Testament is almost limitless, and here we can only suggest a few poems and extracts which may suggest further study and reflection. We have taken the account in St Mark's Gospel, because this is perhaps the starkest and most dramatic of the Passion narratives in the canonical Gospels, and it contains that most haunting of all cries, Jesus's cry of desolation just before his death – 'My God, my God, why hast thou forsaken me?' Terrible and almost inconceivable though it is, it has provided comfort to countless souls who feel that they are beyond the reach of God's mercy – if Jesus himself can feel such desolation, then God's love may reach even to these depths of misery. In fact, the cry is a direct quotation from the first verse of Psalm 22, which begins in misery and ends in an affirmation of God's mercy:

> For he has not despised or abhorred
> the affliction of the afflicted;
> and he has not hid his face from him,
> but has heard, when he cried to him. (verse 24)

We begin with perhaps the most famous of all Anglo-Saxon (early English) religious poems, *The Dream of the Rood*. ('Rood' is an old word for 'crucifix'.) Apart from its considerable literary merit, the history of this poem is remarkable, and indicates the coherence of early Christian Europe. The earliest version of it is found carved in runic characters on a huge stone cross in the church of Ruthwell, Dumfriesshire in Scotland. It was made to celebrate the discovery of a fragment of the True Cross in 701 C.E. by Pope Sergius I while Coelfrith, Abbot of Wearmouth and Jarrow in Northern England was visiting Rome. Other versions from the ninth century are a complete manuscript now in the Cathedral of Vercelli, on the pilgrimage route from England to Rome, and a fragment carved on a silver reliquary made to hold a fragment of the Cross which Pope Marinus gave to King Alfred in 884 C.E. All this indicates that this was a widely known poem across Christendom. In the poem, the dreamer-poet sleeps and dreams that the Cross appears and speaks to him. Written in the pagan literary form of a riddle, the narrative is a remarkable account of the Crucifixion from the perspective of the Cross itself, which suffers with Jesus, feels his blood streaming down its shaft, and is finally abandoned until later Christians ('The Lord's men'), including, presumably, Pope Sergius I, recover it and give it due honour.

The poet of this great poem clearly knew the Liturgy of Passiontide intimately, and it was out of this Liturgy that the great tradition of the English Mystery Plays grew from as early as the tenth century. We have taken lines from one of the greatest of the Miracle Plays, the *Colphizacio* or *Crucifixion* in the Wakefield Pageants of the Towneley Cycle, dating from the early fifteenth century, using a modern translation. Notice that the figure of Jesus speaks only words which are taken from the biblical narratives, though he draws upon two gospels, St Mark (though the words of desolation also appear in Matthew 27: 46), and St Luke. The play also draws upon the legend of the soldier Longinus (here Longeus) who pierces Christ's side with a spear. Although this name is not in the New Testament, it can be traced back to an early apocryphal work, *The Acts of Pilate*, and his conversion which takes place at the foot of the Cross is documented by the Venerable Bede and numerous other medieval authors.

Thus, literature feeds upon the wealth of legend which grew up around the stark biblical narrative of the Crucifixion. Another great devotional work of the Middle Ages, frequently translated from Latin into English and often set to music is the *Stabat Mater Dolorosa*, probably dating from the thirteenth century. Like *The Dream of the Rood*, the *Stabat Mater* dramatically realizes the agony of the Cross by viewing it from a particular perspective, in this case seeing through the eyes of Jesus's Mother as she stands at the foot of the Cross. So popular and powerful was the poem that it became part of the Passiontide Liturgy in the later Middle Ages, was included in the Roman Missal in 1727, and is often sung as a hymn – as in the version we have given here. In this poem we look not so much at the Cross itself as at the sufferings of the Virgin Mary in which we learn to partake as Jesus bleeds for our sins.

In the English Renaissance, John Donne's Holy Sonnet 'Crucifying' employs typical metaphysical play on words to explore the salvation achieved through the shedding of Christ's blood. Using the phrase from the Fourth Gospel (John 3: 14; 'And as Moses lifted up the serpent in the wilderness, so must the Son of man be lifted up'), Donne suggests the Christian call to be 'crucified with Christ' (lifted up), which is also to be raised with him. Poetry here uses its resources to explore the subtleties of atonement theology.

The theme of participation is employed with dramatic effect again in the eighteenth-century nonconformist hymn writer Isaac Watts's poem 'Crucifixion to the World by the Cross of Christ', drawing upon Galatians 6: 14; 'But far be it from me to glory except in the cross of our Lord Jesus Christ, by which the world has been crucified to me, and I to the world'. After the extravagant poetry of medieval devotion, Watts's hymn is simple and restrained in its language, though powerful in its use of image and juxtaposition. He said of his religious poetry that 'I would neither indulge any bold metaphors, nor admit of hard words, nor tempt the ignorant worshipper to sing without his understanding.' Here the gaze is fixed by the poem completely on the Cross, but the drama is inward – as worldly boasting and pride are transformed by the glory of the Passion. In the first word of the third stanza we are bidden to 'see', and our eyes (and meditations) are drawn down the body from head to feet to contemplate the blood which in the next stanza is compared to the crimson robe of a king. In this verse, the reader/watcher also 'dies' with Christ – dies, that is, to the world as all is given to Christ as Christ sacrifices all in his death.

In modern literature the Passion story has increasingly been retold as a frame for contemporary experience, particularly in the genre of the novel. As one theologian and critic, F. W. Dillistone put it in his book *The Novelist and the Passion Story* (1960),

[One] possibility open to the novelist is to write about his contemporary world openly and frankly but with the essential pattern of the Passion narrative forming the inner framework of his own story. It is, of course, impossible for him to do this unless he believes that the successive stages in the recorded life of Jesus do correspond to the general sequence of events which may be traced in the career of every heroic figure who carries out a mission of redemption for his fellow-men.

One well-known example of this is found in Herman Melville's novella *Billy Budd, Sailor*, in which the innocent Budd is hanged from the yard-arm of his ship for the 'murder' of the evil petty officer Claggart. The Great War of 1914–1918, with its terrible slaughter of millions of soldiers, produced a number of hymns and poems which draw a comparison between the sacrificial cross of Jesus and the sacrifice of a soldier's life for his country. Perhaps the best known is Sir John S. Arkwright's 'O Valiant Hearts, Who to Your Glory Came', with its verse:

> Still stands his Cross from that dread hour to this,
> Like some bright star above the dark abyss;
> Still, through the veil, the Victor's pitying eyes
> Look down to bless our lesser Calvaries.

The implications of this, though in intention deeply Christian, are very different from the participatory demands of *The Dream of the Rood* or the *Stabat Mater*. There, the uniqueness of Christ's redemptive suffering on the Cross was carefully preserved in our witness to it. Arkwright seems to suggest that the sacrifice of each soldier in battle is a redemptive 'Calvary' – a danger avoided by the much greater war poet Wilfred Owen in the brief poem given here, 'At a Calvary near the Ancre', which is a meditation upon a French wayside crucifix damaged in war and a reminder all the more, therefore, of the terrible sufferings of Jesus with their Christian teaching of love, not hatred. Owen's poetry was later combined with the Latin text of the Requiem Mass by the English composer Benjamin Britten in his *War Requiem* (1963). (Britten had earlier composed an opera of *Billy Budd* [1951].)

Geoffrey Hill's 'Canticle for Good Friday' follows the ancient tradition of viewing the Crucifixion from a particular perspective, this time that of Thomas, the 'doubter' of John 20: 24–9, who is invited to place his hands on Jesus's wounds so that he may believe in his risen Lord. Like John Donne, Hill uses poetic word-play to transfer the effects of the Cross from Jesus to Thomas, who is 'staggered' and feels its burden as he stands on Calvary – on a cliff-top suggestive of the danger of falling. Thomas (not transfigured) conveys the damp, filthy misery of the scene where both one man, Jesus, and through him all creation 'congeal' into death and decay as the life blood ceases to flow. This sheer misery of Calvary offers a series of images which permeate modern Western literature as it reflects upon our dark century. So, for example, Arthur Koestler's novel *Darkness at Noon* (1940) grimly interprets the logic of the Russian Revolution through the darkness which at the sixth hour (noon) falls over the whole land after the prophecy of Amos 8: 9.

Our two final excerpts are from Irish literature. The first is from the magnificent and terrible hell-fire sermon in James Joyce's autobiographical *A Portrait of the Artist as a Young Man*. As the priest speaks to his schoolboy congregation, he uses the most sadistic images to terrify them into a fear that they, too, may be responsible for Christ's torture and death – another form of participation by what one writer has called 'penny-dreadful word-paintings of phosphorescent charnel-house horrors' against which Joyce himself rebelled from his own schooling in Ireland. The second is from a recent book by a New Testament scholar, Stephen Moore, as he reflects on the power of Good Friday preaching in his youth.

The Crucifixion accounts in the Gospels, theological in purpose and in many ways remarkably restrained as accounts of the physical processes of flogging and execution, have inspired some of the most sublime and some of the most sadistic moments in Western art, literature and music. The complexity of this moment draws us from the depths to the heights of human experience.

——— **Literature** ———

The Dream of the Rood (seventh to tenth century), tr. Michael Alexander, Penguin, 1966

Hwaet!

> A dream came to me
>   at deep midnight
> when humankind
>   kept their beds
> – the dream of dreams!
>   I shall declare it.

> It seemed I saw the Tree itself
> borne on the air, light wound about it,
> – a beam of brightest wood a beacon clad
> in overlapping gold, glancing gems
> fair at its foot, and five stones
> set in a crux flashed from the crosstree.

Around angels of God
  all gazed upon it,
since first fashioning fair.

It was not a felon's gallows,
for holy ghosts beheld it there,
and men on mould and the whole Making shone for it
– signum of victory!
  Stained and marred,
stricken with shame, I saw the glory-tree
shine out gaily, sheathed in yellow
decorous gold, and gemstones made
for their Maker's Tree a right mail-coat.

Yet through the masking gold, I might perceive
what terrible sufferings were once sustained thereon:
it bled from the right side.
  Ruth in the heart.

Afraid I saw that unstill brightness
change raiment and colour
  – again clad in gold,
or again slicked with sweat,
spangled with spilling blood.

Yet lying there a long while
I beheld, sorrowing, the Healer's Tree
till it seemed that I heard how it broke silence,
best of wood, and began to speak:

'Over that long remove my mind ranges
back to the holt where I was hewn down;
from my own stem I was struck away,
  dragged off by strong enemies,
wrought into a roadside scaffold.
  They made me a hoist for wrongdoers.

The soldiers on their shoulders bore me,
  until on a hill-top they set me up;
many enemies made me fast there.
  Then I saw, marching toward me,
mankind's brave King;
  He came to climb upon me.

I dared not break or bend aside
against God's will, though the ground itself
shook at my feet. Fast I stood,
who falling could have felled them all.

Almighty God ungirded Him
    eager to mount the gallows,
unafraid in the sight of many:
    He would set free mankind.
I shook when His arms embraced me
    but I durst not bow to ground,
stoop to Earth's surface.
    Stand fast I must.

I was reared up, a rood.
    I raised the great King,
liege lord of the heavens,
    dared not lean from the true.
They drove me through with dark nails:
    on me are the deep wounds manifest,
wide-mouthed hate-dents.
    I durst not harm any of them.
How they mocked at us both!
    I was all moist with blood
sprung from the Man's side
    after He sent forth His soul.

Wry wierds a many I underwent
up on that hill-top; saw the Lord of Hosts
stretched out stark. Darkness shrouded
the King's corse. Clouds wrapped
its clear shining. A shade went out
wan under cloud-pall. All creation wept,
keened the King's death. Christ was on the Cross.

But there quickly came from far
earls to the One there. All that I beheld;
had grown weak with grief,
    yet with glad will bent then
meek to those men's hands,
    yielded Almighty God.

They lifted Him down from the leaden pain,
   left me, the commanders,
standing in a sweat of blood.
   I was all wounded with shafts.

They straightened out His strained limbs,
   stood at His body's head,
looked down on the Lord of Heaven
   – for a while He lay there resting –
set to contrive Him a tomb
   in the sight of the Tree of Death,
carved it of bright stone,
   laid in it the Bringer of victory,
spent from the great struggle.

   They began to speak the grief-song,
sad in the sinking light,
   then thought to set out homeward;
their hearts were sick to death
   their most high Prince
they left to rest there with scant retinue.

Yet we three, weeping, a good while
stood in that place after the song had gone up
from the captains' throats. Cold grew the corse,
fair soul-house.
   They felled us all.
We crashed to ground, cruel Wierd,
and they delved for us a deep pit.

The Lord's men learnt of it,
His friends found me ...
it was they who girt me with gold, and silver ...'

Stabat Mater Dolorosa (prob. early thirteenth century), Latin
translated by various hands, in *The New English Hymnal*,
Norwich, 1986

   At the Cross her station keeping,
   Stood the mournful Mother weeping,
     Close to Jesus at the last.
   Through her soul, of joy bereavèd,

Bowed with anguish, deeply grievèd,
  Now at length the sword hath passed.

O, that blessèd one, grief-laden,
Blessèd Mother, blessèd Maiden,
  Mother of the all-holy One;
O that silent, ceaseless mourning,
O those dim eyes, never turning
  From that wondrous, suffering Son.

Who on Christ's dear Mother gazing,
In her trouble so amazing,
  Born of woman, would not weep?
Who on Christ's dear Mother thinking,
Such a cup of sorrow drinking,
  Would not share her sorrow deep?

For his people's sins, in anguish,
There she saw the victim languish,
  Bleed in torments, bleed and die:
Saw the Lord's anointed taken;
Saw her Child in death forsaken,
  Heard his last expiring cry.

In the Passion of my Maker,
Be my sinful soul partaker,
  May I bear with her my part;
Of his Passion bear the token,
In a spirit bowed and broken
  Bear his death within my heart.

May his wounds both wound and heal me,
  He enkindle, cleanse, anneal me,
  Be his Cross my hope and stay.
May he, when the mountains quiver
From that flame which burns for ever
  Shield me on the judgement day.

Jesu, may thy Cross defend me,
And thy saving death befriend me,
  Cherished by thy deathless grace:
When to dust my dust returneth,

Grant a soul that to thee yearneth
In thy Paradise a place.

Colphizacio, from *The Wakefield Pageants* (early fifteenth century), modernized by John Gassner, Bantam Books, 1968

(*They sit down to play dice for* Jesus' *garment.*)

THIRD TORTURER (*looking up at the figure on the cross*). If thou be Christ,
as men thee call
Come down now among us all
    And bear not thy dismay!

FIRST TORTURER. Yea, and help myself that we may see
And we shall all believe in thee,
Whatsoever thou say.

SECOND TORTURER. He calls himself God of might,
But I would see him display the might
    To do such a deed.
He raised Lazare out of his sleep
But he cannot help himself
    Now in his great need.

JESUS. Eli, Eli, lama sabachthani!
My God, my God! wherefor and why
    Has thou forsaken me?

SECOND TORTURER. Now, hear ye not as well as I
How he can upon Eli cry
    Upon this wise?

THIRD TORTURER. Yea, there is no Eli in this country
Shall deliver him from this misery
    No, in no wise.

FIRST TORTURER. I warrant you now at the last
That he shall soon yield the ghost,
    For bursten is his gall.

JESUS. Now is my passion brought to end,
Father of heaven, into thy hand
    I do commend my soul.

FIRST TORTURER. Let one prick him with a spear,
And if it should do him no wear
    Then is his life near past.

SECOND TORTURER. This blind knight may best do that. (*He pushes*
    Longeus, *a blind Knight forward.*)

LONGEUS. Make me not do, save I know what.

THIRD TORTURER (*forcing his hand upward*). Naught,

but strike up fast.
LONGEUS (*having thrust his spear into* Jesus' *side*).
　　Ah! Lord, what may this be?
Once I was blind, now I can see;
God's son, hear me, Jesu!
For this trespass of mine thou rue.
For, Lord, other men me made
That I thee struck unto the heart,
I see thou hangest here on high,
And diest to fulfill the prophecy.
FIRST TORTURER. Go we hence, and leave him here
For I shall be his bail this year
　　He feels now no more pain ...
　　Nor gets his life again.
(The Torturers *depart*. Christ's *followers are left alone*.)

John Donne, *Holy Sonnets*, 'La Corona' (*c*.1610–1611), 5 'Crucifying'

> *By miracles exceeding power of man,*
> He faith in some, envy in some begat,
> For, what weak spirits admire, ambitious, hate;
> In both affections many to him ran,
> But Oh! the worst are most, they will and can,
> Alas, and do, unto the immaculate,
> Whose creature Fate is, now prescribe a fate,
> Measuring self-life's infinity to a span,
> Nay to an inch. Lo, where condemned he
> Bears his own cross, with pain, yet by and by
> When it bears him, he must bear more and die.
> Now thou art lifted up, draw me to thee,
> And at thy death giving such liberal dole,
> *Moist, with one drop of thy blood, my dry soul.*

Isaac Watts, 'Crucifixion to the World by the Cross of Christ', Galatians 6: 14

> When I survey the wondrous Cross
> Where the young Prince of Glory died,
> My richest gain I count but loss,
> And pour contempt on all my pride.

THE CRUCIFIXION

Forbid it, Lord that I should boast
Save in the death of Christ my God;
 All the vain things that charm me most,
 I sacrifice them to his blood.

See from his head, his hands, his feet,
Sorrow and love flow mingled down;
 Did e'er such love and sorrow meet?
 Or thorns compose so rich a crown?

His dying crimson like a robe
Spreads o'er his body on the Tree,
 Then am I dead to all the globe,
 And all the globe is dead to me.

Were the whole realm of nature mine
That were a present far too small;
 Love so amazing so divine,
 Demands my soul, my life, my all.

Herman Melville, *Billy Budd, Sailor* (1924)

THE night so luminous on the spar deck, but otherwise on the cavernous ones below, levels so like the tiered galleries in a coal mine the luminous night passed away. But like the prophet in the chariot disappearing in heaven and dropping his mantle to Elisha, the withdrawing night transferred its pale robe to the breaking day. A meek, shy light appeared in the East, where stretched a diaphanous fleece of white furrowed vapor. That light slowly waxed. Suddenly *eight bells* was struck aft, responded to by one louder metallic stroke from forward. It was four o'clock in the morning. Instantly the silver whistles were heard summoning all hands to witness punishment. Up through the great hatchways rimmed with racks of heavy shot the watch below came pouring, overspreading with the watch already on deck the space between the mainmast and foremast including that occupied by the capacious launch and the black booms tiered on either side of it, boat and booms making a summit of observation for the powder-boys and younger tars. A different group comprising one watch of topmen leaned over the rail of that sea balcony, no small one in a seventy-four, looking down on the crowd below. Man or boy, none spake but in whisper, and few spake at all. Captain Vere – as before, the central figure among the assembled commissioned officers – stood nigh the break of the poop deck facing forward. Just below him on the quarter-deck the marines in full equipment were drawn up much as at the scene of the promulgated sentence.

At sea in the old time, the execution by halter of a military sailor was generally from the foreyard. In the present instance, for special reasons the mainyard was assigned. Under an arm of that yard the prisoner was presently brought up, the chaplain attending him. It was noted at the time, and remarked upon afterwards, that in this final scene the good man evinced little or nothing of the perfunctory. Brief speech indeed he had with the condemned one, but the genuine Gospel was less on his tongue than in his aspect and manner towards him. The final preparations personal to the latter being speedily brought to an end by two boatswain's mates, the consummation impended. Billy stood facing aft. At the penultimate moment, his words, his only ones, words wholly unobstructed in the utterance, were these: 'God bless Captain Vere!' Syllables so unanticipated coming from one with the ignominious hemp about his neck – a conventional felon's benediction directed aft towards the quarters of honor; syllables too delivered in the clear melody of a singing bird on the point of launching from the twig – had a phenomenal effect, not unenhanced by the rare personal beauty of the young sailor, spiritualized now through late experiences so poignantly profound.

Without volition, as it were, as if indeed the ship's populace were but the vehicles of some vocal current electric, with one voice from alow and aloft came a resonant sympathetic echo: 'God bless Captain Vere!' And yet at that instant Billy alone must have been in their hearts, even as in their eyes.

At the pronounced words and the spontaneous echo that voluminously rebounded them, Captain Vere, either through stoic self-control or a sort of momentary paralysis induced by emotional shock, stood erectly rigid as a musket in the ship-armorer's rack.

The hull, deliberately recovering from the periodic roll to leeward, was just regaining an even keel when the last signal, a preconcerted dumb one, was given. At the same moment it chanced that the vapory fleece hanging low in the East was shot through with a soft glory as of the fleece of the Lamb of God seen in mystical vision, and simultaneously therewith, watched by the wedged mass of upturned faces, Billy ascended; and, ascending, took the full rose of the dawn.

In the pinioned figure arrived at the yard-end, to the wonder of all no motion was apparent, none save that created by the slow roll of the hull in moderate weather, so majestic in a great ship ponderously cannoned.

Wilfred Owen, 'At a Calvary near the Ancre', *The Collected Poems*, ed. C. Day Lewis, Chatto & Windus, 1963

> One ever hangs where shelled roads part.
>   In this war He too lost a limb,
> But his disciples hide apart;
>   And now the Soldiers bear with Him.
>
> Near Golgotha strolls many a priest,
>   And in their faces there is pride
> That they were flesh-marked by the Beast
>   By whom the gentle Christ's denied.
>
> The scribes on all the people shove
>   And brawl allegiance to the state,
> But they who love the greater love
>   Lay down their life; they do not hate.

James Joyce, *A Portrait of the Artist as a Young Man* (1916)

O, my dear little brethren in Christ Jesus, will we then offend that good Redeemer and provoke His anger? Will we trample again upon that torn and mangled corpse? Will we spit upon that face so full of sorrow and love? Will we too, like the cruel jews and the brutal soldiers, mock that gentle and compassionate Saviour Who trod alone for our sake the awful winepress of sorrow? Every word of sin is a wound in His tender side. Every sinful act is a thorn piercing His head. Every impure thought, deliberately yielded to, is a keen lance transfixing that sacred and loving heart. No, no. It is impossible for any human being to do that which offends so deeply the divine majesty, that which is punished by an eternity of agony, that which crucifies again the Son of God and makes a mockery of Him. – I pray to God that my poor words may have availed today to confirm in holiness those who are in a state of grace, to strengthen the wavering, to lead back to the state of grace the poor soul that has strayed if any such be among you. I pray to God, and do you pray with me, that we may repent of our sins. I will ask you now, all of you, to repeat after me the act of contrition, kneeling here in this humble chapel in the presence of God. He is there in the tabernacle burning with love for mankind, ready to comfort the afflicted. Be not afraid. No matter how many or how foul the sins if you only repent of them they will be forgiven you. Let no worldly shame hold you back. God is still the merciful Lord who wishes not the eternal death of the sinner but rather that he be converted and live.

– He calls you to Him. You are His. He made you out of nothing. He loved you as only a God can love. His arms are open to receive you even though you have sinned against Him. Come to Him, poor sinner, poor vain and erring sinner. Now is the acceptable time. Now is the hour.

Geoffrey Hill, 'Canticle for Good Friday', *For the Unfallen: Poems, 1952–1958* (1959)

The cross staggered him. At the cliff-top
Thomas, beneath its burden, stood
While the dulled wood
Spat on the stones each drop
Of deliberate blood.

A clamping, cold-figured day
Thomas (not transfigured) stamped, crouched.
Watched
Smelt vinegar and blood. He,
As yet unsearched, unscratched,

And suffered to remain
At such near distance
(A slight miracle might cleanse
His brain
Of all attachments, claw-roots of sense)

In unaccountable darkness moved away,
The strange flesh untouched, carrion-sustenance
Of staunchest love, choicest defiance,
Creation's issue congealing (and one woman's).

Stephen D. Moore, *God's Gym: Divine Male Bodies of the Bible*, Routledge, 1996

My own father too was a butcher, and a lover of lamb with mint sauce. As a child, the inner geographical boundaries of my world extended from the massive granite bulk of the Redemptorist church squatting at one end of our street to the butcher's shop guarding the other end. Redemption, expiation, sacrifice, slaughter ... There was no city abattoir in Limerick in those days; each butcher did his own slaughtering. I recall the hooks, the knives, the cleavers; the terror in the eyes of the victim; my own fear that was afraid to show; the crude stun-gun slick with grease; the stunned victim collapsing to its knees; the slitting of the throat, the filling of the basins with blood; the skinning and evisceration of the carcass; the wooden barrels overflowing with entrails; the crimson floor littered with hooves.

I also recall a Good Friday sermon by a Redemptorist preacher that recounted at remarkable length the atrocious agony felt by our sensitive Saviour as the spikes were driven through his wrists and feet. Crucifixion, crucifixation, crucasphyxiation ... Strange to say, it was this sombre recital, and not the other spectacle, that finally caused me to faint. Helped outside by my father, I vomited gratefully on the steps of the church.

Bibliography

Anderson, David. *The Passion of Man in Gospel and Literature* (London: BRF, 1980).

Bennett, J. A. W. *Poetry of the Passion* (Oxford: Clarendon Press, 1982).

Crossan, John Dominic. *Jesus: A Revolutionary Biography* (San Francisco: Harper, 1995), chs 6 and 7.

Dillistone, F. W. *The Novelist and the Passion Story* (London: Collins, 1960).

Moltmann, Jürgen. *The Crucified God*, tr. R. A. Wilson and John Bowden (London: SCM, 1974).

Moore, Stephen D. *God's Gym: Divine Male Bodies of the Bible* (London: Routledge, 1996).

Jesus and Mary in the Garden
John 20: 10–18

[10] Then the disciples went away again unto their own home.

[11] But Mary stood without at the sepulchre weeping: and as she wept, she stooped down, and looked into the sepulchre,

[12] And seeth two angels in white sitting, the one at the head, and the other at the feet, where the body of Jesus had lain.

[13] And they say unto her, Woman, why weepest thou? She saith unto them, Because they have taken away my Lord, and I know not where they have laid him.

[14] And when she had thus said, she turned herself back, and saw Jesus standing, and knew not that it was Jesus.

[15] Jesus saith unto her, Woman, why weepest thou? whom seekest thou? She, supposing him to be the gardener, saith unto him, Sir, if thou have borne him hence, tell me where thou hast laid him, and I will take him away.

[16] Jesus saith unto her, Mary. She turned herself, and saith unto him, Rabboni; which is to say, Master.

[17] Jesus saith unto her, Touch me not; for I am not yet ascended to my Father: but go to my brethren, and say unto them, I ascend unto my Father, and your Father; and to my God, and your God.

[18] Mary Magdalene came and told the disciples that she had seen the Lord, and that he had spoken these things unto her.

Notes

Verse 11. Earlier in the chapter (verses 1–2), Mary had found the stone rolled away from the tomb and had left to tell the disciples that Jesus's body had disappeared.

It now seems that she is back at the tomb again, though we are not told that she had accompanied Peter and his fellow disciple. It seems highly likely that two separate stories of the empty tomb have been put together by the author of the Gospel, leaving this awkward seam.

Verse 12. This is the only reference to angels appearing in this gospel although they are referred to by Jesus in chapter 1 verse 51. In the equivalent passage in St Mark's Gospel the reference is to one young man sitting on the right side of the tomb (Mark 16: 5), and in Luke to 'two men in dazzling apparel'.

Verse 13. There is no disrespect implied in the angels' address to Mary as 'woman'. In John 2: 4, Jesus had addressed his own mother in the same manner. Jesus uses the term again in verse 15.

Verse 15. The Greek word for gardener is used only here in the New Testament, although it is not an uncommon term in Hellenistic Greek. In this verse, John uses his favourite device of enlightenment through initial misunderstanding. He has used it earlier, for example, in the narrative of the Samaritan Woman at the well, in chapter 4.

Verse 16. Jesus simply utters Mary's name. Cp. John 10: 3; 'and he calls his own sheep by name and leads them out'. Mary's response is given in early Palestinian Aramaic, 'Rabboni', a word used characteristically of a deity. This is a moment frequently portrayed in religious art.

Verse 17. The difficulty of interpreting this saying of Jesus has led some scholars to suggest that the text may be corrupt at this point, and originally meant something closer to 'Do not be afraid'. But the Latin form, 'Noli me tangere', has become the almost universal way of referring to this moment. The word for 'ascend' here is the same as was used earlier in the Gospel to speak of Jesus being 'lifted up' on the Cross.

Verse 18. Although this Gospel makes Mary the first actual witness to the risen Lord, the narrative is careful to assert that she was not the first to *believe*. That privilege was granted to the two male disciples Peter and 'the one whom Jesus loved'. The early Church was generally very unwilling to accept the testimony of a woman, even Mary Magdalene.

——— Commentary ———

This beautiful Easter narrative of the meeting of Mary Magdalen and the risen Lord in the garden is peculiar to the Fourth Gospel, and has given inspiration to an ancient tradition of art on the theme of the 'noli me tangere' – the saying of Jesus to Mary that she should not touch him for he had not yet ascended to his Father. Fraught with tension between the weeping woman and the man whom she had loved and believed to be dead, it has recently been given much attention in feminist readings of the Bible which have questioned the motives of Jesus in refusing the touch of one who had loved him so dearly and now wished to hold him in a natural embrace of joy at his return.

The character of Mary Magdalen is a composite figure in Christian tradition who has developed out of a number of different gospel women – the sister of Martha and Lazarus in Bethany, the woman caught in the act of adultery and forgiven by Jesus, the woman who anoints Jesus and wipes him with her hair. She is first referred to specifically by name in chapter 15 verse 40 of St Mark's Gospel, probably the earliest of the canonical gospels, as one of the women 'looking on from afar' as Jesus dies on Calvary. There is even an extra-canonical tradition that Mary was Jesus' wife. But also, from very early times, the Mary who meets Jesus in the garden is confused with the Virgin Mary, Christ's mother, perhaps from a sense of the indecorum of the risen Jesus first meeting with the Magdalen whom tradition sees as originally a prostitute. In the early Coptic apocryphal gospel known as *The Book of the Resurrection of Christ by Bartholomew the Apostle*, here given in paraphrase from M. R. James's *The Apocryphal New Testament*, Jesus appears to Mary and her companion Philogenes, not in the guise of a gardener but riding gloriously on 'the chariot of the Father'. The only similarity to this of the account in the Fourth Gospel is Mary's word 'Rabbouni' and the denial to her of the touch of her son. Instead she asks for his blessing upon 'the body in which thou didst deign to dwell'. The survival of these two elements of the story in a narrative otherwise completely distinct from the canonical gospel suggest that they are very ancient indeed.

In the medieval Latin *Meditations* of St Anselm, Archbishop of Canterbury, there is a version of the story in which *both* Marys appear, Jesus first addressing his mother with the words 'Hail, saintly parent'. In a strange sort of mother-in-law/daughter-in-law relationship, the Virgin Mary gives her son permission to leave her and comfort the grieving Magdalen whom he finds lamenting her lost love in words highly reminiscent of the Song of Songs. This literary echo is found even more strongly in Anselm's *Prayer to St. Mary Magdalene*. Here the poet seems almost to criticize the Lord for his unnecessary question 'Why are you weeping?', since, he says, 'Surely you can see?' The poem is a lyrical celebration of Mary's unbounded love for Jesus, and dares at one point to suggest that Jesus's initial apparent incomprehension is reprehensible in him: 'You, her sole joy, Should be the last thus to increase her sorrow'. But then, in a move which became common in literature and theology, Anselm turns Mary's error in thinking that Jesus was a gardener into an allegory describing the human soul which he both 'waters and puts to the test'. The same motif is found in the early sixteenth-century Mystery play, *Mary Magdalen*, in which 'man's heart' is the Lord's garden, sown with virtue, but choked with weeds until Mary's tears of love water it and encourage it to 'smell full sweet'.

The *noli me tangere* theme focuses on the most dramatic moment in the narrative, and has been the most frequently employed motif in literature. While a strongly patriarchal tradition in theology, emphasized by St. Jerome, suggests that Mary was simply unworthy to touch the risen Lord, in a more kindly manner, Walter Hilton (d. 1396) in his *Scala Perfectionis* (*The Scale of Perfection*) presents Mary in her role as a contemplative, this moment preparing her for the final transformation from the sensual to the spiritual life. Sir Thomas Wyatt's sonnet 'Who So List to Hunt' turns the moment to political purpose, as he places the words around the neck of a hunted deer in a covert reference to a mistress of Henry VIII, who is available for the hunt but not to be touched!

Slightly later in the sixteenth century, St Robert Southwell composed his 'Mary Magdalen's Complaint at Christ's Death', probably while in prison and facing his own death. The purpose of this saintly man was to make spiritual love instead of 'unworthy affections', and here he concentrates solely on Mary's lament before the identity of the stranger in the garden is revealed to her. It is a profoundly moving love poem containing an equally profound Christian spirituality.

In a quite different mode is the reference to the *noli me tangere* in Tobias Smollett's picaresque novel of eighteenth century life on the road, *Humphry Clinker*. Smollett picks up the erotic ambivalences of the moment in the discussion between Humphry and his uncle concerning his dreadful aunt, who cannot be lived with and cannot be lived without. The '*noli me tangere* in the flesh' combines two Biblical phrases, the other from 2 Corinthians 12: 7, 'There was given to me a thorn in the flesh.' The aunt is a sore in her husband's flesh who cannot be borne but nor must be 'tampered with'.

There are only occasional references to the passage in nineteenth-century literature, most creatively by Oscar Wilde in his play (written in French) *Salomé* (1894), in which Jokanaan (John the Baptist) refuses the advances of Salomé crying, 'Back, daughter of Sodom! Touch me not. Profane not the temple of the Lord God.'

In D. H. Lawrence's *St. Mawr*, Jesus's words are placed in the mouth of a young woman who is utterly weary of the world and merely wishes to be left alone. The words of the risen Lord have now become a cry of utter exhaustion and a renouncing of the flesh, not for the spiritual life but as an act of pure revulsion. Twice the phrase 'I am not yet ascended unto the father' (which in the text of the Gospel sits somewhat inconsequentially after the 'Do not hold me'), is repeated, but not as an anticipation of a glorious ascension into heaven. Rather it becomes a plea that the world just leaves her alone – and especially in revulsion to the touch of a man. It is the cry, therefore, of one disgusted with sexuality and eroticism.

In the final excerpt in this section, the narrator is Mary Magdalen herself, now the central character in Michèle Roberts's 'fifth gospel', *The Wild Girl*. In her note at the beginning of the novel, Roberts comments on the 'composite character' of Mary in legend, art and literature. Setting out to dissect a myth, she admits that, 'A narrative novel creates a myth in the same way [as the gospels]: I wanted to dissect a myth; I found myself at the same time recreating one.' So a new Mary comes alive in this contemporary feminist fiction, one who cannot understand why she is not allowed to touch her lover. Jesus's response here is more straightforward than in the biblical text: 'I am not in the body as I was before.' She is now meeting the risen Jesus, different from his former self though paradoxically the same. In this modern version, Jesus and Mary sit companionably together on the grass, and even without physical contact, an air of eroticism remains.

The visual arts have constantly returned to this episode, perhaps because of its complex mixture of sexuality, passion, spirituality; the heady encounter between the weeping woman, saint and sinner, and the stranger; the theological power of these first few moments of meeting with the risen Christ. Used since ancient times as the first Gospel of Easter morning in Christian liturgy and worship, this beautifully constructed narrative is a key moment in the New Testament and Western literature.

—— **Literature** ——

The Book of the Resurrection of Christ by Bartholomew the Apostle, from M. R. James, *The Apocryphal New Testament*, Oxford University Press, 1924

Early in the morning of the Lord's day the women went to the tomb. They were Mary Magdalene, Mary the mother of James whom Jesus delivered out of the hand of Satan, Salome who tempted him, Mary who ministered to him and Martha her sister, Joanna (*al.* Susanna) the wife of Chuza who had renounced the marriage bed, Berenice who was healed of an issue of blood in Capernaum, Lea (Leah) the widow whose son he raised at Nain, and the woman to whom he said, 'Thy sins which are many are forgiven thee'.

These were all in the garden of Philogenes, whose son Simeon Jesus healed when he came down from the Mount of Olives with the apostles (probably the lunatic boy at the Mount of Transfiguration).

Mary said to Philogenes: If thou art indeed he, I know thee. Philogenes said: Thou art Mary the mother of Thalkamarimath, which means joy, blessing, and gladness. Mary said: If thou have borne him away, tell me where thou hast laid him and I will take him away: fear not. Philogenes told how the Jews sought a safe tomb for Jesus that the body might not be stolen, and he offered to place it in a tomb in his own garden and watch over it: and they sealed it and departed. At midnight he rose and went out and found all the orders of angels: Cherubim, Seraphim, Powers, and Virgins. Heaven opened, and the Father raised Jesus. Peter, too, was there and supported Philogenes, or he would have died.

The Saviour then appeared to them on the chariot of the Father and said to Mary: Mari Khar Mariath (Mary the mother of the Son of God). Mary answered: Rabbouni Kathiathari Mioth (The Son of God the Almighty, my Lord, and my Son). A long address to Mary from Jesus follows, in the course of which he bids her tell his brethren, 'I ascend unto my Father and your Father', &c. Mary says: If indeed I am not permitted to touch thee, at least bless my body in which thou didst deign to dwell.

St Anselm, 'Prayer to St. Mary Magdalen' (late eleventh century), *The Prayers and Meditations*, tr. Sister Benedicta Ward, SLG, Penguin, 1973

But you, most holy Lord,
   why do you ask her why she weeps?
      Surely you can see;
her heart, the dear life of her soul, is cruelly slain.
   O love to be wondered at;
   O evil to be shuddered at;
   you hung on the wood, pierced by iron nails,
stretched out like a thief for the mockery of wicked men;
   and yet, 'Woman,' you say, 'why are you weeping?'
She had not been able to prevent them from killing you,
but at least she longed to keep your body for a while
   with ointments lest it decay.
No longer able to speak with you living,
   at least she could mourn for you dead.
So, near to death and hating her own life,
   she repeats in broken tones the words of life
   which she had heard from the living.
   And now, besides all this,

even the body which she was glad, in a way, to have kept,
   she believes to have gone.
And can you ask her, 'Woman, why are you weeping?'
   Had she not reason to weep?
For she had seen with her own eyes –
   if she could bear to look –
   what cruel men cruelly did to you;
and now all that was left of you from their hands
   she thinks she has lost.
   All hope of you has fled,
for now she has not even your lifeless body
   to remind her of you.
   And someone asks,
'Who are you looking for? Why are you weeping?'
     You, her sole joy,
   should be the last thus to increase her sorrow.
But you know it all well, and thus you wish it to be,
for only in such broken words and sighs
can she convey a cause of grief as great as hers.
The love you have inspired you do not ignore.
   And indeed you know her well,
the gardener, who planted her soul in his garden.
   What you plant, I think you also water.
   Do you water, I wonder, or do you test her?
In fact, you are both watering and putting to the test ...

   But now, good Lord, gentle Master,
look upon your faithful servant and disciple,
   so lately redeemed by your blood,
and see how she burns with anxiety, desiring you,
   searching all round, questioning,
   and what she longs for is nowhere found.
   Nothing she sees can satisfy her,
since you whom alone she would behold, she sees not.
     What then?
How long will my Lord leave his beloved to suffer thus?
   Have you put off compassion
now you have put on in-corruption?
   Did you let go of goodness
when you laid hold of immortality?
   Let it not be so; Lord.

You will not despise us mortals
   now you have made yourself immortal,
for you made yourself a mortal
   in order to give us immortality ...

   And so it is; for love's sake
he cannot bear her grief for long or go on hiding himself.
   For the sweetness of love he shows himself
   who would not for the bitterness of tears.
The Lord calls his servant by the name she has often heard
and the servant knows the voice of her own Lord.
   I think, or rather I am sure,
   that she responded to the gentle tone
   with which he was accustomed to call; 'Mary'.
What joy filled that voice, so gentle and full of love.
He could not have put it more simply and clearly:
   'I know who you are and what you want;
      behold me;
      do not weep, behold me;
      I am he whom you seek.'
At once the tears are changed;
   I do not believe that they stopped at once,
   but where once they were wrung
   from a heart broken and self-tormenting
   they flow now from a heart exulting.
How different is, 'Master!'
   from 'If you have taken him away, tell me';
   and, 'They have taken away my Lord,
   and I do not know where they have laid him,'
   has a very different sound from,
'I have seen the Lord, and he has spoken to me.' ...

   But how should I, in misery and without love,
   dare to describe the love of God
   and the blessed friend of God?
Such a flavour of goodness will make my heart sick
if it has in itself nothing of that same virtue.
But in truth, you who are very truth, you know me well
and can testify that I write this for the love of your love,
   my Lord, my most dear Jesus.
   I want your love to burn in me as you command
   so that I may desire to love you alone

292

and sacrifice to you a troubled spirit,
  'a broken and a contrite heart'.
Give me, O Lord, in this exile,
  the bread of tears and sorrow
for which I hunger more than for any choice delights.
    Hear me, for your love,
  and for the dear merits of your beloved Mary,
  and your blessed Mother, the greater Mary.
    Redeemer, my good Jesus,
do not despise the prayers of one who has sinned against you
but strengthen the efforts of a weakling that loves you.
  Shake my heart out of its indolence, Lord,
  and in the ardour of your love
bring me to the everlasting sight of your glory
  where with the Father and the Holy Spirit
  you live and reign, God, for ever. Amen.

Sir Thomas Wyatt, 'Who So List to Hunt I Know Where Is an Hind'

WHO SO list to hount I knowe where is an hynde,
  But as for me, helas, I may no more:
  The vayne travaill hath weried me so sore.
I ame of theim that farthest commeth behinde;
Yet may I by no meanes my weried mynde
  Drawe from the Diere: but as she fleeth afore,
Faynting I folowe. I leve of therefore,
  Sins in a nett I seke to hold the wynde.
Who list her hount I put him owte of dowbte,
  As well as I may spend his tyme in vain:
  And, graven with Diamonds, in letters plain
There is written her faier neck rounde abowte:
  Noli me tangere, for Cesars I ame;
  And wylde for to hold, though I seme tame.

Robert Southwell, 'Mary Magdalen's Complaint at Christ's Death'

Sith my life from life is parted,
  Death come take thy portion;
Who survives when life is murdered,
  Lives by mere extortion;

293

JESUS AND MARY IN THE GARDEN

All that live, and not in God,
   Couch their life in death's abode.
Seely stars must needs leave shining
   When the sun is shadowed,
Borrowed streams refrain their running
   When head-springs are hindered:
One that lives by other's breath,
   Dieth also by his death.

O true life! Since Thou hast left me,
   Mortal life is tedious;
Death it is to live without Thee,
   Death of all most odious:
Turn again or take me to Thee,
Let me die or live Thou in me!

Where the truth once was and is not,
   Shadows are but vanity,
Showing wan, that help they cannot,
   Signs, not salves, of misery;
Painted meat no hunger feeds,
Dying life each death exceeds.

With my love my life was nestled
   In the sum of happiness:
From my love my life is wrested
   To a world of heaviness:
O let love my life remove,
Sith I live not where I love!

O my soul! what did unloose thee
   From thy sweet captivity,
God, not I, did still possess thee,
   His, not mine, thy liberty:
O too happy thrall thou wert,
When thy prison was His heart.

Spiteful spear that breakst this prison,
   Seat of all felicity,
Working thus with double treason
   Love's and life's delivery:

Though my life thou drav'st away,
Maugre thee my love shall stay.

Tobias Smollett, *The Expedition of Humphry Clinker* (1771)

These, however, are not the only efforts she has made towards a nearer conjunction with our sex. Her fortune was originally no more than a thousand pounds; but she gained an accession of five hundred by the death of a sister, and the lieutenant left her three hundred in his will. These sums she has more than doubled, by living free of all expence, in her brother's house; and dealing in cheese and Welsh flannel the produce of his flocks and dairy. At present her capital is increased to about four thousand pounds; and her avarice seems to grow every day more and more rapacious: but even this is not so intolerable as the perverseness of her nature, which keeps the whole family in disquiet and uproar. She is one of those geniuses who find some diabolical enjoyment in being dreaded and detested by their fellow-creatures.

I once told my uncle, I was surprised that a man of his disposition could bear such a domestic plague, when it could be so easily removed – The remark made him sore, because it seemed to tax him with want of resolution – Wrinkling up his nose, and drawing down his eyebrows, 'A young fellow (said he) when he first thrusts his snout into the world, is apt to be surprised at many things which a man of experience knows to be ordinary and unavoidable – This precious aunt of yours is become insensibly a part of my, constitution – Damn her! She's a *noli me tangere* in my flesh, which I cannot bear to be touched or tampered with.' I made no reply; but shifted the conversation.

D. H. Lawrence, *St. Mawr* (1925)

'Dearest Mother: I smelt something rash, but I know it's no use saying: How *could* you? I only wonder, though, that you should think of marriage. You know, dear, I ache in every fibre to be left alone, from all that sort of thing. I feel all bruises, like one who has been assassinated. I do so understand why Jesus said: *Noli me tangere* Touch me not, I am not yet ascended unto the Father. Everything had hurt him so much, wearied him so beyond endurance, he felt he could not bear one little human touch on his body. I am like that. I can hardly bear even Elena to hand me a dress. As for a man – and marriage – ah, no! *Noli me tangere, homine!* I am not yet ascended unto the Father. Oh, leave me alone, leave me alone! That is all my cry to all the world.

Michèle Roberts, *The Wild Girl* (1984), Minerva, 1991

As I turned, I saw a man standing at the bend in the path where I had stood earlier, watching me. He wore a rough woollen robe of the same drab colour as mine borrowed from Joseph's maid, and so I took him for one of the servants, and, when I saw that he held a rush basket filled with figs in one hand, I knew him to be the gardener. I did not stop to think of the folly of admitting to him that I was a witness to the opening of the tomb. I could not resist stepping closer to him and putting out my hand in supplication.

– Tell me, friend, I begged him: do you know what they have done with the body? Do you know where they went with it?

He put down his basket and looked at me, and I looked back at him, not having observed his face before this.

– Mary, he said, and stretched out his hand towards mine.

I did not need the scarlet weal on his palm as proof. I knew him.

– Rabboni, I saluted him: Jesus.

I moved nearer him, so that our hands would have met, except that he stepped back.

– Don't touch me, he said, and then smiled at me, to show that he did not mean his words to hurt.

– Why can't I touch you? I blurted, not understanding anything.

– I'm here with you now, he said: and I shall be with you always. I shall never leave you. But I am not in the body as I was before. We cannot love each other now as we did before. You know this already in your heart.

I did not want to hear him say it. My joy at seeing him was mixed with sharp pain, as had so often been the case in the weeks before his death, when I embraced him and tasted the sweetness of his mouth and felt his arms around me and at the same time feared for him, feared for his safety, for the moment when the soldiers would come and take him away. I looked at his face, which was always beautiful to me, and prayed for the courage to accept the truth he offered me. A little came, so that when I spoke my voice was steady.

– Tell me what we should do now, I pleaded: stay with me just for a little while and tell me what we should do.

– I have much to say to you, he answered: and many messages to send. Listen to me, Mary, so that you can carry back to the others the good news. We sat down together on the grass, and I listened while he spoke. I put away from myself as severely as I could my longing to take hold of him, though I knew it would return later with great sorrow and bitterness, and attended to what he said. When he had finished, he stood up, and I with him, and then he raised his hand in blessing and farewell, and was gone. A trace of fragrance of spices and aromatic oil lingered on in the air under the trees. I had no more business there. I turned round and walked steadily back along the path, my face warm and wet with tears, towards the house. But in my heart there began a great beating, the rising and swelling of a joyful and triumphant song: I have seen the Lord. Let all the people rise up and proclaim with me: I have seen the Lord. And so my pace quickened just as the song did, until I was running, careless of the stones that tore my bare feet, and flinging myself in through the doorway of Joseph's house.

Bibliography

Eslinger, Lyle. 'The Wooing of the Woman at the Well: Jesus, the Reader and Reader-Response Criticism', *Literature and Theology*, 1 (1987), pp. 167–83.

Haskyns, Susan. *Mary Magdalen: Myth and Metaphor* (London: Harper Collins, 1993).

Jasper, Alison, 'Interpretative Approaches to John 20: 1–18. Mary at the Tomb of Jesus', *Studia Theologica*, 47 (1993), pp. 107–18.

Moore, Stephen D. *God's Gym: Divine Male Bodies of the Bible* (London: Routledge, 1996).

Warner, Marina. *Alone of All Her Sex: The Myth and the Cult of the Virgin Mary* (London: Picador, 1990).

The Conversion
of St Paul
Acts 9: 1–19

[1] And Saul, yet breathing out threatenings and slaughter against the disciples of the Lord, went unto the high priest,

[2] And desired of him letters to Damascus to the synagogues, that if he found any of this way, whether they were men or women, he might bring them bound unto Jerusalem.

[3] And as he journeyed, he came near Damascus: and suddenly there shined round about him a light from heaven:

[4] And he fell to the earth, and heard a voice saying unto him, Saul, Saul, why persecutest thou me?

[5] And he said, Who art thou, Lord? And the Lord said, I am Jesus whom thou persecutest: it is hard for thee to kick against the pricks.

[6] And he trembling and astonished said, Lord, what wilt thou have me to do? And the Lord said unto him, Arise, and go into the city, and it shall be told thee what thou must do.

[7] And the men which journeyed with him stood speechless, hearing a voice, but seeing no man.

[8] And Saul arose from the earth; and when his eyes were opened, he saw no man: but they led him by the hand, and brought him into Damascus.

[9] And he was three days without sight, and neither did eat nor drink.

[10] And there was a certain disciple at Damascus, named Ananias; and to him said the Lord in a vision, Ananias. And he said, Behold, I am here, Lord.

[11] And the Lord said unto him, Arise, and go into the street which is called Straight, and inquire in the house of Judas for one called Saul, of Tarsus: for, behold, he prayeth,

[12] And hath seen in a vision a man named Ananias coming in, and putting his hand on him, that he might receive his sight.

[13] Then Ananias answered, Lord, I have heard by many of this man, how much evil he hath done to thy saints at Jerusalem:

[14] And here he hath authority from the chief priests to bind all that call on thy name.

[15] But the Lord said unto him, Go thy way: for he is a chosen vessel unto me, to bear my name before the Gentiles, and kings, and the children of Israel:

[16] For I will shew him how great things he must suffer for my name's sake.

[17] And Ananias went his way, and entered into the house; and putting his hands on him said, Brother Saul, the Lord, even Jesus, that appeared unto thee in the way as thou camest, hath sent me, that thou mightest receive thy sight, and be filled with the Holy Ghost.

[18] And immediately there fell from his eyes as it had been scales: and he received sight forthwith, and arose, and was baptized.

[19] And when he had received meat, he was strengthened. Then was Saul certain days with the disciples which were at Damascus.

Notes

Verse 3. It is interesting to see how the theme of 'light' recurs here: originally the first act of Creation in Genesis, and re-deployed by John as the symbol of Christ, light now made into the hallmark of conversion. Paul is dazzled and blinded, as a sign of his spiritual blindness hitherto, and his sight is only restored after three days of darkness (corresponding to Christ's three days between Crucifixion and Resurrection) before being restored to life and light in Christ, by Ananias.

Verse 4. 'Fell to the ground'. Saul suffers the fate of the profaner Heliodorus, on whom also falls a great darkness. See 2 Maccabees 3: 27–8. 'Saul' is a Semitic form, used again by the 'voice' of Jesus in chapter 26: 14 which speaks in the 'Hebrew language' (Aramaic).

Verse 5. 'To kick against the pricks': a 'prick' was a goad used on oxen, which, as late as the end of the nineteenth century were always used as the heavy draft animals – horses were both more expensive and not as strong. The phrase was a standard one as far back as middle English, and its use by the King James Bible in this context preserved it in English as a metaphor long after the object itself had been forgotten. The phrase is omitted from many manuscript versions and is usually left out of modern translations of the New Testament.

Verse 13. 'Saints' (*hagioi*) is the earliest term used to describe members of the young Christian community.

—— Commentary ——

This is the classic conversion story – one that has been adopted as the prime biblical example of, and justification for, every evangelical conversion experience. Ever since the upsurge of evangelical revivalism associated with, but not confined to, Methodism in the eighteenth century, the 'conversion experience' has been an essential element in any personal testimony. It was seen to mark the difference between those for whom their religious practices were simply a matter of social or class observance, and those who had internalized their beliefs into a personal religious experience. In some circles, especially in the U.S.A., such testimony of being 'born again' is nowadays a necessary qualification for calling oneself a Christian at all. It was not, of course, always so. Pre-eighteenth-century commentaries laid stress not so much upon Paul's inner feelings, but on God's action on him. Paul's own references to it suggest that he, too, was much less interested in his own states of mind, than in what he saw as the miraculous reach of God's saving grace.

It was this aspect of Paul's conversion, together with that of St Augustine (345–430), that led some sixteenth-century reformers, and most notably Calvin (1509–1564), to promulgate the doctrine of predestination. This held that we were saved or damned not through any moral efforts of our own, but solely through God's grace. Ever since Paul's Epistle to the Romans this had, of course, been an accepted plank of Christian doctrine, but what was special about the Calvinist doctrine was its insistence that human understanding after the Fall had been so corrupted that divine justification could only appear, to us sinners, as totally arbitrary. God's 'justice', though of course perfect and unquestionable, might well seem to us to be wildly unjust. Though this doctrine had its origins in the quite understandable convictions of Paul, Augustine, and many others that their conversions – in effect, their personal selection by God – were not due to their own innate efforts or qualities, but to the free outpouring of divine grace, and that they had therefore in some wholly mysterious way been earmarked, even 'predestined', to salvation, the effects of this doctrine were frequently questionable, and in many cases disastrous.

To begin with, it drove a wedge between what we perceive as virtue, and what it was in God's eyes. In other words, human beings could not be expected to know right from wrong, and independent moral choice was either impossible, or meaningless, or both. The best we could hope for was some kind of direct 'guidance' from God. This led to great stress being laid on the 'inward witness' of salvation, or being 'born again'.

Those who had shared in such experiences, it was believed, had at least some degree of access to God's will, and could therefore by-pass the dilemma of the fallibility of human judgement. Though responsible theologians always insisted that it was impossible for us to be *sure* that we were saved, or that we were divinely guided in our actions, this was a subtlety that was often ignored by its adherents – especially if they were already confident about the rightness of whatever course of action they were taking. Thus Oliver Cromwell habitually ascribed his military victories in the English Civil War, or later in Ireland, to God's (often closely tactical) instructions, and it undoubtedly led him into some of the worst atrocities of the period – such as the burning alive of the Catholics (including women and children) who had taken refuge during the siege of Drogheda, in the Church. In its most extreme form it gave rise to 'antinomianism': the belief that if one felt one was instructed by God (something so closely allied to a sense of one's own righteousness as often to be indistinguishable from it) then any action whatsoever was justified. Needless to say, it was not only Protestants who showed antinomian tendencies. The Catholic Inquisition was, of course, antinomian in its philosophy, as have been numerous nationalist or Marxist terrorist movements around the world – including, for instance, the IRA.

If it could lead to bigotry and atrocities even among its most sincere believers (few people have accused Cromwell of being a hypocrite) there were many who failed to find in themselves the necessary 'evidences' to give them 'assurance' of salvation, and so, not unreasonably assumed they were probably damned. Samuel Johnson (1709–1784) seems to have been prey to terrible fears of eternal damnation. The poet William Cowper (1731–1800) was another. Though he had lived a relatively blameless life, and had cooperated with his local curate, John Newton (1725–1807), in the village of Olney, to produce a volume of hymns (*Olney Hymns*), Cowper was haunted by the fear of damnation. Partly, no doubt, this was a matter of a clinically depressive temperament (he later went mad) which was made worse by the fact that Newton, the former captain of a slave-ship, had himself undergone just such a 'Pauline' conversion, denounced the evils of slavery, and taken the job of a country parson. Perhaps Cowper's most moving poem is *The Castaway*, a relatively short poem about a man lost overboard from a moving ship, and so drowned. Only in the final stanzas do we get a hint of a second, internal and symbolic narrative running beneath the first:

> I therefore purpose not, or dream,
> Descanting on his fate

To give the melancholy theme
   A more enduring date:
But misery still delights to trace
   Its semblance in another's case.

No voice divine the storm allay'd,
   No light propitious shone:
When, snatch'd from all effectual aid,
   We perish'd, each alone.
   But I beneath a rougher sea,
And whelm'd in deeper gulfs than he.

Calvinist doctrines of conversion and predestination were also obviously an open invitation to liars, hypocrites, and crooks of all kinds. It was this aspect of Calvinism that attracted a number of writers – especially those who had been through, and rejected, family or social pressures to display their 'conversions'. James Hogg's *Confessions of a Justified Sinner* (1824) is a classic supernatural/psychological thriller set in the strictly Calvinist Edinburgh of a hundred years before, where it is unclear if Robert Wringhim, who believes himself a divinely 'justified sinner', and therefore above the moral law, is suffering from psychological delusions, or is actually being led into his crimes by the Devil himself. More clearly autobiographical is Edmund Gosse's *Father and Son* (1907). Gosse's father, the biologist Philip Gosse, was an ardent fundamentalist Plymouth Brother who placed enormous pressure on his son to declare himself converted and saved at an early age; though Edmund obligingly did so, his own reaction led to an eventual loss of faith and estrangement from his family.

Both these works, of course, rely on a quite different reading of conversion from that of Paul. The key figure here, once again, is Augustine. Though Augustine himself was one of the figures on whom the later doctrine of predestination was to be (quite justifiably) based, there was another, quite different psychological strand to his own account of his conversion that stressed not so much the arbitrary and undeserved nature of divine intervention, but his own feelings and state of mind. His autobiography, *The Confessions*, are a literary landmark giving an insight into the development of his own emotions and character that was to be unequalled again until we reach Rousseau's *Confessions*, or Wordsworth's *Prelude*, some fourteen hundred years later. His conversion was a complex and long drawn-out affair, foreshadowed in many ways by earlier events, and finally triggered by an almost insignificant event – a child's voice overheard in a garden. From Augustine, and from his rediscovery by the Romantics, has developed a quite different (but not necessarily contradictory) way of looking at conversion, not as something done by God, but as an inner process explicable in terms of how it meets a pre-existing need in the individual concerned. If modern readers of Acts 9, therefore, have tended to look at Paul's conversion as the culmination of a growing obsession with Christianity, from his witness of the stoning of Stephen (Acts 7) through to his zeal as a persecutor of the Christians, leading finally to the journey to Damascus, as a personal and internalized journey, that has only increased rather than diminished its literary potential. Thus what is, perhaps, the greatest conversion poem of all, Francis Thompson's 'The Hound of Heaven', manages to combine Pauline drama with Augustinian introspection to produce one of the most powerful poems ever to emerge from an age of scepticism.

—— **Literature** ——

John Newton, 'The Rebel's Surrender to Grace', from *Olney Hymns* (1779)

Lord What Wilt Thou Have Me to Do?

Lord, thou hast won, at length I yield;
My heart, by mighty grace compell'd,
 Surrenders all to thee;
 Against thy terrors long I strove,
But who can stand against thy love?
 Love conquers even me.

All that a wretch could do, I tried,
Thy patience scorn'd, thy pow'r defied,
 And trampled on thy laws:
 Scarcely thy martyrs at the stake
Could stand more steadfast for thy sake,
 Than I in Satan's cause.

But since thou hast thy love reveal'd,
And shown my soul a pardon seal'd,
 I can resist no more:
 Couldst thou for such a sinner bleed?
 Canst thou for such a rebel plead?
 I wonder and adore!

If thou hadst bid thy thunders roll,
And lightnings flash, to blast my soul,
  I still had stubborn been;
But mercy has my heart subdu'd,
A bleeding Saviour I have view'd,
  And now I hate my sin.

Now, Lord, I would be thine alone,
Come take possession of thine own,
  For thou hast set me free;
Releas'd from Satan's hard command,
  See all my powers waiting stand,
    To be employ'd by thee.

My will conform'd to thine would move;
  On thee, my hope, desire and love.
    In fix'd attention join;
My hands, my eyes, my ears, my tongue,
  Have Satan's servants been too long,
    But no they shall be thine.

And can I be the very same
Who lately durst blaspheme thy name,
  And on thy Gospel tread?
    Surely each one who hears my case
Will praise thee, and confess thy grace
  Invincible indeed!

James Hogg, *The Confessions of a Justified Sinner* (1824),
Panther, 1970

In this frame of mind was I when my reverend father one morning arose from his seat, and, meeting me as I entered the room, he embraced me, and welcomed me into the community of the just upon earth. I was struck speechless, and could make no answer save by looks of surprise. My mother also came to me, kissed, and wept over me; and, after showering un-numbered blessings on my head, she also welcomed me into the society of *the just made perfect*. Then each of them took me by a hand, and my reverend father explained to me how he had wrestled with God, as the patriarch of old had done, not for a night, but for days and years, and that in bitterness and anguish of spirit, on my account; but that *he* had at last prevailed, and had now gained the long and earnestly desired assurance of my acceptance with the Almighty, in and through the merits and sufferings of his Son. That I was now a justified person, adopted among the number of God's children – my name written in the Lamb's book of life, and that no by-past transgression, nor any future act of my own, or of other men, could be instrumental in altering the decree. 'All the powers of darkness,' added he, 'shall never be able to pluck you again out of your Redeemer's hand. And now, my son, be strong and steadfast in the truth. Set your face against sin, and sinful men, and resist even to blood, as many of the faithful of this land have done, and your reward shall be double. I am assured of your acceptance by the word and spirit of Him who cannot err, and your sanctification and repentance unto life will follow in due course. Rejoice and be thankful, for you are plucked as a brand out of the burning, and now your redemption is sealed and sure.'

I wept for joy to be thus assured of my freedom from all sin, and of the impossibility of my ever again falling away from my new state. I bounded away into the fields and the woods, to pour out my spirit in prayer before the Almighty for his kindness to me: my whole frame seemed to be renewed; every nerve was buoyant with new life; I felt as if I could have flown in the air, or leaped over the tops of the trees. An exaltation of spirit lifted me, as it were, far above the earth and the sinful creatures crawling on its surface; and I deemed myself as an eagle among the children of men, soaring on high, and looking down with pity and contempt on the grovelling creatures below.

Edmund Gosse, *Father and Son* (1907), Penguin, 1976

In dealing with the peasants around him, among whom he was engaged in an active propaganda, my Father always insisted on the necessity of conversion. There must be a new birth and being, a fresh creation in God. This crisis he was accustomed to regard as manifesting itself in a sudden and definite upheaval. There might have been prolonged practical piety, deep and true contrition for sin, but these, although the natural and suitable prologue to conversion, were not conversion itself. People hung on at the confines of regeneration, often for a very long time; my Father dealt earnestly with them, the elders ministered to them, with explanation, exhortation and prayer. Such persons were in a gracious state, but they were not in a state of grace. If they should suddenly die, they would pass away in an unconverted condition, and all that could be said in their favour was a vague expression of hope that they would benefit from God's uncovenanted mercies.

But on some day, at some hour and minute, if life was spared to them, the way of salvation would be revealed to these persons in such an aspect that they would be enabled instantaneously to accept it. They would take it consciously, as one takes a gift from the hand that offers it. This act of taking was the process of conversion, and the person who so accepted was a child of God now, although a single minute ago he had been a child of wrath. The very root of human nature had to be changed, and, in the majority of cases, this change was sudden, patent, palpable.

I have just said, 'in the majority of cases', because my Father admitted the possibility of exceptions. The formula was, 'If any man hath not the Spirit of Christ, he is none of his.' As a rule, no one could possess the Spirit of Christ, without a conscious and full abandonment of the soul, and this, however carefully led up to, and prepared for with tears and renunciations, was not, could not, be made, except at a set moment of time. Faith, in an esoteric and almost symbolic sense, was necessary, and could not be a result of argument, but was a state of heart. In these opinions my Father departed in no wise from the strict evangelical doctrine of the Protestant churches, but he held it in a mode and with a severity peculiar to himself. Now, it is plain that this state of heart, this voluntary deed of acceptance, presupposed a full and rational consciousness of the relations of things. It might be clearly achieved by a person of humble cultivation, but only by one who was fully capable of independent thought, in other words by a more or less adult person. The man or woman claiming the privileges of conversion must be able to understand and to grasp what his religious education was aiming at.

Gerard Manley Hopkins, *The Wreck
of the Deutschland* (1875)

6

Not out of his bliss
Springs the stress felt
Nor first from heaven (and few know this)
Swings the stroke dealt—
Stroke and a stress that stars and storms deliver,
That guilt is hushed by, hearts are flushed by and melt—
But it rides time like riding a river
(And here the faithful waver, the faithless fable and miss).

7

It dates from day
Of his going in Galilee;
Warm-laid grave of a womb-life grey;
Manger, maiden's knee;
The dense and driven Passion, and frightful sweat:
Thence the discharge of it, there its swelling to be,
Though felt before, though in high flood yet—
What none would have known of it, only the heart being hard at bay,

8

Is out with it! Oh,
We lash with the best or worst
Word last! How a lush-kept plush-capped sloe
Will, mouthed to flesh-burst,
Gush! – flush the man, the being with it, sour or sweet,
brim, in a flash, full! – Hither then, last or first,
To the hero of Calvary, Christ's feet—
Never ask if meaning it, wanting it, warned of it – men go.

9

Be adored among men,
God, three numberèd form;
Wring thy rebel, dogged in den,
Man's malice, with wrecking and storm.
Beyond saying sweet, past telling of tongue,
Thou art lightning and love, I found it, a winter and warm;
Father and fondler of heart thou hast wrung:
Hast thy dark descending and most art merciful then.

10

With an anvil-ding
And with fire in him forge thy will
Or rather, rather then, stealing as Spring
Through him, melt him but master him still:
Whether at once, as once at a crash Paul,
Or as Austin, a lingering-out swéet skill,
Make mercy in all of us, out of us all
Mastery, but be adored, but be adored King.

Francis Thompson, 'The Hound of Heaven' (1893)

I fled Him, down the nights and down the days;
I fled Him, down the arches of the years;
I fled Him, down the labyrinthine ways
Of my own mind; and in the midst of tears
I hid from Him, and under running laughter.
Up vistaed hopes I sped;
And shot, precipitated,
Adown Titanic glooms of chasmed fears,
From those strong Feet that followed, followed after.
But with unhurrying chase,
And unperturbèd pace,
Deliberate speed, majestic instancy,
They beat – and a voice beat
More instant than the Feet –
'All things betray thee, who betrayest Me.'

I pleaded, outlaw-wise,
By many a hearted casement, curtained red,
Trellised with intertwining charities
(For, though I knew His love Who followèd,
Yet was I sore adread
Lest, having Him, I must have naught beside);
But, if one little casement parted wide,
The gust of His approach would clash it to:
Fear wist not to evade, as Love wist to pursue.
Across the margent of the world I fled,
And troubled the gold gateways of the stars,
Smiting for shelter on their clanged bars;
Fretted to dulcet jars
And silvern chatter the pale ports o'the moon.
I said to Dawn, Be sudden; to Eve, Be soon;
With thy young skiey blossoms heap me over
From this tremendous Lover!
Float thy vague veil about me, lest He see!
I tempted all His servitors, but to find
My own betrayal in their constancy,
In faith to Him their fickleness to me,
Their traitorous trueness, and their loyal deceit.
To all swift things for swiftness did I sue;

Clung to the whistling mane of every wind,
But whether they swept, smoothly fleet,
The long savannahs of the blue;
Or whether Thunder-driven
They clanged his chariot 'thwart a heaven
Plashy with flying lightnings round the spurn o' their feet: –
Fear wist not to evade as Love wist to pursue.
Still with unhurrying chase,
And unperturbèd pace,
Deliberate speed, majestic instancy,
Came on the following Feet,
And a voice above their beat –
'Naught shelters thee, who wilt not shelter Me.'

I sought no more that after which I strayed
In face of man or maid;
But still within the little children's eyes
Seems something, something that replies;
They at least are for me, surely for me!
I turned me to them very wistfully;
But, just as their young eyes grew sudden fair
With dawning answers there,
Their angel plucked them from me by the hair.
'Come then, ye other children, Nature's – share
With me' (said I) 'your delicate fellowship;
Let me greet you lip to lip,
Let me twine with you caresses,
Wantoning
With our Lady-Mother's vagrant tresses,
Banqueting
With her in her wind-walled palace,
Underneath her azured daïs,
Quaffing as your taintless way is,
From a chalice
Lucent-weeping out of the dayspring.'
So it was done:
I in their delicate fellowship was one –
Drew the bolts of Nature's secrecies.
I knew all the swift importings
On the wilful face of skies;
I knew how the clouds arise
Spumèd of the wild sea-snortings;

309

All that's born or dies
Rose and drooped with – made them shapers
Of mine own moods, or wailful or divine
With them joyed and was bereaven.
I was heavy with the even,
When she lit her glimmering tapers
Round the day's dead sanctities.
I laughed in the morning's eyes.
I triumphed and I saddened with all weather,
Heaven and I wept together,
And its sweet tears were salt with mortal mine;
Against the red throb of its sunset-heart
I laid my own to beat,
And share commingling heat;
But not by that, by that, was eased my human smart.
In vain my tears were wet on Heaven's grey cheek.
For ah! we know not what each other says,
These things and I; in sound *I* speak –
Their sound is but their stir, they speak by silences.
Nature, poor stepdame, cannot slake my drouth;
Let her, if she would owe me,
Drop yon blue bosom-veil of sky and show me
The breasts o' her tenderness:
Never did any milk of hers once bless
My thirsting mouth.
Nigh and nigh draws the chase,
With unperturbèd pace,
Deliberate speed, majestic instancy;
And past those noisèd feet
A Voice comes yet more fleet –
'Lo! naught contents thee, who content's not Me.'

Naked I wait Thy love's uplifted stroke!
My harness piece by piece Thou hast hewn from me,
And smitten me to my knee;
I am defenceless utterly.
I slept, methinks, and woke,
And, slowly gazing, find me stripped in sleep.
In the rash lustihead of my young powers,
I shook the pillaring hours
And pulled my life upon me; grimed with smears,

I stand amid the dust o' the mounded years –
My mangled youth lies dead beneath the heap.
My days have crackled and gone up in smoke,
Have puffed and burst as sun-starts on a stream.
Yea, faileth now even dream
The dreamer, and the lute the lutanist;
Even the linked fantasies, in whose blossomy twist
I swung the earth a trinket at my wrist,
Are yielding; cords of all too weak account
For earth with heavy griefs so overplussed.
Ah! is Thy love indeed
A weed, albeit an amaranthine weed,
Suffering no flowers except its own to mount?
Ah! must –
Designer infinite! –
Ah! must Thou char the wood ere Thou canst limm with it
My freshness spent its wavering shower i' the dust;
And now my heart is as a broken fount,
Wherein tear-droppings stagnate, split down ever
From the dank thoughts that shiver
Upon the sighful branches of my mind.
Such is; what is to be?
The pulp so bitter, how shall taste the rind?
I dimly guess what Time in mists confounds;
Yet ever and anon a trumpet sounds
From the hid battlements of Eternity;
Those shaken mists a space unsettle, then
Round the half-glimpsèd turrets slowly wash again.
But not ere him who summoneth
I first have seen, enwound
With glooming robes purpureal, cypress-crowned;
His name I know, and what his trumpet saith.
Whether man's heart or life it be which yields
Thee harvest, must Thy harvest fields
Be dunged with rotten death?

Now of that long pursuit
Comes on at hand the bruit;
That Voice is round me like a bursting sea:
'And is thy earth so marred,
Shattered in shard on shard?

Lo, all things fly thee, for thou fliest Me!
Strange, piteous, futile thing!
Wherefore should any set thee love apart?
Seeing none but I makes much of naught' (He said)
'And human love needs human meriting:
How hast thou merited –
Of all man's clotted clay the dingiest clot?
Alack, thou knowest not
How little worthy of any love thou art!
Whom wilt thou find to love ignoble thee,
Save Me, save only Me?
All which I took from thee I did but take,
Not for thy harms,
But just that thou might'st seek it in My arms.
All which thy child's mistake
Fancies as lost, I have stored for thee at home;

Rise, clasp My hand, and come!'
Halts by me that footfall:
Is my gloom, after all,
Shade of His hand, outstretched caressingly?
'Ah, fondest, blindest, weakest,
I am He whom thou seekest!
Thou dravest love from thee, who dravest Me.'

Jacques Derrida, *Memoirs of the Blind: The Self-Portrait and Other Ruins*, tr. Pascale-Anne Brault and Michael Naas, Chicago University Press, 1993

– Each time a divine punishment is cast down upon sight in order to signify the mystery of election, the blind become witnesses to the faith. An inner conversion at first seems to transfigure light itself. Conversion of the inside, conversion on the inside: in order to enlighten the spiritual sky on the inside, the divine light creates darkness in the earthly sky on the outside. This veil between two lights is the experience of bedazzlement, the very bedazzlement that, for example, knocks Paul to the ground on the road to Damascus. A conversion of the light literally bowls him over. Oftentimes his horse is also thrown violently to the ground, bowled over or knocked to the ground in the same fall, its eyes sometimes turned like its master's towards the blinding source of the light or the divine word. In Caravaggio's painting (Rome, Santa Maria del popolo), only the horse remains standing. Lying outstretched on the ground, eyes closed, arms open and reaching up towards the sky, Paul is turned toward the light that bowled him over. The brightness seems to fall upon him as if it were reflected by the animal itself ...

Sunflower blindness, a conversion that twists the light and turns it upon itself to the point of dizziness, the blacking out of the one bedazzled, who sees himself go from brightness and clarity to even more clarity, perhaps to too much sun. This clairvoyance of the all-too evident is Paul's madness.

Bibliography

Derrida, Jacques. *Memoirs of the Blind: The Self-Portrait and Other Ruins*, tr. Pascale-Anne Brault and Michael Naas (Chicago: Chicago University Press, 1993).

Dodd, C. H. *The Meaning of Paul for Today* (London: Collins Fontana, 1958).

Hunter, A. M. *The Gospel According to St. Paul* (London: SCM, 1966).

Knock, A. D. *Conversion* (1961).

Poland, L. M. 'Augustine, Allegory, and Conversion', *Literature and Theology*, 2 (1988), pp. 37–48.

Alpha and Omega
Revelation 21: 1–18

[1] And I saw a new heaven and a new earth: for the first heaven and the first earth were passed away; and there was no more sea.

[2] And I John saw the holy city, new Jerusalem, coming down from God out of heaven, prepared as a bride adorned for her husband.

[3] And I heard a great voice out of heaven saying, Behold, the tabernacle of God is with men, and he will dwell with them, and they shall be his people, and God himself shall be with them, and be their God.

[4] And God shall wipe away all tears from their eyes; and there shall be no more death, neither sorrow, nor crying, neither shall there be any more pain: for the former things are passed away.

[5] And he that sat upon the throne said, Behold, I make all things new. And he said unto me, Write: for these words are true and faithful.

[6] And he said unto me, It is done. I am Alpha and Omega, the beginning and the end. I will give unto him that is athirst of the fountain of the water of life freely.

[7] He that overcometh shall inherit all things; and I will be his God, and he shall be my son.

[8] But the fearful, and unbelieving, and the abominable, and murderers, and whoremongers, and sorcerers, and idolaters, and all liars, shall have their part in the lake which burneth with fire and brimstone: which is the second death.

[9] And there came unto me one of the seven angels which had the seven vials full of the seven last plagues, and talked with me, saying, Come hither, I will shew thee the bride, the Lamb's wife.

[10] And he carried me away in the spirit to a great and high mountain, and shewed me that great city, the holy Jerusalem, descending out of heaven from God,

[11] Having the glory of God: and her light was like unto a stone most precious, even like a jasper stone, clear as crystal;

[12] And had a wall great and high, and had twelve gates, and at the gates twelve angels, and names written thereon, which are the names of the twelve tribes of the children of Israel:

[13] On the east three gates; on the north three gates; on the south three gates; and on the west three gates.

[14] And the wall of the city had twelve foundations, and in them the names of the twelve apostles of the Lamb.

[15] And he that talked with me had a golden reed to measure the city, and the gates thereof, and the wall thereof.

[16] And the city lieth foursquare, and the length is as large as the breadth: and he measured the city with the reed, twelve thousand furlongs. The length and the breadth and the height of it are equal.

[17] And he measured the wall thereof, an hundred and forty and four cubits, according to the measure of a man, that is, of the angel.

[18] And the building of the wall of it was of jasper: and the city was pure gold, like unto clear glass.

Notes

Verse 1. The sea is the cosmic sea out of which both heaven and earth were made. It symbolizes primeval chaos, or the abyss. For this writer there are seven elements of the old order which will eventually disappear: sea, death, grief, crying, pain, all under God's curse, and night. At this moment history comes to an end.

Verse 3. The descent of the holy city is described in terms of a wedding, in which the divine and the human will finally become one. The Greek word used for God's 'dwelling' with men (*skênê*) is the same as the word used for the dwelling of the incarnate Word among humans in John 1: 14. It looks back to the dwelling of God in a tent or tabernacle in the wilderness before the building of the Jerusalem Temple by Solomon, and indicates the presence of the Divine among his people. The writer of Revelation here is developing Rabbinic terminology.

'They shall be his people' looks back to the promises of the prophets (e.g. Jeremiah 7: 23, Hosea 1: 9). This whole passage is full of Old Testament overtones.

Verse 4. See Isaiah 25: 6–8. 'He will swallow up death for ever, and the Lord God will wipe away tears from all faces.'

Verse 6. Alpha and omega are the first and last letters of the Greek alphabet. God is at the beginning and at the end, and the conclusion of all things is not an event so much as a person, yet beyond history.

315

'The water of life' is a common image, referred to already here in the episode of Jesus's encounter with the Samaritan woman in John 4. The whole passage is also very reminiscent of the Beatitudes in the Gospel of Matthew 5, and Luke 6.

—— **Commentary** ——

At the very end of the Bible we see this image of a whole new creation. The first verse takes us back to the very first verses of Genesis:

In the beginning God created the heavens and the earth. The earth was without form and void, and the darkness was upon the face of the deep; and the Spirit of God was moving over the face of the waters.

Now this first creation has passed away, and the sea, the element of chaos, is finally abolished. Christ has come into his own as the alpha and omega, the beginning and the end of all things. This reference to the first and last letters of the Greek alphabet is found on two other occasions in the Book of Revelation (1: 8; 22: 13), and probably derives from the Hebrew word for 'truth' whose first and last letters are the first and last letters of the Hebrew alphabet. (A further use of the term in chapter 1 verse 11 in the King James Bible is not warranted by the best manuscript sources.)

This description of God's infinity in time and space goes back to the Hebrew Bible in such passages as Isaiah 44: 6, where the Lord declares, 'I am the first and I am the last; beside me there is no God', and is common in Rabbinic tradition. The ascription of the title Alpha and Omega to Christ is found throughout early Christian writing, and was quickly taken into hymns and worship, no doubt to reflect the true worship in the holy city of John of Patmos's vision in Revelation. One of the most enduring is the hymn of Prudentius from which we have taken some lines here, affirming the eternity and infinity of the Son. It appears also in one of the most popular of medieval Christmas carols, the macaronic (that is, part in English and part in Latin) song 'In Dulci Jubilo' in which the infant born in the stable in Bethlehem is identified with the Son of God in glory.

References to alpha and omega continue to recur obliquely throughout English literature from the Middle Ages, though rarely explicitly. In Milton's *Paradise Lost*, Book V, for example, Adam and Eve in the first Paradise, Eden, celebrate the glories of God's creation in words which reflect Revelation's description of his infinity, 'Him first, him last, him midst, and without end'. As it shall be in the perfection of the new heaven and earth, so was it in the first before the Fall. The Puritan literature of the seventeenth century gives us, however, one of the greatest of all visions of the New Jerusalem in the closing pages of John Bunyan's *Pilgrim's Progress*, as the pilgrims finally cross the perilous waters of the River and ascend Mount Zion and a society clearly inspired by Revelation 21.

Revelation is sometimes also known as the Apocalypse, though it is in fact only one great example of 'apocalyptic' literature within both Jewish and Christian traditions. This literature is, literally, revealing ('apocalypse' is a Greek word meaning revelation) of the end of all things. There are other apocalypses in the New Testament, for example St Mark's Gospel chapter 13, and in the Hebrew Bible, the Book of Daniel. The Romantic poets were fascinated by the apocalyptic and its powerful imagery, emerging, for instance in Samuel Taylor Coleridge's great poem 'Kubla Khan'. The example we have given here is from William Wordsworth's *Prelude*, Book VI, where he describes the scenery of the Alps in typological terms and language taken from Revelation, the Romantic mountains, waterfalls and clouds 'types and symbols of Eternity'. In another great work of English Romanticism, Charlotte Brontë's novel *Jane Eyre*, a nineteenth-century secularization of the Bible image is found in Rochester's great cry for Jane who is the entirety, the alpha and omega, of his heart's wishes. Jane Eyre herself now bears the full burden of that which in the Bible is of God's nature only – the infinity of all things for her lover.

In Wallace Stevens's poetic exploration of 'plain reality' in 'An Ordinary Evening in New Haven', again alpha and omega are utterly separated from their biblical origins, and are now in antagonism with one another. What we prefer to call 'reality' is 'naked Alpha' – childlike and unwilling or unable to face the end, the 'hierophant Omega', that is, Omega as the priest of mysterious or esoteric doctrines. Far from embracing the infinity of Revelation's vision of all things, our sense of reality never moves far from beginnings. We have, it seems, lost the great coherence of the religious vision in which beginning and end are all one in the Lord. Indeed, the opposite is the case, it seems.

In a much lighter vein, W. H. Auden's 'Victor' suffers from religious indoctrination in his childhood, and having murdered his faithless wife, becomes deluded with messianic pretensions. In the final verse he plays at being the God of Genesis 2: 7, who formed man from the dust or clay of the ground, promising, like Jesus Christ, to return in judgement. So the New Testament ends with a cry for the return of Jesus, who is Alpha and Omega: 'Amen. Come, Lord Jesus' (Revelation 22: 20).

The last passage is from Flannery O'Connor's short story 'Revelation'. It is the final vision of Mrs Turpin, a woman secure in her self-righteousness and self-satisfaction, whom a young girl in a doctor's waiting room has just called a 'wart hog from hell'. For Mrs Turpin it is a moment

of revelation, not a pleasant one indeed, but the result is her vision of the
New Jerusalem and its judgement.

—— Literature ——

Prudentius Aurelius Clemens, 'Hymnus Omnis Horae', from *Cathemerinon* (late fourth century), 9: 10–12

corde natus ex parentisante mundum exordium,
   alpha et cognominatus, ipse fons et clausula
omnia quae sunt, fuerunt, quaeque post futura sunt.

('Born of the Father's love before the world's beginning, called Alpha and
Omega, he is both source and end of all things that are or have been or
hereafter shall be.')

'In Dulci Jubilo' (fourteenth-century German/Latin macaronic carol), *The Penguin Book of Christmas Carols*, ed. Elizabeth Poston, Penguin, 1965

In dulci jubilo
Now sing we all I-O, I-O,
   Our most precious treasure
Lies *in praesepio*,
   And as the sun He shineth
Matris in gremio:
Alpha es et O!

John Milton, *Paradise Lost* (1667), Book V, lines 153–65

These are thy glorious works, Parent of good,
Almighty, thine this universal frame,
Thus wondrous fair; thyself how wondrous then!
Unspeakable, who sitt'st above these heavens,
To us invisible or dimly seen
In these thy lowest works, yet these declare
Thy goodness beyond thought, and power divine.
Speak ye who best can tell, ye sons of light,
Angels, for ye behold him, and with songs
And choral symphonies, day without night,
Circle his throne rejoicing, ye in heav'n;

On earth join all ye creatures to extol
Him first, him last, him midst, and without end.

(There is reference here also to Revelation 22: 13, 'I am the Alpha and the Omega, the first and the last, the beginning and the end.')

John Bunyan, *The Pilgrim's Progress* (1687), 'The Celestial City'

Then I saw in my Dream that Christian was as in a muse a while. To whom also Hopeful added his word, be of good cheer, Jesus Christ maketh thee whole: and with that Christian brake out again with a loud voice, Oh, I see him again, and he tells me, When thou passest through the Waters, I will be with thee; and through the Rivers, they shall not overflow thee …

The talk that they had with the Shining Ones was about the glory of the place, who told them that the beauty and glory of it was inexpressible. There, said they, is the Mount Zion, the heavenly Jerusalem, the innumerable company of angels, and the spirits of just men made perfect. You are going now, said they, to the Paradise of God, wherein you shall see the Tree of Life, and eat of the never-fading fruits thereof; and when you come here, you shall have white Robes given you, and your walk and talk shall be every day with the King, even all the days of Eternity. There you shall not see again such things as you saw when you were in the lower Region upon the earth, to wit, sorrow, sickness, affliction, and death, for the former things are passed away. You are now going to Abraham, to Isaac, and Jacob, and to the Prophets, men that God hath taken away from the evil to come, and that are now resting upon their beds, each one walking in his righteousness. The men then asked, What must we do in this holy place? To whom it was answered, You must there receive the comfort of all your toil, and have joy for all your sorrow; you must reap what you have sown, even the fruit of all your Prayers and Tears, and sufferings for the King by the way. In that place you must wear Crowns of Gold, and enjoy the perpetual sight and vision of the Holy One, for there you shall see him as he is. There also you shall serve him continually with praise, with shouting, and thanksgiving, whom you desired to serve in the World, though with much difficulty, because of the infirmity of your flesh. There your eyes shall be delighted with seeing, and your ears with hearing the pleasant voice of the Mighty One. There you shall enjoy your friends again, that are got thither before you; and there you shall with joy receive even every one that follows into the holy place after you. There also you shall be clothed with Glory and Majesty, and put into an equipage fit to ride out with the

King of Glory. When he shall come with sound of Trumpet in the Clouds, as upon the wings of the Wind, you shall come with him; and when he shall sit upon the Throne of Judgment, you shall sit by him; yea, and when he shall pass sentence upon all the workers of iniquity, let them be Angels or Men, you also shall have a voice in that Judgment, because they were his and your Enemies. Also when he shall again return to the City, you shall go too, with sound of Trumpet, and be ever with him.

Now while they were thus drawing towards the Gate, behold a company of the Heavenly Host came out to meet them; to whom it was said by the other two Shining Ones, These are the men that have loved our Lord when they were in the World, and that have left all for his holy Name, and he hath sent us to fetch them, and we have brought them thus far on their desired Journey, that they may go in and look their Redeemer in the face with joy. Then the Heavenly Host gave a great shout, saying, Blessed are they that are called to the Marriage Supper of the Lamb.

William Wordsworth, *The Prelude* (1805), Book VI, 556–72

> The immeasurable height
> Of woods decaying, never to be decay'd,
> The stationary blasts of water-falls,
> And every where along the hollow rent
> Winds thwarting winds, bewilder'd and forlorn,
> The torrents shooting from the clear blue sky,
> The rocks that mutter'd close upon our ears,
> Black drizzling crags that spake by the way-side
> As if a voice were in them, the sick sight
> And giddy prospect of the raving stream,
> The unfetter'd clouds, and region of the Heavens,
> Tumult and peace, the darkness and the light
> Were all like workings of one mind, the features
> Of the same face, blossoms upon one tree,
> Characters of the great Apocalypse,
> The types and symbols of Eternity,
> Of first and last, and midst, and without end.

Charlotte Brontë, *Jane Eyre* (1847)

'I was in my own room, and sitting by the window, which was open: it soothed me to feel the balmy night-air though I could see no stars, and only by a vague, luminous haze, knew the presence of a moon. I longed for thee, Jane! Oh, I longed for thee both with soul and flesh! I asked of

God, at once in anguish and humility, if I had not been long enough desolate, afflicted, tormented, and might not soon taste bliss and peace once more. That I merited all I endured, I acknowledged – that I could scarcely endure more, I pleaded; and the alpha and omega of my heart's wishes broke involuntarily from my lips in the words – "Jane! Jane! Jane!"' …

'As I exclaimed "Jane! Jane! Jane!" a voice – I cannot tell whence the voice came, but I know whose voice it was – replied, "I am coming; wait for me;" and a moment after, went whispering on the wind, the words – "Where are you?"'

Rudyard Kipling, 'The Last Chantey'

'And there was no more sea'

Thus said the Lord in the Vault above the Cherubim,
Calling to the Angels and the Souls in their degree:
'Lo! Earth has passed away
On the smoke of Judgment Day.
That Our word may be established shall We gather up the sea?'

Loud sang the souls of the jolly, jolly mariners:
'Plague upon the hurricane that made us furl and flee!
But the war is done between us,
In the deep the Lord hath seen us –
Our bones we'll leave the barracout and God may sink the sea!'

Then said the soul of Judas that betrayed Him:
'Lord, hast Thou forgotten Thy covenant with me?
How once a year I go
To cool me on the floe?
And Ye take my day of mercy if Ye take away the sea.'

Then said the soul of the Angel of the Off-shore Wind:
(He that bits the thunder when the bull-mouthed breakers flee):
'I have watch and ward to keep
O'er Thy wonders on the deep,
And Ye take mine honour from me if Ye take away the sea!'

Loud sang the souls of the jolly, jolly mariners:
'Nay, but we were angry, and a hasty folk are we.
If we worked the ship together

Till she foundered in foul weather,
Are we babes that we should clamour for a vengeance on the sea?'

Then said the souls of the slaves that men threw overboard:
'Kennelled in the picaroon a weary band were we;
But Thy arm was strong to save,
And it touched us on the wave,
And we drowsed the long tides idle till Thy Trumpets tore the sea.'

Then cried the soul of the stout Apostle Paul to God:
'Once we frapped a ship, and she laboured woundily.
There were fourteen score of these,
And they blessed Thee on their knees,
When they learned Thy Grace and Glory under Malta by the sea!'

Loud sang the souls of the jolly, jolly mariners,
Plucking at their harps, and they plucked unhandily:
'Our thumbs are rough and tarred,
And the tune is something hard –
May we lift a Deepsea Chantey such as seamen use at sea?'

Then said the souls of the gentlemen-adventurers –
Fettered wrist to bar all for red iniquity:
'Ho, we revel in our chains
O'er the sorrow that was Spain's;
Heave or sink it, leave or drink it, we were masters of the sea!'

Up spake the soul of a grey Gothavn 'speckshioner –
(He that led the flenching in the fleets of fair Fundee):
'Oh, the ice-blink white and near,
And the bowhead breaching clear!
Will Ye whelm them all for wantonness that wallow in the sea?'

Loud sang the souls of the jolly, jolly mariners,
Crying: 'Under Heaven, here is neither lead nor lea!
Must we sing for evermore
On the windless, glassy floor?
Take back your golden fiddles and we'll beat to open sea!'

Then stooped the Lord, and He called the good sea up to Him,
And 'stablished its borders unto all eternity,
That such as have no pleasure

For to praise the Lord by measure,
They may enter into galleons and serve Him on the sea.

Sun, Wind, and Cloud shall fail not from the face of it,
Stinging, ringing spindrift, nor the fulmar flying free;
And the ships shall go abroad
To the Glory of the Lord
Who heard the silly sailor-folk and gave them back their sea!

Wallace Stevens, 'An Ordinary Evening in New Haven', Canto II, short version

Reality is the beginning not the end
Naked Alpha, not the hierophant Omega,
Of dense investiture, with luminous vassals.

It is the infant A standing on infant legs,
Not twisted, stooping, polymathic Z,
He that kneels always on the edge of space

In the pallid perceptions of its distances.
Alpha fears men or else Omega's men
Or else his prolongations of the human.

These characters are around us in the scene.
For one it is enough; for one it is not;
For neither is it profound absentia,

Since both alike appoint themselves the choice
Custodians of the glory of the scene,
The immaculate interpreters of life.

But that's the difference: in the end and the way
To the end. Alpha continues to begin.
Omega is refreshed at every end.

W. H. Auden, from 'Victor', *Collected Shorter Poems.* *1927–1957* (to the tune of 'Frankie and Johnny')

Victor picked up a carving-knife,
His features were set and drawn,
Said; 'Anna, it would have been better for you
If you had not been born.'

Anna jumped up from the table,
  Anna started to scream,
But Victor came slowly after her
  Like a horror in a dream.

She dodged behind the sofa,
  She tore down a curtain rod,
But Victor came slowly after her:
  Said; 'Prepare to meet thy God.'

She managed to wrench the door open,
  She ran and she didn't stop.
But Victor followed her up the stairs
  And he caught her at the top.

He stood there above the body,
  He stood there holding the knife;
And the blood ran down the stairs and sang;
  'I'm the Resurrection and the Life'.

They tapped Victor on the shoulder,
  They took him away in a van;
He sat as quiet as a lump of moss
  Saying, 'I am the Son of Man'.

Victor sat in a corner
  Making a woman of clay:
Saying; 'I am Alpha and Omega, I shall come
  To judge the earth one day.'

Flannery O'Connor, 'Revelation', from *Everything That Rises Must Converge* (1956)

In the deepening light everything was taking on a mysterious hue. The pasture was growing a peculiar glassy green and the streak of highway had turned lavender. She braced herself for a final assault and this time her voice rolled out over the pasture. 'Go on,' she yelled, 'call me a hog! Call me a hog again. From hell. Call me a wart hog from hell. Put that bottom rail on top. There'll still be a top and bottom!'

A garbled echo returned to her.

A final surge of fury shook her and she roared, 'Who do you think you are?'

The color of everything, field and crimson sky, burned for a moment with a transparent intensity. The question carried over the pasture and across the highway and the cotton field and returned to her clearly like an answer from beyond the wood.

She opened her mouth but no sound came out of it.

A tiny truck, Claud's, appeared on the highway, heading rapidly out of sight. Its gears scraped thinly. It looked like a child's toy. At any moment a bigger truck might smash into it and scatter Claud's and the niggers' brains all over the road.

Mrs Turpin stood there, her gaze fixed on the highway, all her muscles rigid, until in five or six minutes the truck reappeared, returning. She waited until it had had time to turn into their own road. Then like a monumental statue coming to life, she bent her head slowly and gazed, as if through the very heart of mystery, down into the pig parlor at the hogs. They had settled all in one corner around the old sow who was grunting softly. A red glow suffused them. They appeared to pant with a secret life.

Until the sun slipped finally behind the tree line, Mrs. Turpin remained there with her gaze bent to them as if she were absorbing some abysmal life-giving knowledge. At last she lifted her head. There was only a purple streak in the sky, cutting through a field of crimson and leading, like an extension of the highway, into the descending dusk. She raised her hands from the side of the pen in a gesture hieratic and profound. A visionary light settled in her eyes. She saw the streak as a vast swinging bridge extending upward from the earth through a field of living fire. Upon it a vast horde of souls were rumbling toward heaven. There were whole companies of white-trash, clean for the first time in their lives, and bands of black niggers in white robes, and battalions of freaks and lunatics shouting and clapping and leaping like frogs. And bringing up the end of the procession was a tribe of people whom she recognized at once as those who, like herself and Claud, had always had a little of everything and the God-given wit to use it right. She leaned forward to observe them closer. They were marching behind the others with great dignity, accountable as they had always been for good order and common sense and respectable behavior. They alone were on key. Yet she could see by their shocked and altered faces that even their virtues were being burned away. She lowered her hands and gripped the rail of the hog pen, her eyes small but fixed unblinkingly on what lay ahead. In a moment the vision faded but she remained where she was, immobile.

At length she got down and turned off the faucet and made her slow way on the darkening path to the house. In the woods around her the invisible cricket choruses had struck up, but what she heard were the voices of the souls climbing upward into the starry field and shouting hallelujah.

Bibliography

Bull, Malcolm (Ed). *Apocalypse Theory and the Ends of the World* (Oxford: Blackwell, 1995).

Caird, G. B. *The Revelation of St. John the Divine* (London: Adam and Charles Black, 1966).

Kermode, Frank. *The Sense of an Ending: Studies in the Theory of Fiction* (London: Oxford University Press, 1981).

McKelvey, R. J. *The New Temple: The Church in the New Testament* (Oxford: Oxford University Press, 1969).

Simon, Urich, *Atonement: From Holocaust to Paradise* (Cambridge: James Clark & Co, 1987), ch. 3, 'Visions of Heaven'.

Wainwright, Arthur. *Mysterious Apocalypse: Interpreting the Book of Revelation* (Nashville, TN, 1993).

— GENERAL BIBLIOGRAPHY —

(*Note*. The literature on this subject is vast. We have suggested only a few of the most useful recent books which will help the reader to work with the material provided in this collection.)

Adam, A. K. M. *What is Postmodern Biblical Criticism?* (Philadelphia: Fortress Press, 1995).

Alter, Robert. *The World of Biblical Literature* (London: SPCK, 1992).

Alter, Robert and Frank Kermode (eds), *The Literary Guide to the Bible* (London: Collins, 1987).

Beardslee, William A. *Literary Criticism of the New Testament* (Philadelphia: Fortress Press, 1970).

Charity, A. C. *Events and Their Afterlife* (Cambridge: Cambridge University Press, 1966).

Drury, John (ed.), *Critics of the Bible: 1724–1873* (Cambridge: Cambridge University Press, 1989).

Frye, Northrop. *The Great Code: The Bible and Literature* (London: Routledge & Kegan Paul, 1982).

Gabel, John B. and Charles B. Wheeler. *The Bible as Literature: An Introduction* (New York: Oxford University Press, 1986).

Gros Louis, Kenneth R. R., James S. Ackerman and Thayer S. Warshaw (eds), *Literary Interpretations of Biblical Narratives* (Nashville: Abingdon, 1978).

Habel, Norman. *Literary Criticism of the Old Testament* (Philadelphia: Fortress Press).

Henn, T. R. *The Bible as Literature* (London: Lutterworth Press, 1970).

Jasper, David. *The New Testament and the Literary Imagination* (London: Macmillan, 1987).

Jeffrey, David Lyle (gen. ed.). *A Dictionary of Biblical Tradition in English Literature* (Grand Rapids: William B. Eerdmans, 1992).

Josipovici, Gabriel. *The Book of God: A Response to the Bible* (New Haven: Yale University Press, 1988).

Lampe, Geoffrey and Kenneth Woolcombe. *Essays on Typology* (London: SCM, 1957).

Landow, George. *Victorian Types, Victorian Shadows* (London: Routledge, 1980).

McKnight, Edgar V. *The Bible and the Reader: An Introduction to Literary Criticism* (Philadelphia: Fortress Press, 1985).

Norton, David. *A History of the Bible as Literature* (2 volumes, Cambridge: Cambridge University Press, 1993).

Ostriker, Alicia Suskin. *Feminist Revision and the Bible* (Oxford: Blackwell, 1993).

Prickett, Stephen (ed.). *Reading the Text: Biblical Criticism and Literary Theory* (Oxford: Blackwell, 1991).

Prickett, Stephen. *Origins of Narrative: The Romantic Appropriation of the Bible* (Cambridge: Cambridge University Press, 1996).

Prickett, Stephen. *Words and 'The Word': Language, Poetics, and Biblical Interpretation* (Cambridge: Cambridge University Press, 1986).

Rosenberg, David (ed.). *Congregation: Contemporary Writers Read the Jewish Bible* (San Diego: HBJ, 1987).

Schwartz, Regina (ed.). *The Book and the Text: The Bible and Literary Theory* (Oxford: Blackwell, 1990).

Wadsworth, Michael (ed.). *Ways of Reading the Bible* (Brighton: Harvester Press, 1981).

Watson, Francis (ed.). *The Open Text: New Directions for Biblical Studies?* (London: SCM, 1993).

There are many anthologies of poetry which have been useful in the preparation of this book. Three of the most useful are:

Atwan, Robert and Laurance Wieder (eds). *Chapters into Verse: Poetry in English Inspired by the Bible* (2 volumes, Old and New Testaments, Oxford: Oxford University Press, 1993).

Davie, Donald (ed.). *The New Oxford Book of Christian Verse* (Oxford: Oxford University Press, 1981).

Impastato, David (ed.). *Upholding Mystery: An Anthology of Contemporary Christian Poetry* (New York: Oxford University Press, 1997).

Name Index